DISCOVERING GRAMMAR

An Introduction to English Sentence Structure

Anne Lobeck

Western Washington University

New York   Oxford

OXFORD UNIVERSITY PRESS

2000

Oxford University Press

Oxford   New York
Athens   Auckland   Bangkok   Bogotá   Buenos Aires   Calcutta
Cape Town   Chennai   Dar es Salaam   Delhi   Florence   Hong Kong   Istanbul
Karachi   Kuala Lumpur   Madrid   Melbourne   Mexico City   Mumbai
Nairobi   Paris   São Paulo   Singapore   Taipei   Tokyo   Toronto   Warsaw

and associated companies in
Berlin   Ibadan

Published by Oxford University Press, Inc.,
198 Madison Avenue, New York, New York, 10016
http://www.oup-usa.org

Oxford is a registered trademark of Oxford University Press

Library of Congress Cataloging-in-Publication Data

Lobeck, Anne C.
    Discovering grammar : an introduction to English sentence
structure / Anne Lobeck.
    p. cm.
  Includes index.
  ISBN 0-19-512984-9 (acid-free paper)
    1. English language—Sentences. 2. English language—Grammar. 3.
English language—Syntax. I. Title.
  PE1375 .L63 2000
  425—dc21   99-35472
                                                               CIP

Printing (last digit): 9 8 7 6 5 4 3 2 1

Printed in the United States of America
on acid-free paper

Contents

PART II: CATEGORIES

Preface

Many of you may be victims of *grammar anxiety*, a negative, even fearful reaction to the idea of being faced with the horrifying task of having to *learn grammar*. This fear is not unwarranted; for many of us, our experience with being taught grammar (and for some teachers, the experience of having to teach it) has involved correction, drills, and memorization. Some of us probably did not do very well, and we probably hated anyone who did. When you think about it, it isn't surprising that we might tremble at the thought of an entire *course* on grammar, given that methods of teaching traditional grammar (drill and correction) focus primarily on memorization rather than on critical thinking. Learning traditional grammar is something like learning the parts of an engine or memorizing the periodic table: it involves mastering terminology rather than concepts, using memorization rather than problem solving. Studying grammar in this way does very little to help you actually understand language and its structure, and it is no wonder that the pedagogical benefits of grammar study have been questioned and continue to be at the heart of discussions of how to teach language arts most effectively, in particular writing. It is unfortunate, however, that research on the inefficacy of teaching traditional grammar has also led many to the conclusion that grammar instruction per se is of no use to students.[1] Rather, it is fairly easy to see that our attitudes about language and its "correct" or "incorrect" structure underlie many of our cultural prejudices and stereotypes and thus crucially affect how we think about ourselves and others. Concluding

---

[1]For example, Constance Weaver, in her 1995 book *Teaching Grammar in Context,* states: "Overall, it is difficult to escape the conclusion that teaching formal, isolated grammar to average or heterogeneous classes, perhaps even to highly motivated students in elective classes, makes no appreciable difference in their ability to write, to edit, or to score better on standardized tests" (p. 26). This may be the case, concerning traditional grammar. However, Weaver goes on to say, in response to the question of what options are then left for the teacher, that one such option is to: "[r]estrict the teaching of grammar as a system to elective classes and units, *offered with no pragmatic justification as an incentive, but only for the pleasure and challenge of studying the language.* . . . (emphasis mine) (p. 26).

In other words, because "formal" grammar training does not help students learn to be better writers, according to Weaver, teachers should expect to teach grammar only for fun, since it has no "pragmatic justification."

that the study of the structure of this uniquely human phenomenon is of no demonstrable use thus does both students and teachers a great disservice.

Quite simply, the more we know about the structure of our language the easier it is to recognize and avoid prejudice based on language. If we understand something about grammar we are better equipped to evaluate claims such as "you talk funny" or "you aren't using that verb right," as well as claims such as "French is more romantic than German" or "that person has sloppy speech." All of us have been criticized at one time or another for our language, and all of us have probably criticized others. We also are called upon to use and understand grammatical terminology, though not all of us ever really study it. Teachers, for example, sometimes need to explain why a sentence is "incomplete," but to do so, both teacher and student must understand basic sentence structure, including what a *subject* and a *predicate* are. Students are told not to use *dangling modifiers,* but how many of us even know what a modifier is, or, more to the point, what it means to (syntactically) "dangle?" We hear these terms so often, yet we never really know what they mean.

This book is intended to help you acquire a foundational knowledge of English syntax, or sentence structure. More specifically, we will explore our own knowledge of the English grammatical system, a system made up of interacting components, including syntax (sentence structure), morphology (word structure), semantics (sentence and word meaning), and phonology (the sound patterns of words and sentences). A full discussion of each grammatical component is too much to undertake here. We will focus primarily on syntax, and in somewhat less detail on morphology and semantics.

We will pursue what I call a *linguistic* approach to grammar. Returning once more to the metaphor of the engine, a linguistic approach to grammar as I define it is similar to learning not only the parts of the engine, but how the engine works. You will then be able to build your own engine, take one apart, evaluate another engine you might be thinking about buying, or fix a broken one. In short, you will not only be able to *explain* how grammar works, but you can also *apply* your knowledge to help answer questions you have about language and usage and understand your and other's linguistic prejudices, opinions, and biases and make informed decisions about them. Discovering grammar, rather than memorizing a list of rules, will also help you learn how to think critically, in particular about the structure of language, just as you would in studying any other subject from an analytical perspective. Using the chemistry metaphor, the linguistic approach to studying grammar is something like actually doing chemistry experiments, rather than just memorizing the periodic table.

A Note to Students

This book is on a general level about linguistics, the study of language, and on a more specific level about the structure of sentences, based on their syntax, morphology, and semantics. I hope that it will therefore be of interest to anyone who gets excited about language and wants to know more about it. It is most specifically designed for those with little or no background in linguistics, particularly college English Education and English Studies majors, and for students and teachers of Teaching English as a Second Language. This book is also geared to students with an interest in linguistics, as many of the exercises focus on linguistic analysis and argumentation, and encourage you to think analytically about language.

A Note to Teachers

This book in intended to fill a gap in the literature on introductory syntax. For those of us with a background in linguistics, it is often difficult to strike the right balance in our teaching between theory and practice; we desire to teach students about grammar from a theoretically informed perspective, yet we also want our students to be able to *apply* this knowledge in their everyday lives in a variety of different roles, for example, as teachers, readers, writers. It is my hope that the text and exercises in each chapter of this book work together to integrate linguistic concepts with pragmatic justification. This book is, as I explain in the following section, unique in its approach to sentence analysis in encouraging students to discover grammatical concepts through both problem solving *and* text analysis. Opportunities are also provided for students to explore sentence structure in the context of language change and variation, and to consider how their knowledge can be applied to current language-related controversies including many that apply to education (bilingual education, the "Ebonics" controversy, the English Only movement, etc.) My hope is that this approach will deepen understanding of language as a dynamic part of all of our lives.

The Structure of the Book and the Exercises

This book is divided into three parts. Part One (Chapters 1 through 3) provides an overview of the grammatical system, including definitions of *grammar* and some of its components and organizing principles. Chapter 1 discusses different definitions of grammar, the notion of standard and nonstandard English, and how our perceptions about language influence our opinions and attitudes. Chapter 2 addresses how we organize words into syntactic categories, and how those words form syntactic units, or phrases. This chapter includes an introduction to phrase structure rules, and explores how this notation allows us to express the basic syntactic principles of constituency, hierarchical structure, and recursion. Chapter 3 investigates some of the syntactic evidence for phrases from movement, pronominalization, and coordination, tools we use in later chapters in our analysis of syntactic structure. Part Two of the book (Chapters 4 through 9) investigates in detail each syntactic category—Noun, Verb, Adjective, Adverb, and Preposition. We discuss the basic morphology, syntax, and semantics of each of these *lexical* categories, and introduce along the way a number of *grammatical* categories, including Determiner, Quantifier, Numeral, Degree, and Auxiliary. Part

xii   Discovering Grammar

Three (Chapters 10 through 13) explores the grammatical functions of phrases (noun phrases, verb phrases, adjective phrases, adverb phrases, and prepositional phrases) as subjects, predicates, complements, and adjuncts. In this section we discuss clause structure in some detail, paying particular attention to subordination and the functions of clauses as complements and adjuncts.

The exercises are the backbone of this book. In each chapter (excluding Chapter 1) they follow the same basic pattern. They are designed to be used as they are, or as templates for exercises you can create on your own. The goal of the exercises is to allow you to practice doing actual syntactic analysis of sentence patterns, and then to apply your knowledge to text analysis, of excerpts compiled from a variety of spoken and written sources, including overheard conversations, novels, poetry, newspaper articles, movie marquis, television and film dialogue, and radio broadcasts. The exercises thus involve no drills, memorization, or reproduction of model sentences.

A set of exercises in each chapter also focuses on linguistic diversity, including exercises on different varieties of English, both over time (Old English and Middle English, for example) and space (varieties of English currently spoken in different regions around the United States and the world). Still other exercises target languages other than English, and certain exercises are keyed to different areas of interest. For example, some exercises target students of English Education (encouraging students to create minilessons on phenomena and concepts, for example), and others are more geared for students interested in linguistics. Others are of particular interest to students studying English as a Second Language (as speakers or teachers), and some focus primarily on literary analysis. Still others approach grammatical analysis through comparison of traditional and more current approaches to different phenomena. An appendix, providing lists of resources and guidance for researching topics for these exercises, is included at the end of the book.

Sets of Discovery Problems in each chapter are designed to deepen your understanding of chapter material and allow you to practice linguistic analysis. Certain Discovery Problems, designated with an asterisk (*), introduce new material related to that discussed in the chapter. It is important to work through all *Problems, as this new material is often discussed in later chapters. All of the Discovery Problems provide experience in formulating and supporting hypotheses based on syntactic patterns. In general, these exercises are designed to help you "discover" syntax using the methodology linguists use to analyze sentence structure.

Each chapter ends with a set of chapter review terms and a chapter exercise. This section reviews the terminology and concepts introduced in the chapter, and provides suggestions for a comprehensive exercise, which may also be used as a chapter test. All new terms introduced in each chapter are typed in boldface, and are included in the Chapter Review Terms section. These terms are also found in the glossary at the end of the book.

Acknowledgments

This book would not have been possible without the help of my colleagues, friends, and family, and above all, my students. Western Washington University has been very generous with grants to support this project, and I am indebted to the staff at the Bureau of Faculty Research for their help in preparing the manuscript. My editors at OUP, Peter Ohlin, D. Anthony English, and Benjamin Clark, made assembling this enjoyable rather than daunting. My colleague Bill Smith deserves special thanks for his excellent advice and good humor in guiding me through the publication process. I am also very grateful to Ed Battistella; he has read more drafts of this book than anyone else, and I'm sure he is as happy as I am that it is finally finished. I am also grateful to Rick Emmerson, Rosina Lippi-Green, and Steve Vanderstaay for reading and commenting on parts of the manuscript, and to Claire Foley and Tom Stroik for their excellent detailed commentary. Betsy Ritter also contributed helpful advice and support, as did Chuck Denny, with whom I collaborated on this project in its earliest stages.

As always, my family has been a great source of support and encouragement. In particular, I thank my husband Charlie for his love and partnership, and for his valuable insights as a fellow teacher.

Most of all, I thank my students for teaching me how to teach them. Their comments and confusions have been my guide throughout this project. This book is dedicated to them.

Part 1

The Grammatical System

1

Grammar and Our Knowledge
of Language

The very word "grammar" evokes a visceral response—usually fear.
Patricia T. O'Connor, *Newsweek,* December 9, 1996

Introduction

In this chapter we provide an overview of the notion of *grammar,* and introduce
some of the basic organizing principles of English sentence structure. We clarify
what the term *grammar* will mean to us in this book, and consider in some detail
how our intuitions, or unconscious knowledge, about language can be expressed in terms of a system of interacting linguistic components: syntax, morphology, phonology, and semantics, what we will call *descriptive* grammar. We
discuss how *descriptive* grammar differs from other definitions, particularly *prescriptive* grammar. In the course of this discussion we will explore the notion of
"standard" English, and discuss in some detail the notion of *grammaticality,* in
particular as it relates to ideas of "correctness," to clarify our goals here. We conclude the chapter with a discussion of the methodology we borrow from linguistics to "discover" grammar as we have defined it.

The Components of Grammar

When we speak, we usually form our sentences without consciously thinking
about them. In fact, when asked to analyze our own sentence structure, many of
us would be unable to do so because we aren't familiar with the grammatical
terms and concepts. Yet we all, if physically capable, speak our native language
fluently and at a very early age, without ever being consciously taught. Further,
we have *intuitions* about word and sentence meaning and structure, and about
which sounds occur in our language and which do not. We know, for example,
that the nonsense word *grobs* "sounds" English, as words in English can begin
with *gr-,* end with *-bs,* and have a vowel in between, as in *grabs* or *grubs.* We also
know that *grobs* might be a noun, identifiable by its plural suffix, as in "The
grobs ate the fringles." Or it might be a verb, suffixed by a third person singular

-s, in the same way as *eats* in "Tory eats," occurring in sentences such as "The fringle grobs the yobel." We don't know what the word *grobs* actually means, though we know that in the sentence "All grobs sleep during the day" we are talking about the set of all grobs, and that *all grobs* is the *subject* of the sentence, the things that are doing the sleeping. We thus can extract some meaning from the sentence, regardless of whether we know the actual meaning of each word.

We appear, then, to have intuitions about structure, sound, and meaning in our language. These linguistic components comprise what we might call the unconscious "knowledge of language" that all speakers possess, which allows us to produce and understand the sentences of our language.[1] Below, we discuss each of these components of our linguistic knowledge in more detail.

Syntax

Syntax is in a basic sense the way in which words are ordered and grouped together, and how each group of words functions in a sentence as a syntactic phrase. Syntax also includes the rules or operations that can apply to words or groups of words. For example, consider the sentence in (1).

(1)   The presidential candidate thought that the expensive dinners given in Lee's honor were surprisingly boring.

In (1), you can tell which words seem to "go together." For instance, you probably know that *presidential* and *the* go together in some way with *candidate*, and that *the expensive dinners* also forms a kind of unit. You might also be aware that *given in Lee's honor* goes together with *the expensive dinners* and that *surprisingly* goes with *boring*.

When we look at the functions of some of the words and groups of words in (1), we can separate *the presidential candidate* from *thought that the expensive dinners given in Lee's honor were surprisingly boring*. These two phrases, referred to as the *subject* and the *predicate*, make up what we might think of as the basic building blocks of the sentence, expressing the information the sentence is designed to convey.

The material contained in a phrase, or group of words, can in turn be broken up into smaller units. You might, for example, have observed that *surprisingly* occurs in a position in which it tells us more about *boring*, as in *very boring*, *less boring*, and so on. *Surprisingly* thus "modifies" *boring*. Similarly, *presidential* modifies *candidate*, and *expensive* modifies *dinners*. These modifiers occur in syntactic positions in which we find other modifiers, as in *happy* candidate or *cheap* dinners.

---

[1] I am assuming here that readers are English speakers, with native intuitions about this particular language. All speakers have intuitions about whatever language it is that they happen to speak, and I am assuming English as native here simply for ease of exposition.

Aside from word order, and how words are grouped together into phrases, our syntactic knowledge also allows us to rearrange words and phrases in certain ways. For example, we know that (2a) and (2b) are possible sentences of English, but that (2c) is not (throughout the book we use the convention of marking sentences that are not possible sentences of English with *).

(2) a. The presidential candidate will give an expensive dinner in Lee's honor.
   b. *Will* the presidential candidate give an expensive dinner in Lee's honor?
   c. **Will give* the presidential candidate an expensive dinner in Lee's honor?

In (2), we see that to form a question we can move *will*, but not *will give*, to the front of the sentence. That we know that (2c) is impossible suggests that there is no syntactic rule in English that allows us to form such sentences. There is, however, apparently a syntactic rule, which we all "know," that allows us to form questions of the form in (2b).

There are many other observations we could make about the syntax of the sentences in (1–2), but for now, it is important simply to notice that we have intuitions about sentence structure regardless of whether we have had any formal training in this area. We can all analyze syntax regardless of whether we know labels for syntactic phrases, such as subject, predicate, and modifier or whether we can formally state the syntactic rule that allows us to form questions in English of the sort in (2).

There are other ways in which we might analyze the sentence in (1). We might analyze it in terms of the structure of the *words* (morphology) or the structure of the *sounds* (phonetics and phonology) of those words, or we might analyze the *meaning* (or semantics) of the sentence. Together, these components provide important information about the sentence that we must know in order to understand it. It is possible to show that these different grammatical components (syntax, semantics, phonetics and phonology, and morphology) interact with one another in interesting ways, and also that each can be studied separately.

Morphology

Our knowledge of **morphology,** or the structure of words and how they are formed, allows us to divide words into *morphemes,* or the smallest units of meaning. For example, the verb *drive* has one morpheme, but the noun *driver* has two. In *driver* we recognize both *drive,* a verb, and the *-er* suffix, or *affix* as separate morphemes. The word *presidential* in (1) also has (at least) two morphemes, *president* and *-ial*. In this word, the affix *-ial,* attached to the noun *president,* derives an adjective, *presidential*. Morphological **affixation** thus provides us with clues about the syntactic category of a word as a noun, adjective, verb, and so on. We know, for example, that "the presidential thought that . . ." sounds odd because *presidential* is an adjective, not a noun, and can not follow *the* by itself. "The president thought that . . . ," on the other hand, is syntactically well formed, because *the* is followed by the noun *president.* Morphology in this way interacts with syntax. From *presidential* we also know that the affix *-ial,* or its other form, *-al,* occurs as an affix on many other words such as *bestial, jovial, legal,* and *social,* even though the roots to which *-ial* is attached, namely *best-, jov-, leg-,* and *soc-,* might not be as immediately recognizable as full words in the same way as *president* in *presidential.* We call such base morphemes *roots,* and we have intuitions about the kinds of affixes they can take. We know as well that *-ing* is an affix *boring,* as is *-ate* in *candidate* and *-ly* in *surprisingly.* In addition to recognizing affixes, we know that some seem to attach to certain words but not to others: *-ly* can attach to *surprising,* but not, for example, to *the* or to *thought.*[2]

We as English speakers therefore have unconscious knowledge of affixation and its role in constructing bigger words from smaller ones. Our knowledge of affixation is really quite sophisticated, as we see when we consider the difference between the *-s* affix on *dinners* and the *-ive* affix on *expensive.* When we add *-s* to the noun *dinner,* we *pluralize* the noun, adding grammatical information, namely information concerning number, to the noun. When we add *-ive* to the noun *expense,* on the other hand, we get an entirely new word or part of speech, namely the adjective *expensive.* Linguists call the plural *-s* an **inflectional affix,** one that adds grammatical information. The *-ive* affix is called a **derivational affix,** because its addition "derives" an entirely new word, an entirely new part of speech.

We will rely quite heavily on affixation in subsequent chapters, because it provides useful clues in identifying the syntactic category of a word. Though it is too difficult to list all of the possible derivational affixes in English, there are only a limited number of inflectional affixes in the language. These are given in Table 1.1.

There are a number of other word formation processes we use every day to add words to our language. For example, we form words through **blending** two words together, as in *flying rubber => flubber.* We create new words through **clipping,** or dropping part of a word to create a shorter one, as in *dis,* for *disrespect.* We also form words through **compounding** (*blacklist*), **coining** (adding an entirely new word such as *Yoda*), and through turning **acronyms** into words (*AIDS, NASA*).

There is much more to morphology than we have the space to go into here, and we will explore the morphological characteristics of different classes of words as we work through the book (particularly in Part Two). What is important to observe here is that even if you are not familiar with the names of all the ways in which we form new words, you have some intuitions about differences among the various suffixes and prefixes in your language, and about how to form words in a variety of ways other than through affixation. You thus unconsciously "know" many important things about English words.

---

[2]Words can also be formed by adding prefixes, such as *un-* in *unrealized,* or *dis-* in *disenfranchise.* I limit the discussion of affixes here to suffixes only for ease of exposition.

Table 1.1
English Inflectional Affixes

Verbs	progressive aspect	*-ing*	Mary is eating/sleeping
	perfect aspect	*-en, -t, -ed*	Mary has eaten/slept/walked
	present tense, 3rd person sing.		
		-s	Mary eats/sleeps/walks
	past tense	*-ed, -t*	Mary walked/slept
Nouns	plural	*-s*	dogs/books/comments
	possessive	*-'s*	Mary's dog/the woman's hat
Adjectives	comparative	*-er*	Mary is taller/happier
	superlative	*-est*	Mary is tallest/happiest
Adverbs	comparative	*-er*	Mary runs faster/harder
	superlative	*-est*	Mary ran fastest/hardest

Phonetics and Phonology

Phonetics is the study of the inventory of sounds in a language. That we as English speakers know the phonetics of our language is illustrated by our ability to recognize a sound that is not "English" to us, such as a Bantu click, a Spanish trilled "r" sound, or a pharyngeal consonant in Hebrew or Arabic. **Phonology,** on the other hand, is the study of the sound patterns of a language: how sounds are pronounced in certain environments. Phonological processes vary across different varieties of English, giving rise to what we call different *accents.* For example, in African American Vernacular English there exists a rule that linguists call Consonant Cluster Simplification, in which in a cluster of consonants at the end of a word, such as [st] or [ld], the final consonant is dropped. The pronunciation of the word *missed*, then, is *miss*, as in *He miss the boat*, and *hand* is pronounced *han'*. In the variety of English spoken on Okrakoke Island off the coast of North Carolina, the diphthong pronounced on the mainland as [aj] in words such as *fight* and *high* is pronounced [oj]. An Okrakoke native might therefore pronounce the mainland version of the phrase *high tide on the south side* as *hoi toide on the south soide.*

Phonology also interacts in crucial ways with morphology, because when we "build" words, our pronunciation often changes as a result of phonological rules or processes. For example, the stress on the word *pórous* shifts when we add the affix *-ity,* deriving *porósity,* and it is our knowledge of phonology that makes us pronounce the plural affix *-s* in *dinners* in the sentence in (1) as [z] rather than [s], but the *-s* affix in *candidates* as [s] rather than [z]. Phonology also interacts with syntax, as it sometimes provides us with clues as to the syntactic category, or word class, of a particular word. For example, *tránsfer* is a noun, but *transfér* is a verb. The different syntactic category of the word is reflected by its phonology, more specifically, its stress pattern. Intonation patterns also tell us whether, for example, a sentence is a question or not; if we say *The presidential candidate thought the dinners were boring?* with rising intonation at the end of our sentence, we are asking a question. If we say the same sentence with "falling" intonation, we are simply making a statement.

As with morphology and syntax, our knowledge of the phonetics and phonology of the language we speak natively is typically unconscious. You have probably not been aware, for instance, that you pronounce the plural -*s* in different ways depending on the consonant that precedes it, nor that a simple shift in the stress on a syllable can change a noun into a verb. Phonetics and phonology thus form another crucial component of our knowledge of our language, or our unconscious "grammar."

Semantics

Finally, consider the meaning, or **semantics,** of the sentence in (1). To understand this sentence we have to know what each of the words means: we have to know what a *candidate* is, and what *boring* means, for example, to fully interpret this sentence. Semantics is far more than simply word meaning, however. We must also have a deeper understanding of meaning to explain the contrast in meaning between, for example, (3a) and (3b).

(3) a. *The* presidential candidate thought that the expensive dinners given in Lee's honor were surprisingly boring.
   b. *Each* presidential candidate thought that the expensive dinners given in Lee's honor were surprisingly boring.

When we replace the determiner *the* in (3a) with the quantifier *each* in (3b), the meaning of the sentence changes rather dramatically, though why exactly might be a bit hard for us to explain. *The candidate* in (3a) picks out a particular candidate, say Hortense, who appears to be understood as the same person by both speaker and hearer of the sentence. This is the function of *the* in English, a definite determiner that helps designate a noun as being understood as the same noun by both speaker and hearer. (Compare, for example, *a candidate,* in which it is not necessarily the case that speaker and hearer are both thinking of Hortense, or of any particular person at all.) (3a) therefore means that the candidate, Hortense for example, thought that the dinners given in Lee's honor were boring.

In (3b), on the other hand, *the* has been replaced with the quantifier *each,* with the result that we are now no longer talking about a particular candidate, but rather a *set* of individual candidates. How we interpret quantities in terms of sets of definite or indefinite numbers of members is what linguists call **quantification.** (3b) can therefore mean that Hortense thought that the dinners for Lee were boring, and that Sue thought the dinners for Lee were boring, and that Andy also thought the dinners for Lee were boring. In other words, by replacing *the* with *each,* we change the members of the set referred to by the noun *can-*

didate from a specific candidate (a set of one member, if you will), to a set of individuals, generating a number of different interpretations. We are able to understand the difference between (3a) and (3b) quite readily, as a result of our unconscious semantic knowledge, though we would probably be hard pressed to explain the intricacies of the different semantic properties of the determiner *the* and the quantifier *each*.

Our intuitive semantic knowledge also plays a role in understanding the meanings of the sentences in (4–7).

    (4)   Colorless green ideas sleep furiously.

    (5)   The fertilizer killed the plant but it didn't die.

    (6)   Would you like another sandwich?

    (7)   That class was a long haul.

(4) illustrates how a sentence can be semantically **anomalous,** or nonsensical, but syntactically well formed. All of the words in (4) seem to be in the right place syntactically, but semantically the sentence is meaningless. (5) is similar to (4) in that it is syntactically well formed but semantically a **contradiction;** a sentence cannot be both true and false at the same time. (6) shows that sentences can have implied rather than literal meanings; we understand that the person addressed has already had a sandwich. This is called **presupposition,** another semantic property. (7) illustrates another form of nonliteral speech called **metaphor,** in which we identify one thing as something else to create a figurative image. Here, *the class* is figuratively identified with a long trip, or what in American English we sometimes call *a long haul.* Sentences (3–7) thus demonstrate how we rely on various semantic properties to interpret and produce sentences in our language. Again, this knowledge is unconscious and interacts in interesting ways with other components of our linguistic knowledge, in particular, syntax.

Another example of semantic knowledge, which we will address from time to time in subsequent chapters, is our ability to understand the ways in which sentences and words can be **ambiguous,** or have more than one meaning. For example, consider the following two sentences, both of which are ambiguous.

    (8)   That's a good pitch.

    (9)   Susan wrote a book on a famous antique desk.

(8) is ambiguous because of the different meanings of the word *pitch;* the "good pitch" could be, for example, a good sales pitch, or a good baseball pitch. (8) is therefore ambiguous at the word level, or *lexically ambiguous.* (9), on the other hand, includes no ambiguous words, though it can mean either that Susan wrote a book while sitting at a famous desk, or that she wrote a book about that particular desk. We can thus say that syntactically, the phrase *on a famous antique desk* describes, or modifies, *write* in the first interpretation; it is where she wrote the book. This interpretation is illustrated in (10).

(10)   Susan wrote [a book] [on a famous antique desk].

The phrase *on a famous antique desk* modifies *book* in the second interpretation; it describes the book Susan wrote. We can represent this interpretation as in (11).

(11)   Susan wrote [a book on a famous antique desk].

In (10), the phrase *on a famous antique desk* is syntactically separate from *a book,* and modifies *write*. In (11), on the other hand, *on a famous antique desk* is part of the phrase including *a book,* and forms a unit with it syntactically.

Ambiguity in (9) thus derives from the different possible syntactic structures for the sentence, rather than from the meaning of a single word. A sentence ambiguous because of its syntax is therefore aptly referred to as being *syntactically ambiguous.* Our knowledge of syntax thus overlaps with our knowledge of semantics, or meaning, allowing us to understand ambiguities of the sort in (9). Semantics also interacts with morphology, providing us with a means of understanding the lexical ambiguity in (8).

We also expand our vocabulary by using words that are formed through **semantic shift,** where we assign a new meaning to an existing word. For example, the word *bad* has undergone semantic shift to now also mean *good,* as in *He's bad!* ("He's really incredible!") *Hot* is another example; in addition to expressing temperature, as in *This coffee is really hot!,* this word can mean *impressive,* as in *That new CD is really hot!* And finally, we saw that one way semantics and phonology interact is in cases in which our intonation influences the meaning of our sentences.

To briefly summarize this section, we've seen that our knowledge of language can be divided into at least four components: *syntax, morphology, phonology,* and *semantics.* Though we can study each of these four components in isolation, there is evidence that they also crucially interact with each other to allow us to speak and understand our language.

Descriptive and Prescriptive Grammar

To speak a language we need to know (at least) the interacting rules of its syntax, morphology, phonology, and semantics.[3] This system is what linguists call **descriptive grammar,** the set of rules that describes speakers' intuitions about their language. An informal definition of descriptive grammar is the following:

---

[3]All human languages, whether gestural or spoken, have grammars composed of interacting rules of syntax, semantics, phonology, and morphology. For example, American Sign Language, or ASL, employs gestures in syntactic combinations, and different signs can be analyzed in terms of their form, or morphology. Gestures can also be broken down into even smaller "phonological" units. ASL also has ways of expressing semantic properties just as oral languages do. ASL thus crucially differs from what we call "body" language, or the fixed set of gestures we use to indicate certain feelings and actions. Body language has no grammar in the sense that ASL or other human languages do; the gestures we use in our body language cannot be combined to form new "sentences," nor can they be broken down into morphological or phonological units.

> **Descriptive Grammar:**   The interacting unconscious rules of syntax, morphology, phonology, and semantics that speakers use to speak their language.[4]

Some of you might be thinking at this point that the definition of grammar as a system of interacting components of unconscious knowledge is very different from what you have considered "grammar" to mean in the past. This is not surprising, as descriptive grammar is generally not what we learn in school, nor is it the definition of grammar used by our parents and peers. "Grammar" means different things to different people. For example, teachers of English as a Second Language might include in their definition of "grammar" not only the components discussed above, but also writing conventions such as punctuation, paragraph organization and coherence, and conventions of language use (such as greetings, forms of address, formal and informal speech patterns). A college English composition class may also focus primarily on writing conventions as "grammar," and discuss sentence structure in the context of written, rather than oral, expression. A creative writer might think of "grammar" in yet another sense, as linguistic patterns he or she might invoke for rhetorical effect in written language and dialogue in a novel, poem, or essay.

Though most linguists agree that descriptive grammar includes (at least) syntactic, morphological, phonological, and semantic rules, some point out that there are other things we have to know about language in order to use it, rules that contribute to what the linguist Dell Hymes has called **communicative competence,** or the rules by which we use language in context. For instance, there are many contexts in which the sentence *What did you pay for that dining room table?* is inappropriate; for example, it would make no sense to say this sentence in response to the question *Hi, how are you?* Many linguists study how we use language in society, and the rules of conversation and discourse. These rules are certainly crucial to our understanding of language, and are for some included in their definition of "grammar."

We can see, then, that the term "grammar" is really quite difficult to pin down. For our purposes, we will take the above definition of descriptive grammar as a starting point, though we will not attempt to address the whole of grammatical structure here. We will focus primarily on syntax, and attempt to restrict our discussion of linguistic phenomena as much as we can to sentence

---

[4]Though we will analyze written text throughout this book, I do not include writing in the definition of descriptive grammar simply to avoid addressing the questions of what we "know" when we know how to write. Analyzing the syntax of a text is, I will assume, not necessarily the same as analyzing *how* we write a text, a question beyond our purview here. Prescriptive grammar, which we discuss later in the book, is assumed to be the grammar we use when we write formally. Prescriptive grammar also does not necessarily address the cognitive process of writing, the kinds of grammatical information we access for this process, or the connections between written and oral speech.

structure. In the course of the discussion it will be necessary from time to time to include aspects of semantics and morphology, and when this is the case, the shift from syntax to another grammatical component will, I hope, be made clear. We will not discuss at any length phonology, nor will we consider our knowledge of context and the role it plays in language use in social situations. These areas are certainly worthy of study, but a full discussion of them would be too much to undertake here.[5]

The approach here will therefore be similar in some ways to the approach taken in some more traditional grammars, which also focus on the study of syntax and morphology (and sometimes on semantics, but not as consistently). Our approach differs from these more traditional approaches, however, in also adopting certain contributions of modern linguistic theory. In particular, we will adopt the convention of phrase structure rules, and our approaches to syntactic phenomena of movement and pronominalization are more congruent with modern linguistic approaches than with the more traditional approach based on form and structure. We will focus primarily on formulating hypotheses about sentence structure and use analytical tests to "discover" syntactic patterns and concepts. Our descriptions of these patterns and concepts will often diverge from those of more traditional approaches, and we will sometimes use the divergence as a starting point for exercises and discussion.

A general conception of grammar with which we are probably all familiar is as the set of rules for "correct" or "good" written or spoken English. All of us have been corrected for using "poor" English, or laughed at for saying or writing something "incorrectly." If we choose to speak or write "correctly" we attempt to consciously learn the conventions of correctness prescribed by our speech community. For example, as college students you will probably learn vocabulary and usage consistent with what is expected of you in an academic speech community, particularly in your written work. These "rules" might not be part of the variety of English you speak at home—you may thus become "bidialectal," or skilled at using two (perhaps significantly different) varieties of English.[6] Grammar as a set of "prescribed" rules that we consciously learn is what we will refer to as **prescriptive grammar,** defined below.

Prescriptive Grammar: Linguistic rules arbitrarily designated (by various sources, including dictionaries, textbooks, self-appointed authorities, etc.) as the rules of "correct" grammar.

---

[5]In some theories of grammar, such as functional grammar, the structure of language is crucially influenced by language use. I do not wish to exclude such theories here by defining grammar narrowly; rather, my goal is only to provide a working definition of grammar that you may revise on your own after you have some familiarity with the basics of linguistic structure.

[6]By *dialect* here I simply mean *language variety*. What we call "English" is actually compiled of a number of different varieties of English, which differ systematically in terms

The definition of prescriptive grammar expresses the view that there exists a correct way to speak or write, and that the rules that govern this language variety are those we consciously learn rather than "know" unconsciously. It would be relatively unrewarding, then, to examine a set of prescriptive rules as a means of discovering underlying concepts and principles of syntax, as such rules tell us little about our actual unconscious knowledge of language. Approaching language descriptively, on the other hand, provides us with a way to think analytically about language, and is something we can do on our own, based on our own intuitions and judgment. With a thorough understanding of descriptive grammar you will be in a position to make your own informed judgments about language structure and use, in particular the notion of "correct" grammar, an idea that plays a role in shaping our perceptions of ourselves and others.

Grammaticality

So far, we have chosen to define the rather slippery term "grammar" as clearly and concretely as we can in terms of the two general definitions of descriptive and prescriptive grammar. How do we determine, given these two definitions, whether a sentence is "grammatical" or not? What do we now mean when we say a sentence is "grammatically *correct?*"

When I ask my students to list sentences they consider to be "incorrect" grammar, some of their examples include using *who/whom* in the "right" place, avoiding *ain't* in favor of *isn't*, avoiding double negatives such as *I don't have no money* in favor of *I don't have any money*, and using subject-verb agreement to avoid *He walk to the store*, using instead *He walks to the store*. Students are thus well aware that there is a way to do things "right," and they also readily admit that they are often guilty of doing things "wrong."

The idea that there is a higher authority that determines what is good or bad grammar is something most of us simply accept. When we consider this notion more closely, however, we find it very difficult to determine who this authority actually is, and which grammatical constructions are consistently considered good and which bad. You might, for example, read newspaper columns by James Kilpatrick, William Safire, John Simon, or Edwin Newman, self-appointed authorities on prescriptive grammar who regularly decry the decay

---

of phonology, morphology, syntax, and semantics. Dialects of a language are typically taken to mean varieties of a language that are *mutually intelligible;* speakers of one variety can understand speakers of another variety. This diagnostic becomes problematic for different reasons. For example, though Swedish and Danish are mutually intelligible, they are not called dialects of a single language for political and social reasons. Similarly, what speakers in the West refer to as *Chinese* is actually not a language, but a collection of language varieties that are not, in fact, mutually intelligible. A speaker of Mandarin and a speaker of Cantonese, for example, cannot necessarily understand each other.

of the English language. They base their discomfort on our use of *aggravate for irritate, like* rather than *as,* and *hopefully* as a sentence adverb, as in *Hopefully, I'll get the part in the play.* Some of you might be aware of these "errors," others of you might not be. Most of you may also have found that your teachers vary on the kinds of grammatical constructions they ask you to use or avoid. This again suggests that though we might look at teachers as authorities in such matters, teachers themselves often have different ideas about what they call good and bad grammar.

We are therefore all aware of some notion of correctness in our speech and writing, but on closer examination we can see that this notion is harder to pin down than we may first have thought. Grammatical correctness seems to consist of a set of rules we consciously learn, and we take it for granted that there exist authorities who we can consult for consistent answers to our usage questions (grammar handbooks, dictionaries, teachers, newspaper columnists). This is, however, not the case. Whether a sentence is considered prescriptively correct or grammatical is not as clear-cut as we may have thought, and depends on who we ask.

When we consider the notion of grammaticality from a descriptive perspective, the "authority" we consult is our own intuitions. That is, what can be descriptively grammatical for one speaker may not be descriptively grammatical for another, because speakers of different varieties or dialects of English have, as we might expect, different intuitions about grammaticality. For example, for a speaker from Alabama, the construction *I might could go* is perfectly grammatical, but to a speaker in Michigan or Pennsylvania this construction is completely unfamiliar. For a Cajun speaker from Louisiana *He been try make me mad* may be part of his or her descriptive grammar, but to certain speakers outside of this speech community this construction sounds very strange.

When we analyze a sentence as descriptively grammatical in a particular variety of English, then, it is "correct" in the sense that speakers of that variety recognize it as a possible sentence in their language. We will refrain from using the terms "correct" and "incorrect" here, as they express arbitrary values imposed on language, rather than judgments based on intuitive knowledge. We will instead use the terms *grammatical* and *ungrammatical,* in labeling sentences as part of a speaker's (in particular our own) descriptive grammar or not. We will follow the linguistic convention of marking sentences that are descriptively ungrammatical in English with an *, as in **Mary to John the book gave.*

Standard English

Having explored some of the distinctions between descriptive and prescriptive grammar, we will now address another term that you are probably familiar with, "standard" English. Standard English is the variety of English that we typically think of as "correct," and thus as the version of English that adheres to prescriptive rules. We've seen, however, that prescriptive rules are arbitrary and variable. How does this arbitrariness and variability affect our definition and understanding of standard English? Can we define it at all?

A possible definition of standard English might be that given below.

Standard English: The version of English that you *perceive* as "standard."

This informal definition of standard English expresses the idea that there is no real, monolithic version of this language variety any more than there is agreement over what is prescriptively correct and what is not. Indeed, declarations of what is standard, and hence by definition also nonstandard, are not based on linguistic fact, but rather on speaker's *opinions* about what is linguistic fact.[7]

Some of you might be aware that in the United States, "broadcast English," the idealized "unaccented" English of the national media, is considered by many to characterize standard American English. Many of us also assume that politicians speak standard English, and we might draw this same conclusion about doctors, bankers, and lawyers. "Standard" varieties of the language are also those to which, right or wrong, we attach prestige as a culture, prestige often based on our perceptions of social class, education, ethnicity, and race. For example, many consider standard English synonymous with "educated" English, and nonstandard English as a mark of a speaker's lack of education. Interestingly, we are fairly indiscriminate in our perceptions of the connections between education and standard speech; some of us may be able to recall elementary, secondary, or college teachers who corrected our grammar, and who we simply assumed had the authority to do so. The connections between our notions of standard English and our views about race and ethnicity in this country are also not difficult to ferret out. In the United States, Hawaiian Pidgin English, African American Vernacular English, Chicano English and Pachuco are all highly stigmatized by nonspeakers of these varieties.

The following excerpts from the website "Common Errors in English," by Paul Brians illustrates the typical assumptions behind the idea of standard English. In each excerpt the author responds to frequently asked questions.

What is an error in English?

Here we're concerned only with deviations from the standard use of English as judged by sophisticated users such as professional writers, editors, teachers, and literate executives and personnel officers.

Aren't some of these points awfully picky?

---

[7]There is also debate over the terms *standard* and *nonstandard* themselves. As Rosina Lippi-Green points out in her book on language ideology, *English with an Accent*, nonstandard is, by definition, usually taken to mean *sub*standard. Standard language thus does not simply label a particular variety of English, but also implies that the variety in question has *prestige* over other varieties of the language. The terms standard and nonstandard thus promote a false dichotomy between language varieties, by labeling some as "right" or "good" and others as "wrong" or "bad."

Some common complaints about usage strike me as too persnickety, but I'm just covering mistakes in English that happen to bother me.

What gives you the right to say what's an error in English?

I'm a professor of English and do this sort of thing for a living. True, but my Ph.D. is in comparative literature, not composition or linguistics, and I teach courses in the history of ideas rather than language as such. But I admire good writing and try to encourage it in my students.

Isn't it oppressive of immigrants and subjugated minorities to insist on the use of standard English?

Language standards can certainly be used for oppressive purposes . . . [but the] fact is that the world is full of teachers, employers, and other authorities who may penalize you for your nonstandard use of the English language. Feel free to denounce these people if you wish; but if you need their good opinion to get ahead, you'd be wise to learn standard English. (*Source: Common Errors in English,* by Paul Brians. http://www.homeworkcentral.com/files.htp?fileid=48659&use=hc)

The content of the website actually underscores the arbitrariness of standard English and its status as a powerful myth. For example, for Professor Brians, standard English is a (presumably monolithic) variety of English spoken by "sophisticated" people, who are educated and/or in positions of social power and authority. We can be sure, however, that such users disagree on what is considered "standard." In fact, as Professor Brians states, the only errors he discusses are those that bother *him,* again illustrating the arbitrariness of what we define as "standard." Furthermore, as he points out, his position as an authority on "correct" English is based on his admiration for good writing, rather than on specific academic training or expertise. The website thus promotes the idea that "experts" on "correct" English are often self-appointed, or those recognized as authorities based on their social position and power. Finally, Professor Brians asserts that we would be wise to learn the language of those in power, if we wish to gain their good opinion. Though we certainly judge each other by our language, the ideas advanced in the website do nothing to encourage us to stop this practice, but rather encourage us to validate a system built on inequality.

The Approach to Grammar in This Book

This book is intended to help you understand your own descriptive grammar, and to explore the descriptive grammar of other speakers of English, which may differ from your own. It will, I hope, help you appreciate the dynamic and complex nature of syntax, a foundation upon which you can base your decisions and choices about language and its social role. To achieve this goal, we will focus on how language works, rather than how someone thinks it *should* work.

The approach taken in this book differs markedly from more traditional approaches in that we will not use drill and correction, a method based on students' recreating sentence models provided them. Rather, we will analyze, by hypothesizing and then testing the hypotheses, the syntactic structure of actual texts, taken from newspapers and magazines, popular and traditional fiction and nonfiction, poetry, and dialogue from television, film, and radio. The goal will be to encourage you to think critically about language, in particular syntax, and to construct arguments based on evidence you discover by analyzing a variety of texts. Actual texts are more syntactically complex than the model sentences you find in more traditional textbooks, and although sometimes you may wish fervently that you had a simple model to follow, I think you will find, in the long run, analysis of actual text more rewarding and also more fun.

Another result of the method of analysis we will use here, which I have found sometimes takes time to get used to, is that you will find that in syntactic analysis there is not always a "right answer." There will be times when you may disagree with someone else's analysis of a particular construction, on the basis of competing evidence. This is to be expected, as grammar is a complex and dynamic system that we use very creatively. It is helpful, then, to think of learning about grammar as an exploration of concepts and principles, where we tend to construct arguments based on evidence, rather than search for a "right answer." We don't know everything about grammar any more than we know everything about physics or chemistry. Scientists, like linguists, are forever experimenting and formulating hypotheses that they then test against even more data. It is perhaps more useful to think of studying grammar as a means of *discovering* more about the principles and basic structure of human language, rather than as a search for right answers.

Summary

In this chapter we discussed some different definitions of **grammar,** exploring in particular differences between **descriptive grammar,** or our intuitions about our language, and **prescriptive grammar,** our perceptions of what we consider "correct" grammar. We briefly considered some aspects of the interacting components of descriptive grammar. **Syntax,** the study of sentence structure, involves analysis of word order, phrases, and operations that apply to them. **Morphology** is the study of word structure and word formation rules including **derivational** and **inflectional affixation, clipping, blending, compounding, forming acronyms,** and **coining,** among others. The study of **phonetics** and **phonology** involves identifying the inventory of sounds in a language and the rules that apply to them, the accents, and the different stress and intonation patterns. **Semantics** concerns word and sentence meaning, including phenomena such as **quantification, presupposition, metaphor, anomaly, contradiction, ambiguity,** and **semantic shift.** Though we will focus on certain components of grammar in our subsequent discussions in this book, we also introduced the idea that crucial to a complete understanding of language *use* as a social tool is the notion of **communicative competence.**

We discussed the notion of **grammaticality** we will use in this book as meaning "a possible sentence of English." This notion of grammaticality is based on descriptive rather than prescriptive grammar, and thus avoids notions of "correctness." We discussed in some detail the notion of **standard English,** and how this language variety can be defined only relatively, as notions of "standard" versus "nonstandard" language vary from speech community to speech community.

DISCOVERY PROBLEMS

Problem 1. Morphology Exercise

In the following chapters we will discuss the morphological characteristics of words in some detail, as morphological information provides important "clues" in identifying a word's syntactic category, or "part of speech" (as noun, verb, adjective, etc.). This exercise is designed to give you some practice in morphological analysis.

Divide the following words into morphemes. Try to identify the affixes you find as either inflectional or derivational.

a. differences	i. catsup
b. lens	j. dignity
c. dinner	k. grammaticality
d. tallest	l. elephants
e. transformation	m. thickened
f. serenity	n. capable
g. dancing	o. dangerous
h. walks	p. paper

List two examples each of words (that you find on your own) created by the following processes.

a) coining
b) clipping
c) blending
d) compounding
e) forming acronyms
f) semantic shift

Find some examples of ways in which morphology is used in advertising to create a catchy phrase or brand name. Try to identify the word formation rule or type of affixation being used to create an effect. Bring one or two examples to class for discussion.

Problem 2. Lexical and Syntactic Ambiguity

We have seen that one way in which syntax and semantics interact is to create ambiguity, or sentences with more than one meaning. Ambiguity can be a result of the structure of the sentence (syntactic ambiguity expressed in terms of the different ways in which words can be grouped together) or of a particular word meaning (lexical ambiguity). See if you can identify the type of ambiguity— syntactic or lexical— in the following newspaper headlines. (You may try to bracket groups of words together as we have in the text to illustrate syntactic ambiguities.)

    a) Enraged cow injures farmer with ax.
    b) Squad helps dog bite victims.
    c) Eye drops off shelf.
    d) Buyers want a car to stand out a bit from the crowd.
    e) St. John tracing his grandfather's footsteps.
    f) Doctor testifies in horse suit.
    g) Talkeetna begins Moose Dropping Contest.

Problem 3. Grammaticality

Put a * in front of any of the following sentences that you find (descriptively) ungrammatical. Then try to "fix" the sentences to make them possible sentences in your variety of English. Compare your results with those of your classmates. Did you all have fairly consistent judgments about which sentences are ungrammatical, and did you all "fix" them in basically the same way?

    (1)   a. John is eager for Mary to meet Bill.
          b. John is eager for Mary to meet.

    (2)   a. There is a unicorn in my garden.
          b. There is the unicorn in my garden.

    (3)   a. It is clear that Mary should stop smoking.
          b. That Mary should stop smoking is clear.
          c. Mary should stop smoking is clear.

    (4)   a. Who does Mary like?
          b. Mary likes him.
          c. Who does Mary like him?

What you probably found is that your intuitions about sentences and how you would "fix" them are fairly consistent with those of your classmates. This is what we might expect, if descriptive grammar includes knowledge we all share as English speakers. Also, observe that you can "fix" sentences on the basis of your intuitions, without conscious knowledge of syntactic rules.

Problem 4. Have You Been "Corrected?"

Make a list of three sentences that you have been told are incorrect, improper grammar, sloppy speech, and so on. Who corrected you, and did you accept his or her judgment? Why or why not? Try to determine whether the sentences you were corrected for are in fact part of your descriptive grammar. That is, are they sentences you would normally say, even if you think that they are "improper grammar?" Is your characterization of them as "incorrect" based on what you think someone else might think of them? If you find this question hard to answer, list some reasons why. Write a short essay discussing your responses, and talk about your ideas together in class.

Problem 5. Have You "Corrected" Others?

Make a list of three things you have corrected or made fun of others for saying. Try to analyze *why* you think these things are ungrammatical. Can you think of any beliefs or possible stereotypes that underlie your opinion? Are these linguistically based or socially based?

Problem 6. Dialects and Ungrammaticality

We have all heard people speak with dialects other than our own, and we may have formulated judgments about such speakers based on the way they talk. Think of some examples of when this has been the case for you. Can you remember what you thought about such speakers' accents, vocabulary, and/or sentence patterns? How would you evaluate the differences in terms of descriptive and prescriptive grammar? Have your thoughts about this changed given the two definitions for grammar we have discussed here?

Problem 7. Standard English: Definitions

Books on English grammar and introductory linguistics often contain definitions of standard English. Find two such definitions, and try to determine the ideological assumptions that underlie each. Bring your definitions to class for discussion. What kinds of generalizations can you make about definitions of standard English on the basis of your sample? (You can also use the Internet as a resource.)

Problem 8. Language Attitudes

Make up a "language attitudes survey" in class by listing a number of stereotypes and beliefs you have about language. Some examples might include:

I use sloppy speech sometimes.

French is a very romantic language.

One language can be more complex than another.

Then discuss whether they are based on linguistic fact or cultural belief. How might a deeper understanding of how language works help dispel some of your linguistic stereotypes and prejudices?

Problem 9. Language Stereotypes

Find examples in the media (movies, videotapes, advertising, radio, etc.) of how people are stereotyped by their language (accent or other dialectal differences associated with ethnicity, race, etc.) Disney movies are a good place to look (Jafar in *Aladdin* has a British accent, as does Scar in *The Lion King*. The heroes, Aladdin and Simba, respectively, speak unstigmatized varieties of American English). Try to determine what kinds of grammatical differences distinguish those portrayed positively, and those portrayed negatively. Do you notice any ways in which gender, race, or class is expressed through linguistic stereotypes?

Problem 10. "Foreign" Languages

Make up a list of languages, and write down the stereotypes you have about each one. Get in groups and compare them, and then discuss them in class. What do your findings show about our language attitudes? What are your opinions about other languages based on? What languages are on your list, and what does that tell you about your world view?

TEXT ANALYSIS

1. The Components of Grammar

Rewrite the following paragraph, from *Huckleberry Finn*, in what you consider to be standard English. What changes did you make? Use the following questions as a guide.

- Did you make changes in vocabulary (morphological changes)?
- Did you make any phonological changes that affect how a word might be pronounced?
- What observations can you make about how the dialect is represented here in terms of spelling?
- Do the spellings themselves have any effect on you as the reader?
- Did you make any syntactic changes, (having to do with word order)?
- What sense do we get of the speaker (Jim) from your revision, and how is it different from the sense of him conveyed by the original version?

In this excerpt, Jim responds to Huck's question about the existence of good-luck (as opposed to bad-luck) signs.

"Mighty few—an' dey ain' no use to a body. What you want to know when good luk's a-comin for? Want to keep it off? . . . Ef you' got hairy arms en a hairy breas', it's a sign dat, you's agwyne to be rich. Well, dy's some use in a sign like dat, 'kase it's so fur ahead. You see, maybe you's got to be po' a long time fust, en so you might git discourage' en kill yo'sef 'f you didn't know by de sign dat you gwyne to be rich bymeby."

Source: *Adventures of Huckleberry Finn,* by Mark Twain.

2. More on Grammatical Components

In the following paragraph the writer uses different components of grammar to create a particular stylistic effect. Read the text and answer the following questions.

O, what a world of unseen visions and heard silences, this insubstantial country of the mind! What ineffable essences, these touchless rememberings and unshowable reveries! And the privacy of it all! A secret theater of speechless monologue and prevenient counsel, an invisible mansion of all moods, musings and mysteries, an infinite resort of disappointments and discoveries.

Source: *The Origin of the Consciousness and the Bicameral Mind,* by Julian Jaynes.

- What semantic properties does the writer rely on in his use of phrases such as *unseen visions and heard silences* and *speechless monologue?* What property does he use in the phrase *insubstantial country of the mind?*
- How does the writer use phonology to create a stylistic effect or tone with lines such as *ineffable essences, invisible mansion of moods, musings and mysteries,* and *disappointments and discoveries?*
- Consider the author's word choice in the phrase *touchless rememberings and unshowable reveries!*. Put this phrase into your own words, and then try to analyze the morphological and semantic differences between your

word choice and the author's. What role does morphology play in creating a certain stylistic effect?

- What observations can you make about word order or syntax in the text? Are there any orders you would change to make the text sound more natural in your own speech? What is the effect of the syntax of the text on the reader?

3. Poetry Analysis

In a poem of your choice, discuss three or four instances of how word order, the structure of particular words, their sounds, and their meanings play a role in creating a poetic effect. That is, in what ways do syntax, morphology, phonology, and semantics contribute to the overall effect of the poem? Bring a copy of the poem to class for discussion.

LANGUAGE DIVERSITY EXERCISES

1. Earlier Englishes

It is natural for us to think that a sentence construction we are unfamiliar with is actually ungrammatical, since it is not part of our own dialect and thus not part of our own descriptive grammar. Descriptive grammars therefore vary from speech community to speech community. Descriptive grammars also vary over time—the descriptive grammars of dialects of Old and Middle English, earlier versions of English spoken in Britain, differ quite dramatically from the varieties of English spoken today.

Find three sentences of Old or Middle English or Early Modern English. Try to analyze each sentence, and explain why it differs from your own speech, or more precisely, your own descriptive grammar. Does the difference come, for example, from vocabulary (morphology), word order (syntax), and/or word meanings (semantics)?

2. Modern Englishes

Find a few sentences of a variety of modern English other than your own, and bring them to class for discussion. Write your sentences on the board and try to discuss the syntactic differences between them and your own variety of English. Explain how you can analyze different varieties as "English." What do they have in common? Discuss the dialect differences in terms of prescriptive and descriptive grammar—what kinds of judgments might you make if you were to hear someone use the sentences in your sample?

3. Prescription in Other Languages

Different groups have tried to regulate language use, sometimes by forming a language "academy" that attempts to codify the language. For example, *L'A-*

cadémie Française was formed in France to maintain the purity of the French language by attempting to limit the number of English words that come into the French language. Write a brief essay on one such academy or institution, and discuss its effectiveness. Are such academies able to control language in the way they propose? Who decides what is to be allowed, and what disallowed, and what methods are proposed to enforce these decisions? What is the status of descriptive grammar in such an institution?

4. Standard Languages

In a short essay, discuss the notion of "standard" language as it applies to a language other than English. Does German, for example, have a "standard" language variety? Who decides which variety is considered standard, and why? What is the status of varieties of the language that are not considered standard? Can the standard language variety be clearly defined, or is it, as in English, what speakers "perceive" to be standard? Does the notion of a standard variety of the language vary from community to community? You may want to interview native speakers of the language in question for your answer, and compare and contrast their views with those you find in written texts that address this issue.

5. The Language Mavens: Prescriptive Grammar

In newspapers and magazines we sometimes find articles by writers whom Steven Pinker, author of *The Language Instinct,* calls "language mavens." These authors (Edwin Newman, William Safire, James Kilpatrick, John Simon, among others) often discuss grammatical "errors" and provide (sometimes derisive) advice concerning how to "correct" these problems. Find an example of such an article, and write a short response to it. Do you agree/disagree with the author's view? Why or why not? How does the piece reflect issues discussed above concerning prescriptive and descriptive grammar, and the notion of standard English?

CHAPTER REVIEW TERMS

different conceptions of the term "grammar"
components of grammar

  syntax (order of words and phrases, operations that apply to sentences)

  phonology (phonetics, phonological rules, accent, stress, intonation)

  morphology (coining, blending, clipping, forming acronyms, compounding, inflectional and derivational affixation)

  semantics (quantification, presupposition, metaphor, contradiction, anomaly, lexical and syntactic ambiguity, semantic shift) descriptive grammar, communicative competence, prescriptive grammar, grammaticality, standard English

CHAPTER REVIEW EXERCISES

1.Approaches to Grammar

As we've mentioned in the chapter, approaches to grammar vary rather widely across different disciplines. Analyze the approach to grammar in textbooks from different disciplines (you might divide into groups to do this, with each group choosing a category). Look at approaches to grammar in textbooks for:

- English composition, technical writing, rhetoric
- Teaching English as a Second Language
- Learning a "foreign" language
- English grammar "handbooks"
- English grammar textbooks

How is "grammar" defined in these books, and how are these definitions different from or similar to the definitions of prescriptive and descriptive we have discussed in this chapter? What approach, if any, do these texts take to standard English? Is there a notion of "authority" expressed in the text, either explicitly or implicitly? Compare your analyses with those of other classmates/groups.

2. Class Reports/Papers/Debates:

There are many different topics for short papers, roundtables and debates, or reports that can be based on the issues brought up in this chapter. Students can do different kinds of projects on the Ebonics controversy, the English Only movement, bilingualism, use of accent in films and on television, origins of different dialects in the United States or elsewhere, attitudes toward grammar and prescription in non-Western societies, and so on. See the Appendix for guidance in researching these topics.

3. Prescription and Standardization in the Schools

Some of you using this book are prospective teachers, and some of you may already be teachers. Coming to terms with the pros and cons of prescriptive grammar is particularly difficult for teachers, since we want to prepare our students the best we can for the "outside world," a world in which they may be expected to speak "correctly." Write a short essay of what you think about this issue at this point, before we have delved very deeply into the study of descriptive grammar.

- How would you approach this issue in your own classroom, and what would you hope to be the result?
- What strategies might you use to reach your pedagogical goals? What kind or problems might you encounter?
- If you have already had experience in the classroom with this issue, discuss that experience, and what you have learned from it, what you see that needs to be changed, or maintained, and so on.

You might like to formulate your essay as a response to a parent who comes to you with the question: *What are you going to do to teach my child to "talk right"?* It might be useful to revisit your essay from time to time as you work through the book, as your ideas about this complex issue perhaps develop and change.

2

Some Syntactic Fundamentals

Categories and Phrases

Phrase structure, clearly, is the kind of stuff language is made of.
From *The Language Instinct* by Steven Pinker

Introduction

Before we begin our more detailed study of the syntax of English, in this chapter you will become acquainted with some of the basic concepts and terminology we will be using throughout the book. The material discussed here builds on what you already know about some of the organizing principles of language. These ideas will therefore probably not be as foreign to you as the labels we will assign to them may make them seem.

This chapter introduces the basic notion of *syntactic categories*, the classes into which words can be divided on the basis of their different characteristics. We all have ideas about what a *noun* or a *verb* is; we might think of a noun as "a person, place or thing," and a verb as "an action or state." But beyond this, we may not have given these classes of words much thought. In Part Two of the book we will systematically analyze different classes of words in terms of their syntax, semantics, and morphology. In this chapter we will discuss a more general division between word classes, *grammatical* and *lexical categories*. For example, the syntactic category Noun is, as we find in Chapter 4, a lexical category, but determiners, such as *the/a/this*, words that introduce members of the lexical category Noun, are members of a grammatical category, Determiner. We will see that lexical and grammatical categories have distinct syntactic, semantic, and morphological properties that provide insights into how grammar is organized.

In this chapter we also introduce *phrase structure rules*, a notational convention that allows us to express some fundamental properties of syntactic structure. This convention is used by linguists to represent syntactic categories and how they are grouped together into larger units, or *phrases*. Phrase structure rules also, as we shall see, allow us to express syntactic principles of *hierarchical structure* (how one phrase can be contained inside another one) and *recursion* (how phrases can "regenerate" themselves). We will call upon phrase structure in our discussions in later chapters as a means of visually expressing the organization of sentences, an organization that is not necessarily apparent in a sequence of words.

Syntactic Categories

You may already be somewhat familiar with the idea of **syntactic categories,** though most of you have probably heard them called "parts of speech," or "word classes." We will see here that words can be classified in a number of different ways. They can be divided according to what they mean, a semantic classification. For example, as mentioned above, you are all probably familiar with the sentence: *a noun is a person, place, or thing,* or have heard that adjectives *describe* nouns. Words can also be divided into classes on the basis of their structure, or morphology: nouns, for example, can be recognized by certain endings, or affixes, that change complete words or roots into nouns. When we add *-ion* to *digest,* or *-er* to *write,* we form the nouns *digestion* and *writer.* Adjectives can be recognized by the suffix *-al,* as in *legal,* or the endings *-er/-est,* as in *taller/tallest.* Words can also be classified by their syntax—by the order in which they occur, and the kinds of syntactic operations that apply to them.

Grammatical and Lexical Categories

Before considering each different syntactic category in detail, it is useful to become familiar with two basic subclasses of syntactic categories, **grammatical** and **lexical categories.** Some lexical categories with which you may be familiar are Noun, Verb, Adjective, and Adverb. Grammatical categories include "little words" such as *the, very,* and *too.* Here we discuss a systematic approach to the differences between these two basic classes of words.

Semantic Clues

One defining characteristic of lexical categories is that they have certain semantic properties in common. For example, members of these categories all have lexical *content,* or intrinsic meanings of their own, such as you would find in a dictionary entry. Other types of words are classified in terms of their grammatical *function,* rather than in terms of their intrinsic meaning. We say that these latter types of words have "grammatical" meanings.

For example, the word *dog* "means" to us a four-legged mammal that we may keep as a pet. In the phrase *the dog,* on the other hand, the word *the* has no such intrinsic meaning. Rather, it has the grammatical function of making the noun *dog* definite. *The dog* thus refers to a definite dog, known to both the speaker and hearer of the phrase. *A dog,* on the other hand, refers to an indefinite dog, whose identity is unknown to the speaker and perhaps to the hearer as well. This grammatical distinction between *the/a dog* is encoded in the words *the/a: the* is a definite determiner, and *a* is an indefinite determiner. Determiners thus form a category of words whose meanings are grammatical, rather than lexical.

In the phrase *very strong, strong* has intrinsic meaning, and is a member of the lexical category Adjective. Other members of this category include words such as *huge/red/fantastic.* The word *very* in the phrase *very strong,* however, expresses information about the degree of strength. *Very,* like *the/a,* has a grammatical meaning, namely degree. *Very* is a member of the grammatical category Degree, along with other degree words such as *so/too/less/quite/rather.*

To further illustrate the meaning difference between lexical and grammatical categories, compare the dictionary definition of the noun *ghost* in (1) with that of the definite determiner *the* in (2).

(1) ghost: the spirit of a dead person, thought to haunt living persons or former habitats. . . .
(2) the: used before singular or plural nouns and noun phrases that denote particular, specified persons or things.

As the contrast between (1) and (2) shows, the noun *ghost* has intrinsic meaning, meaning that is not defined in terms of grammatical function. The determiner *the,* on the other hand, is defined in terms of the grammatical information it contributes to a following noun, namely number and definiteness.

Morphological Clues

Grammatical and lexical categories are also distinguished morphologically. Recall that morphology is the component of grammar that includes word-formation rules such as derivational affixation, compounding, blending, coining, and so on. Grammatical categories typically do not undergo these processes. As a result, they are "closed" morphological classes, ones to which we do not add new members. Imagine, for example, coming up with a new determiner to add to *the/a/that/this/these/those.* To add another member to the list, we would have to come up with a new grammatical relation, something we rarely do. Lexical categories, on the other hand, productively add new members, and are thus "open" classes of words. Some words that have recently come into the language include the nouns *Internet, cyberspace,* and *hypertext* from computer technology and the verbs *mindmeld* and *shapeshift* from the Star Trek television series. The adjectives *sweet* (as in *No test! Sweet!*) and *fly* (as in *That movie was fly!*) are now part of many American English speakers' lexicons. It is easy to find other examples in movies (*Wayne's World* and *Clueless* are prime examples) and television (*Saturday Night Live, The X-Files, Seinfeld,* commentary on sports, politics, etc.).

Syntactic Clues

To help us identify syntactic categories we also rely on our intuitions about the different syntactic classes to which words belong. We all have such intuitions, even though we might not know the conventional labels for different word classes. For example, consider the word *singing*. This word might look at first glance like a verb because of its morphology: it ends in *-ing*, an ending that we typically associate with verbs. Further, when we see the word *singing* in a sentence such as *Rosanne was singing the national anthem*, we think of that word as a verb in part because of its position: it is preceded by *was*, an auxiliary or "helping" verb we recognize from constructions such as *was hoping* and *was leaving*. Further, *was singing* follows the subject, *Rosanne*, in a position in which we find other verbs, as in *Rosanne stars in a television show*, and semantically expresses what the subject is doing. When we see *singing* in certain other positions in the sentence, however, we assign it a different category, regardless of its morphology. In the sentence *The singing really got on my nerves*, for example, *singing* occurs in the same position as other nouns and is preceded by *the*, and is itself the subject of the sentence. Thus, we know that *singing* has a different syntactic function in each sentence on the basis of its position, even though it has the same morphological form. When we analyze the syntactic category of a word in context in a sentence, rather than in isolation, we rely at least in part on syntactic clues, or evidence, to help us.

To further explore our intuitions about syntactic categories, consider the first line of Kate Chopin's novella, *The Awakening*.

(3)   A green and yellow parrot, which hung in a cage outside the door, kept repeating over and over: "Allez-vous-en! Allez-vous-en! Sapristi!

In (3), *parrot* is preceded by *a*, and the words *green* and *yellow*, words that describe it. We thus understand from this syntactic information (a preceding article, and two adjectives) that *parrot* is of the category Noun, a member of the same category as a word such as *decision* in *a good decision*. We use this same unconscious knowledge in deciphering Lewis Carroll's nonsense poem *Jabberwocky*, in which we encounter, for example, the phrase *the slithy toves*.

(4)   T'was brillig and the slithy toves

Even though we have no idea what either *slithy* or *toves* means, we still understand *toves* to be a member of the same category of words in which we would include *parrot* in (3). Though you may not be able to state the reasons for your analysis in formal syntactic terms at this point, your intuitions tell you that *toves* is a noun because it is preceded by a determiner, *the*, and a word that can be analyzed as an adjective, *slithy*. *Toves* therefore occurs in the same position as *frogs*, for example, in *the slimy frogs*.[1]

---

[1] There are morphological and phonological clues here too, which we no doubt call upon unconsciously in our analysis of the syntactic category of *toves* or *slithy*. For example, *toves* ends in *-s*, a plural affix on nouns, and *slithy* ends in *-y*, which we might recognize as the affix on *slimy* or *icky*. Further, *slithy* "sounds like" an adjective, namely *slimy*, and we might use that information to identify *slithy* as an adjective.

Just like the word *singing, parrot* can function as a syntactic category other than a noun, depending on its syntactic position. To illustrate, consider (5).

(5)   The child would *parrot* his mother's every word.

In (5) *parrot* is a member of another syntactic category, namely the category Verb. Verbs, but not nouns, occur after *would*, which we know from the impossibility of **I would baseball*, and the grammaticality of *I would play baseball*.[2] *Parrot* in (5) is also followed by an "object," namely the phrase *his mother's every word*, a property of verbs but not of nouns. That is, we hear and say *the enemy destroyed the city*, and *Juanita arranged the meeting*, in which the verbs *destroy* and *arrange* are followed by objects. We don't hear or say **the destruction the city*, or **the arrangement the meeting*, in which the nouns *destruction* and *arrangement* are followed by objects. We therefore identify *parrot* in (5) as a verb, based on its syntactic position.

The distinction between lexical and grammatical categories we make here will sometimes contrast with that of more traditional approaches to word classes. In some grammars of English, for example, degree words such as *so/very/too* are labeled as members of the lexical category Adverb, and thus fall together with words such as *quickly/happily/fast*. Members of the grammatical category Quantifier, words such as *all/both/every*, are also sometimes labeled as members of the lexical category Adjective, a category that is also sometimes assumed to include determiners such as *the/a/this/that/these/those*. These arbitrary labels do not reflect syntactic, morphological, or semantic differences among grammatical and lexical categories, which we will discuss, and thus they miss important generalizations about differences among word classes. For example, when we label degree words such as *so/very/too* as Adverbs, we miss the generalization that degree words do not in fact function syntactically in the same way as adverbs such as *quickly/happily/fast*. (You can run *fast*, but you can't **run very*.) Similarly, quantifiers such as *all/both/every* do not function in the same way as adjectives such as *tall/disgusting/unequivocal*. (You can say *Michael Jordan is tall*, but not **Michael Jordan is every*.)

We can thus distinguish lexical and grammatical categories on the basis of both their semantics and their morphology. We can distinguish these two categories on the basis of syntactic differences as well, which we discuss in more detail in later sections. First, we introduce phrase structure.

Phrase Structure

In the previous section you were introduced to syntactic categories, or the ways in which we classify words depending on various kinds of grammatical infor-

---

[2]Of course, *I would baseball* might be grammatical for some speakers when understood as including an omitted verb, as in *You would play basketball and I would baseball, if only we had the time*. What is relevant here is *I would baseball* without such a context is ungrammatical.

mation from syntax, semantics, and morphology. In this section we investigate how words of different categories can be combined into larger syntactic units, or *phrases.* As we will see, every sentence can be diagrammed in terms of its *phrase structure,* which provides us with a useful means of representing syntactic relationships among words. Phrase structures are generated by *phrase structure rules,* which allow us to express some important properties of sentence structure, including *hierarchical structure,* the means by which one phrase can contain another phrase, and *recursion,* the property of generating an infinite number of sentences from a finite set of rules.

Phrases and Hierarchical Structure

You may remember from Chapter 1 that sentences can be lexically or syntactically ambiguous. Lexical ambiguity arises when a particular word has more than one meaning, and syntactic ambiguity arises from the different ways in which a sentence can be constructed. For review of this idea, consider (6).

(6)   The journalist interviewed the actor in a tuxedo.

We understand (6) to mean that the journalist was wearing a tuxedo while interviewing the actor, or that the actor was wearing the tuxedo while being interviewed. These two meanings are represented using brackets as in (7a–b), respectively.

(7)   a. The journalist interviewed [the actor] [in a tuxedo].
      b. The journalist interviewed [the actor [in a tuxedo]].

That we can bracket different groups of words to express ambiguity indicates that sentences have some kind of structure beyond simple linear order. Linguists express this structure in terms of syntactic **phrases.** For instance, in (7a), *the actor* and *in a tuxedo* form separate phrases, and we thus don't understand *in a tuxedo* as describing the actor. In (7b), on the other hand, *in a tuxedo* forms a phrase with *the actor,* and is included in the description of the actor. The **phrase structure** of the sentence thus provides us with important clues for interpreting its meaning, meaning we would be at a loss to explain without the concept of phrases, represented by the brackets as in (7).

We can make this notion of phrases more precise by labeling the brackets in (7) according to their syntactic category, (and thus using what linguists aptly call "labeled brackets.") *The actor* in (8a) is what we will call a *noun phrase,* a phrase that has a noun *actor* as its main word, or **head.** *In a tuxedo* is what we will call a *prepositional phrase,* a phrase that is headed by a preposition, in this case, *in.* Using labeled bracket notation, we represent the ambiguities in (7) as in (8).

(8)   a. The journalist interviewed [the actor] [in a tuxedo].
                                    NP   PP
      b. The journalist interviewed [the actor [in a tuxedo]].
                                    NP   PP

The labeled brackets in (8) allow us to express yet another syntactic property, that of **hierarchical structure,** or the ways in which a phrase can contain another one. In (8a), the prepositional phrase *in a tuxedo* is not included in the noun phrase *the actor,* but in (8b) it is. The prepositional phrase in (8b) is therefore contained in a larger phrase, namely the noun phrase *the actor in a tuxedo.* The prepositional phrase is thus a **constituent,** or part, of the larger noun phrase. (8b) illustrates that phrases have **hierarchical structure:** a phrase can contain another phrase, which can contain another phrase, and so on. We say that the noun phrase in (8b) **dominates** the prepositional phrase contained within it.

Syntactic structure is therefore more complex than we might at first imagine; sentences consist not of simple linear orderings of words, but rather of words organized into phrases headed by different syntactic categories. (We have so far introduced noun phrases and prepositional phrases, for illustration.) Phrases themselves have hierarchical structure; one phrase can be dominated by another. In the following section we discuss a way to represent phrases other than by labeled brackets. This new notation provides a more complete description of a mechanism that we can use to diagram sentences, and it also provides us with some insights into how we actually produce, or "generate" hierarchical sentence structure.

Phrase Structure Rules

We saw above that noun phrases can have different structures. The noun phrase in (8a) is made up of [determiner (*the*) + noun (*actor*)], and the noun phrase in (8b) is of the structure [determiner (*the*) + noun (*actor*) + prepositional phrase (*in a tuxedo*)]. We might assume, on the basis of these two examples, that noun phrases contain a noun and also a determiner and possibly also a prepositional phrase. We represent these generalizations about the structure of a noun phrase, or NP, with the **phrase structure rule** in (9), where parentheses indicate a constituent is optional. (We abbreviate the category Determiner here as DET.)

(9)   NP => DET N (PP)

The rule in (9) basically says that noun phrases have the structure [determiner + noun + optional prepositional phrase]. (9) thus allows us to produce or *generate* both of the noun phrases in (8). The rule in (9) also expresses the generalization that phrases have heads; a noun phrase, for example, is headed by, and thus must always dominate, a noun. Observe also that within the noun phrase, the head is preceded, or introduced, by a grammatical category, namely *the,* a member of the grammatical category Determiner. This illustrates an important distinction between grammatical and lexical categories; lexical categories *head* phrases, and grammatical categories typically *introduce* lexical ones.

We can now use phrase structure to illustrate the differences between the sentences in (8a) and (8b). (10a) is the phrase structure of the relevant part of (8a), in which the prepositional phrase, headed by the preposition *in,* is not a constituent of (it is not dominated by) the noun phrase headed by the noun *actor.*

In (10b), on the other hand, the prepositional phrase is dominated by, and is a constituent of, the noun phrase.

(10) a.

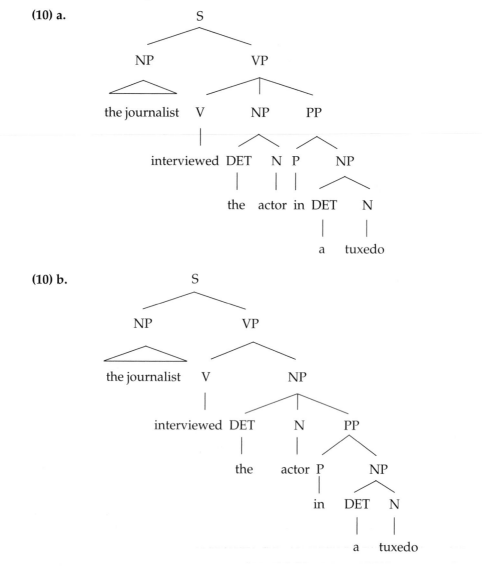

We thus can express the syntactic ambiguity in (8) in terms of two different syntactic structures; in one representation the noun phrase dominates a prepositional phrase, but in the other it does not.

As you might have observed, the phrase structure rule in (9) as written fails to accommodate all the possible structures for noun phrases that we can think of. For example, (9) as it stands doesn't allow us to have noun phrases that do *not* include determiners, such as *homework*, in the sentence *Homework gets on my nerves.* Nor can we diagram noun phrases introduced by quantifiers as in *both boys*, or numerals, as in *six goats.* Some other examples of noun phrases that cannot be generated by (9) are given in (11) and illustrated with labeled brackets in (12).

(11) Lee ordered *lasagna, red wine,* and *two salads.* Cary ordered *some spaghetti.*

(12) a. *lasagna* [noun]
             NP
        b. *red wine* [adjective + noun]
             NP
        c. *two salads* [numeral + noun]
             NP
        d. *some spaghetti* [quantifier + noun]
             NP

The examples in (12) illustrate our earlier generalization, namely that lexical categories, in this case nouns, head phrases. Grammatical categories introduce lexical ones; in (12c–d), *two* and *some* are members of the grammatical categories Numeral and Quantifier, respectively. These two words contribute grammatical information, namely information about number or quantity, and do not have lexical content in the same way as the nouns they introduce, *salads* and *spaghetti,* respectively. We do not add new numerals or quantifiers to the language, indicating that these words are members of morphologically closed classes.

We will not attempt to formulate a comprehensive phrase structure rule to account for all of the possibilities in (12). Nevertheless, it is important to notice that if we wanted to, we could in fact formulate a detailed phrase structure rule that would allow for the possibilities in (12), among others as well. We return to the structure of noun phrases in more detail in Chapter 4.

One issue that bears brief mention has to do with the noun phrase in (12a). Observe that in this case, a noun phrase is made up of a single head noun, *lasagna.* It may at first seem odd to think that a single noun can also be a phrase, but as we will find in the following chapter, a phrase dominating only a head, such as *lasagna* in (12a), has the same syntactic properties as a larger phrase and is therefore best analyzed as a noun phrase rather than as a noun. We will thus diagram *lasagna* in (12a) as in (13).

(13)

The noun phrase in (13) can be generated by the phrase structure rule in (9) only if we revise the rule to make determiners (such as *the*) optional. We do this by putting DET in parentheses, as in (14).

(14)   NP => (DET) N (PP)

The phrase structure rule for noun phrases in (14) allows noun phrases to contain a single head noun, as in (13). We can now diagram the italicized words in (15) as full noun phrases, even though they each dominate only a single head noun.

(15)   a. *They* want to vacation in the *Galapagos*.
           b. *Jim* will become famous for studying *genes* and *DNA*.

We will discuss evidence for the "phrasehood" of the italicized nouns in (15) momentarily. Below, we explore yet another property of sentence structure that we can express in terms of phrase structure rules.

Recursion

The phrase structure rule for the noun phrase in (14), as we know, includes in its expansion another phrase, a prepositional phrase, or PP. Further, PP itself has the structure [preposition + noun phrase]. By including a prepositional phrase in the phrase structure rule for noun phrase, then, we include a means for a noun phrase to generate *another* noun phrase. This is illustrated in (16), where we have given the phrase structure rules of both noun phrase and prepositional phrase.

(16)   a. NP => (DET) N (PP)
           b. PP => P NP

According to (16a), a noun phrase can possibly dominate a prepositional phrase. Prepositional phrases, according to (16b), dominate noun phrases. From this it follows that the phrase structure rule for noun phrase in (16a) is *recursive*; it allows a noun phrase to "regenerate" itself ad infinitum. The rule for prepositional phrases in (16b) is recursive as well; a prepositional phrase can dominate a noun phrase, which in turn can dominate another prepositional phrase.

The property of phrase structure rules to generate phrases of the same category is called **recursion,** illustrated by the phrase structure tree in (17).

(17) Recursion

the frog on the bump on the log in the hole in the bottom of the sea

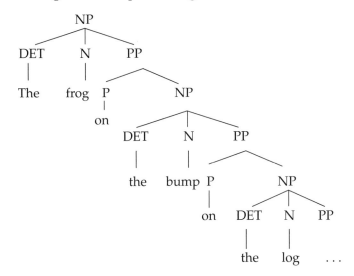

In (17), the highest noun phrase dominates a prepositional phrase, which itself dominates another noun phrase. (17) thus illustrates noun phrase recursion. (17) also exemplifies prepositional phrase recursion; the highest prepositional phrase dominates a noun phrase that in turn dominates another prepositional phrase. The phrase structure rules for noun phrase and prepositional phrase in (16) are thus both recursive rules.

Recursion, captured by phrase structure rules, expresses the property of language that we can generate phrases of indefinite length. It is recursion as well that allows us to generate sentences of infinite length, by allowing one sentence to dominate another. An example of sentence recursion is given in (18).

(18) [The jury decided [that the defendant was guilty]].
　　　S　　　　　　　　S

The sentence *The jury decided that the defendant was guilty* includes a shorter one: *(that) the defendant was guilty.* We can conclude that the phrase structure rule for the expansion of the phrase structure rule for *Sentence,* what we will abbreviate as S, as in (19), must be recursive.

(19) S => NP VP

You have probably heard somewhere along the line that sentences are composed of a "subject" and a "predicate." In (19), these semantic relations are represented in terms of phrase structure by a noun phrase and a verb phrase, respectively. To make (19) recursive, we must somehow ensure that an S can dominate another S. We do this by proposing (20) as one possible expansion of the phrase structure rule for verb phrase.

(20)   VP => V S

According to (20), the verb phrase, or predicate, of a sentence can itself domi-nate another sentence. This allows us to generate the sentence in (18), in which the verb phrase headed by the verb *decide* dominates another sentence, *(that) the defendant was guilty*. The phrase structure for (18) is given in (21), where the high-est S dominates a verb phrase, within which occurs another S.

(21)

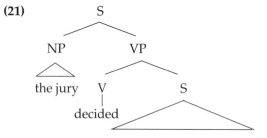

that the defendant was guilty

As we saw with the phrase structure rule for noun phrase in (14), the phrase structure rule for verb phrase in (20) represents only one possible expansion of VP, and does not include options for the array of other possible structures of this phrase. For example, according to (20) we would not be able to generate verb phrases that dominate anything other than a verb and a sentence, as illustrated in (21). There are, of course, many other options for material following the verb in the verb phrase other than sentences. Some examples are given in (22) through (24).

(22)   Many people consider [Leonardo DiCaprio] [a good actor].
                                 NP   NP

(23)   Leonardo DiCaprio took [the part].
                                  NP

(24)   The actor talked [to the reporter].
                           PP

As we can see from (22–24), the phrase structure rule for VP must allow for the following possibilities:

(25)   a. VP => V NP NP
       b. VP => V NP
       c. VP => V PP

We can amend (20) to express the different expansions for VP in (22–24) by using another notational convention, namely "curly" brackets, which allow us a means of "listing" the possible options for expanding a particular phrase structure rule. To illustrate, consider (26).

$$\textbf{(26)} \quad \text{VP} => \text{V} \begin{Bmatrix} \text{S} \\ \text{NP (NP)} \\ \text{PP} \end{Bmatrix}$$

According to (26), VP can be expanded as [V + S], giving us (21). It can also be expanded as [V + NP (NP)]; this option allows us to either have verb phrases of the structure [V + NP], as in (23), or [V + NP + NP], as in (22). The second NP is in parentheses, and thus optional. (26) also allows us to generate verb phrases with the structure [V + PP], as in (24). We can thus look at curly brackets as a means of expressing a number of different *possible options* for the expansion of a verb phrase. Observe once again that the phrase structure rule for VP in (26) is itself recursive; VP can expand as [V + S], with S expanding as [NP + VP]. The verb phrase can therefore generate another verb phrase, because it can generate a sentence.

One might ask at this point, given the evidence that language allows sentences of infinite length, why aren't the sentences we speak infinitely long? What makes us end our sentences at all, if our phrase structure rules are recursive? We do often use sentences of great length, but the limits of our memories, and therefore the ability to understand and keep track of extremely long sentences, keeps us from generating them. Phrase structure rules can therefore be viewed as a finite set c´ ˉules with infinite power: a single rule for prepositional phrase, verb phrase, noun phrase, or sentence can give rise to an infinite number of different phrases and sentences, of varying lengths. Factors independent of phrase structure rules, namely memory limitations, interact with our grammatical knowledge to limit the actual length of our sentences and phrases.

Summary

In this chapter we have introduced the notion of **syntactic categories** and how these categories can be divided into two basic types, **lexical categories** and **grammatical categories.** Grammatical and lexical categories are distinguished semantically, morphologically, and syntactically, as expressed in Table 2.1.

In this chapter we also discussed some fundamentals of phrase structure, first using labeled bracket notation, then moving on to **phrase structure rules,** the notation linguists use to capture a number of different kinds of generalizations about the structure of sentences. These generalizations are listed in Table 2.2.

In the following chapter we continue the discussion of phrase structure, investigating some ways we can "test" whether a group of words forms a syn-

Table 2.1
Characteristics of Lexical and Grammatical Categories

	Lexical Categories	**Grammatical Categories**
Semantics	They have lexical content.	They have grammatical meanings or functions.
Morphology	They are open classes, and therefore admit new members.	They are closed classes, and do not admit new members.
Syntax	They head phrases.	They introduce a lexical category (usually the head of a phrase).

Table 2.2
Phrase Structure Rules

- Show us relationships not expressed by linear order of sentences, such as phrases and heads of phrases

- Allow us to diagram any sentence in our language

- Provide us with a way of expressing the hierarchical structure of phrases and sentences

- Provide us with a way of expressing how syntactic structure is recursive

tactic phrase on the basis of evidence from movement, pronominalization, and coordination.

DISCOVERY PROBLEMS

Problem 1. Be a Word

In class, form groups of three or four. Each group should then make up a sentence of reasonable length and assign each word to a member of the group. Each group should then attempt to "act out" to the rest of the class each word in their sentence, in a version of "sentence charades." The class tries to guess the sentence, and write it on the blackboard. As you will find, miming a grammatical category is much harder than miming a lexical one. Discuss why this is so, and try to formulate a list of the different types of meanings of grammatical and lexical categories. Have a dictionary on hand to look up the "meanings" of grammatical categories you identify, and compare them with the "meanings" of the lexical categories.

Problem 2. Sentence Diagrams

You are now familiar with a partial set of phrase structure rules for the categories NP, PP, VP, and S, as follows:

S => NP VP
NP => (DET) N (PP)

$$VP => V \begin{Bmatrix} S \\ NP \ (NP) \\ PP \end{Bmatrix}$$

PP => P NP

Practice using this set of phrase structure rules by diagramming the following sentences. (We will assume here that DET, or Determiner, includes *the/a/this/that/these/those* and prepositions include words such as *down/from/in/on/out* etc.)

a) The students in the class consider the assignment a bore.
b) Those apples came from stores down the street.
c) The parents think the child on the playground is a bully.
d) The cat ran out the door.
e) Doctors give patients medicine.

When you have finished diagramming the above sentences, make up four sentences on your own that can be generated by the above phrase structure rules and diagram them.

Problem 3. Reading Phrase Structure Rules

Below is a list of phrase structure rules that are a bit different from those in Problem 2. Using this new set of rules, determine which of the sentences in (a–e) can be generated by these rules (there may be more than one).

S => NP VP
NP => (DET) N (PP)

$$VP => V \begin{Bmatrix} NP \\ (PP) \end{Bmatrix}$$

PP => P NP

a) The woman slipped on the pavement.
b) People from cities know about traffic.
c) The senator in the room laughed.
d) Big animals need space.
e) Mary met John at the theater.

Make a list of four sentences of your own, in which at least two can be generated by the phrase structure rules just given. Exchange sentences with a classmate, and try to determine which sentences can be generated by the phrase structure rules, and which cannot be.

Problem 4. Writing Phrase Structure Rules

As discussed above, there are a great many possible phrase structure rules; we talked only about a very small fragment of this larger set. Examine the data given below and, on the basis of only this information, try to write a possible phrase structure rule for NP. Your rule should allow only the noun phrases given here to be generated. Use parentheses to indicate which elements are optional and curly brackets to indicate different possible expansions of the rule. (The word *ugly* is an adjective and *seven* is a numeral or NUM.)

> the frog
>
> the ugly frog
>
> the ugly frog on the log
>
> the ugly frog on the old log
>
> the seven ugly frogs
>
> seven frogs
>
> frogs

Try to come up with a possible rule for VP that would allow only the following possible expansions of VP to be generated. Follow the same basic instructions as given above for writing the noun phrase rule.

> play the bongos
>
> play the bongos for Sue
>
> play for Sue
>
> play

TEXT ANALYSIS

1. Finding Phrases

In the sentences below, do the following.

- Circle at least two phrases in each of the sentences. Do not try to label the category of the phrase, just try to identify which groups of words appear to form a kind of syntactic unit.
- Find at least two examples of phrases that contain other ones, to illustrate hierarchical structure.
- Identify at least three examples of words that are members of grammatical categories, and three that are members of lexical categories. (Don't try to label the categories at this point.)

a) Today, keeping a safe distance, I followed the woman I love when she walked on a carpet of pond lilies.
b) She walked for a long time, saying what must be wonderful things to herself.
c) Then in the middle of the pond she stopped, because a man had stood up suddenly in front of her.
d) He said things to her and I couldn't make them out, but he said them to her so forcefully that drops of brown water sprang from his mouth.

Source: Wingless, by Jamaica Kincaid.

2. Recursion

Find two sentences from texts of your choice that you think illustrate recursion in noun phrases, prepositional phrases, or sentences. Bring them to class to write on the board. Try as a class to identify the recursion. Some examples are given here. In (a), we find a long prepositional phrase, within which is contained a smaller one. In (b), we find two noun phrases, both of which dominate other ones (within prepositional phrases).

a. My first cousin Greg and I came down
[with the same obscure bone disease [in the same knee]]
PP   PP
b. In [less generous regions of [the greater American culture]]
      NP   NP
[the sound of [Appalachian dialect]] has come to signify ignorance
NP   NP

Source: "The Quare Gene," by Tony Earley, *The New Yorker,* September 21, 1998.

Try to find two or three similar examples, using labeled brackets, circles, or tree diagrams to show where recursion occurs.

3. Syntactic Ambiguity: Movie Titles and Advertising

Advertising often takes advantage of ambiguity to attract the consumer's attention. For example, the movie title *Good Will Hunting* is ambiguous (*Grosse Pointe Blank* is another example). We understand it as meaning a kind of hunting, *hunting for good will,* where *good will* modifies *hunting,* a noun. We also understand it as meaning *good Will Hunting,* where *good* is an adjective describing *Will Hunting,* a name, and thus a noun. We represent the possible interpretations with brackets, as follows.

[Good Will] Hunting (hunting for good will)

Good [Will Hunting] (Will Hunting, a person, is good)

See if you can find at least three examples of syntactic ambiguity in advertising, from magazines, television, or in some other media. Illustrate the ambiguities you find as best you can in terms of phrase structure, circles, or brackets (don't try to label categories at this point).

LANGUAGE DIVERSITY EXERCISES

1. Grammatical Categories in Old and Middle English

You are somewhat familiar now with the grammatical category Determiner, whose members include *the/a/this/that/these/those.* Investigate the syntax, morphology, and semantics of one or two of these words (you may find them identified as *articles* or *demonstratives*) in Old or Middle English. Are they best analyzed as grammatical or lexical categories, given the criteria in Table 2.1? How do they differ from their modern counterparts? Give examples to illustrate your points.

2. Lexical Categories in Old and Middle English

Investigate three different Old or Middle English nouns or verbs. How do they differ from their modern counterparts in terms of semantics, syntax, and morphology? Do they satisfy the criteria for lexical categories given in Table 2.1?

3. Phrase Structure in a Language Other Than English

You may be familiar with another language, in which case you can do this exercise without much more than your own knowledge. You might, however, need to consult a grammar textbook on a particular language.

Find at least two examples of ways in which the word order in a language of your choice differs from modern English word order. Try to diagram the differences, based on what you now know about phrase structure. Do not try to be specific about your labels for different categories; you may in fact use no labels at all, if you wish. What is important here is that you try to draw the structure of the sentence or phrase, and compare it with the structure of modern English.

For example, in French, certain adjectives follow the noun, as in *jupe rouge* ("skirt red") in contrast to English, where adjectives typically precede nouns (as in "red skirt"). You might express the difference between English and French by diagramming noun phrases as follows:

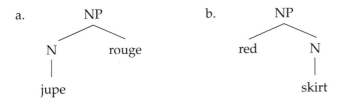

4. Grammatical and Lexical Categories in Other Languages

Using a language other than English that you are familiar with, or researching one you don't know, discuss, using the criteria in Table 2.1, one lexical and one grammatical category in the language. For example, if you choose nouns in French, you might list a number of nouns and their definitions, to illustrate how they have lexical rather than grammatical meanings. You might also list some recently formed nouns in French, to show that the category Noun is an open class. (Examples might include nouns formed by clipping, blending, compounding, etc.) You might then also give some examples of nouns as heads of phrases. Do the same for a grammatical category, giving examples of how it fulfills the criteria in Table 2.1.

CHAPTER REVIEW TERMS

syntactic categories, grammatical categories and lexical categories, heads and phrases, phrase structure, phrase structure rules, hierarchical structure, constituent, dominate, recursion

CHAPTER REVIEW EXERCISE

Choose all or a selection of the following suggestions for analyzing the text that follows.

a) List any grammatical categories you find in the text, using the criteria in Table 2.1.
b) List at least three different examples of lexical categories you find in the text, using the criteria in Table 2.1.
c) List at least four different phrases you find in the text.
d) List at least four examples of phrases contained in other phrases in the text, as examples of hierarchical structure.
e) List two or three examples of prepositional phrase or noun phrase recursion.

f) Make a list of five words from the text that have derivational and or inflectional affixes. Divide the words on your list into morphemes, and label any affixes as derivational or inflectional.

> You could have paved your driveway with Willy's voice, which was smoother than dirt, but not as even as asphalt. The gravel in it made him sound naturally surly, even when he said hello.
>
> Lois did her best to ignore him. After all, he was her ex-husband. But here they were, rocking like good friends on the porch swing, drinking whiskey out of paper cups, the dogs resting at their feet. Willy drank more than his share while Lois stared into the grayness of the dirt road in front of their yard.
>
> In the field across the road, a ruby light blinked on top of the radio tower, and somewhere overhead she could hear the buzzing of a small plane. Her head felt soggy with liquor. Her thoughts wouldn't focus, but banged away at her forehead like the bugs batting the screen door. She could hardly pay attention to what Willy said.
>
> *Source: The Last Studebaker*, by Robin Hemley.

3

Evidence for Phrases

Movement, Pronominalization, and Coordination

> *As far as I'm concerned, "whom" is a word that*
> *was invented to make everyone sound like a butler.*
> Calvin Trillin

Introduction

In the previous chapter we discussed some of our intuitions about the structure
of sentences, and how sentences can be broken up into phrases of different syntactic categories. In this chapter we investigate syntactic evidence for phrases.
One type of evidence comes from *movement;* we find that groups of words move
as syntactic units. Another type of evidence for phrases derives from *pronominalization,* the means by which a pronoun, or more accurately, a *proform,* replaces
an entire phrase. A third kind of evidence involves *coordination,* the means by
which we connect two or more syntactic elements with the conjunctions *and, or,
but, nor,* and so on. The syntactic operations of movement, pronominalization,
and coordination provide us with an important tool of sentence analysis we will
use throughout the book. We consider movement first.

Movement

In the last chapter on phrase structure, we saw that a sentence comprises the
basic units noun phrase and verb phrase. The verb phrase dominates at least a
verb, and possibly other phrases, such as a noun phrase, a prepositional phrase,
or a sentence. The phrase structure rule for S(entence) is repeated in (1a), and a
possible expansion of VP is given in (1b).

(1) a. S => NP VP

b. VP => V $\begin{Bmatrix} S \\ NP\ (NP) \\ PP \end{Bmatrix}$

The rules in (1) suggest that the *basic* word order in English is subject first, verb second, object (a noun phrase or some other kind of phrase) third. Languages such as English, with this type of basic order, are called *Subject-Verb-Object,* or *SVO,* languages. As we might expect, not all languages are SVO. Though Swahili, English, Hausa, and Thai are SVO, Irish Gaelic, classical Arabic, and biblical Hebrew are VSO. German, Persian, Eskimo, and Japanese are SOV. OVS, VOS, and OSV languages also exist.

Even though we think of English as an SVO language, many other orders of phrases are in possible English sentences. Some examples are given in (2).

(2)   a. At the store, *her best friend* bought some new shoes.
      b. What did *her best friend* buy at the store?
      c. Shoes, *her best friend* would never buy.
      d. Will *her best friend* buy shoes?

In all of these sentences, something precedes the subject noun phrase *her best friend.* None of these sentences can therefore be generated by the phrase structure rules in (1) alone. Rather, the syntactic component of our descriptive grammar appears to also include rules that allow us to rearrange the orders of words and phrases in a sentence in certain ways. These **movement** rules are also quite specific, as they do not allow us to move just anything anywhere. We do not, for instance, recognize *shoes buy will her best friend as a sentence of English. Our syntactic knowledge thus appears to include not only knowledge of syntactic categories and phrases, but also information about specific kinds of movement operations that can apply to phrase structures.

Movement rules explain a fundamental fact about language acquisition, namely that children seem to acquire linguistic rules at a very early age, without instruction. Many of us have observed firsthand that children are impervious to correction, and that they come up with words and syntactic constructions that others around them never say. (At age 4, my son analyzed the verb *behave* as *being have,* and his sister at 3 "overgeneralized" the preposition *to,* using it as a substitute for any preposition at all. Her utterances included *Wait to me!* and *Save this to later.* Neither child had heard these constructions, yet both uttered them nonetheless.) Children would not be able to achieve this feat if linguistic rules were not somehow learnable.[1] Learning a rule is more efficient than learning a list of sentences; it is far easier to learn a finite number of ways in which word order can be rearranged than to learn every sentence in the language separately. A movement rule is thus similar in this respect to, say, multiplication, a mathematical operation that allows us to multiply any number by another. We don't learn how to multiply by memorizing *all* of the possible multiplication tables (though some of you may remember trying to learn multiplication this

---

[1]Drawing on work by linguist Noam Chomsky of the Massachusetts Institute of Technology, many linguists argue that our ability to acquire language derives in part from our *innate* knowledge of certain basic grammatical principles. Just which principles are innate, and how they might be formulated, is a subject of much current linguistic research and debate.

way). Rather we learn rules or operations, and then apply these rules to come up with different combinations.

Passive

Turning now to a specific example of a movement rule in English, consider the sentence in (3).

(3) a. The ungrateful lout stole *the anchovy pizza.*
b. *The anchovy pizza* was stolen by the ungrateful lout.

(3a) is an *active* sentence, in which the agent of the action, *the ungrateful lout,* occurs as the subject, and the object of the action, *the anchovy pizza,* occurs to the right of the verb *stole.* (3a) means the same thing as (3b), even though the sentences differ in word order. In each one, the ungrateful lout steals the anchovy pizza. Under the assumption that we learn rules rather than lists of sentences, we might hypothesize that we "derive" (3b) from (3a) by moving groups of words around in a specific way. We would thus not necessarily have to *hear* both (3a) and (3b) in order to utter them. Rather, we learn that English is a language in which we can change the order of words in a particular way, to create passive sentences from active ones. On an intuitive level, then, active and passive sentences are related to each other by *movement.*

The movement rule that derives (3b) from (3a) is what linguists call **Passive,** a rule that moves the subject noun phrase, in this case *the ungrateful lout,* to the right, and the object noun phrase, *the anchovy pizza,* to the left, as illustrated in (4). (We again use triangles to represent phrases, as the details of the structure of the noun phrases in question is not relevant to us here.) Passive also has other important features which we will not discuss here (they are taken up in our discussion of verbs in chapters 5 and 6).[2] For example, we will simply assume that the preposition *by* is inserted as part of the Passive rule, and that the form of the verb changes as well, as a predictable result of the fully formulated Passive rule.

(4)

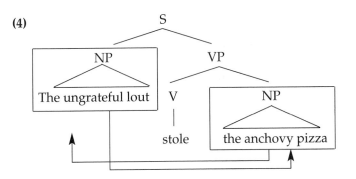

---

[2]The descriptions of movement rules given here are not necessarily consistent with their more current incarnations in different theoretical frameworks. Their more current descriptions, however, also depend on analyzing groups of words as phrases, which is the relevant point here.

Now consider what exactly has moved around in (3a), to produce (3b). Notice that the heads of the noun phrases *the ungrateful lout* and *the anchovy pizza,* namely the nouns *lout* and *pizza,* respectively, do not move by themselves. Rather, the entire noun phrases, *the ungrateful lout* and *the anchovy pizza,* move. The Passive movement rule thus appears to operate on phrases rather than heads, and specifically, on noun phrases. We cannot explain this simple fact unless we assume that syntactic structure is organized into phrases, and that movement rules can apply to them.

We further check our hypothesis by applying the Passive rule to other sentences, and we find that even very large noun phrases appear to move as syntactic units, as in (5). This supports the idea that this movement rule applies to phrases, and thus that the notion *phrase* is part of our unconscious knowledge of syntax.

(5)   a.   [Scientists with a variety of interests] created [the lunar landing
            NP   NP
            module].

      b.   [The lunar landing module] was created by [scientists with a
            NP   NP
           variety of interests].

Again, observe that in (5), Passive does not apply to the heads of the subject and object noun phrases, namely *scientists* and *module.* Rather, the rule applies to the noun phrases [*scientists with a variety of interests*], and [*the lunar landing module*].

Particle Shift

Not all movement rules necessarily move phrases; some may move only heads. Nevertheless, movement of heads provides evidence for phrases, because heads must move *around* phrases. For example, English has a rule that moves a head, what we will call a **particle** (abbreviated here as Prt), around an adjacent noun phrase. This movement is illustrated by the sentences in (6, 7), where the particles *out* and *in* move to the right over noun phrases *the light* and *their exams,* respectively. A phrase structure tree to illustrate this kind of movement rule is given in (8).

(6)   a.   The nurse turned [out] [the light].
                            Prt   NP
      b.   The nurse turned [the light] [out].
                            NP   Prt

(7) a. The students handed [in] [their exams].
                            Prt NP

    b. The students handed [their exams] [in].
                              NP   Prt

(8)

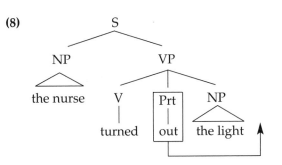

Notice that as a result of what we will call **Particle Shift,** the particle moves over the entire noun phrase, not just a part of the noun phrase. We thus do not find sentences of the sort illustrated in (9), where the particle moves to the right only over part of a phrase.

(9)

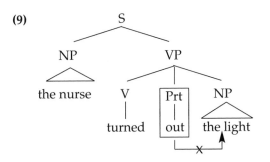

Again, we appear to have evidence from Particle Shift that movement involves phrases. In this case, we have evidence that a head, namely a particle, must move *around* a phrase. We thus explain the contrast between (8) and (9) by assuming that sentences are organized into phrases, and that movement rules are somehow sensitive to the distinction between heads and phrases.

Indirect Object Movement

A final example of movement of phrases we will discuss here is illustrated in (10, 11).

(10) a. Hortense sent [a letter] to [her mother].
                         NP   NP

    b. Hortense sent [her mother] [a letter].
                         NP   NP

(11)   a. Lionel bought [tickets] for [his friends].
                         NP   NP

   b. Lionel bought [his friends] [tickets].
                         NP   NP

We will call the movement rule illustrated here **Indirect Object Movement.** In this operation, the indirect object (*her mother* in (10a) and *his friends* in (11a)) changes places with the direct object (*a letter* in (10a) and *tickets* in (11b)). This kind of movement operation, in which both the indirect object and the direct object move, is illustrated in (12).

(12)

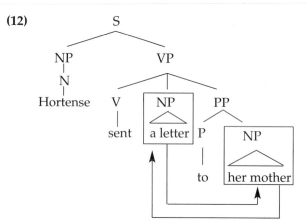

When this movement rule applies, the preposition *to* or *for* is omitted. Putting this detail aside for the moment, what is relevant to us here is that to derive the (b) sentences in (10–11) from the (a) sentences, noun phrases, rather than single nouns, must be rearranged. As (13) illustrates, Indirect Object Movement does not operate on single nouns.

(13)

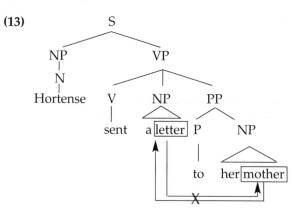

To summarize this section, phrase structure rules alone do not express the possible orders of phrases and words in English sentences. Phrase structure rules must therefore be supplemented by additional syntactic rules, namely movement rules that apply to heads or phrases to rearrange word order in specific ways. We have considered three such movement rules here, **Passive, Particle Shift,** and **Indirect Object Movement,** which illustrate some of the ways in which the basic order of English sentences can be reorganized. Evidence from movement supports the hypothesis that sentences are organized into syntactic phrases, rather than linear strings of words without any kind of hierarchical structure. Movement also provides us with some insights into how language as a system is acquired, and the role syntactic operations or rules play in language acquisition. Children don't learn all sentences separately in order to say them; rather, they learn operations, such as the movement rules of Passive, Particle Shift, and Indirect Object Movement. They can then apply these rules to create any number of different sentences, ones they may never have heard or said before.

Pronominalization

Pronominalization, the means by which syntactic material is replaced by a pronoun, or as we shall see, a **proform,** provides us with further evidence for phrases. This is because proforms replace phrases, rather than heads, and are thus words that "stand for" phrases.

The proforms we are most familiar with are **pronouns,** words that substitute for, or replace, noun phrases. Some examples of pronouns are given in (14).

(14) a. [Books by Chomsky] are on sale at Barnes and Noble and Carrie
NP
wants to buy *them.*

b. [The cat] broke [the antique vase from the Ming Dynasty]
NP   NP
when *she* knocked *it* to the floor.

We can see that pronouns replace noun phrases, and not just nouns, by the ungrammaticality of the sentences in (15). Here, we have constructed sentences in which only the head noun has been replaced by a pronoun.

(15) a. *[*Books* by Chomsky] are on sale at Barnes and Noble and Carrie
NP
wants to buy [*them* by this well-known linguist].
NP

b. *[The *cat*] broke [the antique *vase* from the Ming Dynasty] when
NP   NP
[the *she*]
knocked [the fragile *it* that was a real treasure] to the floor.
NP

We would expect the sentences in (15) to be grammatical if pronouns could replace nouns as well as noun phrases. That they cannot is illustrated by the phrase structure in (16).

(16)

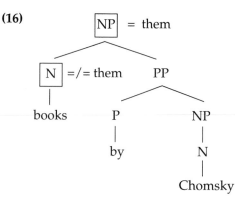

Several different types of pronouns can replace noun phrases in English. Pronouns are a closed class of words; we don't coin new ones, even though attempts have been made to do so (for example, the gender-neutral pronoun *thon* was once proposed to replace "generic" *he*.) A list of pronoun types is given in Table 3.1.

To further explore how we can use evidence from pronominalization as evidence for phrases, consider the sentences in (17).

Table 3.1
Pronoun Types

Personal pronouns: *I/me, he/him, she/her, you* (plural and singular)/, *we/us, they/them*

Possessive pronouns: *mine/yours* (singular and plural) /*his/hers/its/ours/theirs*

Reflexive pronouns[3]: *myself/himself/herself/itself/yourself/ourselves/themselves/yourselves*

Reciprocal pronouns: *one another/each other*

Interrogative pronouns: *which/whose/who(m)/what/when/where/how*

Indefinite pronouns: *it, someone, something, somewhere, anyone, anything, anywhere, no one, none, nobody, nothing, nowhere, etc.*

Relative pronouns: *that/who/when/where/why/which/whose*

---

[3]Not all varieties of English use pronouns of the form in Table 3.1. In some varieties we hear forms such as *hisself, theirself,* and *theirselves.* You can see that such forms are derived systematically; speakers attach *self* to *his* and *their,* just as others do to *him* and *them.* Speakers of the first variety are thus systematically attaching *self* to what we analyze in Chapter 4 as *possessive determiners.*

(17) a. *Lions* are fierce, but *they* are not as dangerous as dairy bulls.
     b. *John* bought *chocolate* for his mother but then *he* ate *it*.

The sentences in (17) illustrate an interesting point about phrases, one which we originally encountered in our discussion in Chapter 2 of the noun *lasagna* and its status as a noun phrase in the sentence *Lee ordered lasagna, red wine, and two salads.* You can see that *lions, chocolate,* and *John* are apparently replaced by pronouns, namely *they, it,* and *he,* respectively. The grammaticality of the sentences in (17) might at first suggest that pronouns can replace single words, but we saw this should not be possible, given the ungrammaticality of the sentences in (15). We can conclude then that pronouns seem only to be able to replace noun phrases. This suggests that *lions, chocolate,* and *John* are not in fact functioning syntactically as single nouns, but rather as full noun phrases. We can represent this hypothesis in terms of phrase structure as in (18).

(18)   NP = they   NP = it   NP = she
           | | |
           N ≠ they   N ≠ it   N ≠ he
           | | |
           lions   chocolate   John

Every pronoun has an **antecedent,** either a **linguistic antecedent,** an actual linguistic phrase, or an understood or **pragmatic antecedent,** which is contextual rather than linguistic. The pronouns in (17), for example, all have linguistic antecedents within the preceding sentence. In (19), on the other hand, the first *him* has a pragmatic antecedent, implied from context. The second *him* is interpreted as referring to the linguistic antecedent, *Francisco.*

(19)   Hortense and Lionel are sitting on the porch and a man walks by and Hortense says: I think I know *him.* Lionel responds: That's Francisco. We met *him* at the bookstore the other day.

Pronouns are also interesting in English because they are some of the few words in which we can still see evidence of morphological inflection of case, person, and number. As we find in later chapters, English is not a "highly inflected" language, that is, it does not morphologically express inflections such as **person, number,** and **case** in a very regular way. To give an example, verbs in many varieties of English express person and number inflection in the third person singular; speakers of these varieties say *I walk* but *she walks.* Pronouns also express person and number, as we see in Table 3.2 for the English personal pronouns.
     Pronouns also express case inflection, or the morphological expression of grammatical function as subject, object, indirect object, and so on. This is why we hear "*I* talked to Jane," but "Jane talked to *me.*" The pronoun *I* is in what we call *nominative* case (also referred to as *subjective* case), because it is the subject of the sentence. *I* becomes *me* in the object position, where it reflects *accusative* or *objective* case. A third kind of case expressed by pronouns in English is *genitive,*

Table 3.2

Person and Number Inflection of English Personal Pronouns

Person	First	Second	Third
Singular	I	you	he/she/it
Plural	we	you	they

or *possessive* case, the form of the pronoun in a sentence such as "the book is *mine.*" (We discuss such as "my book" in Chapter 4.)

Table 3.3 illustrates the case inflections of the personal pronouns.

Pronouns also have different forms that correspond to the **gender** of their antecedents (*she/he,* etc.). Pronouns thus express what linguists call "natural," or biological gender. They do not, however, express grammatical gender in English, as the nouns they replace do not express grammatical gender either. Grammatical gender shows up in languages such as German, French, and many others, in which nouns are either masculine, feminine, or neuter (German nouns express all three, but French nouns only masculine and feminine). Noun phrases in such languages are morphologically marked for gender, though gender in this case is not biological, nor does it derive from any connection to biological gender (contrary to some folk linguistic beliefs).

Some French and German examples of noun phrases marked with grammatical gender, which shows up on the determiner or article, are given in (20–22).

(20)   a. der Tisch (German) "the (Masc) table"
        b. la table (French), "the (Fem) table"

(21)   a. der Mond (German), "the (Masc) moon"
        b. la lune (French), "the (Fem) moon"

(22)   a. das Auto (German), "the (Neuter) car"
        b. la voiture (French), "the (Fem) car"

Table 3.3

Case Inflection of Personal Pronouns in English

	Case		
	Nominative	Accusative	Possessive
Singular	I	me	mine
	you	you	yours
	he/she/it	him/her/it	his/hers/its
Plural	we	us	ours
	you	you	yours
	they	them	theirs

As you can see in (20–22), the equivalent of *the* in German and French expresses gender through changes in its morphological form. The gender of this determiner element reflects the gender of the noun. The determiner *the* in English, on the other hand, does not change form, since nouns in English do not have grammatical gender. You can also see in (20–22) that the assignment of a particular gender to a particular noun is arbitrary, it is not biologically based.

Pronouns and Movement: WH-Movement

The interaction of pronouns and movement provides interesting evidence for the claim that pronouns replace phrases. As we would expect, pronouns can undergo the movement rules discussed above. Examples from Passive and Indirect Object Movement are given below.[4]

(23) a. The dogs chased *her.*
        b. *She* was chased by the dogs. (Passive)

(24) a. The students gave their homework to *him.*
        b. The students gave *him* their homework. (Indirect Object Movement)

Another example of movement involving pronouns that we have not yet discussed is illustrated in (25). The noun phrase *The English Patient* in (25a) is replaced by the phrase *what* in (25b), and is moved to the front of the sentence in (25c). (The _____ indicates the position from which the phrase has moved.)

(25) a. Lionel saw *The English Patient.*
        b. Lionel saw *what?*
        c. *What* did Lionel see _____?

The movement rule illustrated in (25c) is called **WH-Movement,** and it has the effect of moving a phrase that has been replaced by an interrogative pronoun to the front of the sentence to form a question. In (25), WH-Movement applies to the direct object noun phrase, the noun phrase immediately following the verb. WH-Movement can also apply to noun phrases in other positions, as we see in (26).

(26) a. Lucy gave a book to *Linus.*
        b. Lucy gave a book to *who?*
        c. *Who* did Lucy give a book to _____?

---

[4]We will leave Particle Shift aside here, as movement of a pronoun gives rise to sentences that sound odd for phonological reasons. For example, *The child picked up it* sounds strange, but *The child picked it up* does not, for reasons having to do with stress.

In (26), WH-Movement has operated on the indirect object, the object of the preposition *to*. WH-Movement can also operate on the subject noun phrase, though it is not immediately obvious that the phrase actually moves.

(27)   a. *Lucy* gave a book to Linus
        b. *Who* gave a book to Linus?

We can hypothesize, however, that WH-Movement in *all* cases involves movement of an interrogative pronoun to the same sentence-initial position. This rule operates in a systematic way in all sentences, and is therefore easier for a child to acquire. WH-Movement involving a subject or an object thus involves movement as illustrated in (28–29).

(28)

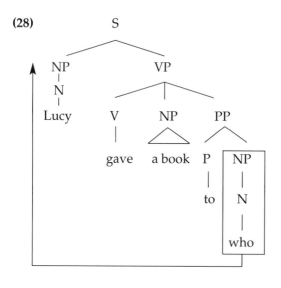

(29)

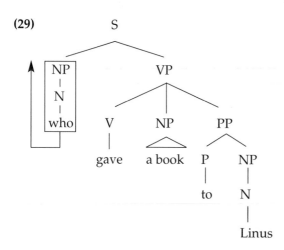

As we can see in (28–29), WH-Movement applies to move a noun phrase to sentence-initial position, even if that movement is essentially "invisible" as it does not change the linear order of words. WH-Movement thus applies in parallel fashion to both subject and object noun phrases.

WH-Movement can also apply to phrases that *dominate* an interrogative pronoun, as in (30).

(30) a. The article discussed [the defendant's appeal to the grand jury].
$\qquad\qquad$ NP

$\qquad$ b. The article discussed [*whose* appeal to the grand jury]?
$\qquad\qquad$ NP

$\qquad$ c. [*Whose* appeal to the grand jury] did the article discuss?
$\qquad$ NP

In (30b), the interrogative pronoun *whose* appears within a larger noun phrase, *whose appeal to the grand jury.* The entire noun phrase moves to the front of the sentence, as in (30c), illustrated in (31). (We also add a form of *do* to the sentence, for reasons we discuss in Chapter 6.)

(31)

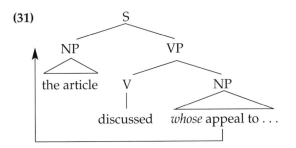

Here, WH-Movement is still applying to a phrase, in this case a phrase that *dominates* an interrogative pronoun.

WH-Movement thus provides us with an example of a movement rule that specifically involves pronouns, namely interrogative pronouns that replace noun phrases. We also saw that WH-Movement applies to noun phrases that dominate an interrogative pronoun, moving the noun phrase to the same sentence-initial position in all cases.

Pronouns Versus Proforms

As we mentioned at the beginning of this section, there are other kinds of pronouns that are not included in Table 3.1, and that do not necessarily replace noun phrases. Pronouns are therefore members of a larger, more general class of **proforms,** including proforms that replace phrases other than noun phrases.

Consider, for example, the sentences in (32), and the use of the proform *so.* Try to determine the syntactic category of the antecedent of this proform.

(32) a. The movie *The English Patient* was actually quite long, but it didn't appear *so* because it was very engrossing.

b. The real estate market isn't very good right now, but it might become *so* after summer begins.
c. They had always been friends, and hoped to remain *so* forever.
d. *The English Patient* is *so* called because the main character is assumed to be English.
e. The Grand National Horse Race was cancelled because of a bomb threat. It said *so* in the newspaper today.
f. Do you think the IRA was responsible for the bomb threat? Some people believe *so*, but my uncle doesn't.

You can probably tell that the proform *so* can replace quite a variety of different kinds of phrases, even if you don't know the category labels for these phrases. The categories that *so* pronominalizes in (32) are given in (33). (It should be noted here also that there are other uses of the word *so*; not every use of this word is as a proform. For example, in *John was being obnoxious, so I left*, the word *so* is a conjunction.)

(33)   *so* replaces
    a. *quite long* = adjective phrase
    b. *very good* = adjective phrase
    c. *friends* = noun phrase
    d. *The English Patient* = noun phrase
    e. *(that) the Grand National Horse Race was cancelled because of a bomb threat* = sentence
    f. *(that) the IRA was responsible for the bomb threat* = sentence

From (33) we see that *so* can replace at least adjective phrases, noun phrases, and sentences.

It is another proform that can actually replace categories other than noun phrases. Others proforms are *here* and *there*. Some pronominal properties of the proform *it* are illustrated in (34), and some of the properties of *here* and *there* are given in (35) and (36).

(34)   a. Hortense smokes constantly, and *it* really bugs me.
    it = that Hortense smokes constantly (sentence)
    b. John is really obnoxious today. I know *it*.
    it = that John is really obnoxious today (sentence)

(35)   Lionel parked the new minivan on the roadside. "You should park it *here*," Cary yelled from the garage.
    here = (in the garage, prepositional phrase, with pragmatic antecedent)

(36)   I put my new Bryan Adams CD on the desk, and now it's not *there!*
    there = on the desk (prepositional phrase)

Pronominalization is therefore the means by which we create syntactic "placeholders" for phrases that can be linked to either a syntactic or pragmatic antecedent. Some grammar books designate PRONOUN as a syntactic category, because it is possible to make a list, such as that in Table 3.1, of words that appear to form a particular class of elements. The larger class of proforms, a class including pronouns, does in fact form a morphologically closed class of elements; we do not add new proforms to our vocabulary in any productive way. This class of words, however, is not necessarily a separate syntactic category. Rather, proforms *replace* phrases of different categories. It is perhaps more accurate to think of pronominalization not in terms of proforms as a syntactic class but as a process that applies to phrases of different syntactic categories.

Coordination

In this section we turn to the process of **coordination** (also called *conjunction*), the means by which phrases and heads can be syntactically linked to form a larger unit of the same category. Coordination allows us to make phrases and sentences longer and more complex. Coordination differs, however, from other processes we use to increase the length and complexity of our sentences. For example, recursion allows us to generate phrases of an indefinite length, by regenerating a particular category. Sentence recursion is called *subordination*, a process discussed in detail in Part Three. We will see here that coordination provides important evidence for phrases, and it will be a useful tool in our subsequent discussions of syntactic categories and phrases.

Conjunctions

Coordination is, in general, the process by which words or phrases are connected to form larger syntactic units. Words and phrases are coordinated by the following list of words, called **conjunctions.** It may be useful for you to use the acronym FANBOYS to remember them.

(37) **Conjunctions**
for   and   nor   but   or   yet   so

Examples of different kinds of coordination using the conjunctions are given in (38).

(38) a. [Julia decided not to eat peanut butter], *for* [she found it too sticky].
          S   S

      b. The girls [played in the water] *and* [swam under the bridge].
                     VP   VP

      c. The children weren't [in their rooms] *nor* [on the porch].
                               PP   PP

d. She was [poor], *but* [quite happy].
           AP   AP   (AP = adjective phrase)

e. Many people drink [beer] *or* [wine].
                       NP   NP

f. [Horatio drinks martinis], *yet* [they make him ill].
      S   S

g. [Linda craves chocolate], *so* [she eats it whenever she can].
      S   S

As we can see in (38), phrases of different syntactic categories, including sentences, can be coordinated by members of the FANBOYS, making sentences more complex. The phrase structures of a few of the sentences in (38) are given in (39–41).

(39)

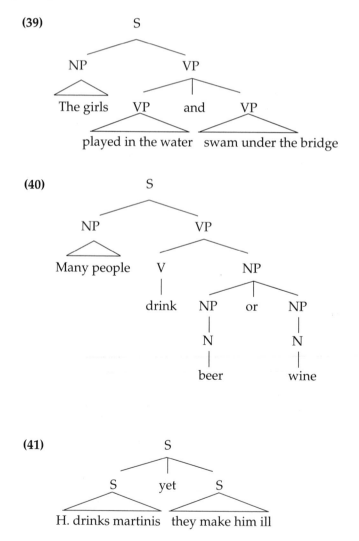

(40)

(41)

In these phrase structure trees, a conjunction links two categories: two verb phrases in (39), two noun phrases in (40), and two sentences in (41). In each case, the coordinate structure itself forms a larger phrase. In (39), for example, the two coordinated verb phrases form a larger verb phrase, in (40) the two coordinated noun phrases form a larger noun phrase, and so on.

Movement and Pronominalization of Coordinate Constituents

Given that coordination gives rise to a larger, more complex phrase, we might expect such phrases to undergo operations that apply to other, less complex phrases. This is to some extent the case, with an important exception that we discuss momentarily.

For example, the highest noun phrase in (40) can undergo WH-Movement, as illustrated in (42).

(42)   a. Many people drink [beer or wine].
                        NP

       b. Many people drink [what]?
                        NP

       c. [What] do many people drink _____?
          NP

We derive (42c) by replacing the coordinate noun phrase in (42a) with the interrogative pronoun *what* as in (42b). We then move this phrase to sentence-initial position, deriving (42c), illustrated by the phrase structure in (43).

(43)

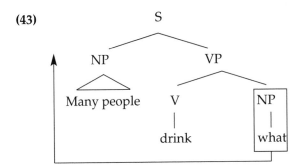

(42) illustrates that *beer and wine* together behave as a larger noun phrase, undergoing both pronominalization and movement.

The sentences in (44) demonstrate a similar point, based on evidence from the Passive movement rule.

(44)   a. Many people drink [beer or wine].
                        NP

       b. [Beer or wine] are drunk by many people.
          NP

The sentences in (44) show that again, *beer or wine* together behave as a single noun phrase, undergoing movement to form a passive sentence from an active one.

As we might by now expect, the phrase *beer or wine* can also be pronominalized, as we see in (45).

(45)   Many people drink [beer or wine], but some people don't like the
                                        NP
           taste of *them* at all.

Now consider (46). This set of sentences illustrates another fact about the interaction of movement and coordination. The relevant phrase structure is given in (47).

(46)   a. Many people drink [*beer* or wine].
                                        NP
           b. Many people drink [*what* or wine]?
                                        NP
           c. *What* do many people drink [_____ or wine]?
                                              NP

(47)

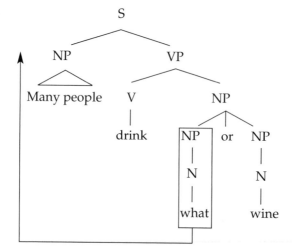

When we compare the sentences in (42) with those in (46), we see that first of all there is a difference between how pronominalization and movement work in a coordinate structure. We can pronominalize either an entire coordinated noun phrase, as in (42b), or only one noun phrase in the coordinate, as in (46b). Movement, however, applies only to the *entire* coordinate structure. (42c) is thus grammatical, but (46c) is not.

That movement must involve the entire coordinate structure is further supported by evidence from Passive. Recall that *beer or wine* can undergo Passive as a full noun phrase, as we saw in (44). (48) illustrates that Passive cannot apply to part of the coordinate structure, namely to only the noun phrase *beer*.

(48) a. Many people drink [*beer* or wine].

        NP

   b. **Beer* is drunk [_____ or wine] by many people.

        NP

Linguists argue that coordinate structures are subject to the Coordinate Structure Constraint, which prohibits movement of *part* of a coordinate structure. We will not pursue this constraint in any more detail here; what is relevant to us is that it underscores the idea that coordinate structures are themselves larger phrases, as it is only these larger structures that undergo movement. Further, it shows us that movement rules do not apply arbitrarily; rather, they apply in restricted ways, subject to certain constraints.

Coordination of "Like" Categories

We saw above that evidence from movement and pronominalization of coordinate structures suggests that such structures are themselves larger phrases. Coordination is also a tool we can use to identify the syntactic category of a phrase. This is because typically, only phrases of "like" categories can be coordinated.

To illustrate the "parallelism" constraint on coordination, consider the following sentences, in which phrases that are *not* of the same category have been coordinated. (AP is the phrase structure notation for "adjective phrase," with which you are not yet familiar; the relevant issue here is that an adjective phrase cannot be conjoined with a phrase of a different category, namely a prepositional phrase.)

(49) a. Mary likes [apples] and [any kind of cookie].

        NP   NP

   b. *Mary likes [apples] and [eating bananas].

        NP   VP

(50) a. Lee went [to the store] and [across the bridge].

        PP   PP

   b. *Lee went [to the store] and [crazy].

        PP   AP

We can therefore use coordination to help us identify the category of a phrase; if we know one member of the coordinate structure is a noun phrase, we can be fairly sure that the other member of the coordinate is also a noun phrase, and so on. If we know, for example, that *eating bananas* is a verb phrase, then we know that *swimming,* with which it can be coordinated as in (51), is also a verb phrase.

(51) Mary likes [eating bananas] and [swimming].

        VP   VP

The parallelism constraint on coordination also allows us to explain the ungrammaticality of the sentence in (52).

(52) *Lee went [to the store] and [off his rocker].
                 PP   PP

You may wonder why (52) is ungrammatical, given that coordination involves two prepositional phrases. Notice, however, that the second PP is synonymous with the adjective phrase in (50b), *crazy*. Parallelism thus appears to involve more than syntactic parallelism; the coordinated phrases must be semantically parallel as well.

The parallelism constraint on coordination thus provides us with a means to determine whether two phrases are of the same syntactic category, and also parallel in meaning in a certain way. We can therefore use properties of coordination as diagnostics not only for phrases, but also for syntactic category and for semantic similarity.

Coordination of Single Words

So far, we have only discussed coordination of phrases, such as noun phrases, verb phrases, and prepositional phrases. As we find below, single words can also be coordinated. These words might be the heads of lexical categories (nouns, verbs, etc.) or members of grammatical categories (determiners, numerals, etc.). Sometimes syntactic ambiguity arises when a construction can be interpreted as involving both coordination of single words and coordination of phrases.

For example, consider (53).

(53) Mary likes green apples and pears.

The sentence in (53) is syntactically ambiguous. It could mean that Mary likes green apples and pears of some other color, or that Mary likes green apples and green pears. We have, as we expect with syntactic ambiguity, more than one way to diagram the sentence. (54) represents the first meaning, and (55) the second.

(54)

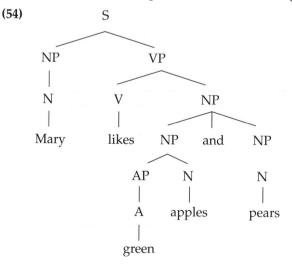

(55)

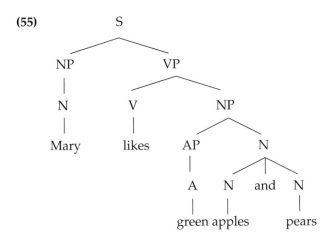

In (54), *green apples* is a noun phrase, as is *pears*. *Green* modifies only *apples* and not *pears*. In (55), on the other hand, *green* modifies both of the coordinated nouns, *apples* and *pears*. The ambiguity of (53) arises because we can interpret the sentence as involving either coordinated noun phrases or coordinated nouns.

Another example of coordinated heads, in which ambiguity does not arise, is given in (56), whose phrase structure is given in (57).

(56) The plane flew to and from Tokyo.

(57)

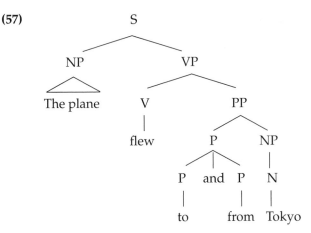

Here, two prepositions are coordinated, rather than two prepositional phrases. No ambiguity arises because we interpret both prepositions as taking the same object, the noun phrase *Tokyo*.

We can also coordinate words that are not heads. For example, the sentence in (58) involves coordinated determiners, and in (59), coordinated numerals.

(58) I would buy either [this or that CD player], but certainly not the one
                               NP
         the salesperson recommends.

(59) [Six or seven children] were playing in the yard.
          NP

The phrase structures of the coordinate noun phrases in (58–59) are given in
(60–61), where *this/that* are dominated by DET (Determiner) and *six/seven* are
dominated by NUM (Numeral).

(60)

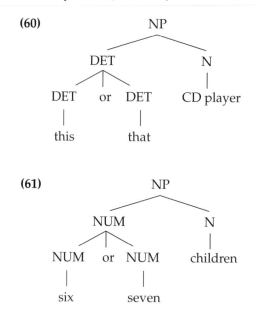

(61)

   We see, then, that coordination can involve either lexical or grammatical categories, applying to either phrases or single words, as long as the parallelism
requirement is met.

Summary

In this chapter we have examined a number of different kinds of evidence for
syntactic phrases. We found that certain **movement** rules, such as **Passive** and
Indirect Object Movement, move phrases to other positions in the sentence.
Other rules, such as **Particle Shift,** apply to heads (namely particles), and move
them *around* phrases. We also discussed the syntactic process of **pronominalization,** through which a phrase is replaced by a **pronoun** or more accurately, a

proform. Pronouns replace only noun phrases, and are one of the few examples of words in English that express inflectional morphology of **number, person** and **case** (nominative, accusative or genitive, for example). Pronouns can also express biological **gender;** *she* is female, while *he* is male. Biological gender differs from "grammatical" gender, an inflection that does not correspond to biological sex. Proforms have either **linguistic** or **pragmatic antecedents,** and are a class of words that replace phrases of a range of different syntactic categories, including, but not limited to, noun phrases. The movement rule of **WH-Movement** provided us with evidence of both movement and pronominalization of phrases, and is another useful tool for determining the status of a group of words as a phrase. We concluded the chapter with a discussion of **coordination,** a process by which phrases or heads can be linked by the **conjunctions** *for, and, nor, but, or, yet, so,* or FANBOYS. We saw that both phrases and words (members of either lexical or grammatical categories) can be coordinated. Coordination appears to be constrained by a syntactic and semantic parallelism requirement, and by the Coordinate Structure Constraint, a condition that blocks movement of a part of a coordinate structure.

The evidence that coordination, movement, and pronominalization operate on phrases shows us that syntactic structure is not simply made up of linear strings of words, but rather is organized into hierarchical structure. These three processes also provide us with a means of determining whether a group of words forms a phrase. We will rely on evidence from coordination, movement, and pronominalization in later chapters in our investigation of sentence structure.

DISCOVERY PROBLEMS

Problem 1. Movement

For practice, first identify whether Passive, Particle Shift, or Indirect Object Movement has applied to derive the (b) sentences from the (a) ones.

(1) a. Suzy bought a new sweater for her sister.
  b. Suzy bought her sister a new sweater.

(2) a. Aaron put out the cat.
  b. Aaron put the cat out.

(3) a. The police found the money.
  b. The money was found by the police.

Now identify which, if any, of these movement rules have applied in each of the following sentences. (Here you don't have pairs—you will essentially have to determine whether any of the following are parallel to the (b) sentences above, in which movement rules have applied.) To make things a bit more challenging, in some sentences none of these movement rules has applied.

a) The Mariners were beaten by the other team.
b) The umpire yelled at the catcher.
c) The catcher handed the ball over.
d) The shortstop threw the first baseman the ball.
e) Peanuts were sold by the vendor.
f) My friend bought us peanuts.
g) Griffey picked up a bat.

Problem 2. Create Your Own Exercise: Movement

Create your own list of sentences in which one of the three movement rules we
have discussed in this chapter has applied in each sentence. You may also, if you
wish, add a few sentences in which the rules have not applied, to make your
exercise more challenging. Exchange exercises with a classmate, and identify
the movement rules that have (or have not) applied in each sentence.

Problem 3. Proforms and Movement

As mentioned above, WH-Movement is a movement rule that also involves
pronominalization: it applies to phrases replaced by an interrogative pronoun.
In English, the interrogative pronoun moves to sentence-initial position, and the
sentence is interpreted as a question. An example follows.

(1)   a. Cary met [the radio talk show host from Milwaukee, Wisconsin].
                NP
      b. Cary met [who]?
                NP
      c. [Who] did Cary meet _____?
          NP

Recall that sometimes, a part of a phrase can be replaced by an interrogative pronoun. When this happens, the larger containing phrase undergoes WH-
Movement. For example, *Hortense's* in the larger noun phrase *Hortense's uncle,*
can be replaced by interrogative *whose.* When this happens, the entire noun
phrase, *whose uncle,* moves.

(2)   a. Cary met [*Hortense's* uncle].
                NP
      b. Cary met [*whose* uncle]?
                NP
      c. [*Whose uncle*] did Cary meet _____?
          NP

Convert the following italicized phrases into interrogative pronouns, and
apply WH-Movement. Briefly discuss other syntactic effects of this movement
operation. Are there any other changes in the sentences other than the fronting
of the WH-phrase to sentence-initial position? Are these changes systematic?

(3) a. We went to "Amistad" *at 7 p.m.*
       b. We went to *"Amistad"* at 7 p.m.
       c. Lee discussed *the movie* with my mother's friend from Poughkeep-sie.
       d. Lee discussed the movie with *my mother's friend from Poughkeepsie.*
       e. *Lee* discussed the movie with my mother's friend from Pough-keepsie.
       f. Lee discussed the movie with *my mother's* friend from Poughkeep-sie.
       g. *My mother's* friend thought the acting was only so-so.
       h. *My mother's friend* thought the acting was only so-so.
       i. Her mother's friend thought *the story* was very compelling.
       j. Lee bought popcorn for *her mother.*

Problem 4. Pragmatic Antecedents

Invent three different scenarios in which a pronoun has to be interpreted pragmatically. Find at least one example of a pragmatically interpreted pronoun in a text (advertising, a novel, a poem, etc.). What supplies the context in which the pronoun is interpreted? Bring your examples to class for discussion.

Problem 5. Diagramming Coordinate Structures

Draw phrase structures for each of the following sentences. If a sentence is ambiguous, draw as many different phrase structures as you need to represent its different meanings. Remember to use phrase structures in which the coordinate structures are themselves part of a larger phrase. Don't try to label all of the nodes in your trees. The point is to illustrate as best you can which phrases or words are coordinated. An example is given below.

The movie had good actors and music.

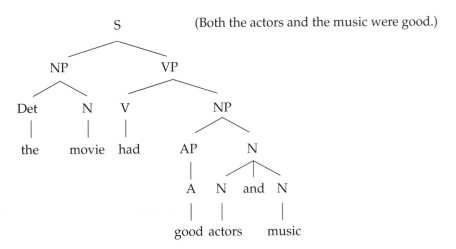

(Both the actors and the music were good.)

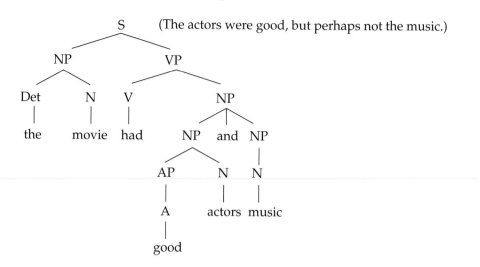

(The actors were good, but perhaps not the music.)

a) The child drew big triangles and boxes.
b) He played the piano with his fingers and toes. (*his* = DET)
c) Six or seven people came to class.
d) She danced the mambo and the tango.
e) The cat goes in and out the door.
f) The teacher wears shoes and socks.
g) Mary scratched and patted the cat.
h) The collie ran up the road and over the bridge.
i) John and Mary passed the test.
j) She likes red shirts and scarves.

*Problem 6. Correlative Conjunctions

Another way we coordinate sentences other than using members of the FAN-BOYS is to use *correlative conjunctions,* such as *neither . . . nor, either . . . or, both . . . and.* Some examples are given in (a–c).

a) She ate *both* her broccoli and her mashed potatoes.
b) She ate *neither* her broccoli *nor* her mashed potatoes.
c) She ate *either* her broccoli *or* her mashed potatoes.

Create three examples of coordination using correlative conjunctions, using in each example phrases of different categories. (For example, in your first sentence, coordinate noun phrases; in your second, verb phrases; and in your third, prepositional phrases.) It is not necessary to label the categories of the phrases, just try to use different ones in each example.

Then attempt to coordinate, using correlative conjunctions, phrases of *different* categories in the same sentence. Give three such sentences and discuss whether your evidence supports the hypothesis that conjunction must involve elements of the same category.

TEXT ANALYSIS

1. Poetic Syntax

We often find syntactic constructions in poetry that differ from what we might consider everyday spoken English, as poets often employ different usage for rhetorical effect. Choose a short poem, or a few lines of a longer one, and analyze how the poet uses movement to create some kind of effect. Find at least three examples of sentences or phrases in which word order is other than SVO. Try to "reconstruct" the sentences into their original order. Discuss your findings in class. What kinds of patterns can you observe? Can you make any generalizations about the kinds of phrases that are moved?

2. Examples of Movement

Find, in texts you choose on your own, at least three examples of sentences in which Passive, Particle Shift, or Indirect Object Movement has applied. Clearly label your examples, and bring them to class for discussion. (The newspaper is a good place to look for examples of passive sentences.)

3. Proforms and Antecedents

To practice finding proforms and to see how they refer back to antecedents, read the following text fragment. Circle any proforms you find, and list their antecedents.

John had not much affection for his mother and sisters, and an antipathy to me. He bullied and punished me; not two or three times in the week, nor once or twice in the day, but continually; every nerve I had feared him, and every morsel of flesh on my bones shrank when he came near. There were moments when I was bewildered by the terror he inspired, because I had no appeal whatever against either his menaces or his inflictions; the servants did not like to offend their young master by taking my part against him and Mrs. Reed was blind and deaf on the subject; she never saw him strike or heard him abuse me, though he did both now and then in her very presence; more frequently, however, behind her back.

Source: Jane Eyre, by Charlotte Brontë.

4. Finding Proforms

Find examples of sentences that illustrate at least three different types of pronouns from Table 3.1. Identify each pronoun according to its type. Also, find its antecedent and circle it. If the pronoun has a pragmatic antecedent, try to explain what it is. Then, in sentences from a text of your choice, find at least three examples of proforms other than pronouns listed in Table 3.1. Find and circle their antecedents if you can. Bring your sentences to class for discussion.

5. Pronouns and Their Rhetorical Effects

In the following paragraph, noun phrases are repeated for rhetorical effect. Which noun phrases can you replace with pronouns, and how does this change the tone of the text?

> All Pueblo tribes have stories about such a person—a young child, an orphan. Someone has taken the child and has given it a place by the fire to sleep. The child's clothes are whatever the people no longer want. The child empties the ashes and gathers wood. The child is always quiet, sitting in its place tending the fire. They pay little attention to the child as they complain and tell stories about one another. The child listens although it has nothing to gain or lose in anything they say. The child simply listens.
>
> *Source: Private Property,* by Leslie Marmon Silko.

6. Analyzing Coordinate Structures

In the text below, circle the phrases or words coordinated by the highlighted conjunction. It is not necessary to label the categories of the phrases, but you may if you wish. A practice example follows.

The world was grey, like a fog, *and* the deathly grey was reflected in the night by the snow.

Phrases conjoined by *and:*

The world was grey, like a fog (sentence)

and

the deathly grey was reflected in the night by the snow. (sentence)

a) They walked up the road together to the old man's shack *and* went in through its open door.
b) The old man leaned the mast with its wrapped sail against the wall *and* the boy put the box *and* the other gear beside it.
c) The shack was made of the tough budshields of the royal palm which are called guano *and* in it there was a bed, a table, one chair, and a place on the dirt floor to cook with charcoal.

Source: The Old Man and the Sea, by Ernest Hemingway.

LANGUAGE DIVERSITY EXERCISES

1. Earlier English Word Order

The word order in Old English was very different from the order in its modern counterpart, and this order underwent certain important changes in the development of Middle English, with the coming of the French to England after the Norman Invasion of 1066. Trace the development of word order in Old English and Middle English. Provide two or three examples to illustrate how this order differs from the SVO order of modern English. Can these earlier orders be captured by the phrase structure rule for modern English S => NP VP? Try to write phrase structure rules for S in Old English and Middle English.

2. Old English Pronouns

In a textbook on the history of the English language, look up the origins of the pronoun system in Old English. From which languages did we acquire some of the current pronouns in Table 3.1? How did they differ from their modern counterparts? In particular, discuss their inflectional morphology, and compare them with their modern English counterparts.

3. Double Negatives in English

Speakers of English differ as to whether they use the indefinite pronouns *anyone/anwhere/anyhow* or *no one/nowhere,* and so on. African American Vernacular English speakers, for example, use the *no* variety of indefinite pronoun, versus the *any* variety. This gives rise to what are called *double negative* constructions, such as *I don't know no one/I'm not going nowhere,* versus *I don't know anyone/I'm not going anywhere.* Dialects such as African American Vernacular English that employ the *no-* word rather than the *any-* word strategy are often stigmatized for forming double negatives on the ground that "two negatives make a positive," and under the assumption that double negatives are "sloppy" or "lazy" speech.

Investigate the use of indefinite pronouns in African American Vernacular English (most introductory linguistics books have information on this; see the Appendix). You will find that the use of such *no-* indefinite pronouns is completely systematic. Try to formulate in your own terms the rules that a speaker of each variety (the *no-*variety and the *any-*variety) must have as part of his or her descriptive grammar. Comment on the claim that double negatives are "incorrect" because two negatives make a positive. Is this the case? What do you think about the claim that such usage is "sloppy speech" after you have researched this linguistic rule? On what assumptions is such a claim based?

CHAPTER REVIEW TERMS

Movement, Passive, Particle Shift, Indirect Object Movement, pronominalization, pronouns, proforms, antecedents (pragmatic and linguistic), WH-Movement, coordination and conjunctions.

CHAPTER REVIEW EXERCISE

Choose from among the following options to create a chapter exercise. You may wish to add options from previous chapter exercises to make this exercise more comprehensive.

1. Identify all the proforms in the text and label their type, if they have one (from Table 3.1). Circle their antecedents.
2. Find any conjunctions in the text, and circle the phrases or words they coordinate.
3. Apply WH-Movement to the following italicized phrases, in sentences taken from the following text excerpt.

a) June Kashpaw was walking down *the clogged main street of oil boomtown Williston, North Dakota.*
b) She was *a long-legged Chippewa woman.*
c) *A lot of people* looked familiar to her.
d) He hooked *his arm.*
d) *She* might tip down one or two with him.
e) She might tip down one or two with *him.*

The morning before Easter Sunday, June Kashpaw was walking down the clogged main street of oil boomtown Williston, North Dakota, killing time before the noon bus arrived that would take her home. She was a long-legged Chippewa woman, aged hard in every way except how she moved. Probably it was the way she moved, easy as a young girl on slim hard legs, that caught the eye of the man who rapped at her from inside the window of the Rigger Bar. He looked familiar, like a lot of people looked familiar to her. She had seen so many come and go. He hooked his arm, inviting her to enter, and she did so without hesitation, thinking only that she might tip down one or two with him and then get her bags to meet the bus.

Source: Love Medicine, by Louise Erdrich.

Part 2

Categories

4

Nouns

I have a map of Dixie on my tongue.
From *Dust Tracks on a Road* by Zora Neale Hurston

Introduction

So far, you have been briefly introduced to syntactic categories, and we have considered some reasons to divide these categories into two subclasses: grammatical and lexical categories. We have also seen that sentences can be divided into phrases, groups of words that form syntactic units, headed by a lexical category. We became familiar with some ways to test whether a group of words forms a phrase or not, using movement, pronominalization, and coordination. In this part of the book (chapters 4 through 9) we focus in more detail on individual syntactic categories, discussing each lexical category Noun, Verb, Adjective, Adverb, and Preposition in turn. In the course of the discussion we will analyze the syntax of grammatical categories as well, because, as we discussed briefly in Chapter 2, one of the characteristics of grammatical categories is that they typically introduce lexical heads.

In this chapter, we address the basic semantic and morphological characteristics of the syntactic category *Noun.* We will also discuss in some detail the structure of *noun phrases,* focusing in particular on the array of grammatical categories that precede nouns in noun phrases, including *Determiner, Numeral,* and *Quantifier,* and formulating a basic phrase structure rule for the noun phrase, or NP. You will also have the opportunity to apply the tests for phrases introduced in Chapter 3, namely pronominalization, coordination, and movement, in analyzing noun phrases.

Semantic Classes of Nouns

You may be familiar with the old saying: *A noun is a person, place, or thing.* While this characterization expresses the general meaning of nouns as "names" for things, it does nothing to deepen our understanding of the more complex semantic, morphological, and syntactic properties of nouns. That is, it does not explain to us how we know that the nonsense words *clons* and *naflings* in (1) are nouns.

(1)   Seven *clons* yarked the *naflings.*

We know intuitively that *clons* and *naflings* are nouns, because we know that syntactically, *the* precedes only nouns in English. We also know that nouns can be morphologically affixed by plural -*s,* and by -*ing* as well, as in *the clans* and *the ducklings.* Morphology and syntax thus provide important clues about the syntactic category of the nonsense words in (1), even though we have no idea what the words mean.

Nouns are typically thought of as names of both abstract and concrete things and events, such as *neighbor, joy, the Statue of Liberty, Courtney Love, vacations,* and *prejudice.* There are several different semantic classifications of nouns (abstract, concrete, mass, proper, common), some of which have distinctive syntactic and morphological properties as well. These (often overlapping) semantic classifications are given in Table 4.1, and each is discussed in more detail below.

Abstract nouns refer to intangibles such as emotions and states, while concrete nouns refer to things in the world that we can see and point to. Proper nouns are names for specific members of a set; the name *Luke Skywalker* consists of two proper nouns that together refer to a particular person. Proper nouns are thus *definite,* or nouns whose identity is presumed to be known by both the speaker and hearer. This is why proper nouns are typically not introduced syntactically by a definite determiner such as *the,* which is usually the way we introduce definite, common nouns in English, in phrases such as *the buildings* and *the students.* Proper nouns are already definite, as they pick out a specific entity, such as *Catwoman, Batman,* and *Robin.* Exceptions, of course, are things whose actual names include *the,* as in *The Joker, The Chunnel,* and *The Empire State Building,* or when we refer to groups such as *The Sonics, The Spice Girls,* or *The Windsors.* Common nouns, in contrast, are labels we give to sets of things (*dolls, toys*) or members of those sets that are not referred to by a special name (*the doll, the toy*). Mass and count nouns differ basically in terms of how they can encode *number,* or plural-

Table 4.1
Nouns: Semantic Classifications

---

abstract: love, poverty, insincerity

concrete: horse, taxicabs, computer

common: craziness, dog, spaghetti, language

proper: The Chunnel, Hanukkah, Mr. Potatohead, Susan B. Anthony

mass: water, rice, mud

count: table, television, grammar

---

ity. Mass nouns cannot be morphologically pluralized (they are "uncountable"), and thus do not take, for example, an *-s* ending, as we see by the oddity of *waters/rices.* Count nouns can be morphologically plural, and thus affixed with *-s* (*hurricanes* and *tornadoes*) or have irregular kinds of plurals (*women, men,* and *foci*). Mass nouns can also be turned into count nouns if we can imagine them as members of a countable set. For example, the plural nouns *waters/rices* in the sentences *I like only those waters bottled by Evian,* or *There are a number of different rices available in stores these days: jasmine, basmati, calrosa,* and *aborio,* are count nouns in this context, because they refer to members of a countable set.

The Morphology of Nouns

Derivational and inflectional morphology also provides us with ways to identify nouns. As we saw above, many nouns in English morphologically express **number** by the presence or absence of the plural *–s* inflectional affix. Other express number through irregular plural endings such as *–en* in *oxen* and *children,* and *–i* in *foci* and *syllabi.* We can also pluralize nouns without using any affix at all, by changing an internal vowel, as in *goose/geese, mouse/mice, woman/women.* There are thus several different ways in English in which a noun can morphologically express number *-s.*

Nouns can also express **case,** which reflects the grammatical function of a noun phrase as a subject, object, indirect object, instrument, and so on. (Case was briefly introduced in the discussion of pronouns in the previous chapter.) English is a language that has few examples of morphologically realized case marking. A brief illustration of case in English is the difference between the personal pronouns *I* and *me* in (2).

(2) a. *I* met the woman.
       b. The woman met *me.*

In (2a), the first person pronoun *I* morphologically expresses nominative, or subjective case. In (2b), the first person pronoun *me* is in accusative, or objective case. The form of the pronoun changes, depending on its grammatical function as subject or object. Subjects typically occur to the left of the verb in English, and objects to the right—we identify *the woman* as the subject or object in (2a) and (2b) on the basis of the *position* of the noun phrase rather than on its morphology. Case in English is therefore often *structural,* based on position, rather than *morphological,* based on the form of the noun or a particular morphological ending.

There is one way in which morphological case in English is expressed in the form of an affix, namely when nouns are affixed with possessive–*s.* This affix tells us that a noun phrase is a *possessor.* An example is given in (3).

(3) The student from Burkina Faso's hat

In (3), *the student from Burkina Faso's* is a noun phrase that is morphologically marked as possessive (with what we call "genitive" case), by the case affix–*s.*

Observe that the head noun of the noun phrase, *student*, is not affixed with–s, evidence that -'s attaches to the right most word in a noun phrase, rather than to the *head* of the noun phrase.

Nouns can also be affixed by *derivational* endings, endings that derive nouns from words of other categories. For example, we derive from the verbs *instruct* and *excite* the nouns *instruction* and *excitement* by adding derivational affixes *-ion* and *-ment*, respectively. Nouns formed through dervational affixation are called **nominalizations.** The term *nominalization* is thus itself a nominalization, as *-ion* is added to *nominalize* (the extra syllable *-a* and *-t* are added for phonological reasons we don't need to go into here). Other examples of nominalizations include *worker* (*work/-er*) and *divinity* (*divin/-ity*).

Nouns can also be formed through **compounding,** the morphological process of combining two (and sometimes more) words to form a single word. Compounds such as *X Files, firefighter,* and *snowboard* can be differentiated from two-word combinations by the "stress test." Compounds are typically stressed on the first word, as in *X Files* versus *large files,* and *firefighter* versus *injured fighter,* and *snowboard* versus *snowy board.* This tells us that compounds, though they may be hyphenated or spelled as two separate words, are nevertheless syntactically single words. Compound nouns such as *White House* and *teddy bear* are thus single nouns and not two separate words, like their counterparts *red house* and *angry bear.* Compounds can be of several different categories of word, as you can see in the following list:

(4) a. verbs: browbeat, download, spoonfeed
     b. adjectives: bedridden, tone deaf, downgraded
     c. prepositions: inside, outside, underneath

Nouns can also be coined as new words (*Ewok, Klingon*), or derived from words of other categories through functional shift (we can *ride* in a car, but a car can now also be a nice *ride.*). We can also derive new nouns by blending (we can watch *infomercials* and work in *McJobs*), clipping (we can *fax* things and we can be *proles*), and changing the meanings of an existing noun by semantic shift (we can now eat *wraps,* when we used to just wear them). There are other morphological processes by which we form nouns (from names and acronyms, etc.) which we will not pursue in any more detail here.

Table 4.2 summarizes our basic discussion of the derivational and inflectional morphology of nouns.

We can see from the above discussion of nouns that the morphology of a noun does not always clearly reflect its semantic classification. For example, both concrete and abstract nouns can be morphologically pluralized by affixing *-s,* and there is no particular morphological ending on common nouns that differentiates them from proper ones. Morphology and semantics together provide us with different kinds of information we use to identify a word's syntactic category.

Table 4.2
Derivational and Inflectional Morphology of Nouns

Derivational affixation: *-ion, -ment, -er, -ness, -ship,* etc.
  action/disagreement/teacher/friendliness/horsemanship (nominalizations)

Regular inflectional affixation: plural *-s,* possessive case *-'s*
  chairs, my cousin's friend

Irregular inflectional affixation: *-en, -i, -a,* etc.
  ox/oxen, child/children, focus/foci, medium/media

Other inflectional morphology: internal vowel change to show plurality
  man/men, woman/women, foot/feet

The Syntax of the Noun Phrase

What kind of evidence for the syntactic category of a noun do we derive from syntax? That is, what clues do we have from a word's position in a phrase? The word *loves,* for example, when not put into a syntactic context, appears to be an abstract noun affixed with the plural *-s,* as in *She has many loves.* It might also be a verb, affixed with the third person singular *-s,* as in *She loves many people.* Syntactic information, such as position, therefore provides crucial clues to a word's syntactic category.

Notice, for example, that the word *stone* in (5) can function differently in the sentence, depending on its syntactic position.

  (5) a. In some countries, a mob will *stone* someone for committing a
      crime.
      b. The man was hit by a *stone.*

In (5a), *stone* functions as a verb, because it follows the subject and indicates what the subject is doing. In (5b), *stone* functions as a noun, following the determiner *a,* a word that introduces only nouns. (5) illustrates, then, that in addition to morphological and semantic information, we rely on the position of a word to provide us with further clues about its syntactic category. Also, depending on the position of the word, its category, and hence its meaning, can change, and in different positions this word might have different morphological endings. Our intuitions about words thus involve a range of interacting grammatical information.

In the following section we examine the syntax of nouns in more detail, and in particular, the types of grammatical categories that precede nouns in English. We find that syntax involves more than just the position of a word; it also involves processes that apply to single words or to phrases. From this information we not only can identify nouns, but also larger units *headed* by nouns, **noun phrases.**

Categories That Introduce Nouns: Determiners, Numerals, and Quantifiers

Nouns in English can typically be preceded by a number of different kinds of words, with which they form a syntactic unit. Some examples are given in (6).

(6) a. *the/a/this/that/these/those* chairs
   b. *the chief executive's/whose* chair
   b. *four* chairs
   c. *all six* chairs
   d. *some/both* chairs
   e. *the many* chairs

The *prenominal* words in (6) can be characterized as members of the grammatical categories **Determiner, Numeral,** or **Quantifier.** In this section we outline some basic characteristics of these grammatical categories, and then discuss in more detail their syntax, in particular the various orders in which they occur. We show in the following sections that they form phrases with the noun they precede. For now, we will simply assume this without argument.

The grammatical categories Determiner, Numeral, and Quantifier in English all encode some kind of grammatical information, such as **definiteness, number,** and **case.** This information is sometimes, but not always, expressed morphologically by a particular inflectional affix.

Determiners in English include *the/a/this/that/these/those.* Determiners express definiteness or indefiniteness, and also number. This is illustrated in (7), where we see that *a/this/that* are singular, and *the* is morphologically unspecified for number: its form does not change, whether it is followed by a singular or a plural noun. The determiners *these/those* are plural.

(7) a. *A/this/that* dog/*dogs
   b. *the* dog/dogs
   c. *these/those* *dog/dogs

The/this/that/these/those are definite: they pick out a particular noun that is known to both speakers in a conversational exchange. This is not the case with the indefinite determiner *a;* the noun following this determiner is not necessarily known to both participants in the conversation. This is illustrated by the differences between (8) and (9).

(8) A. I found the dog.
   B. I'm glad. We really missed him.

(9) A. I found a dog.
   B. What kind is it?

The claim *I found the dog* in (8A) suggests that speaker (A) and hearer (B) both have a particular dog in mind. The response in (8B) assumes knowledge of the dog discussed in (8A), and is thus appropriate. The response *what kind is it?* would in this case be inappropriate, as it assumes that speaker B does not know the identity of the dog. The response in (9B) to (9A), on the other hand, makes sense because neither the speaker nor the hearer knows the identity of the dog. It would be odd, then, to respond to (9A) with (8B).[1]

This/that and *these/those* are also, respectively, singular and plural. They differ from definite *the* and indefinite *a* in an important way. *This/that/these/those* are called *demonstratives*, from the Latin *monstrare*, "to show," and are words that allow us to verbally "point" to things. *This/that*, for example, are both singular and definite, and differ only in proximity; *this dog* in (10) is "closer" to the speaker than *that dog*.

(10)   Mary bought *this* dog, but not *that* dog.

The plural demonstratives *these* and *those* are also definite, and again differ only in proximity; *these tarantulas* in (11) are closer to the speaker than *those tarantulas*.

(11)   Mary bought *these* tarantulas, but not *those* tarantulas.

We will diagram noun phrases in which the noun is introduced by a determiner as in (12), consistent with the phrase structure rule in (13), with which you are already somewhat familiar from our discussion in Chapter 2.

(12)

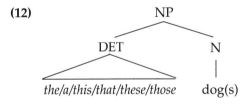

(13)   NP => (DET) N

The phrase structure rule in (13) expresses the generalization that noun phrases include at least a noun, (the head), that can be preceded by an optional determiner.

Numerals express (rather obviously) number, and are typically indefinite. For example, if we say *Four people came into the room*, it could be any four people. Notice, however, that if we say *The four people came into the room*, we assume that the speaker, and probably also the hearer, knows the four people who entered. The addition of the definite determiner *the* to the noun phrase with a numeral thus has the effect of making the noun phrase definite.

---

[1]Noun phrases with *the* are typically definite, and those with *a* are typically indefinite. This is not always the case, however, as the sentence *Sue married a sailor, and we really like him*, suggests. Here, we understand *a sailor* to be a person who we know. Many other such puzzles exist, and definiteness is far more complicated than I have let on here.

Numerals can be *cardinal*, as in *one/two three*, or *ordinal*, as in *first/second/third/twentieth*. Other words, sometimes called *general ordinals*, include *latest/next/additional/past/last/sole/only*, as in *the latest movie, the sole survivor, the only person, the next page*. We will assume that these words are of the grammatical category Numeral when they occur in the prenominal position occupied by numbers, which we will designate as NUM as in (14).

(14)

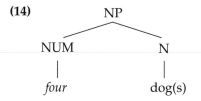

How then do we rewrite the phrase structure rule for noun phrase in (13) to include the option for a numeral to precede the noun? We can see from the following noun phrases that numerals are optional in the noun phrase, and that they must follow a determiner if there is one.

(15)   a. the four dogs (*four the dogs)
         b. a fourth dog (*fourth a dog)
         c. these four dogs (*four these dogs)

We express this order of determiners and numerals by rewriting (13) as (16):

(16)   NP => (DET) (NUM) N

According to (16), numerals follow determiners in the noun phrase. Both determiners and numerals are optional, allowing for a range of different syntactic combinations of these elements.

Quantifiers such as *all/each/every/both/some/several/few/many* pick out members of a set, typically in noncountable ways (except *both*, which we interpret as a set of two members.) Certain quantifiers, like determiners, are definite, and others are indefinite. Consider, for example, the noun phrases in (17).

(17)   a. *all/some/no* Studebakers

All Studebakers refers to a definite set of Studebakers, namely all of them, but *some Studebakers* refers to a partial and indefinite set of cars of this type. *No Studebakers* is indefinite, as it picks out no particular members in a set of Studebakers.

Quantifiers also have the interesting semantic property of taking wide or narrow *scope* over the members of the set they "quantify over." To see what this means, consider (18).

(18)   Everybody loves somebody.

There are at least two ways to interpret (18), a sentence that is ambiguous because of the scope relations of the quantifiers *every* and *some*. The sentence can mean that everybody loves a particular someone; John, Cary, and Lee all love Mary, for example (what we call the *group* interpretation). It can also mean that everybody loves a *different* someone; John loves Mary, Cary loves Pete, and Lee loves Willie (the *individual* interpretation). Observe that we don't get this kind of ambiguity in sentences without quantifiers; that is, (19) is unambiguous, lacking the kind of group and individual readings we get in (18).

(19)   The boys love someone.

The sentence in (19) simply means that there is some person all the boys love. It does not mean that each boy loves a different person. *The boys* thus does not interact with the scope of *someone* to create ambiguity.

There are many other ways to express *quantity* in English without necessarily involving the semantic property of quantification. For example, consider the examples in (20).

(20)   a. a *bunch* of gladiolas
   b. a *gaggle* of geese
   c. a *herd* of horses
   d. a *peck* of peppers

The boldface words in (20) all express amounts, but semantically they are not quantifiers, since they do not give rise to scope ambiguities such as we saw in (18). For example, consider (21).

(21)   The bunch of geese loves someone.

The sentence in (21) can mean only one thing, namely that the geese (members of the bunch) love the same person. *The bunch of geese* contains no quantifier; hence it does not interact with the scope of *someone* to create ambiguity.

The syntax of the phrases in (21) is quite complex, and we will not pursue it in detail here. Rather, we will assume that *a bunch of* and so on are "complex" determiners that are dominated by the symbol DET. We will use triangle notation, as in (22), to express them.

(22)

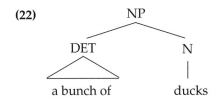

Similar kinds of complex constructions arise with quantifiers, as in (23).

(23) a. *all* (six) (of) the ducks
     b. *certain* of the ducks
     c. *both* of the ducks
     d. *few* of the ducks

Again, we will leave aside a detailed analysis of the complex constructions in (23), and diagram them as in (24), using triangle notation as a means of expressing what we will assume is a kind of complex quantifier.

(24)

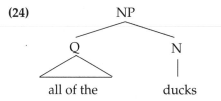

Other noun phrases in which the quantifier precedes the noun, as in (17), we will diagram as in (25).

(25)

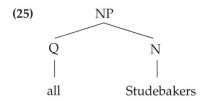

How then are we now to state the phrase structure rule in (16) to accommodate noun phrases with quantifiers? We know that quantifiers, like determiners and numerals, are optional in noun phrases. It remains, however, to determine the possible orders of these categories. Things get quite complicated at this point, because not all quantifiers occur in the same position with respect to other prenominal elements in noun phrases. To illustrate why, consider the noun phrases in (26).

(26) a. all six trucks
     b. *many six trucks

(26) illustrates that *all*, but not *many*, can occur before a numeral. A phrase structure rule in which quantifiers precede numerals thus allows (26a), but fails to block (26b).

    Another issue arises with the noun phrases in (27).

(27) a. the many trucks
     b. *the all trucks

As you can see in (27), *many* can follow a determiner, but *all* can't. Formulating the appropriate phrase structure rule would have to reflect this difference.

In view of the complexity of the syntax of quantifiers in noun phrases, we will adopt the general phrase structure rule in (28).

(28)   NP => (DET) (Q) (NUM) N

(28) allows us to diagram most noun phrases with quantifiers, though it does not block the ungrammatical cases in (26b) and (27b). We will assume that such constructions are ruled out for independent reasons that are beyond us here.

Returning once again to our list of the grammatical categories that occur in noun phrases, nouns can also be introduced by *possessive determiners, my/his/her/your/their/our*. These prenominal elements express *genitive* or *possessive case*. As we mentioned briefly in the discussion of noun morphology, morphological case reflects the grammatical function of a noun phrase as subject (nominative case), object (accusative case), indirect object (dative case), and so on. In English, case is typically determined by the position of the noun phrase in the sentence, and is thus structural rather than morphological. A noun phrase in the subject position thus has structural nominative case, and an object to the right of the verb has structural accusative case.

Possessive determiners in English are one of the few elements that do express morphological case, in particular possessive, or genitive, case. Like the determiner *the*, possessive determiners also appear to be unspecified for number; the form of the determiner remains the same when followed by a plural or singular noun: *her book(s)*.

As for position, possessive determiners are so called because they fill the same position as other determiners in the noun phrase. As we might therefore expect, they occur before numerals, and they do not co-occur with other determiners.

(29)   a. her six books
       b. *her the/this book

By classifying possessive determiners as members of the category DET, we have no need to further complicate our phrase structure rule for noun phrase in (28).

Possessive determiners are sometimes called *possessive pronouns* or *possessive adjectives*, but as we will discuss in the Discovery Problems at the end of the chapter, they clearly differ in both form and function from possessive pronouns *mine/yours/his/hers/ours/theirs*, and from the lexical category Adjective.

Possessive noun phrases are full noun phrases that precede nouns and express morphological possessive case in the form of the affix *-'s*. Some examples of possessive noun phrases are given in (30).

(30)   a. *Parliament's* agreement with Sinn Fein
       b. *France's* victory in the World Cup
       c. *The Hague's* decision

As we might by now expect, a possessive noun phrase can be made up of only a single noun (*Clinton's* decision) or a more complex noun phrase (*the American*

President from Little Rock's decision). Possessive noun phrases are diagrammed in (31).

(31)

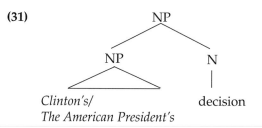

Possessive noun phrases, like possessive determiners, occur in the same position as the determiners *a/the/this/that/these/those*. We draw this conclusion on the basis of evidence that possessive noun phrases cannot co-occur with determiners, and that possessive noun phrases, like determiners, precede numerals. These patterns are illustrated in (32).

(32)   a. *Toni Morrison's the novel
         b. Toni Morrison's five novels

We might thus assume that possessive noun phrases occur in the same position as other determiners, as members of the category Determiner. The phrase structure of possessive noun phrases, however, is clearly different from that of determiners; possessive noun phrases are full *phrases,* rather than single words. Identifying them as members of the cateogory Determiner is thus not completely explanatory. In some traditional grammars, possessive noun phrases, like possessive determiners discussed above, are classified as *adjectives.* This classification arises because possessive determiners and noun phrases in some sense "describe" the noun and precede the noun just as adjectives do in a noun phrase such as *terrific novels.* As we will see, possessive noun phrases differ syntactically, morphologically, and semantically from adjectives, and again, are full phrases rather than lexical heads. To analyze them as adjectives thus runs us into problems similar to those that arise if we identify them as determiners. We will therefore differentiate possessive noun phrases from both determiners *and* adjectives.

We will assume that a noun can be preceded by a possessive noun phrase that occurs in the same position as a determiner, but is not a member of that grammatical category. Our phrase structure rule in (28) must therefore be revised as (33).

(33)   NP => $\left| \begin{matrix} \text{(DET)} \\ \text{(Poss NP)} \end{matrix} \right|$ (Q) (NUM) N

According to (33), a possessive noun phrase can precede a noun in a larger noun phrase, in the same position as a determiner would occur. Possessive noun phrases are not, however, analyzed as either lexical heads or members of grammatical categories (for example as members of DET), but rather as full noun phrases.

We can now diagram noun phrases including possessive noun phrases as in (34). The possessive noun phrase itself has the same phrase structure as any other noun phrase, with the difference that it is affixed with -'*s* and occurs to the left of a noun in a larger noun phrase.

(34)

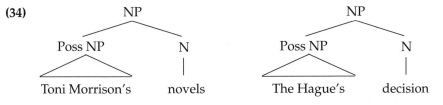

Finally, we turn to *WH-determiners* such as *whose/which/what*. These determiners question something about the noun they precede. For example, *whose lunch* questions the possessor of a particular lunch, and *which lunch* questions which member of the set of *lunches* we are talking about. *What lunch* can also have this interpretation, and the additional one of rhetorically questioning the existence of a particular lunch at all (*What lunch? You think I have time to eat lunch with all the work I have to do?*). These determiners occur in the Determiner position in the noun phrase, as we can see by their incompatibility with other members of the category Determiner and the evidence that they precede numerals.

(35)   a. You like *which roses?*
      b. *Which roses* do you think are the prettiest?
      c. **Which the roses* do you think are the prettiest?
      d. *Which six roses* do you think are the prettiest?

As with possessive noun phrases discussed above, a question arises when we characterize WH-determiners as members of the category Determiner. Consider (36) for example.

(36)   Whose novel did you buy?

In (36), we might assume that *whose* replaces the possessive noun phrase *Toni Morrison's*, and thus that the phrase structure of this noun phrase is the same as in (34). One difference is that the possessive noun phrase has been replaced with a pronoun. This would give rise to the phrase structure in (37) for *whose novels*, where *whose* has pronominalized a full noun phrase.

(37)

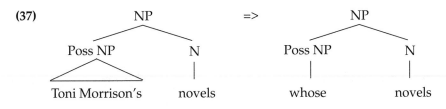

Alternatively, we might assume that *whose* in (36) replaces the possessive determiner *her* rather than a full noun phrase. The phrase structure of *whose novels*
might thus be (38).

(38)
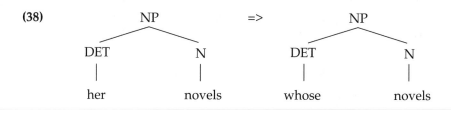

We will opt for the structure in (38) here, as it most easily explains the other uses
of WH-determiners that are *not* possessive, namely interpretations in which the
WH-determiner questions another determiner, as in (39).

> **(39)** a. *Which* book do you like? I like *this* book.
> b. *Which* street do you live on? We live on *the* street with all the
>   elm trees.

The most explanatory way, then, to include WH-determiners in our phrase
structure rule in (33) is to analyze these elements as members of the grammatical category Determiner. We will thus diagram noun phrases such as *which person* and *which person's paper* as in (40) and (41), respectively.

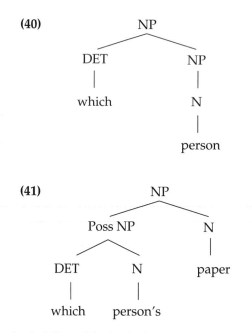

(40)

(41)

In both (40) and (41), *which* is a determiner. In (41), however, *which* happens to
be the determiner in a noun phrase that is itself a possessive noun phrase.

Let us now consider an assumption we have made all along, namely that the categories Determiner, Numeral, and Quantifier are all grammatical, rather than lexical categories.

Recall that lexical categories are morphologically "open," meaning that they allow new members quite productively, new members that can be added through any number of different morphological processes including blending, derivational affixation, compounding, and so on. Nouns are clearly a lexical category in this sense, as we add new nouns to the language all the time. We do not, on the other hand, add new determiners, numerals, and quantifiers to the language, making these classes of words "closed" classes.

Semantically, members of a lexical category have semantic content, or intrinsic meaning. Grammatical categories, in contrast, have grammatical meanings, but not intrinsic content of their own. This is best illustrated by comparing the dictionary definitions of the noun *labyrinth* in (42) with the indefinite article *a* in (43).

(42)   **labyrinth** (*n*) 1. An intricate structure of interconnecting passages through which it is difficult to find one's way: maze. . . .

(43)   **a** (*indefinite article*) 1. Used before nouns and noun phrases that denote a single, but unspecified, person or thing: *a region; a man.* . . .

As we can see by comparing (42) and (43), the determiner *a* has no intrinsic meaning, unlike the noun *labyrinth*. The meaning of the determiner can only be stated in terms of its grammatical function, that of expressing the indefiniteness of a following noun.

We have also seen that syntactically, determiners, numerals, and quantifiers pattern together as *prenominal* elements, and are thus syntactically distinct from nouns, and for that matter, from each other. They introduce a lexical head, namely a noun, another characteristic of grammatical categories.

We thus have a range of evidence that suggests that these elements are members of different grammatical categories, which we will label Determiner, Numeral, and Quantifier. Our final version of the phrase structure rule for noun phrase is given in (44).

(44)   NP => $\begin{Bmatrix} \text{(DET)} \\ \text{(Poss NP)} \end{Bmatrix}$ (Q) (NUM) N

The grammatical categories that occur before nouns in noun phrases are listed in Table 4.3.

Summary

We have seen that nouns come in a variety of different semantic types, including *abstract, concrete, common, proper, mass,* and *count.* Nouns also have a number

Table 4.3
Grammatical Categories in Noun Phrases

Grammatical Category	Members
Determiners:	articles (*the/a*)
	demonstratives (*this/that/these/those*)
	possessive determiners (*my/your/our/his/her/their*)
	WH-determiners (*which* teacher /*whose* class)
Numerals	cardinal (*eight, fifteen, ninety-six*)
	ordinal (*fifth, seventh, sixteenth*)
	"general" ordinal (*last, next, previous*)
Quantifiers	definite (*all/each/both/every*)
	indefinite (*many/some/few/most/several*)

of different morphological characteristics. We use derivational affixation to form **nominalizations,** and inflectional affixation on nouns, namely the plural -*s*, is one way to express **number.** Noun phrases can also express *possessive* or *genitive case* when affixed with possessive -*s*. Other grammatical information in noun phrases is expressed by the morphological form of the grammatical categories that syntactically precede nouns in noun phrases, in different orders that we attempted to capture with the phrase structure rule in (44). These prenominal elements, of the categories **Determiner, Numeral,** and **Quantifier,** express grammatical information of definiteness, number, and case. These three grammatical categories differ from lexical categories in all the ways expressed in Table 2.1; they have grammatical meanings, they do not admit new members, and they syntactically introduce a lexical category, Noun.

DISCOVERY PROBLEMS

Problem I. Phrase Structure Practice

Diagram the following noun phrases using the phrase structure rule in (44) (repeated here). Label the semantic type of each noun in your phrase structures using Table 4.1. (There may be more than one label per noun.)

$$\text{NP} => \begin{vmatrix} \text{(DET)} \\ \text{(Poss NP)} \end{vmatrix} \text{(Q) (NUM) N}$$

a) the forty thieves
b) their homework

c) all six articles
d) the child's two brothers
e) a few elephants
f) hatred
g) Aladdin's lamp
h) a cete of badgers
i) both of the books
j) our territory

Problem 2. More Phrase Structure Practice

Write a brief paragraph in which you include ONLY noun phrases that are generated by the phrase structure rule in (44). (Try to include as many different examples as you can in four or five noun phrases.) Exchange paragraphs with a classmate. Check whether they conform to the phrase structure rule. Label the semantic type of each noun in the text according to Table 4.1.

Problem 3. Beyond Our Phrase Structure Rule

Write a brief paragraph in which you include not only noun phrases that conform to the phrase structure rule in (44), but also others that do NOT conform to this rule. Do as above—exchange paragraphs with a classmate, and attempt to identify and diagram the noun phrases that you find. Which ones conform to (44), and which ones do not? Discuss how we might amend (44) to account for any "new" phrase structures for noun phrases you discover.

Problem 4. Recursion

Some of you may have noticed that (44) is recursive. Why is this? Give three examples of noun phrases that illustrate recursion. Diagram each of your examples as best you can. Use triangles rather than fully drawn structures if you need to.

Problem 5. Compounds as Heads of NP

Compounds are, as we have discussed, combinations of words that function syntactically as single words. A compound noun therefore behaves as a single noun, and can head a larger noun phrase. You are familiar with several different ways to "test" whether a word is syntactically part of a larger phrase, using coordination, movement, and pronominalization. You are also somewhat familiar with the object and subject noun phrase positions and can use these in your analysis of a word as a noun phrase as well.

Present evidence that the compound *backlash* is a noun phrase, even though it may appear to be a single word rather than a phrase. Some hints on how to approach this problem are as follows:

a) Does *backlash* occur in the same position as other noun phrases (as a subject, direct object, or indirect object, for example)?

b) Can *backlash* undergo any of the movement rules that involve other noun phrases (Passive, Indirect Object Movement, Particle Shift)?

c) Is it possible to coordinate *backlash* with other noun phrases?

d) Can *backlash* be replaced by a pronoun, like other noun phrases?

When you have finished your analysis of *backlash,* make a short list of at least three other compound nouns that function syntactically as noun phrases rather than as single words.

*Problem 6. Prenominal Adjective Phrases

Absent from the discussion of the phrase structure of noun phrases so far has been the role adjectives play in modifying nouns. Some examples of prenominal adjectival modifiers of the noun *story* are:

the *happy/gruesome/entertaining/short/boring* story

Now that you have some idea of the phrase structure of noun phrases, as formulated in (44), try to determine the position of adjectives in the noun phrase. How would you incorporate them into our phrase structure rule, and on the basis of what kinds of evidence? Provide examples of the phrases you use in systematically determining the position of prenominal adjectives. Do they occur in the same position as determiners? As quantifiers or numerals? Why or why not?

*Problem 7. Gerunds

You will find that words ending in *–ing,* what you might think of as verbs, can actually also function as nouns. Some examples of *–ing* words, or *participles* that function syntactically as nouns are given in (a–c).

a) Chris likes being a realtor, but sometimes the constant *telephoning* gets on her nerves.

b) Lionel had a good *feeling* about the new president of the company.

c) *Reading* is Sandi's favorite pastime.

Knowing what you now know about nouns and the syntax of noun phrases, give two syntactic arguments for analyzing the participles in (a–c) as nouns, or **gerunds.** Think about their syntactic positions, the words that occur before and after them, and provide as much data in your answer as you can. Make up three or four other sentences that have gerunds in them.

*Problem 8. Another Prenominal Modifier

Consider the following italicized words: *suede* shoes, *iron* lung, *nylon* stocking, *brick* building, *leather* saddle Are these modifiers adjectives, or are they of some other syntactic category? What kinds of syntactic, morphological, and semantic evidence can you use in determining their syntactic category? Do we need to amend the phrase structure rule in (44) to include these words? How might we do that? Try to formulate (44) to include this kind of prenominal modifier. (It is a good idea to complete Problem 6 before doing this one.)

Problem 9. Possessive Determiners and Pronouns

As mentioned in this chapter, there is reason to distinguish possessive determiners from possessive pronouns. Possessive determiners are listed again in (a), and possessive pronouns are given in (b).

  a) possessive determiners: *my/you/his/her/their/your/our* book
  b) possessive pronouns: That book is *mine/yours/his/hers/theirs/yours/ours.*

How do the two sets of elements differ morphologically (and how are they the same)? How do they differ syntactically? Think about the following paradigms when considering the second question.

  c) *my/you/his/her/their/your/our* book
     *mine/yours/his/hers/theirs/yours/ours book
  d) *The book is *my/you/her/their/your/our.*
     The book is *mine/yours/his/hers/theirs/yours/ours.*
  e) *The teacher's* book => *her* book/**hers* book
  f) The book is *the teacher's.* => The book is *hers.*/*The book is *her.*

When thinking about this latter question, consider the positions each type of element can occur in. Are they completely interchangeable syntactically? Also, think about what these elements *pronominalize,* or replace. What reasons can you give, for and/or against, analyzing one as a determiner and one as a pronoun?

Problem 10. Count Versus Mass Nouns

Count nouns have some interesting properties that distinguish them from mass nouns. This exercise gives you a chance to try to figure these differences out on your own, given different kinds of data. First, consider the data in (a–c) for the noun *telephone.*

  a) a telephone/telephones
  b) more telephones/fewer telephones
  c) *(too) much telephone/*less telephone/*little telephone

Telephone is a count noun, as we can see by the option for it to be morphologically plural, for it to be preceded by the indefinite article *a*, and by its failure to co-occur with quantifiers that relate to mass, such as *much/less/little.* Now compare *telephone* with *milk*, using the same criteria.

  d) *a milk/*milks
  e) *more milks/*fewer milks
  f) (too) much milk/less milk/little milk

In contrast to *telephone, milk* is a mass noun—it cannot be pluralized nor can it occur with the indefinite article *a* or as a plural noun with *more/fewer*.

Now consider the following nouns and determine, on the basis of the preceding tests, whether they are count or mass. Some may have uses as *both* mass and count. Be sure to give complete patterns of evidence for your conclusions.

housework beer happiness light beauty paper homework

*Problem 11.“Zero” Plurals

An interesting set of nouns in English, sometimes called *zero* plurals, do not change form at all, whether singular or plural. Some examples are:

fish deer sheep fowl moose elk

Can these nouns be classified as mass or count, according to the tests we used in Problem 7? How would you classify them? Show how you would test your hypothesis based on patterns of data.

Problem 12. Analyzing New Nouns

Find, either in texts of your own choosing, a movie or television show, in speech you overhear, advertising, and so on, at least three examples of nouns that you think have come into the language relatively recently. Explain why you categorize each word as a noun, answering the following questions.

a) What does your noun mean? Does it have lexical or grammatical meaning?
b) Which semantic class or classes does it belong to? Why?
c) In what ways can your noun express inflectional morphology? Give examples.
d) Can your noun head a noun phrase? Can it be preceded by prenominal elements?
e) Can your noun, and the noun phrase it heads, undergo movement that applies to noun phrases? (Passive, Indirect Object Movement, for example?) Construct relevant examples.

Practice Example

You might choose from *Star Wars* the noun *Wookiee,* and analyze it as follows:

a) Definition: Wookiee—a tall furry animal, one of whom is the companion to Han Solo, one of the movie's heroes. (lexical meaning)
b) Semantic type:
   common noun: Wookiees make good companions.
   concrete noun: I saw a Wookiee at the mall.
   count noun: It takes only one Wookiee to save Han Solo.

c) Inflectional morphology:
   number: one Wookiee, two Wookiees
   possessive *-s:* The Wookiee's hair is very long.
d) Wookiee as head of a noun phrase:
   all eight Wookies, these Wookiees
e) Movement: Passive
   The Wookiee helped Han Solo.
   Han Solo was helped by *the Wookiee.*

Conclusion: *Wookiee* is a noun.

Problem 13.The *one/none of the* Construction

Complex *"one/none of the"* constructions, such as *one of the men, none of the books,* raise an interesting issue for prescriptive grammarians. Such constructions have, in effect, two possible elements, one singular and one plural, with which a following verb might agree, as illustrated in (a).

a) One of the men was/were in the garden.

This same "agreement" issue arises with phrases such as *a bunch of roses.*

b) A cloud of mosquitoes was/were in the garden.

We hear both of the cases illustrated in (a) and (b), where the verb *be* agrees with either singular *one/cloud* or with plural *men/mosquitoes.*

James Kilpatrick, a self-appointed grammar expert, whose column *The Writer's Art* appears in national newspapers, often writes about prescriptive conundrums such as the one illustrated in (a–b). In a column that appeared on July 5, 1998, in the *Seattle Times,* Kilpatrick discusses the following sentences, which illustrate the *one of the* agreement issue.

c) "I am *one of those people* who *believes* that the tobacco companies should advertise in newspapers to get their message of brotherhood across."
d) "I am *one of those people* who *find* American rodeo clowns wildly more admirable than Spanish bullfighters."

In both (c) and (d) we find the phrase *one of those people,* but in (c) the verb is singular and in (d) it is plural. Kilpatrick defers to R. W. Burchfield, editor of *The New Fowler's Modern English Usage,* who recommends using plural verbs in such constructions "unless particular attention is being drawn to the uniqueness, individuality, etc., of the *one* in the opening clause." In other words, either usage is "correct," depending on what you wish to focus on in the sentence.

Prescriptive grammarians are far stricter, however, about their view of the construction *none of the* illustrated in (e).

e) None of the men was/were at the rally.

They generally agree that *none* is singular (like *one*), and thus that the verb must be singular as well. *Was* in (e) is thus "correct," and *were* is "bad grammar."

What can we learn about prescriptive grammar from this discussion of the *one/none of the* construction? How does Kilpatrick's discussion of *one of the* reflect attitudes about prescriptive grammar discussed in Chapter 1? (In particular, think about notions of "authority.") What conclusions about the arbitrariness of prescriptive rules can you draw by comparing Kilpatrick's response to *one of the* with the "stricter" approach to *none of the*? You may wish to look the *one/none of the* construction up in some grammar handbooks, to determine whether these two constructions are treated consistently, and if there is consensus among prescriptivists as to how to treat the verb agreement "problem." You might wish to answer this question from the point of view of a teacher. How would you approach this "conundrum" in the classroom, based on the information discussed here?

TEXT ANALYSIS

1. Identifying Nouns

Circle all the nouns in the following paragraphs, and for each one explain the kinds of semantic, morphological, and syntactic evidence you used to determine its syntactic category. Also, label any prenominal elements according to the table in 4.3, and label any possessive noun phrases. Identify and label any pronouns, using Table 3.1 in Chapter 3.

> The affluent, educated, liberated women of the First World, who can enjoy freedoms unavailable to any women ever before, do not feel as free as they want to. And they can no longer restrict to the subconscious their sense that this lack of freedom has something to do with—with apparently frivolous issues, things that really should not matter. Many are ashamed to admit that such trivial concerns— to do with physical appearance, bodies, faces, hair, clothes—matter so much. But in spite of shame, guilt, and denial, more and more women are wondering [if it isn't that they are entirely neurotic and alone] but rather that something important is indeed at stake that has to do with the relationship between female liberation and female beauty.
>
> *Source: The Beauty Myth*, by Naomi Wolf.

> ... as a writer I have never felt that medicine interferred with me but rather that it was my very food and drink, the very thing which made it possible for me to write. Was I not interested in man? There the thing was, right in front of me. I could touch it, smell it. It was myself, naked just as it was, without a lie, telling itself to me in its own terms ... it was giving me terms, basic terms with which I could spell out matters as profound as I cared to think of. . . .
>
> *Source: The Practice,* by William Carlos Williams.

2. Nouns and Poetic Convention

Discuss the use of nouns in the following poem. Identify the semantic class and morphology of each noun, using Tables 4.1 and 4.2. How does the choice of nouns in the poem affect its overall tone or message?

> In the modern fiefdom of Fred Meyer*, the walled city,
> where all things necessary exist, & nothing changes—
> not in housewares, the supermarket, the pharmacy, the clothing store—
> I hear the PA system cry out for Betty Rogers to return
>   to Playland,
> & I wonder who Betty Rogers is, & why she ever left there.
> How human, to wander from a place called Playland.
>
> *Source: See it all as Bardo,* from the collection *Bardo* by Suzanne Paola.
>
> (*Fred Meyer* is the name of a chain of stores that includes groceries as well as housewares, sports, and garden equipment.)

3. Pronominalization as a Test for Noun Phrases

We have now established that noun phrases can be generated by the phrase structure rule in (44), but we have yet to "test" this hypothesis beyond our intuitions. We can, however, invoke the diagnostics for phrases from Chapter 3, namely movement, pronominalization, and coordination, to support our initial intuitions about noun phrases.

Consider the following paragraph, and circle as many of the noun phrases as you can. Some may have structure that you are not yet familiar with, but should nevertheless appear to form a unit of some kind.

We were sitting in the cafeteria of the fitness center at George Lucas's Skywalker Ranch, in Marin County, California, where Redford was completing his new film, "The Horse Whisperer." For Redford, "The Horse Whisperer" is an unusual project. Until now, he has acted in twenty-nine films; he has directed four ("Ordinary People," a tearjerker about family guilt and repression, won two Oscars in 1980, and "Quiz Show," a perfectly judged backward glance at the game-show scandals of the later nineteen-fifties, gained him a nomination in 1994); he has produced and acted in three; but "The Horse Whisperer" is the first in which he's tried to do it all—direct, produce, star.

Source: "Existential Cowboy," by Richard Rayner, *The New Yorker*, May 18, 1998.

Now replace as many of the noun phrases as you can with pronouns. Were your intuitions correct?

4. Movement as a Test for Noun Phrases

Choose five of the noun phrases you identified from the text in (4). Construct sentences to show that each noun phrase you chose can undergo movement. For example, you might choose the noun phrase *Redford*. Construct a sentence in which this noun phrase undergoes movement, using, for example, Passive or some other rule you are now familiar with.

a) *Redford* rode the horse.
b) The horse was ridden by *Redford*.

That *Redford* can undergo movement in this way provides evidence that this word is functioning as a noun phrase. Construct your own examples using Passive, Indirect Object Movement, Particle Shift, and WH-Movement, as discussed in Chapter 3.

LANGUAGE DIVERSITY EXERCISES

1. Old English Determiners

The Old English determiner system differs quite dramatically from its modern English counterpart, especially with respect to inflectional morphology. That is,

Old English had much more inflection that does modern English. Textbooks on the history of the English language usually outline in some detail the determiner system of Old English, and you can find such discussions by looking up *possessive pronouns, demonstratives,* and *articles* in the index.

For this exercise, find three examples of Old English determiners and discuss how they differ morphologically, syntactically, and semantically from their modern counterparts. Be as detailed as you can, and diagram noun phrases if it helps you clarify certain points. Pay particular attention to the ways in which determiners in Old English express inflection.

2. Old English Nouns: Gender

We have discussed in the text the inflections *number, definiteness,* and *case,* the only inflections modern English nouns and determiners express morphologically by the affixes -s and -'s, or by a particular form, such as *the* versus *a.* Old English nouns, on the other hand, also expressed **gender,** and could be masculine, neuter, or feminine. For example, the noun *scip,* or "ship," was neuter, and the noun *bat,* or "boat," was masculine. The noun *brycg,* or "bridge," was feminine.

Investigate, again using a textbook on the history of the language, what is meant by "gender" in this case. Does gender correlate with biological sex? Is there some reason "ship" is neuter and "bridge" feminine in Old English? Why then would "boat" be masculine? In your answer, you will be addressing the differences between grammatical and natural, or biological, gender. Give some examples of different nouns and their genders to illustrate your points, and discuss the ways in which gender inflection is morphologically expressed by Old English nouns and determiners.

3. Middle English Nouns

During the Middle English period (1100 AD => 1400 AD), English borrowed a number of new nouns from French, the language with which English came into heavy contact in the aftermath of the Norman invasion. Most history of the English language textbooks give extensive examples of such nouns. For this exercise, compile a list of nouns borrowed into English during the Middle English period. Discuss, in particular, their meanings. What kinds of nouns were borrowed, and why? For example, from French English borrowed a number of culinary terms, which describe French cooking techniques, foods, and labels for things that might already have had Old English names as well.

dinner, boil, fry, sauce, salad, gravy, beef, pork, mutton, mustard

In Old English, then, one ate *cow,* but after the coming of the French, one ate *beef.* Find a few such lists of new vocabulary borrowed into English from French, and discuss their different meanings. What kinds of synonyms did such borrowings give rise to (such as *cow/beef*)?

4. Kennings

Old English had an interesting way of forming compound nouns, called *kennings*. Examples are *helmet-bearer* for *warrior* and *whale-road* for the sea, from *Beowulf*. Others are *wave-horse* for *ship*, and *laughter-smith* for *minstrel*. Explain what a kenning is, and try to explain how Old English compounding differs from compounding in modern English. Bring three examples of kennings to class for discussion.

5. Pidgin Compounding and Extension

Pidgins are "contact" languages that operate with limited vocabularies and less grammatical complexity than other languages. Pidgins are also distinct from "full" languages in being nonnative; children might grow up speaking a pidgin, but they will have another native language as well. There are a number of other interesting characteristics of pidgins that we will pursue in other chapters.

One way in which pidgin languages form new words using a limited vocabulary is by compounding. For example, a pidgin might form compounds using the word *baby* for the young of animals, such as *cow-baby* and *horse-baby*. Pidgins also adopt a strategy called *extension*, by which they extend the meaning of a noun such as *stick* to mean not only "part of a tree," but also "flagpole" and "pencil," among other things. Such examples are usually discussed in introductory linguistics textbooks, in addition to references on pidgins that you might find by doing some research. Find four or five such examples of pidgin nouns that are formed in these or any other ways. Also, discuss the inflection of nouns in pidgin, and how it compares with inflection of nouns in English. How, for example, does the particular pidgin you are researching form a plural or a possessive noun phrase?

6. The German Determiner System

In German, determiners (such as *der/die/das*, etc.) express case, number, and gender. Find some examples of this (in a German grammar textbook) and explain how the German determiner system differs from the English one in this way. Give contrastive examples from English and German to illustrate your point.

Languages with morphological case also typically allow somewhat freer word order than languages with only structural case. This is because structural case crucially depends on the position of the noun phrase. For example, one reason we know that in *Cary saw Mary, Mary* is the direct object because this noun phrase occurs to the immediate right of the verb. In languages with morphological case, on the other hand, expressed by the form of the determiner, fewer restrictions on order appear to hold, because the grammatical relation of the noun phrase (as subject, direct object, indirect object, etc.) is clear from its morphology. What kind of language is German in this respect? That is, can you find any evidence that noun phrases in German have more "flexible" order than noun phrases in English?

CHAPTER REVIEW TERMS

Semantic classes of nouns: abstract, concrete, common, proper, mass, count
Morphology: nominalizations, gerunds, inflectional affixation: (plural-*s*, possessive- *'s*, and irregular plurals), definiteness, number, case (accusative, nominative and genitive)
Prenominal elements: determiners, numerals, quantifiers, possessive noun phrases, prenominal adjective phrases and noun modifiers
gerunds

CHAPTER REVIEW EXERCISE

Choose from among the following options to create a chapter exercise. You may wish to add options from previous chapter exercises to make this exercise more comprehensive. In the following text excerpts:

1. List all nouns and label them according to their semantic type (use Table 4.1).
2. Identify and label all prenominal elements (using Table 4.3.) Also identify any noun or adjectival modifiers of nouns.
3. Identify any nominalizations, gerunds, and nouns with inflectional affixes.
4. Circle at least four noun phrases, and replace them with pronouns, using Table 3.1 in Chapter 3.

> Claude drove out the Canada highway eight miles, then off on the county road that went between the fields and past my house toward the west mountains a hundred miles away, where there was still snow and it was cold. My house flashed by in back of its belt of olive trees—just a square gray two-story house, unprotected toward the east. Claude was driving to Mormon Creek, I knew, though we were only doing what his father had told us to and not anything on our own. We were only boys, and nothing about us would interest a woman, or even a girl the age of this girl. You aren't ignorant of the fact when it is true about you, and sometimes when it isn't.
>
> *Source:* "Children," a story from *Rock Springs,* by Richard Ford.

Mrs. Sanstad was Lovborg's revenge on his mother. Also a critical woman, she began life as a trapeze artist with the circus; his father, Nils Lovborg, was the human cannonball. The two met in midair and were married before touching the ground. Bitterness slowly crept into the marriage. By the time Lovborg was six years old his parents exchanged gunfire daily. This atmosphere took its toll on a sensitive youngster like Jorgen, and soon he began suffering the first of his famous "moods" and "anxieties," rendering him for some years unable to pass a roast chicken without tipping his hat.

Source: Without Feathers, by Woody Allen.

5

The Forms and Meanings of Verbs

*The only language men ever speak perfectly is the one they
learn in babyhood, when no one can teach them anything!*
Maria Montessori

Introduction

You may have learned somewhere along the line that verbs express actions or
states. This meaning-based definition is not really adequate, as adjectives and
nouns can also express states (the *happy* camper, my *annoyance*) and nouns can
express actions (the *fight/battle/altercation*, a *kiss*, etc.) As we saw with nouns in
the previous section, a more productive way to analyze a particular syntactic
category is by sorting out its various semantic, morphological, and syntactic
properties. These components of grammar contribute different "clues" that help
us make more principled decisions about category membership. In the next two
chapters we will discuss the semantics, morphology, and syntax of grammatical
and lexical *verbs*. This chapter focuses on the semantics and morphology of
verbs. In the course of the discussion we will discover ways to differentiate
among *main verbs*, *auxiliary verbs* such as *have* and *be*, and *modals* such as
will/shall/might. We will also become familiar with the different *forms* of verbs,
including *past tense, present tense, infinitival*, and *participial* forms. We will discuss
in some detail the *tense* and *aspect* of the sentence, or its relative time frame, and
how the forms of the verb reflect this grammatical information. We conclude the
chapter with a discussion of reasons to think that the category Verb can be
divided into two subclasses, lexical main verbs and grammatical auxiliary and
modal verbs, on the basis of their morphological and semantic differences. We
pursue this distinction in Chapter 6, when we examine syntactic differences
between these two types of verbs.

The Semantics of Verbs

Semantically, verbs can be organized into different classes. For example, we
might make the classification *active* and *stative* verbs, in which the former
includes *hit/strike/play/load* and the latter includes *sleep/remain/seem*. Within the

large class of active verbs, however, we might form a smaller subset including only verbs of *motion*, such as *run/walk/climb/drive/crawl*. Another class of verbs might include emotive verbs such as *annoy/disgust/repel/bother*, and still others, verbs of perception, such as *watch/hear/observe*, and sense, such as *taste/feel/smell*. In short, when it comes to classifying verbs on the basis of their meanings, there are numerous possibilities.

Verbs are semantically related to other parts of the sentence. As illustrations, consider (1–2).

(1)   Mary asked Jill for money.

(2)   John seems sick.

In (1), *Mary* is the doer, or *agent*, of the action of the verb *ask*, and *Jill* is what undergoes the action, or the *theme*. *Money* is the *goal* of the action. Semantically, then, the verb *ask* can have associated with it three different semantic roles: agent, theme, and goal. In (2), *John* is not an agent, or performer, of an action. Rather, he is the *theme* of the verb *seem* (or perhaps more accurately, the theme of the larger predicate *seems sick*). *Seem* is therefore a verb that "assigns" only one semantic role, in this case, the role of *theme*.

Another example of the semantic properties of verbs is illustrated in (3–4).

(3)   Mary is a doctor.

(4)   Mary saw a doctor.

In (3), *a doctor* is a noun phrase, in a position directly to the right of the verb, in this case *is*. The same is true in (4); in this case the verb is *see*. (3) and (4) are thus *syntactically* identical.

Notice, however, that the sentences differ in terms of their *semantics*. In (3), *a doctor* is a noun phrase that describes the subject noun phrase *Mary*. This is not the case in (4); here, *a doctor* takes the action of the verb; it is what Mary saw. The semantics of sentences that are syntactically identical differ, depending on the choice of verb.

We can say, then, that verbs themselves encode a wide range of different meanings, and that they also play a crucial role in determining the semantics of the sentence itself. Verbs therefore appear to be members of a lexical category, as they have intrinsic semantic content. This is illustrated by the dictionary definition for the verb *spatter* in (5).

(5)   **spatter** (*v*) 1. To scatter (a liquid) in drops or small splashes. 2. To spot, splash, or soil. 3. To sully the reputation of; defame. . . .

Not all verbs have lexical meanings, however. Consider, for instance, the definition of the modal *can* in (6).

(6)   **can** (*aux. v*) Used to indicate: a. Physical or mental ability: *I can meet you today.* b. Possession of a specified power, right, or privilege: *The*

President can veto congressional bills. c. Possession of a specified capacity or skill: *He can tune the harpsichord as well as play it.* . . .

As we can see in (6), the meanings of modals are quite different from those of verbs such as *spatter* in (5). Modals provide information about *modality,* or volition, necessity, ability, permission, and so on, information that defines the mood of the sentence. They do not provide the verbal meaning of a sentence; that meaning is supplied by a main verb that follows the modal, such as *meet, veto, tune,* as we see in the example sentences in (6).

Modals are therefore semantically distinct from main verbs in that they express grammatical information rather than having intrinsic meaning. Modals thus appear to be members of a grammatical rather than a lexical category, at least on the basis of their semantics, suggesting that the category Verb comprises two different subclasses, lexical verbs and grammatical verbs. We will clarify the distinction between lexical and grammatical verbs in later sections of the chapter. Now, however, we turn to some of the morphological properties of verbs, in particular their inflectional morphology.

The Morphology of Verbs

Derivational Morphology

As we have seen in our discussion of nouns in the previous chapter, derivational morphology provides us with a number of clues for determining the syntactic category of a word. In the case of main verbs, they can be formed by adding suffixes such as *-ize* to adjectives (*regularize, legalize*), *-ate* to roots (*masticate, regulate, pontificate*), or *-ify* to other roots or words (*deify, rarify, ratify*). Main verbs can also be formed through **blending** (*electronic mail => email*), **clipping** (*facsimile => fax*), **functional shift** (*father, mother, impact*), and compounding (*sleepwalk/spoonfeed/mainline*).

The evidence that we productively form new main verbs through various word formation processes again suggests that main verbs form a lexical category, a category to which we productively add new members, rather than a grammatical category, to which we do not. We thus have further evidence for the distinction between grammatical and lexical verbs, in terms of derivational morphology and participation in other word formation processes.

Inflectional Morphology

The inflectional morphology of main verbs encodes information about person, number, tense, and aspect. Inflection can be expressed morphologically through affixation or through internal changes in the form of the verb. Still other verb forms are created through *suppletion,* a process by which we come up with an entirely unrelated form to express a grammatical feature. We discuss each of these processes in turn below, in sections on *tense* and *aspect.*

Tense.   As you may be aware, **tense** is the grammatical expression of the time of an event. In English, main verbs can be affixed with inflectional endings that express *present* or *past tense,* as in (7).

> **(7)** a. Hortense dances the lambada.
>   b. Hortense danced the lambada.

In (7a), the main verb *dances* is affixed with the third person singular *-s*, the only morphological affix that appears on verbs in the present tense in English. Verbs can also be inflected for past tense, affixed with *-ed* as in (7b). This affix is sometimes realized phonologically as a *-t* on other verbs, as illustrated in (8).

> **(8)** a. Lionel bought the Thunderbird.
>   b. The dog caught the frisbee.

Another way in which verbs express tense morphology in English is through internal vowel changes. For example, the verbs *run, sing,* and *drink,* all express tense in this way.

> **(9)** a. Carlos *sings* Barry Manilow songs only in the shower. (present tense)
>   b. Carlos *sang* Barry Manilow songs only in the shower. (past tense)

Still other verbs have past tense forms that are completely unrelated to their present tense forms, and these are called *suppletive* forms. Tense is in this case expressed by **suppletion.**

> **(10)** a. Rudi *goes* to school in Canada. (present tense: affixation)
>   b. Rudi *went* to school in Canada. (past tense: suppletion)

Some verbs combine vowel changes with affixation, as we just saw with examples such as *buy/bought* and *catch/caught.* In these cases, tense is expressed by both an internal vowel change and an affix, *-t.* Table 5.1 summarizes the tense, person, and number inflections of main verbs in English.

Aspect.   English verbs can also morphologically express **aspect,** or information concerning the *duration* or *completion* of an event. Consider (11), for example.

> **(11)** a. Hortense *has* written a letter.
>   b. Hortense *is* writing a letter.

Observe that the forms of the main verb *written/writing* in (11) are not inflected for tense, unlike the main verbs *dance, bought,* and *caught* in (7–8). Rather, the **auxiliary,** or "helping," verbs *have* or *be* that precede the forms of the main verb *written/writing* are inflected for present tense.

That tense is expressed by the auxiliary verbs rather than main verbs in such sentences is further illustrated by comparing (11) with (12):

Table 5.1
Person, Number, and Tense Morphology of English Verbs

	Singular	Plural
First Person	I walk	we walk
Second Person	you walk	you walk
Third Person	he/she/it walks	they walk

	Present Tense	**Past Tense**
Affixation	she walks	she walk**ed**
	she plays	she play**ed**
Vowel change	she runs	she **ran**
Suppletion	she goes	she **went**
Vowel change	she buys	she **bought**
and affixation	she brings	she **brought**

> **(12)** a. Hortense *had* written a letter.
> b. Hortense *was* writing a letter.

In (12a), *had* is a past tense form of *have,* and in (12b), *was* is a past tense form of *be.* Though the tense of the sentences in (11) has changed, the form of the main verb, *written/writing,* remains the same. One characteristic of auxiliary *have* and *be,* then, is that they by definition precede main verbs, and are thus not main verbs themselves. Another characteristic is that when they are the only auxiliary in the sentence, they express past or present tense.

Morphologically, then, the differences between (11–12) are that in the former, the auxiliary verbs are in their present tense forms, followed by *written/writing.* In the latter, the auxiliary verbs are in their past tense forms, again followed by *written/writing.* When we compare the semantics of the sentences, however, we notice that although both (11a) and (12a) occur in past time, (12a) was *completed* further in the past than (11a), a difference we can attribute to the past tense of the auxiliary verb *had.* (11b) and (12b) also express more than just tense; (11b) expresses an event that is *ongoing* in the present and (12b), an event ongoing in the past. We call the grammatical information of *completion* and *duration* expressed by verbs *aspect.* Aspect is illustrated in (13).

> **(13)** a. Hortense has written a letter. (past, completed)
> b. Hortense is writing a letter. (present, duration)
> c. Hortense had written a letter. (further past, completed)
> d. Hortense was writing a letter. (past, duration)

Summarizing the main points made above, the expression of aspect, or the completion or duration of an event, is separate from past or present *tense,* the time at which an event occurred. Morphological, or "grammatical," tense is encoded in the forms of the auxiliary verb; the examples just discussed included present and past *has/had* and *is/was*. The main verb following an auxiliary verb does not express tense. Main verbs following auxiliary *be* occur in a specific morphological form, namely that affixed with-*ing*. Main verbs following auxiliary *have* occur in their -*en*, -*ed*, or -*t* form, as in (14).

> **(14)** a. The blast has/had knocked the door down.
> b. The cat has/had caught/eaten the mouse.

The main verbs in their -*ing* or -*en*/-*ed*/-*t* forms are called **participles.**

The terminology associated with discussions of aspect seems designed to create confusion, and we will try to sort it out here. Duration, illustrated in (13b,d), is what is traditionally referred to as **progressive aspect.** Completion, illustrated in (13a,c), is called **perfect aspect.** In the progressive aspect, main verbs are affixed with -*ing*, a form of the verb called the **present participle.** In the perfect aspect, the form of the main verb is called the **past participle.** What is unfortunate about this terminology is that as we have seen, the participial form of the verb, labeled *past* or *present*, actually lacks tense; the auxiliary verb reflects morphological tense, and the participle expresses aspect.

Though present participles are easy to identify by their regular -*ing* endings, recognizing past participles can be a bit more problematic. This is because the *past tense* form of a main verb can be identical to its *past participle* form. Some examples are given in (15–16).

> **(15)** a. Hortense *walked* over to the store. (past tense)
> b. Hortense has *walked* over to the store. (past participle)
>
> **(16)** a. The company *hired* the person from Chicago. (past tense)
> b. The company has *hired* the person from Chicago. (past participle)

As we can see, the past tense forms *walked* and *hired* are identical to their past participial forms *walked/hired*. Other past tense forms are more easily distinguishable from their past participial forms, as we see in (17–18).

> **(17)** a. The lion *ate* the hyena. (past tense)
> b. The lion had *eaten* the hyena. (past participle)
>
> **(18)** a. Carl Lewis *ran* the race. (past tense)
> b. Carl Lewis has *run* the race. (past participle)

We can thus analyze verbs in terms of their different morphological *forms* as present tense or past tense, present participles, or past participles. Some past tense forms of verbs are identical to their past participle forms; we will explore ways to distinguish between the two in subsequent chapters. For now, a good rule of thumb is to determine whether the main verb is preceded by an auxiliary or whether it is the main verb itself that is tensed. In the former case, the main verb will be in its participial form, and in the latter, its tensed form.

Table 5.2
Aspectual Morphology of English Verbs: Regular Affixation

Perfect	I have walked/eaten/bought (verb form = past participle)
Progressive	I am walking/eating/buying (verb form = present participle)

The regular inflectional affixes that express aspect on English verbs is summarized in Table 5.2.

"Unpredictable" Verb Forms.   We saw above that in addition to inflectional affixation, English verbs can express tense through internal vowel changes and through suppletion. The same is true of aspect; some past participles in English are formed through internal vowel changes, and some are suppletive. Verbs that change form without affixation are sometimes called "irregular" verbs, but this is actually a misnomer; suppletive forms are truly "irregular," but verbs whose forms result from vowel changes actually derive from classes of verbs that followed predictable patterns in earlier versions of English. The forms of such verbs were, at one time, completely predictable, but in modern English the full range of such verb classes no longer exists, and this regularity is therefore sometimes hard to see.

For example, as illustrated in Table 5.3, the verb *be* in English has various suppletive forms that express different person, number, and tense forms. Aspect is, however, expressed by the "regular" affixes *–en* and *–ing*.

Examples of English verbs that express inflection through internal vowel changes are given in Table 5.4. As you can see, they appear irregular, but note

Table 5.3
English *be:* An Example of Suppletion

	Singular	Plural
Present Tense		
First Person	I am	we are
Second Person	you are	you are
Third Person Number	he/she/it is	they are
Past Tense		
First Person	I was	we were
Second Person	you were	you were
Third Person	he/she/it was	they were
Aspect		
Perfect:	I have been	
Progressive:	I am being	

Table 5.4
Verbal Inflectional Morphology: Internal Vowel Changes

	Person/Number (first sg./third sg.)	Tense (present/past)	Aspect (perfect/progressive)
Run	I run/he runs	I run/ran	I have run/am running
Sing	I sing/he sings	I sing/sang	I have sung/am singing
Drink	I drink/he drinks	I drink/drank	I have drunk/am drinking
Choose	I choose/she chooses	I choose/chose	I have chosen/am choosing
Find	I find/she finds	I find/found	I have found/am finding
Bring	I bring/she brings	I bring/I brought	I have brought/am bringing
Keep	I keep/she keeps	I keep/kept	I have kept/am keeping

that *sing* and *drink,* for example, follow the same pattern of predictable vowel alternations. Notice also that these changes surface predominantly in the past tense and past participle forms of the verb. Other forms of the verb follow regular affixation patterns.

Table 5.4 also illustrates that as we have seen, some verbs employ *both* affixation (of a suffix, -*t,*) and internal vowel changes to express inflection: *bring* and *keep* in Table 5.4 are two examples of this, with *brought/kept* as past tense forms. English thus has what we might call a "mixed" inflectional system, involving suppletion, affixation, and internal vowel changes.

Traditionally, verbs that undergo internal changes to express inflection are called **strong verbs,** and those that express inflection through regular affixation are called **weak verbs.** English seems to be evolving from a language with strong verbs to one with predominately weak ones; varieties of Old English had far more classes of strong verbs than we have now in current varieties. (Overall, however, Old English still had more weak verbs than strong ones.) We can see this shift in progress when we consider how new verbs coming into the language express inflection. When we adopt a new verb, we inflect it by regular affixation as exemplified in Tables 5.1 and 5.2, rather than by the internal changes illustrated in Table 5.4, or by suppletion such as we saw with *be* in Table 5.3. For example, we *fax* things today, *faxed* them yesterday, and the day before we *had faxed* them. English thus appears to be moving in the direction of inflectional affixation rather relying on internal vowel changes, but this is not necessarily the evolutionary pattern that all languages follow.

Another feature of the verbs listed in Table 5.4 is that, as some of you may have noticed, the forms listed do not necessarily conform to those you might actually use, as part of your own descriptive grammar. Table 5.4 expresses an idealized, prescriptive version of verbal inflection. Some of you may use or may have heard the following patterns, which differ from those in the table.

(19) a. They *drunk* six beers. (past participle as past tense)
   b. They had *drank* six beers. (past tense as past participle)

(20) a. Hortense *sung* the Marseillese. (past participle as past tense)
   b. Hortense has *sang* the Marseillese. (past tense as past participle)

(21) a. I *seen* it around here somewhere. (past participle as past tense)
   b. They *come* here and then left. (past participle as past tense)

In some varieties of American English, speakers interchange past participles and past tense forms of the verb, in effect using past tense forms as participles. This is what gives rise to sentences such as those in (19b–20b). Speakers of English also sometimes use past participles for past tense forms, as illustrated in (19a, 20a, and 21a–b). Using a past tense form as a participle or a participle for a past tense form is considered "nonstandard" or "poor grammar" English by certain speakers. Nevertheless, this pattern is common in different varieties of modern English, and occurred as well in earlier varieties of the language. Notice also that using one form of the verb for both past tense and past participle in fact follows the same pattern speakers use with verbs such as *bring* and *keep*. As you can see, the past tense forms (*brought* and *kept*) and past participle forms (*brought* and *kept*) are identical. That speakers might "analogize" or extend this pattern to other verbs is a predictable linguistic phenomenon, rather than the result of "sloppy" grammar.

Semantic Tense and Aspect

We will now discuss ways in which sentences express tense and aspect either without, or in spite of, inflectional morphology. That is, tensed and aspectual *forms* of the verb do not always correspond to the actual semantic tense and aspect interpretations of the sentence.

Not all aspect is reflected by a particular morphological form of the verb. For example, **habitual aspect,** which expresses an action or event that continues indefinitely, can be expressed in a variety of ways, as we can see by the sentences in (22).

(22) a. Her days begin when the cat jumps on her.
   b. Dogs eat meat.
   c. Class starts promptly at 9 a.m.

The interpretation of the sentences in (22) as habitual is not reflected by morphological endings on verbs. In fact, observe that the verbs in (22) are in their present tense forms, though the sentences are semantically interpreted as representing actions or states that occur in a kind of perpetuity rather than in the present moment.

Languages differ in how they express tense and aspect, and we will consider some of these differences in more detail in the Discovery Problems. As you can see from the above discussion, in certain varieties of English habitual aspect is reflected semantically, rather than syntactically or morphologically. In African American English, however, habitual aspect is syntactically expressed by the addition of habitual *be*. Some examples are given in (23).

(23) a. She be late. (She is always late.)
b. My uncle be working at Macy's. (My uncle works at Macy's every day.)
c. The truck be leaking oil. (The truck leaks oil all the time.)

In (23), *be* marks the sentences for habitual aspect; without *be*, the sentences have no such interpretation, as illustrated in (24). (The sentences below lack *be* altogether for reasons we will not go into here.[1])

(24) a. She late. (right now/today/*always)
b. My uncle working at Macy's (right now/today/*always)
c. The truck leaking oil. (right now/today/*always)

African American Vernacular English thus expresses habitual aspect syntactically by inserting *be*, while other varieties of English express this aspect only semantically.

The following sentences illustrate that the past or present tense morphology on the verb does not necessarily correspond to the semantics of the temporal interpretation of the sentence.

(25) a. Mary *leaves* at seven this evening. (present morphology, future tense)
b. The Rolling Stones *are* playing next week. (present morphology, future tense)
c. Mary said that she *was* leaving tomorrow. (past tense morphology, future time)
d. John *is* going to try out for the team. (present tense morphology, future time)
e. Hortense *leaves* for Boston this week. (present tense morphology, future time)
f. Hortense *left* for Boston today. (past morphology, present time)

---

[1]The absence of *be* in (24) is a result of *be*-deletion, another syntactic rule of some dialects of English, including African American Vernacular English. This rule operates only on tensed forms of the verb. The source sentences for those in (24) are therefore the ones below, which do not include habitual *be*.
a. She is late.
b. My uncle is working at Macy's.
c. The truck is leaking oil.

(25) also illustrates that aspect is not necessarily predicted by the form of the verb. In (25c), for example, *she was leaving tomorrow* is, morphologically, in past tense and progressive aspect. The interpretation, however, is not past progressive but rather future tense. In (25d), *is going* is in progressive aspect and present tense, but in fact expresses future tense, rather than an event that is present and ongoing.

We pursue the discussion of the semantic and morphological expression of tense and aspect in the following section, where we investigate the properties of modals, words that often affect the temporal interpretation of a sentence.

Future Tense and Modals

As we saw in the previous section, English morphologically expresses tense through the affixes *–s* and *–ed/–en/–t*, by an internal change in verb form, or by a suppletive form of the verb. Tense can also be interpreted semantically, and may not correspond to the morphological form of the verb at all. We express future tense in English in yet an entirely different way, by adding a word to the sentence. This is illustrated in (26), where *will* and *shall* form the future tense *syntactically* rather than morphologically. (This strategy is therefore similar to that of African American Vernacular English, in which *be* is added to express habitual aspect.)

(26) a. Mary attends the ballet class.
　　 b. Mary *will* attend the ballet class.
　　 c. Mary *shall* attend the ballet class.

Will and *shall* are **modals,** members of a set of words in English that have distinctive semantic and morphological properties. The English modals include *shall/should, may/might, can/could, will/would,* and *must.* As we saw briefly in the introduction to this chapter, modals express semantic modality, or the notion of possibility, volition, permission, necessity, and so on. This is exemplified in (27), where the sentences are ambiguous with respect to their different modalities.

(27) a. You *may* not get elected. (possibility or permission)
　　 b. *Can* I have the car tonight? (ability, permission)
　　 c. He *should* get home soon. (prediction, obligation)
　　 d. You *can* have the car tonight, but *may* you is the question.
　　　 (*can* = permission/ability, *may* = permission)

Morphologically, modals are inflected for neither person nor number, and they lack *–s* and *–ed/–t* present and past tense forms. They also have no participial (*-ing* or *–en/–ed/–t*) forms. The morphological differences between modals and other verbs is illustrated by the impossible forms in (28).

(28) a. She can/* cans go.
　　 b. *shalled/*maying, etc.

Even though they have no forms affixed with -s or -ed, modals are often assumed to have past and present tense forms: *shall/may/can/will* are present tense forms, and *should/might/could/would* are past tense forms. These forms do not necessarily clearly correlate with past and present time; although in (26) *will* and *shall* express future time, the sentences in (29–31) illustrate that the morphological form of the modal does not necessarily correlate with its past or present tense interpretation.

(29)　a. I *will* do that now. (present morphology, present time)
　　　　b. I *will* do that tomorrow. (present morphology, future time)

(30)　a. I *would* do that tomorrow, if I were you. (past morphology, future time)
　　　　b. I *would* do that now, if I were you. (past morphology, present time)

(31)　a. I *could* do that (back when I was a child). (past morphology, past time)
　　　　b. I *could* help you with that right now. (past morphology, present time)
　　　　c. I *could* help you with that tomorrow. (past morphology, future time)

Modals thus differ from main verbs in lacking the same range of morphological forms, as well as differing semantically in expressing modality rather than lexical content. For this reason they always occur *with* main verbs but never *as* main verbs. As we discussed above, modals appear to fall into a class of grammatical verbs that are distinct in morphology and semantics (and as we shall see later, syntax) from lexical main verbs.

Infinitives

Modals are similar to auxiliary verbs such as *have* and *be* in occurring in construction with a main verb. As illustrated in Table 5.2, *have* occurs before the past participle form of the verb, its *–en/–ed/–t* form. *Be* introduces the present participle form of the main verb, its *-ing* form. Examples are given in (32).

(32)　a. Lionel has *left* for Borneo.
　　　　b. Linda was *watching* the World Cup.

The form of the main verb following a modal, on the other hand, is not a participle, but rather an **infinitive**. Infinitives are the "base" form of the verb, lacking inflection of any kind. (*Infinitive* means, technically, *not finite*, or lacking tense). The forms of the main verbs in (33) are thus *infinitival* forms.

(33) a. The French could *win.*
     b. This ice could *melt.*

Modals are followed by what we call the *bare infinitive* form of the verb. Infinitives can also be preceded by *to* in English, what we will call a *to-infinitive*, illustrated in (34).

(34) a. I want *to go.*
     b. They expect *to buy the car.*

Infinitives, both *bare* and *to-*, occur in a number of different kinds of syntactic positions in English that we discuss in more detail in Part Three of the book. For now, we will simply add infinitives to our list of forms of the main verb in English. These forms are summarized in Table 5.5, with examples to illustrate forms derived through affixation, internal vowel changes, and suppletion, and cases in which verbal morphology draws on both internal change and regular affixation.

Grammatical Verbs: Auxiliaries and Modals

From the above discussion we can conclude that modals and auxiliary *have* and *be* express inflectional morphology, and have grammatical meanings: auxiliary *have/be* express tense, aspect, and in some cases person and number, and modals express tense and modality. Main verbs also express tense, aspect, person, and number, but they differ from auxiliaries and modals in also having lexical meanings. That auxiliaries do not have lexical meanings is illustrated by the difference between the dictionary definitions in (35) for auxiliary *have*, with grammatical meanings, and the definition in (36) for main verb *have*, with lexical meanings.

(35) *have (aux)* Used with a past participle to form the following tenses indicating completed action: a. present perfect: *has gone for good.* b. past perfect: *regretted that he had lost his temper.* c. future perfect: *will have finished by the time we arrive.*

Table 5.5
English Morphological Verb Forms

infinitive	(to) walk	(to) eat	(to) drink	(to) go	(to) bring
present tense	walks	eats	drinks	goes	brings
past tense	walked	ate	drank	went	brought
present participle	walking	eating	drinking	going	bringing
past participle	walked	eaten	drunk	gone	brought

(36)   *have (v)* a. to be in possession of: *already had a car.* b. to possess as a characteristic, quality, or function: *has a beard; had a great deal of energy,* . . . .

We also know that the class of verbs including modals and auxiliaries is morphologically closed: we do not add new modals or auxiliaries to the language. These elements thus again differ from lexical main verbs. We can therefore hypothesize, based on this evidence, that modals and auxiliaries form a class of grammatical rather than lexical verbs.

In the following chapter we discuss the syntax of the verbal system in English. There we pursue the distinction between grammatical and lexical verbs, and conclude that grammatical auxiliary verbs *have* and *be*, along with modals, and the auxiliary verb *do* introduced in that chapter, form a grammatical category distinct from main verbs that we will call *Auxiliary.*

Summary

In this chapter we have examined the semantics and morphology of English verbs. We found that main verbs are members of a lexical category, from evidence that they have intrinsic meanings, and that we productively add new main verbs to the language. Main verbs have five basic morphological forms, derived by **suppletion, internal vowel changes,** and **regular affixation.** The forms of the verb in English include **past tense, present tense, past** and **present participles,** and **infinitives.** One of the functions of verbs is to express **tense** and **aspect,** or the time frame of a sentence. Tense and aspect can be grammatical, expressed by the morphology of the verb, or semantic, in which case tense and aspect do not necessarily correlate with the morphology of the verb.

We found that **auxiliary verbs** and **modals** differ from main verbs in lacking intrinsic meanings. Rather, these verbs have grammatical meanings, expressing tense, aspect, and in the case of modals, modality. These grammatical verbs form a closed morphological class, and thus appear to be members of a grammatical category. We concluded that category Verb actually comprises two subclasses, lexical and grammatical verbs.

DISCOVERY PROBLEMS

Problem 1. Verb Forms

We have seen that modals and auxiliary verbs occur in certain sequences, as illustrated in (a–b).

a) Hortense [might have been singing] the Marseillese.
b) Hortense [has sung] the Marseillese.

Using (a) as a starting point, make a list of sentences in which you try to express all of the possible logical combinations of *might, have, be* and the main verb *singing*, from longest to shortest. Identify the form of each verb in your list, using the five forms in Table 5.5. The longest sentence you will have is the form in (a) above, and the shortest, the form in *Hortense sang the Marseillese.* What other orders of verbs are possible?

Problem 2. Verb Forms

Formulate example sentences that conform to the following possible orders of modals, auxiliary verbs, and main verbs. Vary your choices of main verbs and modals as much as you can in constructing your sentences.

    a) modal + main verb
    b) modal + *have* + *be* + main verb
    c) *have* + *be* + main verb
    d) *be* + main verb
    e) main verb
    f) *have* + main verb
    g) modal + *have* + main verb
    h) modal + *be* + main verb

Label the form of each verb, using Table 5.5. Then supply a brief context for each sentence, and identify the tense and aspect of the sentence within that context. Try to create examples in which tense and aspect are not necessarily reflected by the morphology of the verb.

Problem 3. Gerunds

Recall that words with *-ing* affixes can function as nouns, as in the examples in (a–c) below.

    a) *Running* is good for your health.
    b) Sue likes her job, but all the meetings make her tired.
    c) Mary likes *dancing.*

How can we distinguish gerunds from participial verbs also ending in *-ing*? One way is to use morphological and syntactic "tests" that distinguish nouns from verbs. Some ways in which we are now able to distinguish nouns from verbs are the following.

-ing Nouns

- can occur with determiners, quantifiers, and numerals
- can be modified by prenominal adjectives
- can be affixed with plural *-s,* and possessive *-'s*

-ing Verbs

- can be modified by adverbs, such as *quickly, softly, happily*
- can be preceded by auxiliary *be*

Use these criteria to determine the category of the *-ing* words in (a–c). On what basis do you analyze them as nouns? Illustrate your conclusions with examples.

Now, determine whether the *-ing* words in (d–i) are nouns (gerunds) or verbs. On what kinds of evidence do you base your conclusions?

d) The *crying* baby woke up the neighbors.
e) *Driving* down the interstate takes a lot of patience.
f) Jim is *training* for the race.
g) *Training* for the race means *running* five miles a day.
h) He will be *running* the Boston Marathon.
i) The fifth *running* of the marathon will be held next week.

Problem 4. Inflecting New Verbs

As mentioned in the text, we constantly add new verbs to the language, and tend to inflect them using regular affixation, illustrated in Tables 5.1 and 5.2. Think of three or four examples of verbs that you think have recently come into the language (they can be coinings, verbs you consider "slang," computer terms, terms you have heard used on television shows or in movies, etc.). Use them in sentences to illustrate all of their possible forms (refer to Table 5.5). Label each form. Are the verb forms regular?

*Problem 5. The Form of the Verb in Passive Sentences

You are by now quite familiar with the movement rule of Passive, whereby the subject noun phrase and the object noun phrase change position. We have put aside in our earlier discussions the details of an additional effect of this rule: the change in verb form. This change is illustrated below.

a) Beowulf *killed* Grendel.
b) Grendel *was killed* by Beowulf.

In (a), *killed* is in its past tense form. What is the form of *killed* in (b), and how is it unexpected, based on what we have discussed about participles in this chapter?

Create four or five other active/passive pairs, and examine the form of the main verb. Try to formulate an informal statement about the change in the verb phrase triggered by the Passive movement rule.

Then, apply Passive in the following sentences. What form of the verb *be* must you add in each case?

c) Beowulf had hunted Grendel.
d) Beowulf might hunt Grendel.
e) Beowulf is hunting Grendel.
f) Beowulf might have been hunting Grendel.
g) Beowulf had been hunting Grendel.
h) Beowulf might have hunted Grendel.

Problem 6. Participles and Language Change

As mentioned in the chapter, English speakers sometimes interchange participial and past tense forms, a process of change that has been going on for hundreds of years. Some examples of verbs whose past participles and past tense forms are interchangeable are given below.

infinitive	past tense	past participle
hang	hung	hanged/hung
freeze	froze	frozen/froze
mown	mowed	mowed/mown
forget	forgot	forgot/forgotten

Think of some forms of verbs that you might use or have heard, that appear to have two possible ways of forming the past participle. Is one form more "preferred" than another? Is that preference linguistically or socially based? Why or why not?

TEXT ANALYSIS

1. Identifying Verb Forms

In the following text, try to identify and list all of the main verbs, auxiliary verbs, and modals. Identify any gerunds. Then identify the form of each verb, using Table 5.5.

a) The rain turned perceptibly to a deluge, the thick, warm drops penetrating his clothes and running in rivulets down his back and face.
b) The wild trees and plants of the Pacheco garden nodded and drooped, leaves glistening dully in the half-light.
c) The pink walls darkened as the water soaked into them, eating at the plaster.
d) The LeNoir window was black; he remembered some claimed to have seen a white-faced figure in army uniform standing there at night.
e) The story had provided mystery back then, a real haunted house, and on a rainy afternoon schoolboys could feel their spines tingle as they aimed their stones.

Source: *There Are a Lot of Ways to Die*, by Neil Bissoondath.

2. More on Verb Forms

Do the same as in (1) for the following text. In addition, identify any passive sentences.

> a) The Iraqi military announced today that it had dispersed captured allied airmen "among scientific and economic targets."
> b) The Iraqi statement indicated that the captured pilots were being used as so-called human shields to deter allied air attacks.
> c) It would not be the first time that Iraq had used such a strategy.
> d) After the Aug. 2 invasion of Kuwait, thousands of foreigners were prevented from leaving Iraq.
> e) Some were held at military bases and strategic sites before the last were freed in December.
>
> *Source: The New York Times, January 22, 1991, p. 1.*

3. Interpreting Tense and Aspect

In a text of your choice, identify all the verbs you find and label them according to the Table in 5.5. Be sure to identify any gerunds, if there are any. Then identify the tense and aspect of each sentence in your sample. Are tense and aspect semantic, or morphological?

LANGUAGE DIVERSITY EXERCISES

1. The Origins of Suppletive *Be*

The suppletive forms of the verb *be* in Table 5.3 have an interesting history; they derive from forms of a number of different verbs. Trace the origins of suppletive forms of the verb *be,* and discuss the original meanings and functions of this verb, and whether they have shifted. Make a chart illustrating your findings.

2. Old English Inflectional Morphology

Choose two Old English verbs, and describe how they were inflected for person, number, and tense. Is this inflection expressed by affixes, vowel changes, suppletion, or in some other way? How is aspect reflected? How does the Old

English system differ from our modern English one, based on your verb sample? Try to choose verbs that have different inflectional patterns.

3. Middle English Tense

Choose two Middle English verbs and describe how tense is expressed. Is tense morphological (affixes, internal vowel changes, suppletion), syntactic (adding a word), semantic (based on meaning only)? Illustrate your findings with clear examples, and try to discuss a few ways in which the Middle English and modern English verb systems differ.

4. Middle English Verbal Semantics

With the coming of the French to England after the Norman Invasion in 1066, English took on a number of French verbs, some of which had English counterparts and some of which did not. Look up seven or eight such French verbs (they will be discussed under *French loanwords* or *French vocabulary* or *borrowings*, or some similar heading in history of English textbooks), and discuss their meanings. Did they have English counterparts, and are these still in existence? How have their meanings shifted or remained the same?

5. Strong and Weak Verbs

As mentioned in the text, Old English had a number of strong verb classes, as well as many weak verb classes. Choose one weak class and a strong class, and contrast them. How is each class inflected for tense and aspect in Old English? Are there modern verbs that still show the same patterns you find with their Old English counterparts?

6. Old English Verbs: From Strong to Weak

Trace the historical development of two of the following verbs from Old English to modern English. These verbs have all changed from strong verbs to weak verbs. Illustrate this process with examples showing the different strong and weak forms of the verb. Discuss any cases of semantic shift.

   bow, brew, chew, creep, crowd, flee, lie (prevaricate), lose, reek, rue

7. Modals in Languages Other Than English

Modals in languages other than English behave as main, rather than auxiliary, verbs. In Spanish, French, and German, for example, modals can be the only verb in the sentence, and they can be inflected in ways that English modals can't be. Find two or three examples of modals in a language of your choice, and investigate their inflectional morphology. Do they show more inflection than their English counterparts? Do they have lexical or grammatical meanings? Would you classify them as lexical verbs, or as members of a grammatical verb class? Support your answer with examples.

8. German Strong and Weak Verbs

Modern German (which comprises a number of varieties, just as "modern" English does) has both weak and strong verb classes, similar to the situation in Old English (unsurprisingly, as both are Germanic languages). Find two examples of weak verbs in German, and two of strong verbs. Discuss reasons for classifying them as such, and illustrate your discussion with examples. Why is a particular verb classified as strong? What are its vowel alternations and what are some other verbs in the same class? Do the same for some weak verbs, to try to discover some of the basic inflectional patterns of German verbs.

9. Pidgin and Creole Verb Systems

Pidgin and creole languages often have different ways of expressing tense and aspect from those we have discussed here. For example, in Hawaiian Creole, the tense and aspect system includes the following forms:

a) he walk (he walked)
b) he bin walk (he had walked)
c) he go walk (he will/would walk)
d) he stay walk (he is/was walking)
e) he bin go walk (he would have walked)

Explore the tense and aspect system of a creole or pidgin language of your choice. Try to make a list of different verb forms, and of the kinds of "strings" of verbal elements that occur in the language, to express different tenses and aspects. Are tense and aspect expressed syntactically, semantically, or morphologically? Support your answers with detailed examples.

CHAPTER REVIEW TERMS

main verbs, auxiliary *have,* auxiliary *be,* modals

verb forms: infinitive (bare and *-to*), past tense, present tense, past participle, present participle

morphological, syntactic, and semantic tense and aspect

inflectional morphology: affixation, internal vowel changes, suppletion, affixation combined with internal vowel changes

weak and strong verbs

CHAPTER REVIEW EXERCISE

Choose from among the following options to create a chapter exercise. You may wish to add options from previous chapter exercises to make this exercise more comprehensive. In the text below:

1. Identify all verbs as main, auxiliary, or modal and also give their forms, using Table 5.5 There are some forms of *do* in the text. Try to identify their forms, and whether they are main or auxiliary verbs. (*Do* is discussed in more detail in Chapter 6.)
2. What tense is each sentence in? Is tense grammatically (morphologically), semantically, or syntactically expressed?
3. Identify any sentences with aspect, and identify the aspect as *habitual, durative,* or *completed.* Is aspect grammatical or semantic?
4. This paragraph is taken from the children's book *Corduroy,* by Don Freeman. A comment on the dust jacket of the book is, "The art and story are very direct and just right for the very young." Discuss the complexity of the paragraph, using your understanding of tense and aspect, and forms of verbs. What conclusions can you draw? How might you rewrite the passage to make it more "adult?" Discuss, in grammatical terms, any changes you would make.

Corduroy is a bear who once lived in the toy department of a big store. Day after day he waited with all the other animals and dolls for somebody to come along and take him home. The store was always filled with shoppers buying all sorts of things, but no one ever seemed to want a small bear in green overalls. Then one morning a little girl stopped and looked straight into Corduroy's bright eyes. "Oh, Mommy!" she said. "Look!! There's the very bear I've always wanted." "Not today, dear." Her mother sighed. "I've spent too much already. Besides, he doesn't look new. He's lost the button to one of his shoulder straps."

Corduroy watched them sadly as they walked away.

"I didn't know I'd lost a button," he said to himself. "Tonight I'll go and see if I can find it."

Source: Corduroy, by Don Freeman.

6

The Syntax of the Verb Phrase

To have another language is to possess a second soul.
Charlemagne

Introduction

In the previous chapter you became acquainted with the forms and meanings of
main verbs, auxiliary verbs, and modals. We addressed in detail the forms of the
verb that morphologically express tense and aspect. In this chapter, we focus on
the syntax of the verb phrase. We will explore ways to diagram the rather complex system we introduced in Chapter 5, involving strings of tensed auxiliary
verbs and modals and the main verbs that follow them. As we will see, it is possible to syntactically distinguish main verbs from auxiliary verbs and modals,
further supporting our claim in Chapter 5 that auxiliary verbs and modals form
a separate class of grammatical verbs, what we will label as the category *Auxiliary.* We find that certain syntactic rules apply only to auxiliary verbs and
modals, namely *Negative Contraction, Subject Auxiliary Inversion,* and *Tag Question Formation.* In cases in which there is no auxiliary verb or modal present, an
auxiliary element must be added to the sentence. This gives rise to sentences
with the *pleonastic* auxiliary verb *do.* We thus add to our list of syntactic rules a
rule of *Do-Insertion,* and add to the category Auxiliary the pleonastic auxiliary
verb *do.* We conclude the chapter with a discussion of a possible phrase structure of sentences in which tensed auxiliaries, modals, and *do* are generated in an
AUX, rather than V position. We further propose that, to account for certain
facts about the order of untensed auxiliary verbs and *not,* untensed auxiliaries
can optionally move from V to AUX by *Verb Raising.*

A Phrase Structure Rule for Verb Phrase

We begin our analysis of the syntax of the verb system by considering once
again our phrase structure rules for sentences and verb phrases, given in (1). As
you can see, we have one invariant position for the verb, at the left periphery of
the phrase. (Other constituents that may follow V are left unspecified, and simply represented by four ellipsis points [. . . .].)

(1) S => NP VP
VP => V. . . .

(1) leaves us without a way to generate verb phrases with more than one verb, and thus without a way to generate sentences with auxiliary verbs or modals.

We can rectify this situation, however, by rewriting the rule for the verb phrase as in (2).

(2) VP => V (VP)

As stated in (2), the phrase structure rule for VP is *recursive;* the rule allows us to optionally generate any number of verb phrases, as illustrated in (3). (Of course, other phrases can occur after V, such as NP and PP, and we could complicate (3) to handle them, but we will leave them aside here, and focus only on verb phrases in VP.)

(3)

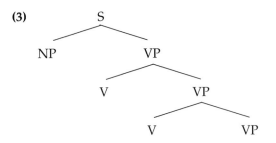

We might assume, then, that we can insert under V the auxiliaries *have/be,* modals, and main verbs in their respective orders, as in (4).

(4)

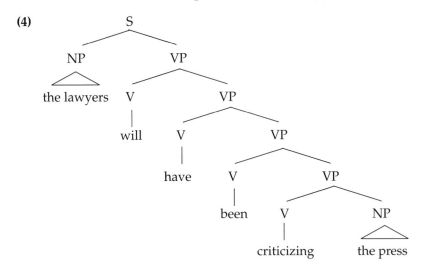

For now, we will adopt (2) as a possible phrase structure rule for VP, to be revised later. Notice that according to this rule, there is no structural distinction among verbs other than in terms of their hierarchical structure: we can distinguish "the highest verb" in the verb phrase, "the lowest verb," and so on. In the following section we address some of the syntactic differences among the verbs in a structure such as (4), and show that in fact, there are syntactic processes that apply to modals and tensed auxiliary verbs but not to main verbs. We thus have syntactic evidence for a distinction between modals and auxiliary verbs on the one hand, and main verbs, on the other.

Negation and *Do*-Insertion

We negate sentences in English by adding the word *not*. *Not* usually occurs to the right of the first (tensed) auxiliary/modal. This is illustrated in (5).

(5) a. Toby is *not* painting the piano white.
b. Toby has *not* been painting the piano white.
c. Toby might *not* have painted the piano white.

(6) shows that negation in sentences with only main verbs operates somewhat differently. In such sentences, the main verb occurs to the right of *not*. Further, an auxiliary verb *do* is inserted to the left of *not*, in the position of the tensed auxiliaries in (5).

(6) Toby did *not* paint the piano white.

Do in this case is what we call a **pleonastic** or "dummy" auxiliary verb, as it has no intrinsic meaning and is inserted simply to do the work of an auxiliary verb in a sentence without one. In negative sentences in English, for example, tense must always be realized on an auxiliary element to the left of *not*. That is, we never hear or use sentences of the form in (7).

(7) *Toby not painted the piano white.

We "fix" (7) by adding *do*, an auxiliary element that can realize tense. In (6), *do* is in past tense. In (8), it is in present tense.

(8) Toby does *not* paint the piano white.

Before exploring other cases in which *do* is inserted, it is first important to point out that the use of auxiliary *do* in negative sentences differs from another use of *do* as a means of adding emphasis. As we see in (9), *do* occurs in a sentence without *not*. *Do* in this case differs from *do* in (6) because it is stressed for emphasis.

(9) a. Toby DID paint the piano white!
b. But I DID finish my homework!

Emphatic *do* sounds strange when unstressed, as we can see by the oddity of (10), where the *do* of (9b) is unstressed.

(10) I did finish my homework.

Nonemphatic *do* in (6), on the other hand, sounds odd when stressed, as we see in (11).

(11) Toby DID not paint the piano white.

We can thus differentiate pleonastic *do* inserted in negative sentences from emphatic *do,* inserted to indicate emphasis. Pleonastic auxiliary *do* sounds odd with stress, and emphatic *do* sounds odd without it.

It appears, then, that one difference between main verbs and others is that in negative sentences, the main verb must occur to the right of *not* and a pleonastic auxiliary, namely *do,* must be inserted. Why might this be?

Observe that auxiliary *do* is tensed, and thus seems to have the same syntactic function as other auxiliaries, namely to realize tense inflection in sentences in which the main verb is untensed. For example, in (12), tensed *have/be* are followed by (untensed) participles, and the tensed modal *might* by a bare infinitive.

(12) a. School has started already.
 b. School is starting in September.
 c. School might start late this year.

As for *do,* consider the pair of sentences in (13).

(13) a. School *starts* here in September.
 b. School does not *start* here until September.

In (13a) *start* is in its present tense form. In (13b), however, *start* is in its bare infinitival form, lacking *-s* or any participial ending (*-ed/-t/-en/-ing*). We can conclude that in sentences with the pleonastic auxiliary *do,* the main verb is untensed, in its bare infinitival form.

Suppose, then, that we formulate the "rule" for the presence or absence of *do* in terms of its role in realizing tense in negative sentences that otherwise lack auxiliaries or modals. We can informally state the role of pleonastic *do* in English, then, as in (14), a rule we will call **Do-Insertion.**

(14) *Do*-**Insertion** (preliminary formulation): In negative sentences with only a main verb, insert pleonastic *do* to the left of *not,* in the position of other tensed auxiliaries or modals, to realize tense inflection.

According to (14), *do* occurs in the same position as tensed auxiliaries. We can make this a bit more precise by considering the phrase structures of negative sentences in more detail. A negative sentence with a single tensed auxiliary has the structure in (15) according to our assumptions. *Not* occurs in a position to the right of the tensed auxiliary.

(15)

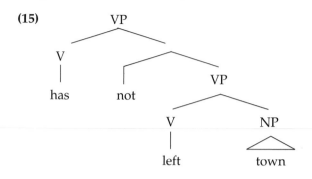

A parallel structure for negative sentences with modals is given in (16).

(16)

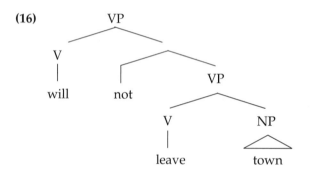

Sentences with more than one auxiliary verb can be diagrammed as in (17–18), with *not* in the same position as in (15) and (16), to the right of the tensed auxiliary/modal.

(17)

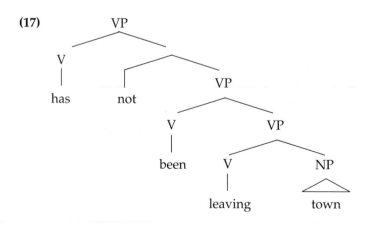

(18)

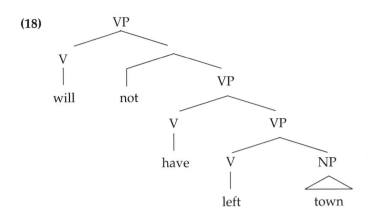

As for sentences with main verbs and *do*, we can diagram them as in (19), where *do*, inserted by *Do*-Insertion, occurs in the same position as the tensed auxiliary verbs and modals in the other phrase structures discussed above.

(19)

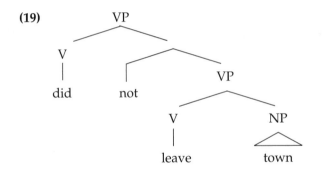

It appears, then, that English has a syntactic rule of *Do*-Insertion whereby a pleonastic auxiliary verb occurs in the same position as other tensed auxiliaries and modals in negative sentences. Tensed auxiliaries, including *do*, and modals thus syntactically differ from main verbs by occurring to the left of *not*. We will henceforth include *do* as a member of the set of auxiliaries, based on the evidence that its sole function is as an auxiliary element in construction with a main verb. (We discuss main verb *do*, as in *Let's do lunch*, in more detail in the Discovery Problems.)

Not Contraction

Evidence from the contraction of *not* with auxiliary verbs and modals supports our claim that these verbs differ syntactically from main verbs. To illustrate, consider the following sentences.

(20) a. The kids will not be home until later.
        b. The kids *won't* be home until later.

(21) a. They *are* walking home.
        b. They *aren't* walking home.

(22) a. Sam fixed his bicycle.
        b. Sam *didn't* fix his bicycle.

As we can see in (20–22), *not* can contract with a tensed auxiliary, modal, or *do*, which is what we might expect if contraction occurs between *not* and an element to its left. We can state this rule informally as in (23).

(23) *Not* **Contraction** (preliminary formulation): *Not* can contract with an auxiliary verb or modal to its left.

Notice, however, that we need to make (23) even more precise; *not* can contract only with *tensed* auxiliaries, not with their participial forms, even though these forms may occur to the left of *not*, as illustrated in (24–25).

(24) a. John might have *not* been driving the car.
        b. *John might *haven't* been driving the car.

(25) a. Rico will have *not* left.
        b. *Rico will *haven't* left.

Even though *not* can occur to the right of a participial auxiliary verb, it cannot contract with the verb in this case. We must thus revise our rule in (23) as (26).

(26) *Not* **Contraction:** *Not* can contract only with a tensed auxiliary verb or modal to its left.

We have evidence that certain rules apply to tensed auxiliaries and modals only. We can state this in phrase structure terms by saying that such rules apply only to the highest auxiliary or modal in the phrase structure tree. We consider further evidence for this generalization below.

Subject-Auxiliary Inversion and Tag Question Formation

In English, we form *yes/no* questions by moving an auxiliary verb or modal to the front of the sentence, as illustrated in (27).

(27) a. *May* we buy some ice cream?
        b. *Is* the water too hot?
        c. *Have* you been eating potato chips?
        d. *Could* Lucy have been talking to her mother?

As you can see in (27), we move only the tensed auxiliary or modal to the front of the sentence, over the subject noun phrase (as we discussed briefly in

Chapter 3). We do not move the infinitival or participial forms of auxiliary *have* or *be*, nor do we ever front main verbs to form questions.

(28)　a.　**Have been* you eating potato chips?
　　　b.　**Could have been* John talking to his mother?
　　　c.　**Ate* you potato chips?
　　　d.　**Talked* Lucy to her mother?

This rule, what we will call **Subject-Auxiliary Inversion,** appears to operate on tensed auxiliaries alone. It does not apply to main verbs, nor to participial forms of auxiliary verbs. We thus have two rules, Subject-Auxiliary Inversion and *Not* Contraction, that apply specifically to the tensed auxiliary in a longer string of verbs.

Notice that Subject-Auxiliary Inversion can also apparently apply in affirmative sentences in which there are no auxiliary verbs. When this happens, *Do*-Insertion must again occur.

(29)　a.　You finished reading your book.
　　　b.　*Did* you finish reading your book?

That Subject-Auxiliary Inversion applies in (29) might seem surprising; we have discussed above the insertion of *do* as dependent entirely on the presence of *not*. We have also suggested, however, that *do* must be inserted to do the work other tensed auxiliaries do. In negative sentences, a tensed auxiliary must occur to the left of *not*, giving rise to *Do*-Insertion in sentences that otherwise lack auxiliary verbs. In sentences in which Subject-Auxiliary Inversion has applied, a tensed auxiliary must move over the subject. If there is no auxiliary, *do* is inserted. Subject-Auxiliary Inversion is therefore yet another rule that not only applies exclusively to tensed auxiliaries, but also triggers *Do*-Insertion in sentences that lack such auxiliaries.

We can now see that our *Do*-Insertion rule in (14) is inadequate, as it requires the presence of *not* in order for *do* to appear. We must therefore revise this rule as the more general (30).

(30)　***Do*-Insertion** (final formulation): Insert pleonastic *do* in sentences in which a tensed auxiliary is required and none is available.

According to (30), *do* will occur in those positions in which a tensed auxiliary is required to the left of *not* to realize tense inflection and to undergo contraction. In questions, *do* will also be inserted in the absence of a tensed auxiliary required to move to sentence-initial position by Subject-Auxiliary Inversion.

Another kind of question formation in English illustrates similar points. **Tag Question Formation** applies to tensed auxiliary verbs but not main verbs, again distinguishing these two classes syntactically. Tag questions are formed by copying the tensed auxiliary verb and subject (realized as a proform) at the end of the sentence, forming a kind of truncated question. Tags are unique in that they must be opposite in *polarity* from the sentence they occur in. That is, if the sentence is affirmative, the tag question is negative, and vice versa. Some examples are given in (31). Notice that Tag Question Formation operates in sentences with main verbs by employing a form of pleonastic *do*.

(31) a. Nathaniel wandered through the forest, *didn't* he?
    b. Hortense hadn't been talking to John, *had* she?
    c. They will be leaving soon, *won't* they?

Tag questions are impossible with main verbs, as we see in (32a), and with participial auxiliaries, as in (32b–c).

(32) a. *Nathaniel wandered, *wandern't he?*
    b. *Hortense hadn't been talking to John, *had been she/had she been?*
    c. *They will be leaving soon, *won't be they/won't they be?*

As (31–32) illustrate, tag questions provide additional evidence for a syntactic distinction between main verbs and participial auxiliary verbs on the one hand, and tensed auxiliaries and modals on the other, as the rule applies exclusively to the latter set of verbs. Tag Question Formation is another example of a rule that triggers the insertion of pleonastic *do* when no tensed auxiliary is available.

The Grammatical Category *Auxiliary*

The syntactic differences between main verbs, untensed auxiliaries, and tensed auxiliaries and modals are summarized in Table 6.1.

How might we account for the overlap between main verbs and untensed auxiliaries illustrated in Table 6.1? We know that semantically and morpholog-

Table 6.1
Syntactic Differences Between Main Verbs, Auxiliaries, and Modals

	Main Verbs	Untensed Auxiliaries	Tensed Auxiliaries/Modals
Occur to right of *not*	yes	yes	no
Occur to left of *not*	no	yes	yes
Not Contraction	no	no	yes
Subject-Auxiliary Inversion	no	no	yes
Tag Question Formation	no	no	yes

ically, auxiliary verbs *have* and *be,* the modals, and pleonastic *do* can be characterized as members of a closed grammatical category, namely Auxiliary. There appear to be, however, operations that apply exclusively to *tensed* auxiliary verbs and modals, namely *Not*-Contraction, Subject-Auxiliary Inversion, and Tag Question Formation. Untensed (participial or infinitival) auxiliaries overlap with main verbs in failing to undergo these operations. Further, tensed auxiliaries and modals occur to the left of *not,* and main verbs to its right, but *untensed* auxiliary *have* and *be* can occur in either position. Another issue that remains unclear is the phrase structure of auxiliary verbs. Other grammatical categories we have identified (Determiner, Quantifier, and Numeral, for example) occur in specific positions distinct from those in which lexical categories appear (under DET, Q, and NUM, for example) and they introduce a lexical head noun. We have assumed so far, however, that verbs, whether modals, auxiliary, or main, all occur under V in VP.

Auxiliaries and Verb Raising

We can account for the differences between main and auxiliary verbs on the one hand, and the overlap between main verbs and participial and infinitival auxiliaries on the other, by proposing the following phrase structure tree, (where XP is a phrase of any category).

(33)

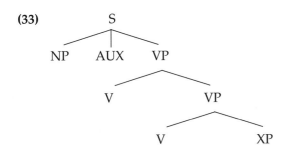

Suppose that tensed auxiliaries and modals are inserted into an **AUX** position in (33), and that untensed auxiliaries and main verbs are inserted under V. We capture this generalization by proposing the phrase structure rule for Auxiliary in (34a). Our phrase structure rule for S will also change, with the addition of an optional AUX position between NP and VP, as in (34b).

(34) a. $\text{AUX} = \begin{Bmatrix} \text{tense} \\ \text{modal} / have/be \end{Bmatrix}$

      b. S => NP (AUX) VP

We will assume that this AUX position is present in all tensed sentences, and dominates either tense inflection, or a tensed auxiliary or modal that realizes tense inflection. All tensed sentences will therefore be generated with an AUX

position. AUX is optional, however, since it does not appear in infinitival constructions, as we discuss in more detail in later chapters.

According to (34), AUX can be filled with a modal or a tensed form of *have*
or *be*. AUX can also be filled with tense inflection only, and *do* may, under circumstances specified by our *Do*-Insertion rule, be inserted to realize this inflection. The rules in Table 6.1 will apply only to elements in AUX, allowing us to
predict that only tensed auxiliaries or modals will undergo *Not*-Contraction,
Subject-Auxiliary Inversion, and Tag Question Formation. Main verbs and participial and infinitival auxiliaries do not occur in AUX, and hence fail to undergo
these operations.

Let us consider AUX in a bit more detail. Suppose AUX is filled only with
tense inflection, as in (35).

(35)

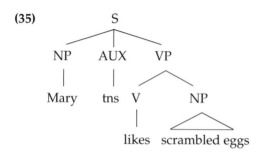

The sentence in (35) has no *not*; hence, *Do*-Insertion will not apply. *Do* will only
be inserted in the event that Subject-Auxiliary Inversion or Tag Question Formation applies. Otherwise, we simply generate a sentence in which the main
verb is tensed.

Now, consider the position of *not* with respect to AUX. We have seen that
not typically occurs as what we can now say is to the immediate right of AUX.
We will assume that when present, *not* occurs in the position in (36).

(36)

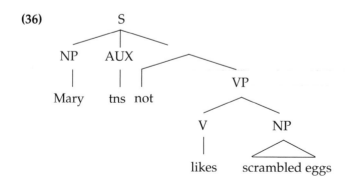

Do-Insertion, and possibly also *Not* Contraction, will apply in (36), generating
Mary does not/doesn't like scrambled eggs.

Sentences with a tensed auxiliary or modal will have the structure in (37).

(37)

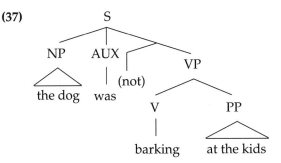

We can also diagram sentences with more than one auxiliary, as in (38).

(38)

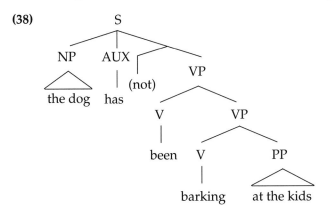

What we so far fail to account for, however, are sentences in which an untensed, rather than a tensed form of the auxiliary verb occurs to the *left* of *not*, as in (39). Here, *have* is a bare infinitive following modal *might*.

(39) The dog might have not been barking at the kids.

Under the assumption that the AUX position is reserved for tensed auxiliary verbs, we have no way of explaining the grammaticality of (39), unless we assume that *not* can occur in more than one position, namely to the right of an untensed verb. This predicts, incorrectly, that sentences such as (40) should be grammatical.

(40) *The dog is barking not.

In (40), *not* occurs to the right of an untensed verb, namely the participial main verb *barking*. It appears then, that we probably want to maintain an approach in which *not* occurs in a single position, to the right of a tensed auxiliary. We must therefore find an alternative explanation for the grammaticality of sentences such as (39).

One way to explain the contrast between (39) and (40) is to propose that participial auxiliary verbs, but not main verbs, can *move* from V position to AUX position, as in (41).

(41)

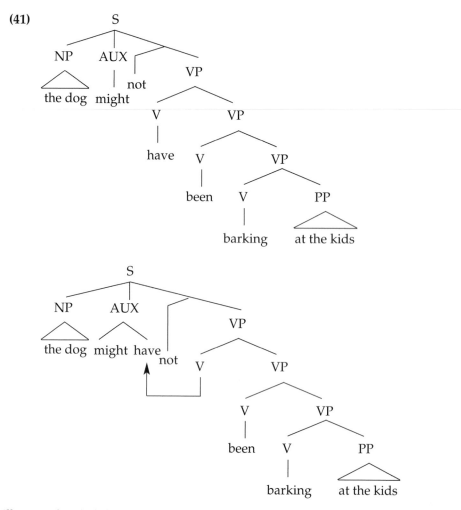

As illustrated in (41), bare infinitive auxiliary *have* can move, or *raise*, from V to AUX, around *not*. We thus derive the order of auxiliaries and *not* in (39), and maintain an approach in which *not* occurs in a fixed position to the right of AUX. We block (40) by assuming that this verb movement rule, which we will call **Verb Raising,** applies only to auxiliary *have/be* in English. We thus predict that it will apply to *have* in (39), but not to *barking* in (40).

By positing an AUX position we can now say that members of the grammatical category Auxiliary introduce a lexical head, namely a verb, parallel to other grammatical categories. Tensed auxiliaries therefore differ syntactically from other forms of auxiliaries, and from main verbs, by being generated in AUX. Participial and infinitival auxiliary verbs also differ from main verbs in being generated under V, but having the option to undergo Verb Raising to AUX. This approach also allows us to propose that *not* occurs in a position to the right of AUX.

In the Discovery Problems we provide further evidence for Verb Raising of auxiliaries in English. You also have the opportunity to investigate the effects of Verb Raising in languages other than English in the Language Diversity Exercises.

Summary

In this chapter we have formulated a few hypotheses about the structure of the verb phrase in English, and the different positions of auxiliary verbs, modals, *do*, and main verbs. On the basis of evidence from a number of rules that apply exclusively to tensed auxiliaries and modals, namely **Not Contraction, Subject-Auxiliary Inversion,** and **Tag Question Formation,** we concluded that auxiliary verbs, modals, and *do* form a separate grammatical category, **Auxiliary.** Members of this category form a morphologically closed class of words with grammatical meanings. Members of the category Auxiliary also differ syntactically from main verbs; tensed members are generated in **AUX,** and the above rules apply exclusively to elements in this position. A further difference between auxiliary verbs and main verbs is that only auxiliary verbs can undergo **Verb Raising** in English, adjoining to the right of a tensed auxiliary, and to the left of *not*.

We have also presented evidence for a rule of ***Do*-Insertion,** a rule that inserts **pleonastic** *do* into AUX in sentences without auxiliaries, in order for the rules mentioned above to apply, and to realize tense inflection. By analyzing auxiliary verbs as members of a separate grammatical category we find that they pattern in the same way as other grammatical categories, Determiner, Quantifier, and Numeral, in introducing a lexical category, in this case, a main verb.

DISCOVERY PROBLEMS

*Problem 1. Main Verb *Be**

We have seen in this chapter that *be* in English patterns with other auxiliary verbs, and is among the members of the grammatical category Auxiliary, in a sentence such as *Mary is lifting weights. Be* can also, however, behave syntactically as a main verb. This is illustrated by the sentences in (a–c), where we see that *be* must be the main verb in the sentence because it is the *only* verb in the sentence.

    a) Hortense *is* a nice person.
    b) They *were* happy to be home.
    c) The two girls *are* best friends.

Interestingly, *be* can also function syntactically as an auxiliary in such sentences. That is, rules that apply to tensed auxiliaries also apply to main verb *be*. Using Table 6.1 as a resource, provide example sentences that illustrate the ways in which main verb *be* might also be classified as an auxiliary. The question is, where is *be?* Under AUX or under V?

We have discussed the motivation for a rule of Verb Raising to account for the position of auxiliary verbs and *not*. Can this rule help us account for the syntactic behavior of main verb *be?* Diagram (a–c) to illustrate your hypothesis.

The sentences in (d–f) illustrate that as we might expect, main verb *be* can occur with other auxiliaries and modals preceding it. Does main verb *be* in these sentences have the same properties of auxiliaries you found for (a–c)? Diagram each sentence.

d) Hortense is *being* a nice person.
e) Hortense had *been* a nice person.
f) Hortense might have *been* a nice person.

*Problem 2. Main Verb *do*

As you now know, *do* is an auxiliary verb that occurs in sentences such as those in (a–c).

a) *Did* you go to the store?
b) I *didn't* go to the store.
c) I went to the store, *didn't* I?

Do can also be a main verb, as we see in (d–g).

d) I *did* the dishes.
e) Charlie *did* the laundry yesterday.
f) What did you *do* about it?
g) Let's *do* lunch!

Does main verb *do* function syntactically in the same way as main verb *be?* That is, can main verb *do* behave as an auxiliary, doing all the syntactic things that auxiliary verbs do? Explain your answer with systematic comparisons between main verb *do* and main verb *be,* based on the criteria in Table 6.1, and on your answers to Problem 1. Does Verb Raising apply to main verb *do?*

*Problem 3: Verb Phrase Ellipsis

There is yet another way in which tensed auxiliary verbs and modals differ from other verbs. To illustrate, consider the following data from a phenomenon called **Verb Phrase Ellipsis** or Verb Phrase Deletion. (The _____ indicates missing material.)

a) Nabokov might have been writing a novel and Dostoyevsky might have been _____ too.

b) Nabokov might have written a novel and Dostoyevsky might have _____ too.

c) Nabokov might write a novel and Dostoyevsky might _____ too.

What constituent has been omitted in the above sentences? Diagram each case, illustrating the omitted material using a triangle. Then answer the following questions.

- State the operation of Verb Phrase Ellipsis informally, using phrase structure rules to illustrate its effect.

- What happens in sentences such as *Nabokov wrote a novel and Dostoyevsky wrote a novel too?* Can Verb Phrase Ellipsis apply? What does this tell us about pleonastic *do?* Is what happens in such sentences consistent with what we might expect, given what we know about pleonastic *do* in other contexts? Why or why not?

- Can Subject-Auxiliary Inversion and Tag Question Formation apply in Verb Phrase Ellipsis contexts? Can *Not* Contraction apply? Give examples to illustrate your answer.

Problem 4. The Morphology of the Category Auxiliary

We saw in the chapter that auxiliaries *have* and *be*, modals, and *do* have grammatical meanings, and that together with modals they appear to form a morphologically closed class of words with only grammatical meanings. We did not, however, discuss the possible *forms* of these verbs, and whether they pattern with main verbs in having five different forms, listed in Table 5.5 in Chapter 5. Using Table 5.5, and Table 5.3 on the forms of *be* as resources, try to determine all the possible forms of the members of the category Auxiliary (*have/be*, modals, and *do*). How do they differ from main verbs and from each other? Does this evidence suggest a further distinction between grammatical verbs and lexical ones, or does it provide support for another kind of overlap between these two categories?

*Problem 5. Semimodals

Sometimes the words *dare, need,* and *ought* are labeled as "semimodals," or words that share properties with modals *will/would/shall/should/can/could,* and so on. With this in mind, consider the following paradigm for *dare.* The same pattern holds for *need.* (In the following sentences, *to leave* can be substituted for *leave,* without any change in the overall analysis.)

We dare leave town.

Dare we leave town?

We dare not leave town.

We daren't leave town.

Daren't we leave town?

Do we dare leave town?

We don't dare leave town.

Don't we dare leave town?

Now answer the following questions.

- Why do you think that *dare* and *need* are considered *semimodals?* Do they have anything in common semantically, syntactically, and morphologically with the modals we have discussed?
- In what ways do *dare* and *need* pattern syntactically with the main verbs and other modals? Be explicit in your answer, discussing syntax, morphology, and semantics.
- Consider the following patterns, involving the semimodal *ought,* and answer the same questions as above for *need/dare.* Does *ought* differ in any way from *dare/need?* Does it behave syntactically as a main verb, or a modal, or does it have properties of each? What are its morphological and semantic properties? Explain, using examples.

Ought he to stop smoking?

He ought to stop smoking

He ought not to stop smoking.

Oughtn't he stop smoking?

He oughtn't stop smoking.

*He doesn't ought to stop smoking.

*Does he ought to stop smoking?

TEXT ANALYSIS

1. Subject-Auxiliary Inversion and Tag Question Formation

The following text is divided into separate sentences. Apply Subject-Auxiliary Inversion or Tag Question Formation in each sentence if you can. If you need to separate coordinated sentences into two separate sentences to apply the rules, do so. Then answer the following questions.

- Does *Do*-Insertion apply? If so, why?
- Label the forms of the verbs in each sentence using Table 5.5 from Chapter 5.

- Label any examples of Verb Phrase Ellipsis (if you have done Problem 3 above).
- Identify any passive sentences, and label the forms of the verbs (again using Table 5.5).

---

a) "It was them, Hank and the others.
a) They wanted me with them but I wouldn't go against Will.
b) First place, I knew he was faster and a better shot, but mostly it was because I always liked his style.
c) He was my kind of man—the kind I'd like to have been . . . I never was anything but a wild kind of hombre with no more sense than the law allows . . ."
d) His voice trailed off, and in another minute Val saw that he was asleep.
e) While the water was getting hot he went outside and led the horses from the corral and picketed them on the grass.
f) Tensleep's horse had evidently been taken away, for there was neither horse nor saddle, and they must have taken his weapons too.

Source: Reilly's Luck, by Louis L'Amour.

---

2. Forming Negative Sentences

In the following set of sentences, negate as many verbs as you can by inserting *not* in an appropriate position. Then apply *Not* Contraction where you can. Now label the forms of each verb, using Table 5.5 from Chapter 5. Then answer the following questions.

- If *Not* Contraction fails, explain why.
- In which cases do you have to add a form of pleonastic *do?* What kind of change in the form of the following main verb is triggered by inserting *do?*
- What is the tense of each sentence, and which verbal element is inflected for tense?

a) Patti Ann had been watching a family, and the inmate smiled at her and waved.
b) It took a second for her to realize that the gesture was directed at her.
c) She smiled awkwardly and tried to place him—slight, sandy hair, a little obsequious even at this distance.
d) Jack had introduced her to him last winter.
e) Now he gave her the thumbs-up and she remembered that he was up for parole too.
f) He had made it.

Source: The Indian Lawyer, by James Welch.

3. "Undoing" Syntactic Rules

Find three or four example sentences, in written texts of your choice, in which at least one of the following rules has applied: Subject-Auxiliary Inversion, Tag Question Formation, *Not* Contraction, and/or *Do*-Insertion. Then *undo* the results of each rule—you will be creating the "source" sentence to which the rule applied. List the rules you have "undone" in each case.

a) Did she believe, truly, that one ought to protest in this way?
b) Wasn't there some other method that might work and prove less disastrous than marching in the street?

Source: Meridian, by Alice Walker.

Undoing the rules:

a) She believed, truly, that one ought to protest in this way. (*Do*-Insertion and Subject-Auxiliary Inversion)
b) There was not (any) other method that might work and prove less disastrous than marching in the street. (Subject-Auxiliary Inversion, *Not* Contraction)

Language Diversity Exercises

1. Negation in Old and Middle English

Negation of sentences in Old English differed rather dramatically from negation of sentences in modern English. For example, Old English had a variety of ways of forming "double negatives," comparable to sentences such as *He won't buy nothing* in modern English. Discuss the basic ways in which sentences could be negated in Old English, and give some examples. Compare them with their modern English counterparts. What kinds of changes did negation undergo in the course of development from Old to Middle English?

2. Negative Contraction in Old English

In Old English, as in modern English, negative morphemes could contract with verbs. Find some examples of this contraction, and compare them with their modern counterparts. Did negative morphemes in Old English contract only with tensed auxiliary verbs, or was negation possible with main verbs as well? Are there any other kinds of contraction involving verbs?

3. British English *Have*

In American English, *have* can be a main verb, as in *I have a dog*. In British English, main verb *have* also patterns with main verb *be* in American English, undergoing rules that apply to tensed auxiliaries. Main verb *have* in American English, on the other hand, does not undergo these rules. Rather, main verb *have* in this language variety patterns with other main verbs.

Research British English *have*, and outline the ways in which it patterns with American English main verb *be*. Use clear examples to compare and contrast these verbs in both varieties of English. Use Table 6.1 and your answers to Discovery Problem 1 as a guide for this exercise. Also, show how main verb *have* in American English differs from British English *have* with respect to the characteristics given in Table 6.1.

4. *Yes/No* Questions in Other Languages

Not all languages, as you may already have guessed or may already know, form yes/no questions through Subject-Auxiliary Inversion. For example, in French the tensed main verb can undergo this process. (The addition of *t* in (b) is not relevant to the discussion here.)

a) Elle *va* au cinéma. ("She goes to the movies.")
b) *Va*-t-elle au cinéma? (Goes-she to movies) ("Is she going to the movies?")

A tensed auxiliary verb, if there is one, can also front in a yes/no question. Here, we see that a tensed form of the auxiliary verb *be*, or *être* in French, has been fronted by Subject-Auxiliary Inversion.

c) Elle *est* allée au cinéma. (She is gone to the movies) ("She went to the movies.")

d) *Est*-elle allée au cinéma? (Is-she gone to the movies?) ("Has she gone to the movies?")

It appears, then, that French differs from English in fronting not only auxiliary verbs but also main verbs. The rule for question formation is therefore not stated in terms of Subject-*Auxiliary* Inversion, but rather as Subject-*Verb* Inversion. Notice also that in French, there is no equivalent of pleonastic *do*, because the tensed main verb can undergo inversion, in contrast to English, where *do* must be inserted.

Choose a language, and investigate how questions are formed. Explain, in general terms, the syntactic distinctions between question formation in the language and Subject-Auxiliary Inversion in English. Give examples, and contrast them with English ones to support your analysis. Does the language you consider have the equivalent of *Do*-Insertion? Is it like French or English, or different from both of these languages?

5. Negation in Other Languages

Choose a language other than English (including, if you wish, a pidgin or creole), and try to explain how simple affirmative sentences are negated (*negation* is a huge topic—focus only on the counterpart of the negative morpheme *not*) and how it compares with the English system. Many languages use "double negatives" to form negative sentences. This kind of syntactic construction (as in *I don't like nobody*) is stigmatized in American English, even though it is a strategy widely used in this and other languages. Does the language you investigate use double negatives? Give some examples, and discuss, if you can, whether such constructions are stigmatized as "poor grammar." You may find it interesting to interview a native speaker about this issue.

CHAPTER REVIEW TERMS

Do-Insertion, *Not* Contraction, Subject Auxiliary Inversion, Tag Question Formation, Verb Raising, the category Auxiliary, the AUX position, grammatical versus lexical verbs, pleonastic and main verb *do*, auxiliary verbs *have* and *be*, modals, main verb *be*, the negative morpheme *not*, Verb Phrase Ellipsis

CHAPTER REVIEW EXERCISE

Choose from among the following options to create a chapter exercise. You may wish to add options from previous chapter exercises to make this exercise more comprehensive.

In the following text excerpt:

1. Make two positive sentences negative by inserting *not* in an appropriate position, and apply *Not* Contraction where you can.
2. Label the forms of each verb in the excerpt, using Table 5.5 from Chapter 5.
3. Identify the morphological tense and aspect of each sentence, and the verbal element that is inflected for tense. Does the semantic tense and aspect of the sentence correspond to its morphological tense and aspect?
4. Apply Subject-Auxiliary Inversion to two sentences in the text.
5. Apply Tag Question Formation to two sentences in the text.
5. In which sentences do you have to apply *Do*-Insertion? What kind of change in the form of the following main verb is triggered by inserting *do?*
6. Identify any uses of main verb *be.*
7. Choose two sentences in which there are no auxiliary verbs. Add a modal, auxiliary *have,* and auxiliary *be* to create the longest possible sequence of verbal elements (as you did in Discovery Problem 2 in Chapter 5). Label the forms of the verbs. How does the original form of the main verb change when you add an auxiliary verb?

a) A young Sioux woman lies on a bed in our house.
b) She is feverish, delirious, and coughing so hard I am afraid she will die.
c) My father kneels on the kitchen floor, begging my mother to help him.
d) It's a summer night and the room is brightly lit.
e) Insects cluster around the light fixtures, and the pleading quality in my father's voice reminds me of those insects—high-pitched, insistent, frantic.
f) It is a sound I have never heard coming from him.
g) My mother stands in our kitchen on a hot, windy day.
h) The windows are open, and Mother's lace curtains blow into the room.
i) Mother holds my father's Ithaca twelve-gauge shotgun, and since she is a small, slender woman, she has trouble finding the balance point of its heavy length.

Source: Montana 1948, by Larry Watson.

7

Adjectives and Adjective Phrases

Introduction

In this chapter we continue the discussion of syntactic categories, exploring in some detail the semantics, the morphology, and in particular the syntax of the lexical category *Adjective*. Adjectives function semantically as *modifiers* or *predicates*, and express particular kinds of derivational and inflectional morphology that help us identify them. Adjectives also occur in construction with members of the grammatical category Degree, forming adjective phrases. We will test our hypothesized phrases using movement, pronominalization, and coordination. We conclude the chapter with a discussion of some of the different syntactic positions adjective phrases occur in, which we can express in terms of phrase structure rules.

The Semantics of Adjectives

We have seen from our previous discussions of nouns and verbs that our first impulse is to describe these syntactic categories in terms of their general meanings: nouns are people, places, and things, and verbs are actions or states. We are probably most likely to define adjectives semantically as well, as words that "describe" nouns, adding additional information to what a noun names or refers to. This semantic definition is in some sense accurate; adjectives do provide descriptive information about nouns, typically in the form of a quality or attribute, a personality trait, nationality, and so on. This semantic function of adjectives can be made even more precise, however. To illustrate, consider the difference between (1) and (2).

(1) the *ecstatic* children jumped into the pool.

(2) the children were *ecstatic*.

In both (1) and (2), the adjective *ecstatic* in some sense "describes" the children, as in each sentence we are talking about children who are ecstatic. *Ecstatic* actually has a technically different semantic function in each case, however. In (1), we interpret the noun phrase *the ecstatic children* as meaning "the set of children who are ecstatic." The adjective *ecstatic* is therefore a **modifier** of the noun *children*, part of the description of the noun *children*. In (2), on the other hand, *children* has no such modifier; rather, the noun phrase *the children* itself denotes a set of children (who may or may not be ecstatic). That these children *are*, in fact, ecstatic, is information that is contributed by the rest of the sentence, namely by the verb phrase *were ecstatic*. In this case, the state of being ecstatic is a *property* assigned to the set of children denoted by the noun phrase *the children*. The adjective (or adjective phrase, as we will see) *ecstatic* is thus in (2) a **predicate,** or property, assigned to, in this case, the subject noun phrase.

We can make the distinction between adjectival modification and predication more precise by comparing the semantics of the following sentences.

(3) Spray the green wall.

(4) Spray the wall green.

In (3), *green* modifies *wall*, and we understand we are to spray a green wall. In (4), on the other hand, the wall in question is not necessarily green at all, but could be purple or yellow. *Green* thus has a completely different semantic function in this case, it is not part of the description of the noun *wall*.

Adjectives are a particularly interesting category in that they can occur in "strings" of more than one, when they precede the noun they modify. That there are different semantic classes of adjectives is also illustrated by the evidence that adjectives occur in certain orders, depending on what they mean. For example, the order of adjectives in (5) and (6) is interchangeable.

(5) the *intelligent, content* woman

(6) the *content, intelligent* woman

Both *intelligent* and *content* express qualities or attributes of the woman and are thus in the same semantic class. When we add an adjectival modifier of a different class, however, such as one that expresses nationality, we find the order of adjectives becomes more restricted.

(7) a. the *content, intelligent, Japanese* woman
     b. *the *Japanese, content, intelligent* woman

Some other examples of ordering restrictions among classes of adjectives are given in (8).

(8) a. the big young man
     b. *the young big man

(9) a. a new German car
         b. *a German new car

(10) a. the great oaken table
          b. *the oaken great table

(8) suggests that size adjectives precede adjectives expressing age, and (9) demonstrates once again that nationality adjectives seem to follow adjectives expressing qualities or attributes. (10) shows that adjectives of material appear to be restricted to following adjectives of size.

Some of the different semantic classes of adjectives are summarized in Table 7.1.

From the semantic evidence we can see that adjectives are members of a lexical category, words with intrinsic meanings. Their lexical content is evident in the following dictionary definitions.

(11) **gracious** (*adj.*) 1. Characterized by kindness and warm courtesy. 2. Characterized by tact and propriety: *responded to the insult with gracious humor.* . . .

(12) **shaky** (*adj.*) 1. Trembling or quivering; tremulous. 2. Unsteady or unsound; weak: *a shaky table* . . .

We now turn to the morphology of adjectives, where we see that their morphological characteristics support the claim that adjectives are members of a lexical category.

The Morphology of Adjectives

Adjectives occur in a variety of different morphological forms. We constantly bring new adjectives into English in various ways, which is what we expect of a lexical category. We use the adjective *bogus* (as in *this is a bogus exam!*), created through both functional and semantic shift. (*Bogus* was originally a noun, the name of a device for making counterfeit money. It now is an adjective meaning *fake* or *ridiculous*.) Through compounding we have added to the language *highbrow/uptown/far out*, as in a *highbrow/uptown/far out* person. Some adjectives we

Table 7.1
Some Semantic Classes of Adjectives

Nationality	Japanese, African, American, Swedish, Filipino
Personal	human/female/rich/poor/healthy/sick/friendly
Material	wooden/oaken/woven
Age/size	young/old/big/fat/small/little/ancient/modern/current
Color	green/orange/purple/blue

have added through semantic shift are *phat* and *sweet*, whose original meaning has shifted to mean *excellent*. (A recent movie is entitled *Phat Beach*, for example. Note also that this particular case of semantic shift is also signaled by spelling, in the case of *phat/fat*). *Bad*, on the other hand, now means *good* in some circles.

We can often recognize adjectives by their derivational affixation. Adjectives can be derived by adding *-ish, -ary, -al, -ic,* among other affixes as in (13).

(13) a. fiend + ish = fiendish   (noun + ish = adjective)
      b. danger + ous = dangerous   (noun + ous = adjective)
      c. discipline + ary = disciplinary (noun + ary = adjective)
      d. leg + al = legal   (root + al = adjective)
      e. artist + ic = artistic   (noun + ic = adjective)

Some adjectives have no recognizable morphological endings at all, as in (14).

(14) *full/fun/cool/happy/slick*

And some adjectives, as we have seen in previous chapters, are **participial.** These adjectives have undergone functional shift, from verbs to adjectives.

(15) *exciting/bored/interesting/fraught*

Adjectives can also end in *-ly,* as in (16).

(16) *friendly/lively/queenly*

These adjectives are sometimes confused with adverbs, such as *quickly/ slowly/quietly,* which also end in *-ly.* We turn to ways to syntactically "test" whether a word is an adjective or adverb in a later section of this chapter and in chapter 8. Here, however, simply note that adverbs cannot occur in prenominal position as modifiers, and in this way they contrast syntactically and semantically with adjectives.

(17) a. the *friendly/lively/queenly* woman
      b. *the *quickly/slowly/quietly* woman

Another way to identify an adjective is through its inflectional morphology. Many adjectives can be suffixed with comparative *-er* and superlative *-est,* as in (18).

(18) *friendlier/friendliest, cooler/coolest, happier/happiest*

Not all adjectives have morphological comparative and superlative forms, however; for some adjectives, this grammatical relationship is expressed by a preceding word, *more/most* or *less/least.*

(19) a. more/less *interesting/enthusiastic/boring/fun/extraordinary*
      b. **interestinger/*enthusiasticest/*boringer/*funner/*extraordinariest*)

It is difficult to predict exactly which types of adjectives can be affixed with *-er/
-est,* and which express comparative and superlative syntactically by being preceded by *more/most, less/least.* We will not attempt to formulate a hard and fast rule here, as it would require examining a wide range of characteristics of adjectives that we are not prepared to do. For example, we cannot formulate a rule based on "number of syllables," as two-syllable adjectives such as *quiet* and *happy* take *-er,* as in *quieter* and *happier,* but two-syllable *boring* and *gracious* do not take this affix, as we see by the oddity of **boringer* and **graciouser.* Monosyllable adjectives are unpredictable as well; while we may think that *fuller/fullest* sound odd, we certainly hear *bluer/bluest,* and so on. I would have said that *funner* was not a form we use, but while writing this book I heard this word used by a reporter on the radio.

Finally, observe that some of the morphological comparative and superlative forms of adjectives are **suppletive.** That is, this inflection is expressed by a completely unrelated form of the word, rather than by a suffix.

(20)   a. *good/better/best*
         b. *bad/worse/worst*

Inflectional and derivational morphology of adjectives thus provides us with a number of clues to help us distinguish them from other syntactic categories. These morphological characteristics are summarized in Table 7.2.

The evidence from morphology and semantics of adjectives suggests that these words are members of a lexical category. In the following section we turn to the syntax of adjectives, or more appropriately the syntax of the adjective phrase. We discuss evidence for such phrases based on movement, pronominalization, and coordination, and become acquainted with a few of the basic positions that adjective phrases occur in. We also discuss evidence that adjectives, like other lexical categories, are introduced by a grammatical category, in this case the grammatical category *Degree.*

Categories That Introduce Adjectives: Degree Words

We saw above that one way to identify an adjective is by a preceding word, *more/most, less/least.* These words supply grammatical information about the

Table 7.2
Derivational and Inflectional Morphology of Adjectives

Derivational affixes: *-ish/-ous/-ary/-ic/-al/-ly,* etc. (churlish, fabulous, incendiary, historic, apocryphal, manly)

Inflectional affixes: *-er/-est* (brown/browner/brownest)

Suppletive forms: good/better/best, bad/worse/worst

adjective they syntactically introduce, namely information about comparison. Other words that introduce adjectives and express grammatical information are given in (21).

(21) Lionel is *very/so/too/quite* tall.

The words *very/so/too/quite* in (21) express the "degree" to which Lionel is tall. (The *too* under discussion here is different from *too* in other uses, such as in *Lionel left too.*) Observe that the words *more/most/less/least* in (22) also express, in addition to comparison, a notion of "degree," in this case, the degree to which the idea is popular.

(22) the *more/most/less/least* popular idea

Some other words that fall into this class are *rather/quite/extremely/ barely/entirely/scarcely*. All of these words express grammatical information about the adjective they introduce, namely information about degree or intensity.

How then are we to classify these "degree words?" In dictionaries, they are usually classified as adverbs, and thus of the same class as words such as *quickly, softly, happily,* and so on. There are several ways in which degree words are distinct from adverbs, which we will discuss in the following chapter. Putting a more detailed discussion of the differences between degree words and adverbs aside, let us focus here on what we do know about degree words, and attempt to formulate a hypothesis about their syntactic category.

Semantically, degree words are similar to determiners or quantifiers in noun phrases, grammatical categories that provide grammatical information about the noun they introduce. Some definitions of degree words are given in (23–24). Compare them with the dictionary definitions of the adjectives in (11–12).

(23) **very** *(adv)* 1. In a high degree: extremely: *very happy.* 2. Truly: absolutely: *the very best money can buy.* 3. Precisely: *the very same one. . . .*

(24) **too** *(adv)* 1. More than enough; excessively: *He studied too much.* 2. Very; extremely; immensely; *He's only too willing to be of service.*

Notice that in these dictionary definitions, *very* and *rather* are considered adverbs; indeed, they are defined as synonyms for different adverbs (*too* is defined as a synonym of *very* in (24), for example). Putting this aside for the moment, observe that degree words nevertheless contribute grammatical information about intensity or degree to an adjective they introduce. Degree words thus also pattern syntactically with grammatical categories such a Determiner, Quantifier, Numeral, and Auxiliary, in introducing members of a lexical category, in this case, Adjective.

The question of whether degree words form a morphologically closed or open class is an interesting one. For example, we have recently coined the degree word *way*, a synonym for *very*, as in (15).

(25)   *The trip was way cool.*

Notice that this new degree word does not have a correspondingly new meaning, but rather is synonymous with an existing degree word. We thus do not
really coin an entirely new word, as we do when we create new nouns and
verbs.
   We can also quite easily form degree words from adjectives:

(26)   a. *absolute, fantastic, complete, incredible* (adjectives)
        b. *absolutely, fantastically, completely, incredibly* (adverbs)

The adverbs in (26b) are all in some sense degree words, and fall together
semantically with the grammatical degree words *very/so/too/quite/less/least/more/*
most in (21–22). That the adverbs can be productively derived from adjectives,
as we see in (26), suggests, on the other hand, that the words in (26b) are members of a lexical category, namely Adverb. The "degree adverbs" in (26b) thus
present us with something of a conundrum, with respect to the distinctions
between grammatical and lexical categories.
   There is reason, however, to analyze the degree adverbs in (26b) as members
of the grammatical category Degree. We will present evidence for this classification in Chapter 8, where we address the properties of adverbs in greater
detail. For now, we will simply be aware that degree adverbs modify adjectives,
just as do members of the grammatical category **Degree.** The category Degree is
morphologically "closed" in the sense that additional members do not have
unique semantic content; rather, new members of this class are basically synonymous with existing members. (Hence, we can create new degree words such
as *way*, but only as synonyms for existing degree words, in this case *very.*)
Degree words introduce members of a lexical category, namely Adjective, and
thus syntactically pattern with other grammatical categories we have discussed,
Determiner, Quantifier, Numeral, and Auxiliary.

The Structure of the Adjective Phrase

We might hypothesize, given our present understanding of phrase structure,
that degree words, combined with adjectives, form adjective phrases as in (27).

(27)

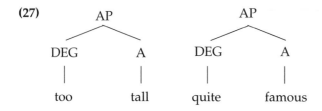

We know that we can test for phrases in different ways, using movement and
pronominalization, and also coordination. Let us now apply these tests to *too tall*

and *quite famous,* to see whether our hypothesized phrase structures in (27) are on the right track.

Turning first to movement, (28–29) illustrate that *too tall* and *quite famous* do in fact appear to act like syntactic phrases by undergoing WH-Movement.

(28) a. Jeff Goldblum is *too tall.*
  b. Jeff Goldblum is *how tall?*
  c. *How tall* is Jeff Goldblum _____?

(29) a. Amelia Earheart was *quite brave.*
  b. Amelia Earheart was *how brave?*
  c. *How brave* was Amelia Earheart _____?

Remember that WH-Movement has the effect of moving a phrase pronominalized by an interrogative proform to the front of the sentence. WH-Movement can also operate on phrases that include interrogative proforms. For example, we saw in our discussion of noun phrases in Chapter 4 that a possessive determiner such as *his/her* can be pronominalized by interrogative *whose.* (This issue was also addressed in the Discovery Problems in Chapter 3.) The noun phrase containing *whose* then moves to sentence-initial position by WH-Movement.

(30) a. Maureen read *his/her* book.
  b. Maureen read *whose* book?
  c. *Whose* book did Maureen read _____?

A similar operation appears to be at work in (28–29). Here, the degree words *very/quite* are pronominalized by interrogative *how.* The entire phrase [*how* + adjective] then undergoes WH-Movement. In fact, this is really the *only* way that an adjective phrase can undergo WH-Movement. The sentences in (31), for example, show that we cannot pronominalize an adjective phrase with a single interrogative proform, such as *what.* Rather, we interpret such proforms as replacing noun phrases.

(31) a. *What* is Maureen?
  b. Maureen is a surgeon/*happy.

We can see evidence for adjective phrases more clearly with examples of movement of larger phrases such as in (32–33). We also can see from the responses to the WH-questions that *how* pronominalizes a degree word.

(32) a. The students are *very eager for help.*
  b. The students are *how eager for help?*
  c. *How eager for help* are the students _____?

(33) a. Michael Jordan is good at baseball.
  b. Michael Jordan is *how good at baseball?*
  c. *How good at baseball* is Michael Jordan _____?

WH-Movement thus provides us with evidence not only that the sequence [degree word + adjective] (and additional material as well, as we see in (32–33)) forms a larger phrase, but also that degree words themselves can be pronominalized, by *how*.

We can also pronominalize entire adjective phrases, as in (34). This is again what we expect if adjectives occur as parts of larger phrases, in the same way as nouns or verbs.

(34) a. The students are *eager for help* and *so* are the teachers.
      b. Michael Jordan is *very good at baseball* and *so* is Cal Ripken, Jr.
      c. Volleyball is *fun* and *so* is tennis.
      d. Our cat is *very content*, and *so* is our dog.

Evidence from movement and pronominalization thus supports the idea that even "small" adjective phrases, such as *fun* in (34c), which consist of a single head adjective, are nevertheless, in terms of phrase structure, adjective phrases.

Coordination allows us to test the above hypotheses we have made about the phrase structure of adjectives, as it clearly illustrates that degree words form phrases with adjectives, and that a single adjective alone can head an adjective phrase. For example, (35) illustrates that adjective phrases of the form [degree word + adjective] can be coordinated, suggesting that both are adjective phrases.

(35) The movie *Titanic* was [too expensive] and [very long].
                                AP   AP

The phrase structure of (35) is given in (36).

(36)

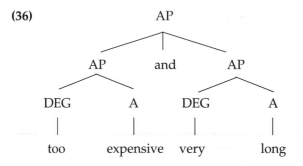

An adjective phrase consisting of a single head adjective can also be coordinated with an adjective phrase of the form [degree word + adjective], as in (37), illustrated in (38).

(37) The movie *Titanic* was [expensive] and [very long].
                                AP   AP

(38)

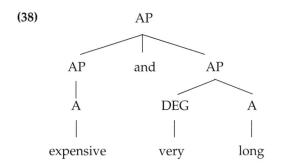

We would expect (37) to be ungrammatical if *expensive* were an adjective but not an adjective phrase, as it should not be able to be coordinated with the adjective phrase *very long*.

Recall that phrase structure allows us to untangle certain syntactic ambiguities. For example, the adjective phrase *very expensive and long* is actually ambiguous; it can mean *very expensive and very long,* or *very expensive* and (some other degree of) *long*. We can diagram these two meanings as in (39) and (40).

(39)

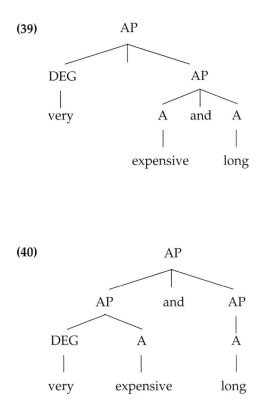

(40)

The phrase structure in (39) reflects an interpretation in which *very* modifies both *expensive* and *long*. In (40), on the other hand, *very* modifies only *expensive*. The adjective phrase *long*, in contrast, has no degree modifier at all.

Based on our above evidence for adjective phrases, we can now formulate a phrase structure rule for adjective phrases as in (41).

(41)   AP => (DEG) A

(41) does not, of course, allow us to generate all of the possible adjective phrases we can actually produce. It does, however, capture the generalizations about adjective phrases discussed so far, in which an adjectival head is introduced by, and forms a phrase with, a degree word. We will return to this phrase structure rule in later chapters, revising it as we discuss in more detail the internal structure of the adjective phrase.

Adjective Phrase Positions

We saw above that movement, pronominalization, and coordination provide different ways to test whether a group of words functions as an adjective phrase. We also formulated a preliminary phrase structure rule for adjective phrases, based on a number of different contrasts. In this section we discuss a few of the different positions adjective phrases can occur in, in order to provide more ways to recognize and understand the function of this syntactic category.

Prenominal Position

We have already seen that adjectives can occur before nouns, in **prenominal** position, as in (42).

(42)   these *ferocious* dinosaurs

We now know that prenominal adjectives such as *ferocious* in (42) are actually adjective phrases; observe that *ferocious* occurs in a position in which we can also have adjective phrases, as in (43).

(43)   these *very ferocious* dinosaurs

Rather than complicating our phrase structure rules to say that nouns can be introduced by either adjective phrases or single adjectives, we will analyze prenominal adjectives as adjective phrases, regardless of whether they contain a single member. We express the option for nouns to be modified by adjective phrases by including in our phrase structure rule for noun phrases a position for prenominal adjective phrases, as in (44).

(44)   NP => (DET) (Q) (NUM) (AP) N

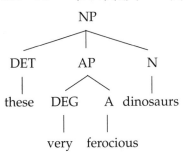

(44) allows us to express not only the generalization that adjective phrases occur in prenominal position, but also that they occur to the *right* of all other prenominal elements, as illustrated in (45).

(45)   a. *very ferocious *six* dinosaurs
　　　　 b. *very ferocious *all* dinosaurs
　　　　 c. *very ferocious *these* dinosaurs

We now have two diagnostics for adjectives. One is that they can be preceded by degree words, such as *very*. Another is that they can occur in prenominal position. Below, we turn to some other positions in which we find adjective phrases, providing us with additional tools we can use to identify them.

After Linking Verbs

Another position in which we often find adjective phrases is within the verb phrase, as in (46), illustrated in (47).

(46)   a. The problem appeared complicated.
　　　　 b. The boys grew taller over the summer.
　　　　 c. The car was bright red.
　　　　 d. The chowder tasted delicious.

(47)

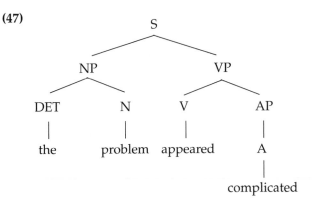

The adjective phrases in (46) are all semantically predicates; they assign a property to a noun phrase, in this case, the subject noun phrase. Such adjective phrases do not form part of the subject noun phrase, and thus do not semantically modify the noun. Adjective phrases in this position typically occur after what we call **linking verbs,** verbs that link the subject noun phrase to a predicate in the verb phrase. A list of linking verbs is given in (48).

(48)   **Linking Verbs**
      a. taste, smell, feel
      b. remain, seem, appear, grow, be, become

All of these verbs have in common that they can be followed by predicate adjective phrases, as in (46).

Categories other than adjective phrases can also be predicates, as we can see from the examples in (49). We discuss these kinds of predicates in more detail in chapters 11 and 12. For now, however, notice that as we might expect, these predicates can occur after linking verbs.

(49)   a. They remained *friends.* (predicate noun phrase)
      b. The couple seemed *in good health.* (predicate prepositional phrase)
      c. She became *a doctor.* (predicate noun phrase)

In all of the sentences in (49), and in those in (46) as well, the predicate adjective phrase, noun phrase, or prepositional phrase assigns a property to the subject noun phrase.

We are now in a position to devise some useful diagnostics for adjective phrases, what we can call the *linking verb test* and the *very test.* Adjective phrases can occur after linking verbs, and can be distinguished from other categories in this position (noun phrases and prepositional phrases, as in (49)) by also being modified by degree words, such as *very.* Neither noun phrases nor prepositional phrases can be so modified, as we seen in (50).

(50)   a. *They remained *very* friends. (predicate noun phrase).
      b. *The couple seemed *very* in good health. (predicate prepositional phrase)
      c. *She became *very* a doctor. (predicate noun phrase)

Adjective phrases after linking verbs, on the other hand, can be modified by degree words, as in (51).

(51)   a. The problem appeared *very* complicated.
      b. The boys grew *much* taller over the summer.
      c. The car was *very* bright red.
      d. The chowder tasted *quite* delicious.

We can use the linking verb test to determine whether a phrase is a predicate adjective phrase, noun phrase, or prepositional phrase. The *very* test allows us to determine whether the predicate in this position is an adjective phrase.

We can now write an (incomplete) phrase structure rule for verb phrases to include an optional adjective phrase after the verb, as in (52).

(52) VP => V (AP)

Finally, we discuss yet another position in which we find adjective phrases, one that has several interesting syntactic properties.

Postnominal Position

Not all adjectival modifiers of nouns occur in prenominal position. As we see in (53), adjective phrases can occur in **postnominal** position, or *after* the nouns they modify.

(53) a. All things *possible* have been done.
  b. You should always give something *useful/interesting/expensive* as a gift.

Postnominal adjectival modifiers have a number of very interesting properties. We will outline some of the questions these constructions raise, and leave further discussion of how they are derived aside. For example, prenominal adjectival modifiers cannot always occur in postnominal position:

(54) a. The *impressive/smart/well-dressed* woman walked in.
  b. *The woman *impressive/smart/well-dressed* walked in.

Further, some adjectival modifiers occur *only* in prenominal position, such as *utter/mere/main*.

(55) a. Lionel is an *utter/mere* fool.
  b. *Lionel is a fool *utter/mere*.

Another interesting fact about postnominal adjectives is that they can occur with *complements,* or phrases of other categories that form part of an adjective phrase. For example, the adjectives *proud* and *fond* can occur with prepositional phrase complements as in (56). (Complementation of adjectives is discussed in more detail in Chapter 10.)

(56) a. proud of her son
  b. happy about their grades

Notice that although *proud* and *happy* can occur in prenominal position, they can include complements only in postnominal position.

(57)   a. a proud woman
        b. happy students

(58)   a. *a proud of her son woman/a woman proud of her son
        b. *happy about their grades students/students happy about
           their grades

It appears, then, that in order to include postnominal adjectival modifiers in our phrase structure rule for noun phrases, we must rewrite (44) as (59).

(59)   NP => (DET) (Q) (NUM) (AP) N (AP)

Alternatively, we might be able to derive the postnominal position of adjectival modifiers in some way, and maintain our more simple phrase structure rule in (44). We might posit, for example, that, rather than complicate our phrase structure rules, in some cases adjectives can *move* to the right around a noun, as in (60).

(60)   *possible* things = things *possible*

Notice, however, that if we opt for such an analysis, we are still left without an account of the data involving complements in (56) and (58). We also have no explanation for the fact that not all prenominal adjectives can also be postnominal, as illustrated in (54–55).

We will not attempt to work through this complicated problem here. We will return to it briefly in Chapter 12 when we revisit the syntax of the noun phrase. For now we will simply assume the phrase structure rule in (59) for noun phrases, keeping in mind that an alternative derivation of the position of adjectival modifiers might also be possible.

Summary

Adjectives are semantically *modifiers* or **predicates,** providing descriptive information about a noun or noun phrase. Information expressed by modifiers is included in the description of the noun, and information expressed by predicates is assigned as a property to a noun phrase. Adjectives appear to fall into different semantic classes, including size, age, nationality, personality traits, material, and so on, which occur in certain restricted syntactic orders. Adjectives have specific morphological properties, expressed by derivational and inflectional affixes specific to this lexical category. Adjectives can also be **participial.** The lexical category Adjective thus productively adds new members with intrinsic meaning. Syntactically, adjectives can be modified by **Degree** words, members of a grammatical category with which adjectives form larger phrases. Members of the category Degree introduce a lexical category, have grammatical meanings, and form a closed morphological class. They thus pattern with other grammatical categories, Determiner, Numeral, Quantifier, and Auxiliary. Adjectives can also be modified by **degree adverbs.** Adjective **phrases** have certain syntactic properties; they undergo syntactic movement, pronominalization, and coordination, and occur in certain positions. Three positions for adjective phrases we discussed here include: **prenominal** position, **postnominal** position, and the position after a **linking verb.** We thus have a number of semantic, morphological, and syntactic ways to "test" whether a word or phrase is of the category Adjective: one useful way is to combine the *very test* with the *linking verb test*—this distinguishes adjective phrases from noun phrase and prepositional phrase predicates.

Discovery Problems

*Problem 1. Nationality Terms

Nationality adjectives such as *German, Japanese, African, Filipino, French, Swedish,* can also in some syntactic contexts function as nouns, giving rise to ambiguity. Specifically, nationality adjectives (as in *She likes German food*) can be confused with the name of a language (*I speak German*) or a noun used to refer to a person in terms of his or her nationality (*She is a German*). Sometimes, the adjectival and nominal forms are distinct: we can eat *Swedish* food, or speak *Swedish,* but one is a *Swede* (noun), or *Swedish* (adjective). Using the tools you now have to identify adjectives, determine the category of the following nationality terms. Give explicit evidence (sets of sentences) that illustrate how you came up with your answer. Explain any ambiguities.

a) Lionel is fond of *Italian* food.
b) He speaks *Arabic.*
c) She married a *Korean.*
d) The *Canadian* border was closed yesterday.
e) No one in the room speaks *Japanese.*
f) The *Chinese* interpreter did an excellent job.
g) *Latin* is a dead language.

Now, come up with three or four different examples on your own of nationality adjectives, and show how you distinguish them from nationality nouns.

Problem 2. Refining Tests for Adjectives

We have said that one way to test for an adjective is to see if it can be introduced by *very*. There are many adjectives, however, that cannot be interpreted in terms of degree—*infinite* and *pregnant* are such adjectives (**Space is very infinite./*Mary is somewhat pregnant.*) Think of five or six other examples, using sentences to show how they do not accept degree words. How might you determine the category of such adjectives? What other test or tests might you use?

*Problem 3. Participial Adjectives

Recall from earlier chapters that participles can function syntactically as nouns (gerunds), verbs, and adjectives in different syntactic contexts. Some examples are:

a) I like *running*. (noun/gerund)
b) The *galloping* horse raced past the barn. (verb)
c) An *excited* student answered the question. (adjective)

You now have two tests for adjectives at your disposal, the *very* test and the linking verb test. Find four examples, in a text of your choice, of sentences with participial adjectives. Show how you use these two tests to support your conclusions. Write out the relevant sets of sentences that illustrate the results of these tests.

*Problem 4. Modifiers of Adjectives

We have seen that adjectives can be modified by degree words, such as *very/so/too*. Now consider the examples below. What is the syntactic category of the words that modify the adjectives *brown, blue,* and *yellow* in these phrases? Provide at least two different arguments in support of your hypothesis.

a) Her dress was a *pretty* blue.
b) The sunflowers were a *pale* yellow.
c) His eyes were a *lovely* brown.

How do we now have to revise the hypothesis that adjectives are typically modified by Degree words? What other category can modify adjectives? How must we revise our phrase structure rule for adjective phrases in (59)?

*Problem 5. More Modifiers of Adjectives

What is the syntactic category of the words *pretty* and *real* in the following pairs of sentences? Explain your answer using syntactic arguments.

a) She was *real/pretty* tired.
b) The human mannequin was *pretty/real*.

How must we further modify (59)?
Now, consider the following sentences.

a) The soldier came in, *dog tired*.
b) Her face turned *beet red* with embarrassment.
d) The doctor's lab coat is *sky blue*.

What is the syntactic category of *dog, beet,* and *sky,* and what syntactic category do they modify here? Again, support your answer with syntactic evidence. How must we further revise our hypothesis about the categories that modify adjectives?

Problem 6. Movement and Pronominalization

As we saw in this section, adjective phrases can undergo both movement and pronominalization. With this in mind, put the adjective phrases below into sentences, and show how each can undergo WH-Movement. To create examples, you may have to include in each example a degree modifier, which you will then replace with *how.* Then apply WH-Movement. The first example is done for you.

a) anxious to be gone

   Mary was very anxious to be gone.

   Mary was how anxious to be gone?

   How anxious to be gone was Mary?

b) honored that he was chosen
c) very pliable
d) generally indisputable
e) certain about the outcome

TEXT ANALYSIS

1. Analyzing Adjective Phrases

In the following text you will find a number of different adjective phrases. First, simply try to find them. Then provide the following information for each adjective.

- Is the adjective semantically a predicate or a modifier?
- Identify any adjective phrases in prenominal position or after linking verbs. Can you identify any other positions adjective phrases occur in?
- What semantic class does each adjective you identify fall into? Do we need to amend the list of semantic classes in Table 7.1 to include any of them?
- Analyze the derivational and inflectional morphology of each adjective. (Use Table 7.2 for reference.) Label any adjectives that are participial.
- Identify any degree words that precede the adjectives in the text.

a) Every invitation was successful.
b) They were all disengaged and all happy.
c) The preparatory interest of this dinner, however, was not yet over.
d) A circumstance rather unlucky occurred.
e) The two eldest little Knightleys were engaged
   to pay their grandpapa and aunt a visit of
   some weeks in the spring, and their papa now
   proposed bringing them, and staying one
   whole day at Hartfield—which one day would
   be the very day of this party.
f) His professional engagements did not allow of
   his being put off, but both father and daughter
   were disturbed by its happening so.

Source: Emma, by Jane Austen.

2. More Analysis

Do the same as in (1) for the following texts.

a) She and the building share the same coloring,
   polished silver and fresh cream.
a) She is quite tall, almost six feet, and she is
   wearing a long, simple, off-white dress.
b) She has put up her hair, but several loose locks
   fall like a cascade of shiny metal over her
   cheeks.
c) No makeup, no perfume, and no jewelry other
   than a silver cross at her throat.
d) An angel. The kind you can trust to guard
   something with a flaming sword.

Source: Smilla's Sense of Snow, by Peter Hoeg.

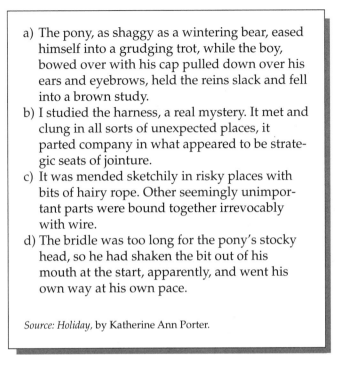

a) The pony, as shaggy as a wintering bear, eased himself into a grudging trot, while the boy, bowed over with his cap pulled down over his ears and eyebrows, held the reins slack and fell into a brown study.

b) I studied the harness, a real mystery. It met and clung in all sorts of unexpected places, it parted company in what appeared to be strategic seats of jointure.

c) It was mended sketchily in risky places with bits of hairy rope. Other seemingly unimportant parts were bound together irrevocably with wire.

d) The bridle was too long for the pony's stocky head, so he had shaken the bit out of his mouth at the start, apparently, and went his own way at his own pace.

Source: Holiday, by Katherine Ann Porter.

3. Finding Adjective Phrases

Do the same as you did in (1–2) above, using an excerpt from a text of your own choice (a poem, newspaper article, magazine advertisement, etc.). Analyze at least five adjective phrases that you find following the above guidelines.

4. Poetry Analysis

Find three examples of unique uses of adjectives in poetry (using a poem you have not yet analyzed elsewhere). Discuss as best you can how the poet makes use of adjectives for rhetorical effect. Why does the author choose to use these words in this particular way? Give as many details about the adjectives you analyze as you can. What are their semantic, morphological, and syntactic characteristics, and how are these manipulated for effect?

LANGUAGE DIVERSITY EXERCISES

1. Old English Adjectives

Adjectives in Old English were highly inflected; they expressed gender, case, and number. Adjectives also fell into strong or weak declension classes; strong adjectives expressed inflection through internal vowel changes, and weak ones through more regular affixation. Discuss two examples of strong and weak adjectives in Old English. Illustrate their inflectional patterns and show how they differ from adjective inflections in modern English. Also find two or three examples of adjectives that have survived into modern English from Old English, and discuss how their meanings have changed over time. Find two or three examples of Old English adjectives that have dropped out of the language. Have they been replaced in modern English by new adjectives?

2. Middle English Adjectives

Adjectival inflection changed after the coming of the French to England in the period after the Norman Invasion (1066). Old English adjectives were highly inflected, and Middle English ones less so. Using two or three examples, compare and contrast the development of adjectival inflection from Old English to Middle English. What kind of changes occurred, and how are they representative of larger developmental changes that were taking place in the language? What are some examples of "new" adjectives borrowed into English from French during the Middle English period?

3. The Historical Development of Degree Words

Trace the development of two grammatical degree words of your choice (choose from the list including *very/too/so/less/much/more/less/least/rather,* etc., but avoid words such as *extremely, incredibly, fantastically,* etc.) Where do these words come from? Do they derive from lexical categories or grammatical ones? What were their earlier meanings? What other characteristics distinguish their modern counterparts from their earlier ones? (You will have good luck using the Oxford English Dictionary for this exercise.)

4. Adjectives in Other Languages

For this exercise, compare the syntax, semantics, and morphology of adjectives in a language other than English with the English adjective system. Do adjectives in the language you choose occur in the same positions as they do in English? What are some of their inflectional and derivational affixes, and in what other ways are they formed? Do adjectives fall into the same kinds of semantic classes that they do in English? Give clear examples to illustrate these and any other interesting comparisons you come across.

5. Adjectives in Dialects of English Other Than Your Own

For this exercise, do the same as in (4), using a dialect of English other than your own. For example, you might look at some of the adjectives in the Pennsylvania Dutch dialect, a variety of English that is heavily influenced by German. How does the adjective system in this variety of English differ from your own (assuming you are not a speaker of Pennsylvania Dutch)? How is it similar?

CHAPTER REVIEW TERMS

Adjectives: as modifiers or predicates

Semantic classes: size, age, nationality, personality traits, material, etc.

Participial adjectives

Modifiers of adjectives: degree words, degree adverbs, nouns, other adjectives

Adjective phrases: prenominal position, postnominal position, after linking verbs

Tests for adjectives: the *very* test, the *linking verb* test

CHAPTER REVIEW EXERCISE

Choose from among the following options to create a chapter exercise. You may wish to add options from previous chapter exercises to make this exercise more comprehensive.
In the following texts:

a) List all adjectives.
b) Is the adjective phrase a predicate or a modifier?
c) What is the semantic class of the adjective (refer to Table 7.1)?
d) What position does the adjective phrase occur in (prenominal, postnominal, after a linking verb, or in some other position)?
e) Analyze the derivational and inflectional morphology of each adjective. (Use Table 7.2 for reference.)
f) Label any adjectives that are participial.
g) List any degree word the adjective is preceded by.

> Could foreign debt be the lever that moves poor countries to save their rain forests? President Bush apparently thinks so. The White House is backing a bold program to channel billions of dollars that Latin American governments owe Washington into local conservation projects. "Debt for nature" swaps are not new. Private groups are already busy raising cash to buy up foreign debt, trading the I.O.U.s back to the financially troubled debtors in return for commitments to acquire parks and conserve environmental resources in eight countries.
>
> Source: *The New York Times*, January 22, 1991, p. B5.

My grandmother gave me bad advice and good advice when I was in my early teens. For the bad advice, she said that I should become a barber because they made good money and listened to the radio all day. "Honey, they don't work como burros," she would say every time I visited her. She made the sound of donkeys braying. "Like that, honey!" For the good advice, she said that I should marry a Mexican girl. "No Okies, hijo"—she would say—"Look, my son. He marry one and they fight every day about I don't know what and I don't know what." For her, everyone who wasn't Mexican, black, or Asian were Okies. The French were Okies, the Italians in suits were Okies.

Source: Like Mexicans, by Gary Soto.

8

Adverbs and Adverb Phrases

*We don't just borrow words; on occasion, English has pursued
other languages down alleyways to beat them unconscious and rifle their
pockets for new vocabulary.*

Booker T. Washington

Introduction

In this chapter we discuss the semantics, morphology, and syntax of the lexical category *Adverb*. Adverbs are sometimes described as words that add "extra" information to sentences, information about where, when, or how an event or state occurs. Some examples are given in (1).

(1) a. They drove to Seattle *often/quickly*.
　　 b. *Now/evidently*, we can really have some fun.

As we will see, adverbs usually function semantically as *modifiers* of verbs or sentences. They are thus in some ways similar to adjectives, another class of words that can be modifiers. They differ from adjectives in crucial ways, however. Recall that semantically, adjectives provide descriptive information about nouns. Adverbs, on the other hand, supply a wide range of other kinds of descriptive information, including possibility, a speaker's attitude, time, manner, and place. Adjectives and adverbs also differ in their syntax, and though they overlap a bit in terms of morphology, there are several ways to distinguish these two categories.

In this chapter we return to the questions raised by degree adverbs such as *fantastically, incredibly, amazingly*. We will propose here that these adverbs are in fact members of the grammatical category Degree.

Semantic Classes of Adverbs

Adverbs have a number of different meanings and can be divided into a number of different semantic classes. Some possible semantic classes are given in Table 8.1.

Table 8.1
Semantic Classes of Adverbs

Possibility (convey information about truth of an action or event): probably, certainly, allegedly, possibly

The truck will *probably* break down if you drive it.

Attitude (convey attitude of speaker): fortunately, hopefully, obviously

Fortunately, the game didn't start on time.

Time (the time at which something occurred): now, then, immediately, sometimes, daily

Let's go *now!*

Aspect (duration, completion, habitual): still, yet, already, anymore, usually

The dishes aren't done *yet.*

Frequency: always, never, sometimes, seldom, often

Lily *never* picks up her socks.

Manner (the manner in which an action was done): quickly, quietly, slowly, carefully

They marched down the avenue *slowly.*

Place (location): here, there

You should put the papers *there.*

Focus: even, only, also, too

Even John knows better than that.

The range of information an adverb contributes to the sentence is thus quite broad. Adverbs can, for example, influence the tense and aspect of a sentence, as we can see in (3–4).

   (3)   a. You should call her.
         b. You should call her *now.*

   (4)   a. We drove about four hours.
         b. We drove about four hours *daily.*

In (3a), the modal *should* is in past tense, yet the tense interpretation could be either future or present. In (3b), with the addition of the adverb *now,* the tense interpretation of the sentence is unambiguously present. In (4a), the form of the verb (*drove*) is past tense, and the sentence is interpreted as past tense, and completed. In (4b), the sentence remains in past tense but its aspect changes from completed to habitual, with the addition of the adverb *daily.*

   Other examples of how the addition of an adverb to a sentence changes its semantics are given in (5).

(5) a. He will be back, *fortunately.*
     b. He will *possibly* be back.

In (5a), *fortunately* adds information about the speaker's attitude or opinion about the proposition *he will be back*. The addition of *possibly* in (5b), on the other hands, adds information about the possibility of his being back.

Adverbs therefore fit the criteria for lexical categories, at least in terms of their semantics. They contribute a number of different kinds of information to sentences they occur in, and alter the semantics of the sentence in important ways. We return to the meanings of adverbs in our discussion on their syntax. First, however, we turn to their morphological characteristics.

The Morphology of Adverbs

Adverbs come into the language in a variety of ways. We derive them from other words, in particular adjectives, through derivational morphology. One way we do this is by adding the affix *-ly* to adjectives, as in (6).

(6) probable, fortunate, hopeful, quick, easy => probably, fortunately, hopefully, quickly, easily

We have a number of other derivational affixes we use to form adverbs, as shown in (7).

(7) a. *-wise:* likewise, clockwise, crosswise
     b. *-ward:* backward, forward, toward, southward
     c. *-ways:* crossways, sideways, this-a-way(s)
     d. *-ally:* demonically, tragically

We also create adverbs by adding *-style* and *-fashion* to other words, as in (8).

(8) a. They ate their dinner *picnic-style* out on the porch.
     b. She wore her hair *punk-fashion,* sticking straight up and dyed black.

This morphological evidence supports the claim that the category Adverb is a lexical, rather than grammatical, category, an open class of words to which new members are productively added.

Flat Adverbs

Though many adverbs end in *-ly*, adverbs do not always have a distinctive morphological form. For example, we saw in Table 8.1 that *often, never, seldom,* and so on, have no particular morphological affix that helps us recognize them as adverbs. In fact, there is an entire subclass of manner adverbs that lacks the

-ly affix. These are called **flat adverbs,** exemplified in (9). As you can see, some
have corresponding *-ly* forms, but some do not.

(9) a. He ran *fast/hard.* (in a fast/hard manner) (He ran **fastly/*hardly.*)
     b. The package arrived *late/*lately.* (*Lately* can of course be an adverb
        with a different meaning: *Have you seen any good movies lately?*)
     c. She turned *sharp/sharply* at the corner.

Flat adverbs are interesting, and potentially confusing, because they can
also function as adjectives when they occur in adjective positions. So in (10a),
the adjective phrases *fast/hard* in prenominal position modify the noun *pitch,*
and in (10b), the adjective phrases *fast/hard* are the complements of *seem,* a linking verb that can be followed by an adjective phrase.

(10) a. The *fast/hard* pitch caught the batter unaware.
      b. The pitch seemed *fast/hard.*

We know that *fast/hard* are adjective phrases in (10) on the basis of evidence
that adverbs do not occur in prenominal position, nor do they occur after linking verbs.

As we saw above, some, but not all, flat adverbs also have-*ly* forms. For
instance, we hear both (11a) and (11b), and some of you, depending on dialect,
may prefer one form over the other.

(11) a. They left the room *quickly/slowly.* (*-ly* adverb)
      b. They left the room *quick/slow.* (flat adverb)

Omitting the-*ly* on an adverb is assumed by some to be "incorrect grammar."
From a descriptive point of view, however, the process of omitting *-ly* is a productive descriptive grammatical rule for a large number of English speakers.

Adverbs are morphologically similar to adjectives in forming their comparative and superlative forms with the inflectional affixes *-er/-est.* Like adjectives,
some adverbs express the grammatical functions of comparison syntactically, by
occurring in construction with degree words *more/most* and *less/least,* or preceded by other adverbs that express degree, as we saw above in the section on
the semantics of adverbs. Flat adverbs tend to form the comparative/superla-
tive by adding the affixes *-er/-est,* and *-ly* adverbs tend to sound more natural
with *more/most* and *less/least.*

(12) a. He talks *fast/faster/fastest.*
      b. He talks* *more/*less fast.*

(13) a. He talks **quicklier/*quickliest.*
      b. He talks *more/less quickly.*

Summarizing this section, we have seen that we form adverbs using a range
of different derivational affixes, including, but certainly not limited to, the affix

-ly. We also coin adverbs. Adverbs express inflectional morphology indicating comparison in much the same way as adjectives. The category Adverb thus clearly patterns with other lexical categories we have discussed in being a category to which we productively add new members.

The derivational and inflectional morphology of adverbs is summarized in Table 8.2.

We turn now to the syntax of adverbs, and in particular, to their status as phrases. We will, as in past chapters, investigate adverb phrases using the tools of movement, pronominalization, and coordination. We then turn to the different positions adverb phrases occur in.

Categories That Introduce Adverbs: Degree Words

Adverbs, like adjectives, can be introduced by members of the grammatical category Degree, including words such as *very/so/too*.

(14)   *very/so/too* quickly

Adverbs can also be introduced by–*ly* words that express degree, words we suggested may be grouped together with *very/so/too* as members of the grammatical category Degree in Chapter 7.

(15)   *amazingly/incredibly/fantastically* quickly

Adverbs thus pattern with adjectives in being introduced by degree words such as *very* and also by **degree adverbs** such as *amazingly*. Let us look at some evidence in support of the claim that these words function here as degree modifiers rather than as members of the category Adverb.

As we mentioned in Chapter 7, most traditional grammars classify *very/so/too* and *-ly* degree words such as *amazingly* as members of the category Adverb.

Table 8.2
Derivational and Inflectional Moprhology of Adverbs

Derivational Affixation:	*-wise:* likewise, clockwise, crosswise
	-ward: backward, forward, toward, southward
	-ways: crossways, sideways, this-a-way(s)
	-ary: secondary, primary
	-ly: madly, disgustedly, demonically, tragically
	-style / -fashion: picnic-style, punk-fashion
Inflectional Affixation:	*-er:* faster, tighter, softer
	-est: fastest, tightest, softest

In fact, we saw in that chapter that *very* and *so* are defined as similar in meaning to–*ly* adverbs such as *amazingly/incredibly*. While this classification makes some sense, as both of these elements syntactically introduce both adverbs and adjectives and both semantically express degree, it does not capture *certain* differences between degree words on the one hand, and -*ly* adverbs on the other.

For example, though both *very/so/too* and *incredibly/terribly/amazingly* can function as degree words, the latter can also function as manner adverbs, as in (16). Degree words, on the other hand, have no such function.

(16)   Wynton Marsalis played *incredibly/terribly/amazingly* yesterday.

(17)   *Wynton Marsalis played *very/so/too* yesterday.

In (16), *incredibly/terribly/amazingly* are manner adverbs, describing the way in which Wynton Marsalis played. No corresponding interpretation is available for *very/so/too*. Notice, however, that the semantics of *incredibly/terribly/amazingly* changes when they introduce adverbs or adjectives; they are no longer interpreted as manner adverbs, but rather, like *very/so/too*, as expressing degree or intensity.

We can further illustrate the semantic difference between *incredibly/terribly/amazingly* in (16), as manner adverbs, and in (15), as degree words, in the following way. Manner adverbs cannot introduce other manner adverbs, as we see in (18).

(18)   *Wynton Marsalis played *softly* assertively.

The degree words *incredibly/terribly/amazingly*, however, *can* introduce manner adverbs, as we see in (19).

(19)   Wynton Marsalis played *incredibly* assertively.

We do not expect (19) to be grammatical, if *incredibly* is interpreted as a manner adverb in this position. It thus appears that when adverbs such as *incredibly/terribly/amazingly* introduce adverbs (or adjectives), they function not as manner adverbs, but as degree words.

We will assume that when they introduce adjectives or adverbs, *incredibly/terribly/amazingly* are actually members of the grammatical category Degree, whose members include *very/so/too*, and others. The manner adverbs *incredibly/terribly/amazingly*, on the other hand, are members of the lexical category Adverb.

We can now formulate a phrase structure rule for adverb phrases, namely (20), which is similar to the rule we proposed for adjective phrases in the previous chapter. We now understand DEG to include *incredibly/terribly/amazingly* as well as *very/so/too*, and so on.

(20)   ADVP => (DEG) ADV

We can diagram some of the above adverb phrases as in (21).

(21)

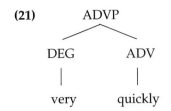

In (21), the degree word and following adverb are constituents of a larger adverb phrase. Syntactically, members of the category Degree pattern with other grammatical categories in introducing a member of a lexical category, in this case, the category Adverb.

To support our claims about the above possible structures of adverb phrases, we once again call on our tests for phrases, movement, pronominalization, and coordination. (22b) illustrates that *very* can be pronominalized by *how*, and (22c) shows that [*how beautifully*] can in turn front to sentence-initial position through WH-Movement.

(22) a. She played *very beautifully.*
      b. She played *how beautifully?*
      c. *How beautifully* did she play?

The patterns in (23) show that the adverb phrase *very beautifully* can also be pronominalized by *how*, and fronted by WH-Movement.

(23) a. She played *very beautifully.*
      b. She played *how?*
      c. *How* did she play?

It appears, then, that on the basis of evidence from WH-Movement, degree words and the adverbs they introduce form syntactic phrases.

We can further substantiate this claim with evidence from coordination. Recall that phrases can be coordinated only with other phrases. We thus expect the sequence [degree word + adverb] to be able to be conjoined with other adverb phrases. That this is the case is illustrated in (24–25).

(24) She played the sonata [very softly and quite expressively].

(25)

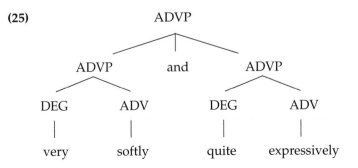

As we also might expect, adverbs can be coordinated, "sharing" the same degree word, as in (26), whose relevant phrase structure is given in (27).

(26)   She played the sonata [very softly and expressively].

(27)

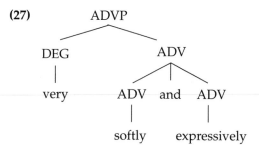

In the following section we turn our attention to the positions that adverb phrases occur in. Interestingly, their positions do not necessarily correlate with their meanings. This provides us with evidence once again for the modularity of grammar, a system in which syntax and semantics interact but are nevertheless also in certain ways distinct.

Adverb Phrase Positions

Adverb phrases appear in a number of different syntactic positions in the clause. They can occur sentence initially, or sentence finally, as in (28).

(28)   a. *Unfortunately,* John ate the last cookie.
          b. John ate the last cookie, *unfortunately.*

They can also occur before or after the first (tensed) auxiliary in the sentence, as in (29).

(29)   a. John *never* could have found the place.
          b. John could *never* have found the place.

They can also occur before the main verb, as in (30)

(30)   John could have *completely* forgotten the test.

The five possible adverb positions illustrated in (28–30) are listed in Table 8.3, along with examples. You may not agree with the distribution of adverbs discussed here (for which I am using my own dialect), but the point is that adverbs occur in these five basic positions, though exactly which ones occur in a specific position might vary from speech community to speech community.

Table 8.3
Syntactic Positions of Adverbs

Position One: sentence initial

> *Nimbly,* the cat leaped from the sofa to the chair.

Position Two: before the first auxiliary

> The criminal *still* could be portrayed as a victim.

Position Three: after the first auxiliary

> The criminal could *never* be portrayed as a victim.

Position Four: before the main verb

> The children could have been *cleverly* hiding from sight.

Position Five: sentence final

> The quarterback dropped the ball *clumsily.*

The positions exemplified in Table 8.3 are numbered for ease of reference in our subsequent discussion.

We might say then, on the basis of the evidence in (28–30), that adverbs can occur in five different positions in the sentence and leave it at that. This is, as you might expect, not the whole story, however. Not all adverbs, it turns out, can occur in *all* of these positions. A few examples to illustrate are given in (31–32), where we see that *yet* does not share the same syntactic distribution as *happily*, and *never* differs in this way from *evidently*. (For the relevant interpretations, the adverbs in final position must be interpreted without comma intonation.)

(31) a. The child must not have **yet/happily* kissed the kitten.
       b. The child must not *yet/*happily* have kissed the kitten.
       c. The child must not have kissed the kitten *yet/happily.*

(32) a. *Evidently/*never,* the child must have kissed the kitten.
       b. The child must **evidently/never* have kissed the kitten.
       c. The child must have kissed the kitten **evidently/*never.*

It would take a detailed investigation of adverb positions to determine exactly which adverbs occur in which positions, and why. We will of course undertake no such comprehensive study here. Rather, we will simply observe that adverbs as a general class occur in the five positions in Table 8.3, which we can express in terms of phrase structure as in (33). Adverb positions are notated only with numbers, corresponding to Table 8.3.

(33)   Adverb Positions

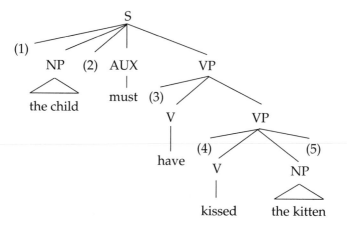

One issue that must be addressed in our discussion of (33) is: how must we rewrite the rules for VP and S to generate sentences with adverbs in the five positions in Table 8.3? We might, for example, propose (34).

(34)   S => (ADV) NP (ADV) (AUX) (ADV) VP (ADV)

According to (34), adverbs occur in five positions. The rule in (34) says nothing about which adverbs can occur where; rather, it predicts, incorrectly, that any adverb can occur anywhere. This suggests that phrase structure rules are designed to encode only the *possible* positions in which a phrase occurs. Details concerning the actual distribution of different kinds of adverbs must be derived from some other grammatical property or principle. We will thus assume that (34) adequately captures only the basic generalizations about the *possible* positions in which adverb phrases occur.

Summary

In this chapter we have seen that **adverbs** fall into a number of different semantic classes, and that morphologically, adverbs are formed by several different processes of derivational affixation, as well as by other word formation rules. Most notably, many adverbs have -*ly* endings, and others, called **flat adverbs,** have no endings at all. Adverbs also express comparative and superlative inflectional morphology, and in this way pattern with adjectives. Syntactically, adverb phrases typically include a head adverb introduced by an optional member of the grammatical category **Degree,** a grammatical category in which we included *very/so/too* and **degree adverbs** such as *incredibly/fantastically/amazingly*. Adverb phrases occur in five different positions in the sentence. Finally, we considered some of the issues that arise when we attempt to write phrase structure rules for the positions in which adverb phrases occur. We found that phrase structure rules can express only broad generalizations about the positions of adverb phrases as a class. They do not predict, for example, the distribution of particular adverb phrases, not all of which occur in the same positions.

DISCOVERY PROBLEMS

Problem 1. Semantics of Adverbs

Find a (short) text in which there are at least three or four adverbs. Write the text out omitting the adverbs, and explain how this omission changes the tone and meaning of the text. What kinds of information do adverbs provide? Analyze the semantic class of each adverb, using Table 8.1.

Problem 2. Flat Adverbs

Are the italicized words in the following sentences "flat" adverbs or adjectives? Explain your answer using semantic and syntactic evidence. For example, is the word a modifier of a noun (an adjective) or a modifier of a verb (an adverb)? What syntactic position does it occur in, and is it one in which adjectives or adverbs occur? What kinds of modifiers does each word take? Use the *very* and *linking verb* tests from Chapter 7 to help formulate your answers.

   a) She hammered the metal *flat*.
   b) She hammered the metal *hard*.
   c) We ate the carrots *fast*.
   d) We ate the carrots *nude*.
   e) He held the ball *tight*.

Think of three more flat adverbs that can also be adjectives, and make up sentences that illustrate this difference. Explain, using semantic and syntactic evidence, why you analyze the adverbs as adverbs, and the adjectives as adjectives.

Problem 3. *bad* and *badly*

We often hear people say that they *feel badly* about something, and we also hear *I feel bad* about something, perhaps just as often. You may also have strong feelings about which is "correct" and which is not, based on what you have been taught. Given what you now know about adjectives and adverbs, analyze the syntactic category of *bad* and then of *badly* when it is used in each of these ways. What conclusions can you draw about your own use of these words and your assumptions about correctness? Consider in your answer the use of (feeling) *well/good*. Can you make any interesting comparisons between *bad/badly* and *good/well* in this context?

Problem 4. Adverb Positions

We mentioned in the text that different adverbs can occur in different positions in the sentence. Try to determine how the adverbs *evidently/easily/probably/completely* differ in their distribution by inserting them into different syntactic positions (summarized in Table 8.3) in the sentence below. I have done *evidently* for you, to illustrate. Do the same with the other adverbs. Do they pattern together? What conclusions can you draw about their meanings and their positions?

    a) *Horatio *evidently* has been arrested.
    b) *Evidently,* Horatio has been arrested.
    c) *Horatio has been arrested *evidently.* (without a pause between *arrested* and *evidently*).
    d) Horatio has *evidently* been arrested.
    e) *Horatio has been *evidently* arrested.

TEXT ANALYSIS

1. Identifying Adverb Phrases:

Label all the adverbs in the following texts, and also identify any degree words that introduce them. Label the semantic class of each according to Table 8.1, and also identify which position they occur in, according to Table 8.3. Are any of these adverbs flat adverbs?

> The cattle hated being forcibly moved during a driving rain. They bawled angrily, and some hung their heads dejectedly and refused to move. Several disheveled, dirty, and wet cowboys urged their tired mounts into the head of distressed bovines, but the horses, feeling beaten and defeated, would often muster only brief spurts of energy, and would usually end up exiting the herd fearfully, to avoid being attacked by an angry steer. The cowboys themselves had never seemed so discouraged and blue. Fortunately, this would be the last drive.

2. Identifying Adverb Phrases

Follow the same instructions as in (1) in analyzing the adverb phrases in the following text.

It shames her how little the man eats, diddling his spoon around in his dish, perhaps raising his eyes once or twice to send her one of his shy, appreciative glances across the table, but never taking a second helping, just leaving it all for her to finish up—pulling his hand through the air with that dreamy gesture of his that urges her on. And smiling all the while, his daft tender-faced look. What did food mean to a working man like himself? A bother, a distraction, perhaps even a kind of price that had to be paid in order to remain upright and breathing.

Source: The Stone Diaries, by Carol Shields.

3. More Adverb Analysis

In texts of your choice, find examples of at least four sentences, each of which contains an adverb phrase. Rewrite each sentence as many ways as you can, to illustrate the possible positions the adverb phrase can occur in. (Use Table 8.3 as a guide.) Draw up your results in the form of a table that outlines the different positions of each of your adverb phrases. Does each occur in all five positions? How do they differ? Can you explain any of their differences based on their meanings?

LANGUAGE DIVERSITY EXERCISES

1. Adverbs in Old English

Research adverbs in Old or Middle English, and outline some of their basic syntactic, semantic, and morphological properties. How do they differ from their modern English counterparts? What kinds of modifiers occur with them, and are they similar to modern degree words?

2. Adverbs in Other Varieties of English

Find three examples of words used for adverbs in varieties of English other than your own, including English pidgins and English creoles. Analyze them according to the criteria in Tables 8.1, 8.2, and 8.3. What semantic classes do they fall under? What syntactic position do they occur in? Finally, discuss their inflectional or derivational morphology, if they have any.

3. Adverbs in Other Languages

As you might expect, adverbs in languages other than English differ in interesting ways from their English counterparts. Discuss the general syntax, morphology, and semantics of adverbs in a language other than English. How do they differ from adverbs in English?

CHAPTER REVIEW TERMS

adverbs and adverb phrases

different semantic classes of adverbs: possibility, attitude, time, aspect, frequency, manner, place, focus

flat adverbs

degree words and degree adverbs as members of the category Degree

the five different syntactic positions of adverb phrases

CHAPTER REVIEW EXERCISE

Choose from among the following options to create a chapter exercise. You may wish to add options from previous chapter exercises to make this exercise more comprehensive.

In the following texts:

a) Label the semantic class of each adverb in your list, using Table 8.1.
b) Identify any inflectional or derivational affixes of the adverbs in your list, using Table 8.2.
c) Identify the position of each adverb, using Table 8.3.
d) Label any flat adverbs.
e) Identify any degree words, including degree adverbs.

---

a) Impulsively, she lies back across the soft down comforter and pulls it around her, shroudlike, burying her face in it, dreaming of long-ago leisure days, of young adulthood and the stasis of contentment and no ambition.
b) "You're eating early." The idea of that glutinous mass in his stomach turns hers.
c) Yet there is a moment when she thinks how warm his body must be, through and through.
d) Twenty-four years together and it still happens like this now and then.

Source: Beyond Deserving, by Sandra Scofield.

There are two Muscle Beaches—separate places, though they're separated more by time than space. One still exists; it's easy to find. Just go down the boardwalk in Venice, a seaside community on the edge of Los Angeles. . . . On certain days, the Pit is filled with nearly naked men and women, competing in body-building. Spectators begin queuing up early in the morning for spaces on the boardwalk beside the Pit. When the body-jousting finally begins, the onlookers stare, gasp and go giddy.

Source: Muscle Beach, by Ken Chowder, *Sunset Magazine,* November 1998.

A word, finally, about the title of this chapter. As I have indicated, the idea of multiple intelligences is an old one, and I can scarcely claim any great originality for attempting to revive it once more. Even so, by featuring the word *idea* I want to underscore that the notion of multiple intelligences is hardly a proven scientific fact: it is, at most, an idea that has recently regained the right to be discussed seriously. Given the ambition and scope of this book, it is inevitable that this idea will harbor many shortcomings. What I hope to establish is that "multiple intelligences" is an idea whose time has come.

Source: Frames of Mind, by Howard Gardner.

9

Prepositions

Only where there is language is there world.
From *The Demon Lover* by Adrienne Rich

Introduction

In this chapter we investigate the syntax, semantics, and morphology of the category *Preposition*. You may recognize prepositions as including words such as *in/out/by/under/for/with*. This class of words raises some interesting questions with respect to the characterization of syntactic categories as lexical or grammatical. We find that although prepositions share certain characteristics with other lexical categories we have studied, they also pattern with grammatical categories in certain ways. For example, prepositions head their own phrases, just as do the lexical categories Adjectives, Adverbs, Nouns, and Verbs. Prepositions can also be introduced by members of a grammatical category, and again pattern in this way with lexical categories. We also find that prepositions, like verbs, can be *transitive* or *intransitive,* and that intransitive prepositions form a subclass of the category Preposition, what we will call *Particle.* Prepositions pattern with grammatical categories, however, in being a closed morphological class, and in having grammatical, rather than lexical, meanings. We will thus leave their status as a lexical or grammatical category open. We will discuss in some detail the syntax of prepositional phrases, including those in which the preposition is followed not by a noun phrase but rather by a clause. We will call such prepositions *subordinating prepositions.* We will also discuss prepositions that are followed by participial phrases, and *complex prepositional phrases,* in which a preposition is followed by another prepositional phrase. We will conclude by formulating a recursive phrase structure rule for prepositional phrases to account for these different structures.

The Semantics of Prepositions

Prepositions are the "little words" in English, such as *on/out/in/at,* that express a number of different kinds of relationships, such as time, space, direction, possession, cause. A preposition can also have more than one meaning; for example, the preposition *by* can be used a number of different ways, as in *by acci-*

dent/by air/by the river/by Maxine Hong Kingston/by the way. We consider the semantic classes of prepositions and their multiple meanings below.

There are a number of different aphorisms aimed at helping us remember the list of English prepositions. One is, "a preposition is anything a rabbit can do to a hill." A partial list of examples of prepositions is given in (1).

(1) The rabbit went
below, under, across, along, beyond, past, by, into, in, behind, down, over, around, up, through
the hill.

The prepositions in (1) are spatial or directional. Notice, however, that prepositions can also have other meanings. The ones in (2), for instance, are temporal:

(2) *since/at/by/until/after* 6:00

Prepositions can express other relationships as well, as we can see in Table 9.1. This table is not meant to include *all* of the possible meanings of prepositions, but rather to give you an idea of some of their possible interpretations.

You may have noticed that some of the prepositions above (more accurately, the prepositional *phrases*) overlap in some ways with adverbs, in expressing, for example, time or manner, as illustrated in (3).

(3) a. We will leave *at 6 p.m./now.*
b. She smiled *with glee/gleefully.*

For this reason, it is not uncommon to see prepositions in traditional grammars classified as *adverbs* in such contexts. You should be well aware by now, how-

Table 9.1
Semantic Classes of Prepositions

Space/direction: The rabbit ran *under* the gate.

Temporal: I have been working *since* this morning.

Cause: He was fired *for* the offense.

Means: We traveled *by* air.

Accompaniment: I would like my gardenburger *with* lettuce.

Support/opposition: We're *for/against* the idea.

Possession: That dog *of* Mary's ate my homework.

Concession: They came *despite* the weather.

Exception/addition: We had a great time *apart from/despite* the hurricane.

Instrument: We cut the cheesecake *with* a knife.

Benefactive: I baked cookies *for* the party.

ever, that such classifications tend to obscure certain important differences among syntactic categories. Prepositions do not, for example, semantically pattern with adverbs in a very consistent way, as we can see by comparing Table 9.1 with Table 8.1 in the previous chapter, which provides a list of some of the semantic classes of adverbs. They are clearly distinct morphologically and syntactically as well, as we shall see below.

Returning now to the semantics of prepositions, we can see from Table 9.1 that these words have a number of different meanings, suggesting that the category Preposition is a lexical category. Upon closer inspection, however, observe that the meanings of prepositions are grammatical; they express a relation between two things. More specifically, they indicate the relation of their noun phrase object to the rest of the sentence. A dictionary definition of the term *preposition* is given in (4), where *substantive* means, for our purposes, a noun phrase. Notice also that the category label for preposition is *Grammatical*.

(4)   **preposition** *(n) Gram.* 1. In some languages, a word that indicates the relation of a substantive to a verb, an adjective, or another substantive, as English *at, by, in, to, from,* and *with* . . .

The definition in (4) captures the generalization that a preposition such as *at*, for instance, indicates location or time of its noun phrase "object," what we will call the **prepositional object** or **object of the preposition.** In the prepositional phrase *at the store*, the preposition is locative, indicating that the prepositional object noun phrase *the store* is a location. In the prepositional phrase *at 6 p.m.,* on the other hand, *at* expresses a temporal relation, and thus the noun phrase *6 p.m.* has a temporal interpretation.

We further illustrate the grammatical/relational meaning of prepositions with the dictionary entry for *by* in (5).

(5)   **by** *(prep.)* 1. Next to; close to: *the window by the door.* 2. With the help of or use of; through: *He came by the back road.* 3. Up to and beyond; past: *He drove by the house* . . .

Prepositions thus have a number of different meanings, but these meanings are nevertheless grammatical in that they indicate a particular relation between a noun phrase and the rest of the sentence. Semantically, then, prepositions seem to pattern with other grammatical categories, in having interpretations limited to (a rather broad range, in this case,) grammatical relationships.

The Morphology of Prepositions

Prepositions are morphologically a closed class; we do not add new members through derivational affixation, blending, clipping, or the like. We do have a number of compound prepositions, such as *inside, outside, underneath, overhead, upside,* but compounding of prepositions is not particularly productive; we rarely create new ones.

Prepositions have no inflectional morphology; they are invariant in form. In fact, in some languages, including English, a preposition itself can indicate inflection, though not through inflectional morphology or any kind of change in morphological form. For example, the preposition *of* in English can express possessive, or genitive case, as we see in (6).

(6) a. the end of the chapter (the chapter's end)
     b. the rotation of the earth (the earth's rotation)

In different varieties of German, certain prepositions can be classified according to the case inflection of their objects. Some prepositions in German are accusative and must be followed by a noun phrase in accusative, or objective, case. Other prepositions are dative; objects that follow dative prepositions must have dative case (the case assigned to indirect objects in German depending on one's dialect). An example is given in (7).

(7) a. der Junge
         the-NOM boy
     b. ohne den Jungen
         without the-ACC boy
     c. mit dem Jungen
         with the-DAT boy

As illustrated in (7), the determiner *der* ("the") in German expresses morphological case; it can be nominative (*der*), accusative (*den*) or dative (*dem*). The case of the noun phrase *der Junge,* and hence the form of the determiner *der* changes, depending on the preceding preposition. The preposition *ohne* requires an object noun phrase with accusative case; hence, *der* shows up as *den*. The preposition *mit*, on the other hand, requires an object with dative case, and *der* must be *dem*.

The property of prepositions to indicate case inflection underscores their function as grammatical, rather than lexical, words, words that express a grammatical relationship between a noun phrase and the rest of the sentence rather than words that have intrinsic meaning or content themselves. The morphology of prepositions thus further supports their classification as a closed grammatical category, and is another way in which they are distinct from adverbs.

Categories That Introduce Prepositions

We have seen above that prepositions typically indicate a relation, namely that of a following noun phrase in the context of the rest of the sentence. This following noun phrase, or prepositional object (also called the object of a preposition), forms part of a larger *prepositional phrase*. A preliminary phrase structure rule for prepositional phrases is (8).

(8)   PP => P NP

We return to (8), and to further discussion of objects of prepositions momentarily. First, however, we will discuss a way in which prepositions, which appear to be members of a grammatical category, pattern with the lexical categories Noun, Verb, Adjective, and Adverb in being introduced by a set of grammatical words.

The grammatical words that introduce prepositions are difficult to label, and their meanings are difficult to define. This very difficulty suggests that such words are grammatical categories, whose meanings in some sense depend on the lexical category with which they occur. Syntactic and morphological evidence supports this claim, as we show below. Further, we will find that the grammatical words that introduce prepositions form a category distinct from others with which we are familiar, namely Determiner, Quantifier, Numeral, Auxiliary, and Degree.

Some examples of the grammatical words that introduce prepositional phrases are given in (9) (some of the examples in (9) may or may not be familiar to you, depending on your dialect).

(9)   The squirrel ran *flat/straight/right/plumb/slap/clear* **up** the tree, and
       all/clean **through** the house.

The words that introduce the prepositions *up* and *through* in (9) are not of the category Degree, which we can see from the evidence that they cannot also introduce adjectives or adverbs.

(10)   a. *The squirrel ran *straight/clear/right* quickly up the tree.
        b. *The squirrel is *straight/clear/right* angry.

(*Right* can be a synonym for *very*, as in *right quickly*, and in some dialects of English *She is right angry* is grammatical. Observe that its meaning in these contexts differs, however, from the meaning of *right* in (9). The point here is that *right* in (10) cannot have the same meaning as *right* in (9).)

Conversely, the degree words that introduce adjectives or adverbs, namely *very/so/too*, cannot introduce prepositions, further evidence that *right/straight/clear* are not of the same category as *very/so/too*.

(11)   a. The squirrel ran *very/so/too* quickly.
        b. The squirrel is *very/so/too* angry.
        c. *The squirrel ran *very/so/too* up the tree.

The above evidence suggests that *right/straight/clear* are not members of the category Degree. Notice, however, that these words can function as adjectives or adverbs themselves. We might hypothesize, then, that they are members of the category Adjective or Adverb.

(12)   a. His back was *straight*. (adjective)
        b. The sky was *clear*. (adjective)
        c. He played it *straight/right*. (adverb)

The meanings of *straight/right/clear* in (12) differ from those in (9), however. In the sentence *The squirrel ran clear up the tree*, for example, *clear* does not mean "without obstruction," as it does in (12b). Similarly, *right* in (12c) has a different meaning from *right* in (9); the former, but not the latter, means *correctly*. Although *straight* in *The squirrel ran straight up the tree* means something similar to *straight* in (12a), such as "in a straight line," or "directly," *straight* in (9) is not functioning syntactically as an adjective, as it cannot in this position be introduced by *very*. Indeed, none of the grammatical words that introduce prepositions can be so introduced, as we see in (13). This again differentiates them from their adjectival counterparts in (12).

(13) The squirrel ran *very flat/straight/right/plumb/slap/clear up the tree.

As illustrated in (14), we see that the adjectives and adverbs *straight/right/clear* can each be introduced by *very/so/too*.

(14) a. His back was *very* straight.
      b. The sky was *very* clear.
      c. He played it *very* straight/right.

Further evidence that *right/straight/clear* in (9) are neither adjectives nor adverbs is that they do not have superlative or comparative forms in this position, as we see in (15). When these words function as adjectives, on the other hand, they can take these affixes. (We omit *more right* from the discussion, because *right* is an adjective that cannot be modified by a degree word for semantic reasons; it is odd to be *more right*.)

(15) a. *straighter/*clearest up the tree.
      b. This is the *straightest/clearest* route.

It appears, then, that when *straight/clear/clean/right*, and so on introduce prepositions, they are functioning as members of a category other than Degree, Adjective, or Adverb. They are also morphologically invariant and lack lexical content (indeed, their meanings are difficult to define). They syntactically introduce another category, namely the category Preposition. They thus satisfy all of the criteria we have proposed for grammatical categories. We will assume that this is what they are. We will refer to them as grammatical **modifiers of prepositions.**

Prepositions: A Grammatical or Lexical Category?

We now are faced with an interesting conundrum, one that emerges in other descriptions of English grammar in a variety of ways. The classification of the category Preposition varies rather widely, for reasons you may already be aware of. Prepositions are considered lexical categories in some grammars (or *content words*, or *major categories*, depending on the terminology), and in others, they are analyzed as grammatical categories (as *structure words,* or *function words,* again depending on terminology). In still other classifications, prepositions are considered members of the lexical category Adverb, at least in certain contexts. The classification of the category Preposition reflects an overlap between what we have defined as lexical and grammatical categories, expressed by the criteria in Table 9.2, repeated from Chapter 2 (where it appeared as Table 2.1).

According to Table 9.2, the category Preposition has many of the earmarks of being a grammatical category; prepositions are members of a morphologically closed class, they are invariant in form, and their meanings are grammatical rather than lexical. Prepositions pattern with lexical categories, however, in being introduced by a class of grammatical words, including *right/straight/clear.* Prepositions also head their own phrases, as reflected by the phrase structure rule in (8). They thus differ from grammatical categories that introduce heads of phrases, such as those illustrated in (16).

(16)

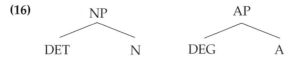

Prepositions are themselves heads of phrases, and are themselves introduced by grammatical modifiers as in (17) (we will use the category label MOD for the grammatical modifiers of prepositions *right/straight/clear,* etc.)

(17)

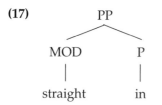

Prepositions thus pattern with lexical categories in heading a phrase and in being introduced by a grammatical category.

The characteristics of prepositions as grammatical and lexical categories are summarized in Table 9.3.

Table 9.2
Characteristics of Lexical and Grammatical Categories

	Lexical Categories	Grammatical Categories
Semantics	They have lexical content.	They have grammatical meanings or functions.
Morphology	They are open classes, and therefore admit new members.	They are closed classes, and do not admit new members.
Syntax	They head phrases.	They introduce a lexical category (usually the head of a phrase).

Table 9.3
Characteristics of Prepositions

Semantics: They have grammatical meanings or functions, like other **grammatical** categories.

Morphology: They are a closed class like other **grammatical** categories.

Syntax: They head phrases like other **lexical** categories.

They can be introduced by a grammatical category, like other **lexical** categories.

Though we might hope for some symmetry in our analysis of syntactic categories, what we find instead is that prepositions exhibit characteristics that cut across our lexical/grammatical distinction. This same asymmetry is also reflected in the diversity of approaches to prepositions in other grammars. This suggests either that prepositions are simply exceptional in this respect, or that our criteria for category membership may need to be revised in such a way as to account for the patterns we see in the category Preposition. For our purposes, it is enough to point out that the category Preposition raises some very interesting questions about the nature of syntactic categories, questions that might lead us to a better understanding of the organization of grammar in general.

The Phrase Structure of Prepositional Phrases

We will now turn to a discussion of the syntax of prepositional phrases. First, our preliminary phrase structure rule for prepositional phrases in (8) can now be revised as (18), given the above discussion.

(18) PP => (MOD) P NP

We have so far taken for granted that a preposition heads a larger phrase that includes a noun phrase object. Let us now test this hypothesis with movement, pronominalization, and coordination.

As we see in (19), prepositional phrases can be pronominalized by *where*, and fronted by WH-Movement.

(19) a. The ship sailed *under the bridge.*
　　　 b. The ship sailed *where?*
　　　 c. *Where* did the ship sail?

The phrase structure in (20) illustrates that the prepositional phrase *under the bridge* can be coordinated with another phrase, *over the dam*, which is what we expect if these two groups of words form larger syntactic phrases.

(20)

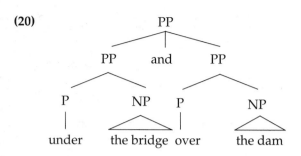

In (21) the prepositions *under* and *over* are coordinated, forming a larger prepositional phrase.

(21)

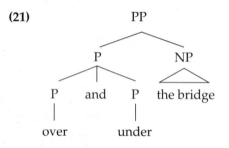

Both of the highest prepositional phrases in (20–21) can undergo WH-Movement, as we see in (22) and (23), respectively.

(22) a. The canoe went *under the bridge and over the dam.*
         b. The canoe went *where?*
         c. *Where* did the canoe go?

(23) a. The water went *over and under the bridge.*
         b. The water went *where?*
         c. *Where* did the water go?

We can conclude from the above evidence that our phrase structure rule for prepositional phrases in (18) correctly expresses the generalization that a preposition and its object (and an optional grammatical modifier introducing the preposition, which you can test for yourself by adding *straight/clear/right* to any of the examples above) form a syntactic phrase.

Intransitive Prepositions: Particles

So far, the examples of prepositions we have looked at have all been **transitive,** prepositions that form a phrase with a noun phrase object. This transitivity is encoded into our phrase structure rule in (18). English also has a class of prepositions that are **intransitive,** that do not take noun phrase objects. Indeed, these prepositions do not form a syntactic phrase with another constituent at all. To distinguish these intransitive prepositions from transitive ones, we will give intransitive ones a different name, **Particle.**

The Syntax of Particles

Some examples of sentences with particles are given in (24).

(24) a. We turned *out* the light.
      b. The students handed *in* the papers.
      c. He put *on* his hat.

As for the syntax of particles, as you can see in (24), *out, in,* and *on* all occur to the right of the verb. They can also, as you may recall from Chapter 3, occur to the right of the direct object of the verb, as in (25).

(25) a. We turned the light *out.*
      b. The students handed the papers *in.*
      c. He put his hat *on.*

In Chapter 3 we accounted for the different orders of particles and noun phrases in (24–25) by proposing a movement rule of **Particle Shift,** whereby the particle moves to the right over a direct object noun phrase of the verb. Transitive prepositions, in contrast to particles, cannot undergo this rule, as we see in (26).

(26) a. We turned *into* the street. => *We turned the street *into.*
      b. The students ran *in* the race. => *The students ran the race *in.*
      c. He put the cap *on* the bottle. => *He put the cap the bottle *on.*

There are various ways we might approach this syntactic difference between prepositions and particles in (24–26). Suppose we assume, for instance, that particles, like other prepositions, head prepositional phrases. The relevant phrase structures are given below. (27) corresponds to (24a), and (28) to (26a).

(27)

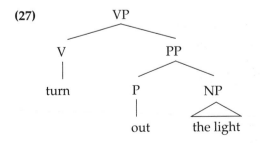

(28)

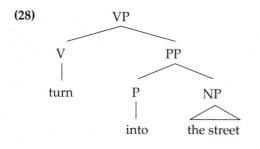

If both prepositions and particles have the same syntactic structure, we have no obvious way to explain why particles, but not prepositions, can undergo Particle Shift. How would a child learn that this operation is possible in (27) but not in (28)? If we propose, however, that particles are intransitive prepositions, and thus occur under P without a noun phrase object, we can distinguish constructions with particles from those with prepositions in the following way:

(29)

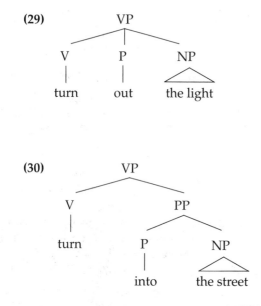

(30)

The particle in (29) is an intransitive preposition: it does not form a constituent with a noun phrase object. Rather, *the light* in (29) is the noun phrase object of the verb. The preposition in (30), on the other hand, is transitive: *the street* is the noun phrase object of the preposition, rather than the noun phrase object of the verb.

We can also assume that particles move to the right over the object via Particle Shift, as illustrated in (31).

(31)

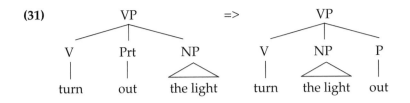

If we assume that Particle Shift applies only to intransitive prepositions, then we explain why it fails to apply to *into* in (30). This preposition is part of a larger phrase, namely PP, and thus not in the appropriate configuration to undergo Particle Shift.

Further evidence in support of this structural distinction between prepositions and particles illustrated in (29–30) comes from the Passive movement rule. Recall that this rule applies to direct object noun phrases, as illustrated in (32).

(32) a. Hortense walked *the dog*. => *The dog* was walked by Hortense.
 b. Baryshnikov danced *the part*. => *The part* was danced by Baryshnikov.
 c. The kids played *the game*. => *The game* was played by the kids.

As we might expect, Passive does not apply to objects of prepositions. We thus cannot passivize the noun phrase *the street* in the sentence in (33).

(33) a. The students turned into *the street*.
 b. **The street* was turned into by the students.

Notice, however, that we can passivize the noun phrase in constructions with particles, as in (34).

(34) a. We turned *the lights* out.
 b. *The lights* were turned out by us.

We explain the contrasts in (33–34) by adopting the structural distinction between transitive prepositions and particles in (29–30). In (29), the noun phrase *the light* is the object of the verb, and hence can undergo Passive. In (30), *the street* is the object of the preposition, and Passive cannot apply to it. Without the structural distinction between prepositions and particles we have no way to explain the syntactic patterns that arise from Particle Shift and Passive.

We capture the distinction between prepositions and particles by proposing the phrase structure rule for prepositions in (35).

(35) PP => (MOD) P (NP)

Again, the phrase structure rule in (35) tells us only so much, namely that some prepositions take objects and that others do not. Information concerning which prepositions are transitive, and which intransitive, must be expressed by some other component of the grammar other than phrase structure rules.

Finally, our analysis of particles as intransitive prepositions is consistent with, and thus supported by, one more piece of evidence about the distinction between prepositions and particles. To illustrate, consider the sentences in (36).

(36)   a. We jumped *up/around/in/down*.
       b. Shut *up*.
       c. Oh come *on!*
       d. She broke *off* right at the good part.
       e. Hortense looked *out*.
       f. They moved *about*.

In (36) the prepositions all lack objects. The verbs also lack objects; hence, Particle Shift cannot apply, as there is no noun phrase for the particle to shift over. Nevertheless, we know the prepositions in (36) are particles, because they are intransitive.

The Semantics of Particles

Particles also differ semantically from prepositions. Particles seem to contribute to the semantics of the verb in a way in which prepositions do not. That is, the semantic unit [verb + particle] has a unique nonliteral meaning, different from the meaning of the verb without a particle. For instance, the presence of a particle changes the meanings of the verbs *run* and *turn* in (37–38) quite significantly.

(37)   a. He ran *up* a big hill (preposition *up*)
       b. He ran *up* a big bill (particle *up*)

(38)   a. The kites turned *in* the wind (preposition *in*)
       b. The students turned *in* their papers (particle *in*)

Up in (37a) is a directional preposition, and *run* is a verb of motion. *Run up* in (37b) has an entirely different meaning, however, namely to *accrue*. In (38a), *turn* is again a motion verb, and *in* indicates location or source. In (38b), on the other hand, *turn in* means to *give*.

That particles and the verbs with which they occur have idiomatic meanings reflects the fact that historically, particles were syntactically part of the verb. This situation is still evident in modern German, a language to which English is closely related.

(39)   a. *mitgehen: mit* = with, *gehen* = to go; "to go with/accompany"
       b. *aufstellen: auf* = up, *stellen* = to set; "to set up"

Furthermore, in traditional grammar, particles and the verbs they occur with are often called *two-word* or *multiword* verbs. These labels are intended to capture the semantic generalization illustrated by the contrasts in (37–38). We have seen, however, that the semantics of verb-particle constructions are not necessarily reflected syntactically; that is, the verb and particle do not form a consituent, even though they appear to be semantically linked. Once again, we have evidence that semantics is not always reflected by syntax, and vice versa.

More Prepositional Phrases

So far we have discussed only transitive and intransitive prepositions, prepositions that either take a noun phrase object after them or nothing at all. Prepositions appear in a number of other kinds of constructions, however, in what we will call *subordinating* prepositional phrases. Some examples are given in (40). Other examples of **subordinating prepositions** include *since, though, although*.

(40) Mary left   *after* she talked to John.
                 because she was depressed.
                 while no one was looking.
                 when her mother called.

The prepositions in (40) are all followed by sentences, or what we will analyze in Chapter 10 as *subordinate clauses*. We discuss these prepositional phrases again in Chapter 12. For now, however, we will simply observe that certain prepositions take clauses rather than noun phrases after them, and have the basic structure in (41).

(41)

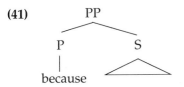

Still other prepositions take verb phrases, or *participial phrases,* after them. These prepositions are not necessarily *subordinating,* because the participial phrases that follow them are not clauses. Some examples are given in (42).

(42) Mary left   *after* watching the last game.
                 before talking to John.
                 by taking a cab.

Some linguists argue that the participial phrases in (42) are in fact clauses, as they have a "concealed" subject position, which we interpret, for example, as *Mary.* We will not pursue this here. Rather, we will simply analyze the prepositional phrases in (42) as ones in which the preposition takes a participial phrase, rather than a noun phrase or clause, and give them the structure in (43), where participial phrases are verb phrases, or VP.

(43)   PP

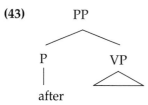

P   VP

after

And finally, (44) illustrates that prepositions can also take other prepositional phrases after them.

(44)   a. Ali pushed Forman *up against the ropes.*
      b. The ice is *over under the bridge.*
      c. Shirley Maclaine is *out on a limb.*
      d. The cows are *over under the trees.*

The **complex prepositional phrases** in (44) have the structure in (45).

(45)   PP

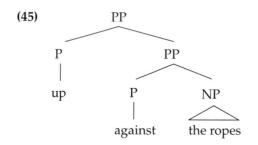

P   PP

up   P   NP

against   the ropes

As you can see in (45), the phrase structure rule for prepositional phrases is recursive, allowing one prepositional phrase to occur inside another. We have also
seen that prepositional phrases can be followed by noun phrases, clauses, and
verb phrases. We must therefore revise the phrase structure rule in (18) as in (46).

(46)   PP => (MOD) P $\left(\left\{\begin{matrix} NP \\ S \\ VP \\ PP \end{matrix}\right\}\right)$

According to (46), prepositions can take a number of different kinds of phrases
after them. They can also take no phrase at all, and thus be intransitive; in this
case the preposition is what we call a *particle.*

Summary

In this chapter we have discussed the semantics, morphology, and syntax of the
category *Preposition.* Prepositions form a morphologically closed class and are

in this way similar to other grammatical categories. Prepositions are also "grammatical" with respect to their semantics, as they express grammatical relationships, typically of noun phrases, to the rest of the sentence. The syntax of prepositions is, we find, rather complex. Prepositions head their own phrases and can be introduced by a grammatical category, what we called grammatical **modifiers of prepositions.** In this way they are similar to other lexical categories, which are also introduced by grammatical categories. Prepositions thus appear to have characteristics of both grammatical and lexical categories.

Prepositions can also be either **transitive** or **intransitive.** Transitive prepositions take noun phrase objects, or **prepositional objects,** and intransitive prepositions take no objects at all. We called intransitive prepositions **particles,** and showed that they differ syntactically from other prepositions by undergoing **Particle Shift.** We supported the syntactic analysis of particles as intransitive prepositions with evidence from Passive. Particles differ from other prepositions semantically as well, by forming an idiomatic semantic unit with a verb. Particles are not, however, syntactically *part* of the verb. The syntax of particles thus does not necessarily reflect their semantic relationship to the verb.

We concluded the chapter with a discussion of some of the prepositions that take phrases other than noun phrases. Here, we introduced **subordinating prepositions,** which take clauses, or more specifically, subordinate clauses, after them. We also saw that prepositions can take other prepositional phrases after them, forming **complex prepositional phrases.** Still others take participial phrases. We proposed a recursive phrase structure rule to account for the distribution of different kinds of phrases with which prepositions form prepositional phrases.

DISCOVERY PROBLEMS

Problem 1. Phrase Structure Practice

Diagram any prepositional phrases you find in the following nursery rhymes, using the phrase structure rule in (46). Use triangle notation to diagram any subordinate clauses and participial phrases that follow prepositions if you wish. List any particles you find, and try to diagram the verb phrases they occur in.

> **Little Jack Horner**
>
> Little Jack Horner sat in a corner
> Eating of Christmas pie.
> He put in his thumb,
> And pulled out a plum.
> And said "What a good boy am I!"

> **The Man In Our Town**
>
> There was a man in our town,
> And he was wondrous wise,
> He jumped into a bramble bush,
> And scratched out both his eyes;
> But when he saw his eyes were out,
> With all his might and main,
> He jumped into another bush,
> And scratched them in again.

Problem 2. More Phrase Structure Practice

Do the same as above for the following sentences, which are a bit harder to analyze than the sentences in Problem 1.

> a) I was reading as I had never read before.
> b) What my eye missed, my hands found and my head construed.
> c) I was flattening sheets of paper, piecing together others carelessly torn up, setting them in piles and filing them in my memory at the same time.
> d) I was doing in hours what once I would have done in weeks, because hours, unless I was mistaken, were all I had.
>
> *Source: Our Game,* by John LeCarré.

Problem 3. Prepositions or Adverbs?

Consider the following sentence, which includes a number of terms typically analyzed in traditional grammar as *adverbs.*

The rabbit hopped *outside/downhill/downstream/around/throughout.* Are the italicized words *adverbs,* according to the criteria for this category we discussed in Chapter 8? Are they prepositions or particles or some other category? Illustrate your answer with the appropriate example sentences to make your point, using the different characteristics of syntactic categories you are now familiar with.

*Problem 4. PP Preposing

A movement rule that applies exclusively to prepositional phrases is called **PP Preposing.** The operation of this rule is illustrated below.

(1)   a.   The fox dashed *over the bridge.*
       b.   *Over the bridge* dashed the fox.

(2)   a.   The cat lay *under the bed.*
       b.   *Under the bed* lay the cat.

Describe what has to happen to derive the (b) sentences from the (a) sentences. Which constituents move? In particular, how does PP Preposing differ from the rule that derives the (a) sentences from the (b) ones in (3–4)?

(3)   a.   The fox dashed *over the bridge.*
       b.   *Over the bridge* the fox dashed.

(4)   a.   The cat lay *under the bed.*
       b.   *Under the bed* the cat lay.

Other data to consider are given in (5–6).

(5)   a.   The fox chased the squirrel *over the bridge.*
       b.   **Over the bridge* chased the fox the squirrel.

(6)   a.   The cat ate the mouse *under the bed.*
       b.   **Under the bed* ate the cat the mouse.

Why does PP Preposing fail in (5–6)? How can you now informally state the rule of PP Preposing, so that it will not produce (3–4) or (5–6) but only (1–2)?

When you are satisfied that you understand the differences among (1–2), (3–4), and (5–6), list in sentences from texts of your own choosing three or four examples of PP Preposing. Poetry is a good place to look for constructions in which PP preposing has applied.

*Problem 5. PP Preposing of Complex Prepositional Phrases

After completing Problem 4 you should have a fairly good idea of how PP Preposing works. Now, apply PP Preposing to the following complex prepositional phrases. Does the rule generate grammatical results? What does this tell you about the phrase structure of complex prepositional phrases?

a)   Forman fell *up against the ropes.*
b)   The ice went *over under the bridge.*
c)   The dog came *in from the storm.*
d)   The cows are *over under the trees.*

Formulate three or four more examples of sentences with complex prepositional phrases that behave in the same way as those in (a–d) with respect to PP
Preposing.

*Problem 6. Particles and PP Preposing

Given what we have said here about the syntax of particles, and what we now
know about PP Preposing after doing Problems (4–5), we can now use PP
Preposing as a test for the status of a preposition as transitive or intransitive (a
particle). To see why this is the case, try to apply PP Preposing to what may
appear to be prepositional phrases in the following sentences. What happens?
How do your results support a syntactic distinction between prepositions and
particles?

a) Lucy turned in her medal.
b) His therapist always brought up very uncomfortable issues.
c) Nadine was wringing out the towel.
d) The president of the university called out the graduating seniors' names.

Problem 7. Coordination of Prepositions and Particles

For this exercise, try to construct your own examples of "tests" using coordination to determine the constituency of prepositional phrases. Construct your
answer on the basis of the following instructions.
Can you:

- coordinate two prepositional phrases, illustrating their status as syntactic units?
- coordinate two prepositions?
- coordinate two prepositional objects?
- coordinate prepositions introduced by a single grammatical modifier?
- coordinate two particles?

How does coordination of prepositions differ from coordination of particles? In
what ways can coordination provide us with evidence for the syntactic distinction between prepositions and particles?

TEXT ANALYSIS

I. Analyzing Prepositional Phrases and Particles

In a text of your choice, find at least four sentences with transitive and/or
intransitive prepositions. Diagram each prepositional phrase and each particle,
and explain, in the case of the particles, why you analyzed them as particles.
Base your answer on both syntactic and semantic evidence.

2. More Analysis

Read the following texts and label all the prepositional phrases, particles, and grammatical modifiers of prepositions.

> The old man dropped the line and put his foot on it and lifted the harpoon as high as he could and drove it down with all his strength, and more strength he had just summoned, into the fish's side just behind the great chest fin that rose high in the air to the altitude of a man's chest. He felt the iron go in and he leaned on it and drove it further and then pushed all his weight after it.
>
> *Source: The Old Man and the Sea,* by Ernest Hemingway.

> When I was growing up I used to think that the best thing about coming from Des Moines was that it meant you didn't come from anywhere else in Iowa. By Iowa standards, Des Moines is a Mecca of cosmopolitanism, a dynamic hub of wealth and education, where people wear three piece suits and dark socks, often simultaneously. During the annual state high school basketball tournament, when the hayseeds from out in the state would flood into the city for a week, we used to accost them downtown and snidely offer to show them how to ride an escalator or negotiate a revolving door.
>
> *Source: Fat Girls in Des Moines,* by Bill Bryson.

3. Poetry Analysis

Find three examples of unique uses of prepositional phrases and/or particles in a poem of your choice. Does the author use these constructions in any particularly interesting way? Also, identify any cases in which an author uses the movement rules that apply to prepositional phrases or particles, such as PP Preposing, or Particle Shift, to create a rhetorical effect.

4. The Semantics of Prepositional Phrases

Find a text that includes four or five prepositional phrases. Try to reword the text without using the prepositional phrases, by using adverbs instead, if you can. What does this tell us about the semantics of prepositional phrases, and how they compare semantically with adverb phrases?

5. Create a Minilesson

Create a minilesson in which you introduce prepositional phrases to students at the secondary or elementary school level. What kinds of diagnostics for prepositional phrases would you use at this level? What would be your goal, and what would you want students to take away from such a lesson? How can you present the material in a creative way (using, for example, rabbits and hills)?

LANGUAGE DIVERSITY EXERCISES

1. The Historical Development of Prepositions

The grammatical information conveyed by prepositional phrases in modern English was in Old English sometimes expressed as noun inflection. As a result, the inventory and function of prepositions in Old English differed from those of modern English. Discuss some of the ways in which prepositions in Old English could show up as inflections on nouns. Also, find some examples of prepositional phrases with syntax comparable to the syntax of prepositional phrases in modern English. In the Middle English period, we find more prepositions exhibiting less inflection, part of an overall loss of inflection during this period. Find some examples of prepositions in Middle English that were in Old English inflections on nouns. What does the historical development of prepositions in English suggest about their status as lexical or grammatical categories?

2. Prepositions in Other Varieties of English

Varieties of English differ in their use of prepositions. For example, in some dialects speakers say *sick* **at** *your stomach,* and in others, *sick* **to** *your* stomach. Find five or six examples of uses of prepositions that differ from your own, and bring them to class for discussion. (Introductory linguistics and sociolinguistics texts are good places to look for such data.)

3. Evidence That Prepositions are Grammatical Categories

Further evidence that prepositions are grammatical categories is that they are lacking in a variety of different linguistic contexts, contexts in which grammatical categories and inflection are also dropped or diminished. For example, people with certain kinds of aphasia drop grammatical categories and inflection, as do children in the early stages of acquiring English. Grammatical categories and inflections are also diminished in pidgin languages.

For this exercise, choose one of the above, aphasia, language acquisition, or pidgin languages, and discuss the status of grammatical categories and inflections in that situation. What is the status of prepositions in these contexts? If they are lexical categories, we expect them to be as productive as adverbs, adjectives, nouns, and verbs. If they are grammatical categories, on the other hand, we expect them to go the way of other grammatical categories and inflections. Use examples to illustrate your answer.

4. Prepositions in Languages Other Than English

Different languages use different prepositions to express similar ideas. For example, in French, you *téléphoner á* someone, or "telephone to" them. In German, a book *by someone* is a book *von*, or "from" someone. Find five or six examples of such differences in a language other than English. Write out the English translation of sentences using these different prepositional constructions to illustrate differences in literal translation, and show how such differences might give rise to miscommunication.

CHAPTER REVIEW TERMS

preposition, grammatical modifiers of prepositions, transitive and intransitive prepositions (particles), prepositional objects or objects of prepositions, Particle Shift, subordinating prepositions, subordinate clauses, complex prepositional phrases, PP Preposing

CHAPTER REVIEW EXERCISE

Choose from among the following options to create a chapter exercise. You may wish to add options from previous chapter exercises to make this exercise more comprehensive.
In the following text:

1. List all the prepositional phrases.
2. Diagram each prepositional phrase.
3. Label any particles.
4. Label any subordinating prepositional phrases, complex prepositional phrases, and prepositional phrases that dominate participial phrases.
5. Identify any grammatical modifiers of prepositions.

Beside them, little pot-bellied men in light suits and panama hats; clean, pink men with puzzled, worried eyes, with restless eyes. Worried because formulas do not work out; hungry for security and yet sensing its disappearance from the earth. In their lapels the insignia of lodges and service clubs, places where they can go and, by a weight of numbers of little worried men, reassure themselves that business is noble and not the curious ritualized thievery they know it is; that business men are intelligent in spite of the records of their stupidity . . . and that a time is coming when they will not be afraid anymore.

Source: The Grapes of Wrath, by John Steinbeck.

Part 3

Grammatical Functions

10

The Sentence: Clause Structure, Subordination, and Coordination

We have really everything in common with America nowadays,
except of course, language.

Oscar Wilde

Introduction

Now that you are familiar with different syntactic categories and phrases, we will in this chapter discuss the various ways in which phrases are combined into sentences. We will address in some detail how to recognize sentences by being able to identify their two basic syntactic parts, the *subject* and the *predicate*, or the noun phrase and verb phrase in (1).

(1) S => NP (AUX) VP

We will also tease out some of the differences among some rather confusing terms. We will make an explicit distinction between the broader notion *sentence* and the more technical syntactic term *clause*, relying on the former to mean our conception of "everything between the capital letter and the period," and the latter to express the syntactic unit in (1). As we will see, though all sentences are clauses, not all clauses are necessarily sentences. We also introduce the phenomenon of *subordination* in this chapter, the means by which a *subordinate* clause can be contained inside a *main* or *independent clause* as a result of recursion, with which you are familiar from Chapter 2. We will oppose subordination and coordination, to show how we can also syntactically connect clauses and other phrases without subordination.

In subsequent chapters in this section of the book we explore the syntactic functions of phrases within sentences. From the discussion of Subject-Auxiliary Inversion in Chapter 6 you are already familiar with how a phrase, in particular a noun phrase, can function as a subject. In this chapter you will see how verb phrases can function as predicates. In Chapter 11 we discuss in detail the ways in which phrases of different categories can also function as *complements*. Complements are phrases that are *selected* by, or typically occur with, a head noun, verb, adjective, adverb, or preposition. Certain verbs, such as *adore* for example, typically occur with direct object noun phrase complements, as in (2).

(2)   She *adores* the Spice Girls.

The basic pattern of complementation in English is illustrated in (3), in which we use adjective phrase and verb phrase examples. (3) shows that, in English, complements typically occur to the right of the head of the phrase that dominates them. This same pattern holds in phrases of other categories as well, including prepositional phrases, noun phrases, and adverb phrases.

(3)

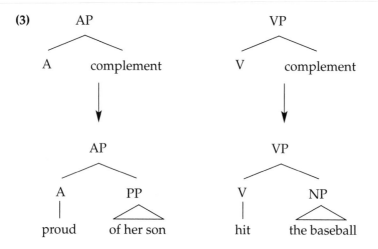

On a more general level, the structure of complementation in English is as illustrated in (4).

(4)

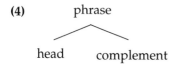

The complement position in (4) can be filled by a phrase of any category, including a noun phrase, verb phrase, adjective phrase, prepositional phrase, or an adverb phrase. Complements can also be clauses, clauses that are by definition subordinate.

In Chapter 12 we discuss another function of phrases, as *adjuncts*, or phrases that are **not** selected by a head. Adjuncts, like complements, can be of any category, including noun phrases, verb phrases, prepositional phrases, adverb phrases, and adjective phrases. Adjuncts can also be clauses of a variety of types. Adjuncts are distinct from complements in not being selected by a head and in occurring in noncomplement positions in a phrase. Adjuncts typically occur to the right of all complements, adjoined to a higher position than complements, as illustrated in (5). (Again, we use only two categories to illustrate, but adjuncts can occur in any category in addition to noun phrases and verb phrases.)

(5)

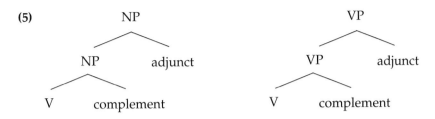

The more general position in which adjuncts occur is illustrated in (6).

(6)

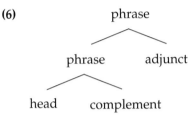

An understanding of the distribution of phrases as complements and adjuncts provides us with a basic understanding of the general sentence patterns of English. In this section of the book, we therefore shift the discussion from syntactic categories and phrases to sentences and clauses and the functions of phrases within them.

The Structure of the Clause: NP and VP

We begin this chapter with a discussion of basic Clause Structure, the noun phrase subject and the verb phrase predicate.

What is a Subject?

You are probably pretty good at intuitively picking out the subject of a sentence, but the definition of **subject** is actually a bit more complex than you might think at first. For example, if asked what the subject of the following sentence is, you might answer "cat."

(7)   The cat stretched and yawned lazily.

Actually, the subject of the sentence in (7) is *the cat,* an entire noun phrase, as *the cat* provides us with important information that *cat* lacks, namely that the feline under discussion is one that both the speaker and hearer have some knowledge of. *The cat,* then, is a *definite* noun phrase, in which definiteness is contributed by the determiner *the.* We typically, however, think of subjects as nouns, the main word in the group of words describing what we think of as the "doer of the action" in some sense. If asked to define "subject" in structural terms, we might also say it is "the first word in the sentence." Intuitively, we probably mean the "first main word," what we usually think of as a noun.

Here, for reasons that will become more clear below, we will define *subject* in terms of position, namely as the position of the noun phrase in (8).

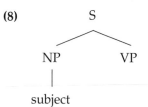

(8)

The noun phrase in (8) is the subject because it is in the subject *position*, not necessarily because it is the (purposeful) doer, or *agent*, of some action. One reason we define subject in structural, rather than semantic, terms is because, as illustrated in (9), the subject noun phrase need not be an agent or performer of some action.

> **(9)** a. *The ivy* climbed the wall.
> b. *A big rock* was rolling down the hill.
> c. *The rain* destroyed the wallpaper.

In (9), the italicized subject noun phrases are not agents,—they are not acting on their own volition, because they have none. The sentences in (9) differ from those in (10), in which the subject is in fact an agent capable of performing an action with volition.

> **(10)** a. *The burglar* climbed the wall.
> b. *Six kids* were rolling down the hill.
> c. *The termites* destroyed the wallpaper.

Another reason we want to define *subject* in terms of syntactic position rather than in terms of meaning, or semantics, is that certain kinds of subjects have no real meaning at all. They are for this reason called *dummy subjects,* or what we will refer to as **pleonastic subjects.** Some examples in English are the proforms *there* and *it,* illustrated in (11).

> **(11)** a. *There* were six linguists at the lecture.
> b. *It's* hot outside.

In (11a), the phrase in the subject position is *there,* but we nevertheless understand the logical, or semantic, subject to be *six linguists.* In (11b), there is no obvious semantic subject at all, because *it* has no intrinsic meaning nor does it refer to a linguistic or pragmatic antecedent. *It,* however, fills the syntactic subject position and thus is, in syntactic terms, the subject of the sentence.

Compare the use of *there* and *it* in (11) with their uses in (12). In (12a), *there* indicates a location, in contrast to *there* in (11a), which has the interpretation "there exists." In (12b), *it* refers to the movie *Nightmare on Elm Street* and is thus a proform with an antecedent, in contrast to pleonastic *it* in (11b).

(12)   a. Lionel took his books to school, and he left them *there*.
   b. Hortense saw *Nightmare on Elm Street* last night, and *it* really scared her.

The contrast between (11–12) shows that *it* and *there* can be either pleonastic proforms or proforms with antecedents. *It* and *there*, then, can be either "referential or nonreferential," and either type can fill the subject position in English.

We have seen that the subject is not the *first word* in the sentence, but rather the *first noun phrase* in the sentence. The sentences in (13–14) show us that the subject is not always the first phrase in the sentence; in the (b) sentences, something else precedes the subject noun phrase, the first phrase in the (a) sentences.

(13)   a. *Hortense* took balloons to the party.
   b. What did *Hortense* take to the party?

(14)   a. *Hortense* will visit Mount Rushmore.
   b. Will *Hortense* visit Mount Rushmore?

In (13–14), movement rules such as those discussed in the preceding chapters have moved phrases to sentence-initial position, in front of the subject. You may recognize WH-Movement in (13), where an interrogative pronoun has been fronted to sentence-initial position. In (14), *will*, a modal, has moved over the subject to form a question by Subject-Auxiliary Inversion, a movement rule introduced in Chapter 6. In both (13–14), however, *Hortense* is nevertheless the subject noun phrase, because it occurs in the noun phrase position in (8), as illustrated in (15–16) below.

(15)

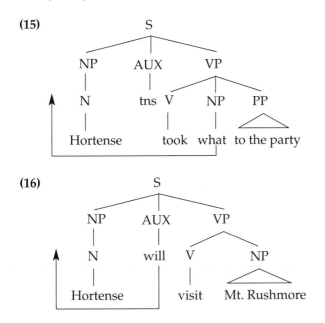

(16)

Evidence from movement therefore allows us to maintain that the subject of a sentence is best defined in terms of a structural position, rather than as the first word, or even the first phrase, in the sentence.

Our structural definition of subject might appear to run into some problems when we consider active and passive sentences, such as those in (17). Recall that the Passive movement rule has the effect of moving the subject noun phrase to the right and the object noun phrase to the left, into the (vacated) subject position. We thus derive (19) from (18).

(17)   a. The Giant chased Jack in the Beanstalk.
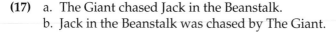
           b. Jack in the Beanstalk was chased by The Giant.

(18)

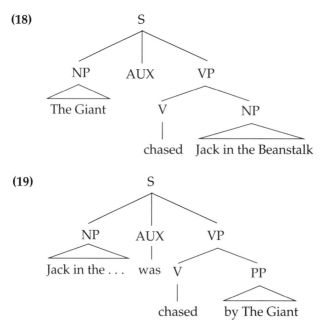

(19)

In accord with our definition of subject as the phrase occupying the noun phrase position in (8), *The Giant* occupies this position in (18). After Passive applies, however, *Jack in the Beanstalk* fills this position, as in (19). Observe, however, that *Jack in the Beanstalk* is not the *logical* or semantic subject of the sentence, any more than *there* is the logical subject of the sentence *There were six linguists at the lecture,* which we discussed in (11a). We thus need to distinguish between **syntactic** and **logical subjects,** if we are to explain cases in which the actual logical subject of the sentence does not, in fact, occur in the noun phrase position as in (8). *Jack in the Beanstalk* in (19) is the syntactic but not the logical subject. In (18), however, *The Giant* is both the logical and the syntactic subject of the sentence.

We will not discuss how to "find" the logical subject of a sentence here; you can rely primarily on your intuitions for this. There is, however, a very clear "test" for syntactic subjects that helps us differentiate between the two. We form *yes/no* questions in English through Subject-Auxiliary Inversion, the operation that moves an auxiliary verb (recall from Chapter 6 that the auxiliaries include *have* and *be,* and pleonastic *do*) or a modal such as *can/could/shall/should/may/might/must/will/would* over the syntactic subject. Subject-Auxiliary Inversion allows us to syntactically identify the subject of a sentence regardless of its semantics, and regardless of its status as a pleonastic proform *it* or *there.*

Examples of Subject-Auxiliary Inversion that illustrate these different cases are given in (20).

(20) **Subject-Auxiliary Inversion.**
   a. *The ivy* climbed the wall. => Did *the ivy* climb the wall? Subject noun phrase is not the agent of the action.
   b. *The burglar* climbed the wall. => Did *the burglar* climb the wall? Subject noun phrase is the agent of the action.
   c. *There* were six linguists at the lecture. => Were *there* six linguists at the lecture? Subject noun phrase is a pleonastic proform.
   d. *It's* hot outside. => Is *it* hot outside? Subject noun phrase is a pleonastic proform.
   h. *The Giant* chased Jack in the Beanstalk. => Did *the Giant* chase Jack in the Beanstalk? Subject noun phrase is also the logical subject.
   i. *Jack in the Beanstalk* was chased by the Giant. => Was *Jack in the Beanstalk* chased by the Giant? Subject noun phrase is not the logical subject.

In our subsequent discussions we will employ Subject-Auxiliary Inversion as a test for determining the subject of a sentence, as it is effective in a variety of syntactic contexts in which other, more semantically based ways of identifying the subject fail. Subject-Auxiliary Inversion clearly shows that there is a difference between syntactic and logical subjects of a sentence and that the syntactic subject is defined as a position, namely the noun phrase position in (8).

Subjects That Aren't Noun Phrases

We conclude this section with a brief discussion of a possibly confusing issue that will arise throughout the following chapters, in particular when we look at examples of written and spoken text. Not all subjects are noun phrases, though they appear to occur in the noun phrase position in (8). Some examples are given in (21).

(21) a. [Under the stairs] seems to be a good place to hide.
      PP
   b. [Cutting trees for sport] is unnecessarily destructive.
      VP

We will from time to time encounter cases such as these, in which the subject position appears to be filled with a phrase other than a noun phrase. It is thus not entirely accurate to say that the syntactic subject of a sentence is always a noun phrase. Nevertheless, the syntactic subject, noun phrase or not, can be identified by our Subject-Auxiliary Inversion test.

> **(22)** a. *Does* under the stairs seem to be a good place to hide?
> b. *Is* cutting trees for sport unnecessarily destructive?

We might assume, as some linguists argue, that the phrase structure of subjects such as in (22) is as in (23), where the prepositional phrase (or verb phrase) is dominated by a noun phrase.

(23)

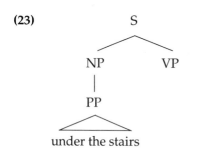

We will not pursue this issue further here, and will leave open whether non-noun phrase subjects are dominated by NP. We will simply assume that phrases other than noun phrases can sometimes occur in the noun phrase position in (8).

What Is a Predicate?

You have most likely heard that a sentence is made up of a *subject* and a *predicate*. Technically, **predicate** is a semantic term for a phrase that assigns a property to another phrase, usually a noun phrase. (You may recall the discussion of predication in Chapter 7, in our investigation of the role of adjective phrases in sentences such as *We painted the wall green.* In this sentence, *green* is a predicate, and a property assigned to *the wall*.) So if we think of the subject as the *topic* of the sentence, the predicate explains what the subject is up to, or the state the subject is in, what is sometimes called the *comment* of the sentence. Thus, in (24), *the cat* is the subject, or topic, and *stretched and yawned lazily* is the predicate, or comment.

(24) The cat stretched and yawned lazily.

Syntactically, the predicate of a sentence is the verb phrase in (25). A sentence is thus a unit whose two essential parts include the noun phrase subject and the verb phrase predicate. AUX is, as we have seen, optional.

(25) S => NP (AUX) VP

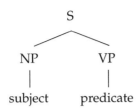

Though the verb phrase in (25) is semantically a predicate, it is not the *only* kind of predicate that we find in a sentence, as we saw in the discussion of *We painted the wall green,* where *green* is a predicate adjective phrase. We will thus try to avoid thinking of the verb phrase in (25) as the only possible predicate. We will discuss other examples of phrases that semantically function as predicates as well, in the following chapters.

We will, however, take (25) to be our syntactic definition of a **clause,** a syntactic unit consisting of a noun phrase, a verb phrase, and an optional AUX. A **sentence,** on the other hand, will be "everything between the capital letter and the period." Further, we will assume that, given the phrase structure rule for sentence in (25), a clause is a kind of *phrase,* for which we retain the label S.

In the following section we discuss further some of the distinctions between clauses and sentences as we have defined them here. We also begin our discussion of subordination, the means by which one clause can be dominated by another one. This gives rise to further distinctions we must make between main, independent, and subordinate clauses.

Independent and Subordinate Clauses

Under our current assumptions, the syntactic subject of the sentence in (26) is the noun phrase *Hortense,* and the rest of the sentence is a verb phrase. (26) is thus in this case defined as a clause, with a verb phrase that begins with *thinks* and ends with *funny.*

(26) [Hortense]
NP
[thinks that the television show *Mad About You* is really funny].
VP

As (26) shows, the verb phrase can actually be quite complex, and can be broken down into smaller units, or phrases. For example, the verb phrase *thinks that the television show Mad About You is really funny* includes, upon closer inspection, a clause: *the television show Mad About You is really funny.* This is an example of sentence (or more accurately, clausal) recursion; the larger clause contains a smaller one, as illustrated in (27). (*That* is what we will call a *complementizer,* a word that introduces subordinate clauses. It's precise position is largely irrelevant to the points being made here. We discuss *that* and other complementizers later in the chapter.)

(27)

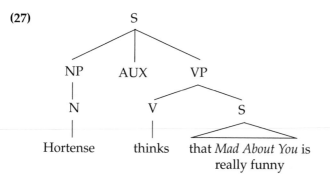

We will call the larger containing clause in (27) an **independent clause,** and the smaller clause inside it a **subordinate clause.** Subordination is thus a process that allows us to combine one clause with another, to form a larger syntactic unit.

Independent clauses are sometimes distinguished from subordinate ones in the following way:

(28) **Independent Clause:** An independent clause is a clause that can "stand alone."

(29) **Subordinate Clause:** A subordinate clause cannot "stand alone."

Although the definitions in (28–29) are accurate in some sense, they are nevertheless confusing. Often, subordinate clauses can in some sense stand alone, as we can see by the grammaticality of (30).

(30) The television show *Mad About You* is really funny.

Here, the subordinate clause in (27) has been made an independent clause. It thus in this case "stands alone." Because some subordinate clauses can "stand alone" in this way, the "stands alone" criterion for independent clauses can be misleading.

Independent and subordinate clauses are more accurately defined as in (31–32).

(31) **Independent Clause:** An independent clause is a clause that is not dominated by another phrase.

(32) **Subordinate Clause:** A subordinate clause is a clause dominated by another phrase.

According to (31–32), we can distinguish between the larger clause in (27) and the smaller one contained in it. The larger clause is an independent clause, and the one inside it, a subordinate clause, as this latter clause is dominated by VP.

We will see in the next section on coordination that the definitions in (31) and (32) must be further refined if they are to be truly explanatory.

Subordination Versus Coordination

A possible confusion arises if we maintain (32) as our definition of subordinate clause. To illustrate, consider the conjoined clauses in (33).

(33)

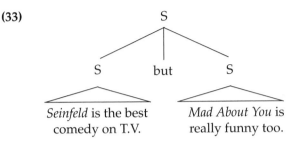

In (33), we have two independent clauses contained inside a larger, independent clause. If we define subordinate clauses as in (32), we might assume that the two coordinate clauses in (33), dominated by another phrase, namely another larger clause, are by definition both subordinate clauses. The clauses are not, however, contained one inside the other as they are in (27). It appears, then, that to distinguish subordination in (27), from coordination, in (33), we need to refine our definition of subordinate clause.

One way in which a subordinate clause can be distinguished from a coordinate clause is in terms of hierarchical structure. Notice that the subordinate clause in (27) is contained inside a verb phrase, a phrase that cannot "stand alone" but is itself *dependent* rather than *independent*. The coordinate clauses in (33), on the other hand, are contained inside a larger clause that is independent, rather than dependent. We capture the relevant distinction between subordinate and coordinate clauses by redefining "subordinate clause" as (34).

(34) Subordinate Clause: A subordinate clause is a clause dominated by a phrase that is dependent.

Because the clause in (27) is dominated by a verb phrase, it is dominated by a phrase that is dependent; a verb phrase must always be dominated by another phrase, in this case S. The clauses in (33), on the other hand, are not dominated by another dependent constituent; the S dominating them is independent. They are thus both independent clauses, under the revised definition of independent clause in (35).

(35) Independent Clause: An independent clause is a clause that is not dominated by a phrase that is dependent.

Let us now look at some other cases of subordinate and coordinate clauses to see whether our definitions need further refinement. First, observe that one subordinate clause can be contained inside another one, as we can see in (36), diagrammed in (37).

(36) The writer hoped that his audience would think that the story was true.

(37)

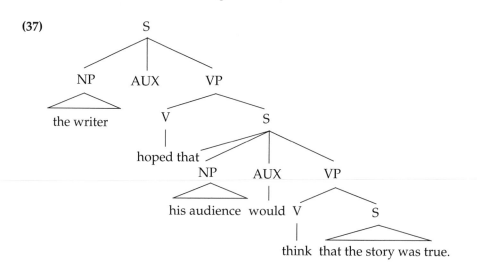

The larger, independent clause in (37) contains two subordinate clauses, as illustrated in (38).

(38)   a. Independent clause: *The writer hoped that his audience would think that the story was true.*
   b. Subordinate clause: *that his audience would think that the story was true*
   c. Subordinate clause: *that the story was true*

Both of the subordinate clauses in (38b–c) fall, as desired, under the definition in (34), since both are dominated by phrases that are dependent. The entire sentence in (38a), however, is an independent clause.

Now consider the sentence in (39).

(39)   The writer hopes that people will read his book and that they will love it.

Here, we have conjoined subordinate clauses, as illustrated in (40).

(40)

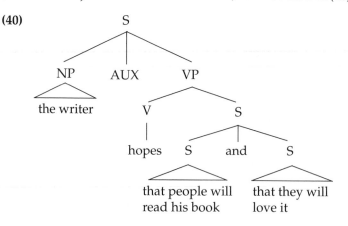

According to our definition, the coordinate clauses in (40) are also subordinate, because they are contained in S, a phrase dominated by a dependent verb phrase. The larger sentence in (40) is of course independent, because it is not contained inside a dependent phrase. Thus, coordinate clauses can be either independent, as in (33), or subordinate, as in (40).

An **independent clause** is for us the same as a **main clause,** another term you have probably heard. The main clause in (40) is thus the highest S. We will try to use the term *independent* rather than *main*, especially when talking about main verbs. As you can see from the above discussion of clauses within clauses, a "sentence," or an independent clause, can actually dominate more than one main verb. We can specifically refer to the main verb of the independent clause, to distinguish it from the main verb of a subordinate clause.

Coordination and Conjunctive Adverbs

We have seen that coordination can operate not only on heads and phrases, but on clauses as well. In fact, a set of coordinating conjunctions, called **conjunctive adverbs,** functions specifically to coordinate independent clauses. A list is given in (41).

(41)   *consequently/thus/therefore/however/nevertheless/moreover,* etc.

Clauses conjoined by conjunctive adverbs are by definition not subordinate. Some examples of independent clauses conjoined by conjunctive adverbs are given in (42).

(42)   a. Alex Rodriguez is the best overall player on the team; *however,* Randy Johnson is the best pitcher.
  b. Mary saw the Indigo Girls in concert; *furthermore,* she bought two of their CDs.
  c. The senators won't back the president; *moreover,* they will not contribute money to his campaign.
  d. Sue likes to talk on the phone; *therefore,* she tries to call only when the rates are low.

Conjunctive adverbs typically conjoin clauses, but they can also sometimes begin sentences, as in (43).

(43)   Mary hates taking the bus to work every day. Nevertheless, she won't buy a car.

We interpret *nevertheless* in (43) as connecting *she won't buy a car* with the previous sentence *Mary hates taking the bus to work every day.* A clause beginning with *nevertheless* is therefore construed as part of a larger coordinate structure, even though it appears to be a separate independent clause.

A final note: though conjunctive adverbs are labeled *adverbs,* they do not share the properties of adverbs you became familiar with in Chapter 8. We will not pursue this here; but observe that conjunctive adverbs, like the FANBOYS conjunctions and the correlative conjunctions discussed in Chapter 3, are grammatical words. That is, they can be defined in terms of their functions (as conjunctions), and they also form a morphologically closed class, to which we do not add new members. Conjunctions thus form a grammatical category. They differ from other grammatical categories we have discussed in not forming phrases with heads they introduce, in contrast, for example, to determiners or degree words. Rather, conjunctions link heads or phrases, and thus have a different syntactic function.

Types of Subordinate Clauses

Tensed Subordinate Clauses

So far, we have discussed only one example of a subordinate clause, namely (26), repeated in (44).

(44) Hortense thinks
[that the television show *Mad About You* is really funny].
S

The subordinate clause in (44) is a tensed subordinate clause, with a tensed main verb, *is* (a form of *be*). Some other examples of tensed subordinate clauses are given in (45).

(45) a. They thought [that Garth Brooks was singing tonight].
                      S
   b. No one knows [that Trisha Yearwood will also be there].
                      S
   c. The fans decided [that the concert surpassed all others].
                      S

In (45), the verbs *think, know,* and *decide* are all followed by *tensed* subordinate clauses. Each contains a tensed (auxiliary or main) verb or a tensed modal (*was, will,* and *surpassed,* respectively).

Another fact about the tensed subordinate clauses in (45) is that each is introduced by *that.* You might also have observed that *that* is optional in these sentences; (45a–c) are grammatical if *that* is omitted.

Notice also that *that* in (45) differs from *that* in (46).

(46) I don't like *that.*

In (46), *that* is being used as a pronoun, which replaces a noun phrase such as "the look she gave me." Crucially, *that* in (45) has quite a different function and meaning from *that* in (46), where it is a pronoun with an antecedent. We call *that* in (45) (and other words like it that we discuss below) a **complementizer,** a word that introduces a subordinate clause complement.

Other subordinate clauses have the phrase structure of a clause, NP-VP, and are thus clauses, but they differ from the clauses discussed above in lacking tensed verbs. Rather, verbs in these subordinate clauses are infinitival or participial. We discuss each in turn below.

Bare Infinitival Subordinate Clauses

Recall from Chapter 5 that modals and *do* are followed by the *bare infinitive* form of the verb, a verb that lacks tense and also person and number agreement. The clauses in (47) are nevertheless *tensed* clauses, because the modal or auxiliary verb is tensed.

(47) a. The defendant will *make* a statement tomorrow.
     b. The plane did not *land* on time.

There also exist *bare infinitival* subordinate clauses, clauses in which there is no tensed verb and the main verb occurs in its bare infinitive form. Some examples are given in (48).

(48) a. Marisa and Lionel heard [B. B. King play the blues].
                        S
     b. The kids saw [the cat catch a bird].
                  S
     b. The climber felt [her strength give out].
                  S

We know that the verbs in the subordinate clauses in (48) are infinitival because they express neither tense nor subject-verb agreement. This is illustrated when we try to make the bare infinitival clauses in (48) into main clauses as in (49).

(49) a. B. B. King play the blues.
     b. The cat catch a bird.
     c. Her strength give out.

In certain dialects of English, the sentences in (49) are completely grammatical. In such dialects, consonant clusters are reduced and the final -s affix is omitted, yet the sentences are nevertheless interpreted as tensed. In other varieties of English, however, the affix -s must be added for the verbs to be interpreted as tensed, as in (50).

(50) a. B. B. King *plays* the blues.
     b. The cat *catches* a bird.
     c. Her strength *gives* out.

We can use the contrast between the subordinate clauses in (48) and the independent clause counterparts in (50) as a diagnostic for bare infinitives. Assuming that subject-verb agreement in the form of -s can (and must, in certain dialects) show up if the verb is tensed, we know that the verbs in the subordinate clauses in (48) are bare infinitives, since they lack this affix, even though they have third person singular subjects.

Bare infinitival subordinate clauses show up quite often as the complements of perception verbs, such as *watch, hear, see, feel,* as in (48). They also show up as complements of *make* and *let,* as in (51).

(51) a. She made [her son clean his room].
      b. He won't let [John use the computer].

We can use the above agreement test to determine the status of the verbs *clean* and *use* as bare infinitives. Observe that as independent clauses, these verbs can be affixed with -s.

(52) a. Her son *cleans* his room.
      b. John *uses* the computer.

Bare infinitival clauses are thus similar to tensed clauses in having the basic phrase structure NP-VP/subject-predicate. They differ from tensed clauses, however, with respect to the form of the verb that heads the verb phrase. They never have an AUX position, as they do not contain tensed verbs. This is illustrated in (53), the phrase structure of (51a).

(53)

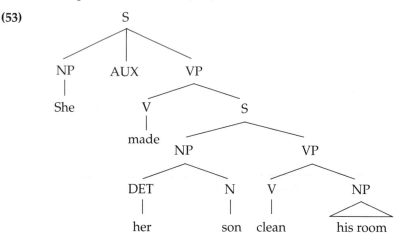

Also, the distribution of bare infinitives is more restricted than that of tensed clauses; though both can be subordinate clauses, only tensed clauses can *also* be independent clauses. Bare infinitival clauses typically follow a limited class of verbs (perception verbs, *make* and *let*) whereas tensed clauses follow verbs of various classes (*think, know, decide, hope, expect,* among others).

As we might expect, *to*-infinitives can also be subordinate clauses, though their syntactic properties are somewhat more complicated than those of bare infinitival clauses. We turn to *to*-infinitives below.

To-*Infinitives as Subordinate Clauses*

Consider the sentence in (54).

(54)   The stockbrokers hoped [to make money for their clients].

The phrase following *hope* in (54) is a *to*-infinitive; the main verb is *make*, preceded by *to*, and is in its uninflected form. How might we diagram (54)? More specifically, what is the phrasal status of the *to*-infinitive in the sentence? Notice that the infinitive is not a prepositional phrase, even though it is introduced by *to*. *To* in (54) is not the preposition *to* that occurs in prepositional phrases such as those in (55).

(55)   a. We walked *to the car.*
　　　　 b. They drove from Stockbridge *to Boston.*

The preposition *to* in (55) is followed by a noun phrase, but *to* in (54) is followed by an infinitival verb. Furthermore, observe that *to*-infinitives also differ from prepositional phrases in sometimes including noun phrase subjects, as in (56a–b).

(56)   a. I want [Hortense to go].
　　　　　　　　　　 S
　　　　 b. We expect [(for) The Mariners to win].
　　　　　　　　　　　　　　　 S
　　　　 c. The children prefer [(for) to eat in the kitchen].
　　　　　　　　　　　　　　　　 S

In each of the sentences (56a–b), the infinitival verb has a subject (*Hortense* and *The Mariners*, respectively). *For* can optionally introduce the subject in some dialects of English. Some varieties of English also allow (56c), with *for* alone, without a subject. It appears, then, that there is reason to analyze at least some *to*-infinitives as clauses, with NP-VP structure. Such *to*-infinitives all have noun phrase subjects and verb phrase predicates and might even be argued to have an optional complementizer, namely *for*. This complementizer is the analog of *that* in tensed subordinate clauses discussed earlier. *To*-infinitival clauses are therefore syntactically parallel to other clauses, with the difference that they contain infinitival, rather than tensed, verbs, verbs introduced by *to*.

We can diagram (56a), for example, as in (57). (We will assume for exposition that infinitival *to* is part of the verb.) Because the clause lacks tense, it lacks an AUX position.

(57)

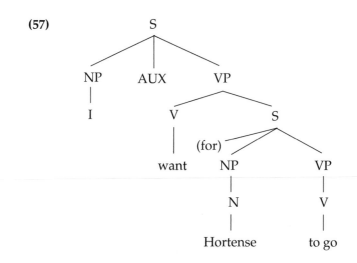

How then might we diagram the *to*-infinitive in (56c), or those in (58) below?

(58)   a. I want _____ to go.
        b. We expect _____ to win.
        c. The children prefer _____ to eat in the kitchen.

In these sentences there is no "overt" noun phrase subject of the infinitive, and it might therefore be dubious that such phrases are clauses. However, we would *like* them to be clauses, because this would provide symmetry to our overall analysis of *to*-infinitives. Furthermore, notice that we in fact *interpret* the *to*-infinitives in (58) as having subjects, namely subjects that are identical to the main clause subject.

(59)   a. I want (myself) to go.
        b. We expect (ourselves) to win.
        c. The children prefer (themselves) to eat in the kitchen.

How then are we to analyze infinitives that do not have expressed noun phrase subjects? How are we to account for the evidence that in such infinitives, no noun phrase subject actually appears, but we nevertheless *interpret* such a noun phrase as being there? We might simply call such infinitives "subjectless infinitives" to distinguish them from infinitival clauses. But this approach is not really explanatory, and implies that infinitives have two different structures: those with subjects are apparently clauses, as in (57) and those without overtly expressed subjects apparently have some other structure.

Some linguists argue, on the basis of a range of data beyond what we are considering here, that *to*-infinitives, with or without overtly expressed subjects, are syntactically clauses. We will adopt this analysis here, since it allows us to provide a unified analysis of different clausal types, including tensed clauses, bare infinitival clauses, and *to*-infinitival clauses.

We will diagram *to*-infinitival subordinate clauses as in (60), where we assume the subject position of the subordinate clause is simply an empty NP position.

(60)

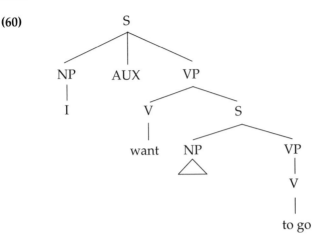

So far, we have seen that subordinate clauses can be either tensed or infinitival. Furthermore, we have seen that infinitival clauses can be bare or *to*-infinitives, with essentially the same basic NP-VP phrase structure as tensed clauses, with the difference that they lack a tensed verb, and consequently also an AUX position.

We turn now to another kind of untensed subordinate clause that is *participial*, rather than *infinitival*.

Participial Subordinate Clauses

Participial subordinate clauses differ from others we have discussed in that the head of the verb phrase is participial, rather than tensed or infinitival. Some examples are given in (61).

(61) a. They watched [the candidate giving a speech].
                          S

      b. We saw [Hortense drinking and driving].
                     S

      c. The protesters heard [the senator jeered by the mob].
                            S

Participial clauses follow a number of different verbs, including perception verbs such as *watch, hear, see* (verbs that also take bare infinitival complements, as we discussed above). Their phrase structure is illustrated in (62). Again the structure of the subordinate clause is NP-VP, with no AUX position.

(62)

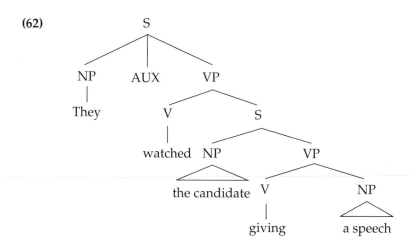

Participial clauses must always be dependent, and thus subordinate. They are not tensed and thus can never be independent clauses themselves, under the assumption that every sentence must be tensed.

Participial clauses are not difficult to identify, but they can sometimes be confused with constructions we discuss in Chapter 13, *reduced*, or *participial*, relative clauses. For example, the sentence in (61a) is ambiguous. It can mean either they watched a particular *event*, namely the event of the candidate, Ms. Jones, giving a speech, or they watched *someone*, namely the candidate who is slated to give a speech that evening. We watched, for example, Ms. Jones (the candidate giving the speech that evening) walking her dog.

The first interpretation of (61a) is diagrammed in (62), where what they watched is an event, represented as a clause. The second interpretation, in which they watched *someone*, is diagrammed as in (63).

(63)

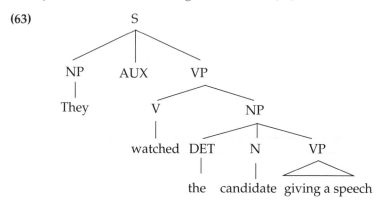

In (63), *the candidate giving a speech* is a noun phrase rather than a clause. As we might by now expect, the noun phrase in (63), but not the clause in (62), can be replaced by a pronoun.

(64)   They watched *the candidate giving a speech* that evening walk in the door.
Then *she* talked to John.

(64) can only be construed with the meaning illustrated in (63), where *the candidate giving a speech that evening* is an NP. It cannot be construed as corresponding to the meaning illustrated in (62), where they watched the *event* of someone in the process of giving a speech. A sentence corresponding to this second interpretation is given in (65).

(65) They watched the candidate giving a speech, and then they saw *it* again that night on television.

In (65), they watched an event that can in turn be replaced by the proform *it*.

Summarizing, we are able to explain the ambiguity of the phrase *the candidate giving a speech* by proposing that the phrase has two different phrase structures, namely (62) and (63). In (62), the phrase has the structure of a clause, and in (63), a noun phrase. This difference in structure is further supported by evidence that the clause can be replaced by the proform *it*, and the noun phrase by the pronoun *she*. Pronominalization thus helps us distinguish between subordinate participial clauses and reduced relative clauses, a construction we address in more detail in Chapter 13.

Summary

Summarizing, clauses have the structure below, generated by the following phrase structure rules.

S => NP (AUX) VP.

$$AUX => \left| \begin{array}{c} \text{tense} \\ \textit{have/be/modal/do} \end{array} \right|$$

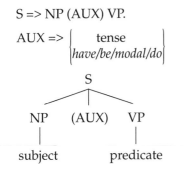

In syntactic terms we defined **subject** as the noun phrase in the above phrase structure and **predicate** as the verb phrase. We saw that the syntactic subject of the sentence is not always also its semantic, or **logical,** subject. For this reason we invoked the Subject-Auxiliary Inversion test to determine whether a phrase, regardless of its semantics (as a **pleonastic subject** such as *it* or *there*, or as a nonagentive noun phrase) is the syntactic subject of the sentence. Semantically, the predicate is the "comment" on the semantic "topic" of the sentence. We distinguished a **clause** from a **sentence** again in syntactic terms; clauses are phrases with the structure NP-VP and are not necessarily tensed. Sentences are tensed clauses that may include more than one clause. Clauses themselves can be **independent** (or **main**), or **subordinate,** as a result of recursive phrase structure rules. We defined subordinate clauses as those dominated by a dependent constituent, in order to differentiate them from not only independent clauses but also coordinate clauses. Coordinate clauses may but need not be contained within a larger dependent constituent. They can therefore be subordinate, or independent. We also briefly discussed in this chapter coordination of (independent) clauses by **conjunctive adverbs,** such as *furthermore, however, nevertheless.* We concluded the chapter with a discussion of various types of subordinate clauses, including *tensed, (bare* and *to-) infinitival,* and *participial* clauses. These clauses all share the basic phrase structure NP-VP, but differ in distribution and in the form of the verb that heads the verb phrase. Participial and infinitival subordinate clauses differ from tensed ones in lacking an AUX position.

DISCOVERY PROBLEMS

Problem 1. Auxiliary Verbs and the Predicate

One issue that arises in identifying predicates is the status of auxiliary verbs, modals, and *do.* That is, we define the predicate as the verb phrase. Assuming that tensed auxiliary verbs, modals, and *do* fill AUX, it follows that these elements are *not* in fact included in the syntactic predicate of a sentence. Recall from Chapter 6, however, that untensed auxiliary *have* and *be* head verb phrases and do not occur under Auxiliary unless they undergo Verb Raising.

Assume that no verb raising has yet applied in the following sentences. Divide the sentences into subjects and predicates. Elements dominated by AUX will not be included in VP, the predicate. Diagram each sentence.

a) Jim might have been running a marathon.
b) Jim has been running a marathon.
c) Jim might run a marathon.
d) Jim is running a marathon.
e) Jim ran a marathon.
f) Jim has run a marathon.
g) Jim might have run a marathon.
h) Jim might be running a marathon.

Now, consider what happens when you have main verb *be,* as in *Jim* **is** *a molecular biologist. Be* raises into AUX by Verb Raising, as we saw in the Discovery Problems in Chapter 6. Assuming that the predicate is a verb phrase, what assumptions must we make about the predicate in such sentences? Does it include *be* or not?

Problem 2. "Diary Drop"

In the following text, what constituents are consistently omitted? What is the effect on you as a reader?

> Wash the white clothes on Monday and put them on the stone heap; wash the color clothes on Tuesday and put them on the clothesline to dry; don't walk barehead in the hot sun; cook pumpkin fritters in very hot sweet oil; soak your cloths right after you take them off . . .
>
> *Source: Girl,* by Jamaica Kincaid.

This paragraph illustrates another syntactic phenomenon in English informally referred to as "diary drop." What constituent is consistently "dropped" in the above text, and under what conditions is it allowed? Why do we not do it in other kinds of writing?

Find a text on your own that has the same stylistic device as the one you identify here. Does your example have the same rhetorical effect? (Recipes and other instructions are usually written in this kind of style.) Bring your example to class for discussion.

Problem 3. Identifying Coordination and Subordination

Identify the bracketed clauses below as *subordinate* or *independent,* and also identify any clauses that are *coordinate.* (Remember that coordinate clauses can be either independent or subordinate.)

a) In 1919, when [President Woodrow Wilson arrived at Versailles for the conference that formally ended World War I], Ho drafted a statement to hand him.

b) Inspired by Wilson's famous doctrine of self-determination, Ho had written that ["all subject peoples are filled with hope by the prospect that an era of right and justice is opening to them . . . in the struggle of civilization against barbarism."]

c) [His appeal to Wilson modestly requested constitutional government, democratic freedoms, and other reforms for Vietnam—conspicuously omitting any reference to independence].

d) [Ho never saw Wilson, whose principles presumably applied only to Europe], but [his gesture attracted the attention of French socialists like Jean Longuet and Léon Blum, later prime minister].

Problem 4. Creating Subordinate and Coordinate Clauses

Make the independent clauses below subordinate clauses by "embedding" each of them in a larger clause you make up on your own. Be sure not to *coordinate*

the clauses; if you do you will not create subordination. To make this exercise more challenging, try to use a different main verb in each independent clause you create.
Examples:

- [Lee is a really funny person]. (independent clause)
- Subordination: I think that [Lee is a funny person].
- Coordination (what you *don't* want): [Mary is rather quiet] but [Lee is a really funny person].

a) I asked for a shot of rum.
b) The senator tried to get elected a second time.
c) It was too bad that The Steelers lost to The Broncos.
d) Hortense married Lionel yesterday.
e) Border collies are considered the smartest dogs around.

Now, *coordinate* each of the sentences in (a–e) with another one. Then try to *subordinate* your coordinated sentences. An example is given below.

- Lee is a really funny person.
- Coordinate independent clauses: [Mary is rather quiet] but [Lee is a really funny person].
- Coordinate subordinate clauses: I think that [Mary is rather quiet] but [Lee is a really funny person].

Problem 5. More Practice

In Problem 3 you created tensed subordinate and coordinate clauses, from the sentences in (a–e). Now create two examples of each of the following:

- an independent clause dominating a bare infinitival subordinate clause
- an independent clause dominating a *to*-infinitival subordinate clause
- an independent clause dominating a participial subordinate clause
- an independent clause dominating coordinate clauses, either infinitival or participial

Problem 6. Subordination: Class Exercise

Make up a "test" for your classmates. Compile a list of sentences from a text of your choice, which includes at least three or four subordinate clauses. Bring your list of sentences to class, and exchange "tests" with a classmate. Take a few minutes to analyze the sentences, and then discuss your analysis with your classmate's for comparison. Be prepared to present arguments to support your answers.

*Problem 7. Subordinate Clauses After Adjectives and Prepositions

We have discussed in the text only examples of subordinate clauses that follow verbs. Subordinate clauses can, in fact, occur in a variety of other positions. For example, the infinitival clause in (a) follows the adjective *able,* and the tensed subordinate clause in (b) follows the adjective *happy.* The participial clause in (c) follows the preposition *with,* and the tensed subordinate clause in (d) follows the preposition *because.*

a) Mary was **able** *to find the book.*
b) Sue was **happy** *that she had been elected.*
c) John left **with** *his head hanging in embarrassment.*
d) The lawyer quit the case **because** *he couldn't take the stress.*

In a text of your choice, find four examples of subordinate clauses that follow some head other than a verb. Label each as tensed, participial, or (bare or *to-*) infinitival. Diagram each sentence as best you can, using triangles for NP and VP positions in clauses if you wish.

*Problem 8. Sentence Fragments

You may be familiar with the term **fragment.** Some of you may have found this term in the margin of a paper you have written. Fragments are incomplete sentences, or more specifically, phrases that do not form independent clauses. Now that you have had some experience in analyzing independent clauses, you are better equipped to also identify fragments. Some examples of fragments are given in (a–c).

a) To talk to Mary. (infinitival clause)
b) Someone looking this way. (participial clause)
c) A hot afternoon. (noun phrase)

Writers often use fragments to create a rhetorical effect or tone in their work. For example, consider the following text:

> The next evening Quoyle was there, gripping paper bags. The front of Partridge's house, the empty street drenched in amber light. A gilded hour. In the bags a packet of imported Swedish crackers, bottles of red, pink and white wine, foil-wrapped triangles of foreign cheeses. Some kind of hot, juggling music on the other side of Partridge's door that thrilled Quoyle.
>
> Source: *The Shipping News,* by E. Annie Proulx.

Try to identify the fragments in the above text. Specifically, look for tensed verbs in each "sentence" to identify an independent clause. What is the syntactic structure of the fragments you find? Do any have the structure of the types of subordinate clauses you are familiar with? Rewrite each fragment as (part of) an independent clause. If you like, you may create a minilesson on fragments that addresses the questions raised here as your response to this problem.

Another text excerpt that contains some fragments is given below, for more practice.

> A pair of tennis shoes and a hammock. What she had taken from others in this war. She would wake under the slide of moonlight on the ceiling, wrapped in an old shirt she always slept in, her dress hanging on a nail by the door. . . .
>
> Her hammock and her shoes and her frock. She was secure in the miniature world she had built; the two other men seemed distant planets, each in his own sphere of memory and solitude.
>
> Source: *The English Patient,* by Michael Ondaatje.

Problem 9. Sentence Combining

Make up a short "story" of at least four or five short independent clauses. Rewrite them, trying to subordinate as many of them to each other as you can. What do you have to do to accomplish this? What changes do you have to make, and how do these changes affect the overall tone of the piece? Discuss the influence of syntax on style or tone.

Problem 10. Conjunctive Adverbs

Create some examples of independent clauses conjoined by conjunctive adverbs. Then, from a text of your choice, find three or four more, write them down, and bring them to class. Try to find some cases in which the adverb occurs in some position other than as a conjunction between two sentences, and try to explain how coordination, if it is coordination, works in such cases.

*Problem 11. *It*-Extraposition

The pleonastic *it* subject we have discussed in the text shows up in a number of different syntactic environments. A common environment in which we find pleonastic *it* is in what linguists call *It*-**Extraposition** constructions. In these constructions, *it* can alternate with a subordinate clause in the subject position.

When *it* occurs in the subject position, the subordinate clause appears at the end of the sentence.
Example:

1a. [That most people don't vote] really bothers Michael Moore, author of *Downsize This!*
  b. **It** really bothers Michael Moore, author of *Downsize This!* [that most people don't vote].
2a. [That Newt Gingrich wants to be president] is obvious.
  b. **It's** obvious [that Newt Gingrich wants to be president].
3a. [To fake your signature] is illegal.
  b. **It** is illegal [to fake your signature].

Practice doing *It*-Extraposition in the following sentences. Then find at least three examples from texts in which this operation has applied, and bring them to class for discussion. Be careful to differentiate between sentences in which *It*-Extraposition has applied and those that simply have pleonastic *it* subjects.

a) To work hard can be rewarding.
b) That Alexander is thinking about quitting his job worries Andrew.
c) That college prices are so high now is distressing to many parents.
d) That Chris works too hard is clear.

TEXT ANALYSIS

1. Finding Subjects

Using Subject-Auxiliary Inversion as a test, identify the *syntactic* (not logical) subjects in the following independent clauses. Are all of them noun phrases? Which of them are pleonastic? You may have to rearrange the structure of the sentence in order to apply Subject-Auxiliary Inversion. For example, in sentences without auxiliary verbs, you will need to add one in order to apply the rule. An example is given below.

Examples:

There was a change in the weather. => Was there a change in the weather?

(No additions necessary. Apply Subject-Auxiliary Inversion. Subject = *there*)

The air became unbearably humid. => The air *had* become unbearably humid

(Add auxiliary *had* in order to apply Subject-Auxiliary Inversion) *Had* the air become unbearably humid?

(Apply Subject-Auxiliary Inversion. Subject = *the air*)

a) Stanley was drenched in sweat.
b) Beads of moisture ran down the handle of his shovel.
c) It was almost as if the temperature had gotten so hot that the air itself was sweating.
d) A loud boom of thunder echoed across the empty lake.
e) A storm was way off to the west, beyond the mountains.
f) Stanley could count more than thirty seconds between the flash of lightning and the clap of thunder.
g) That was how far away the storm was.
h) Sound travels a great distance across a barren wasteland.

Source: Holes, by Louis Sachar.

2. Finding Subjects and Predicates

You now know how to identify subject noun phrases through the application of Subject-Auxiliary Inversion; this test allows you to identify the subject noun phrase. Everything else in the sentence is, presumably, part of the predicate, except material in the AUX position.

- Identify the syntactic subject of each independent clause below, using Subject-Auxiliary Inversion as a diagnostic.
- Label any logical subjects as well, if they do not occur in the syntactic subject position.
- Label any pleonastic subjects.
- Identify the predicate in each sentence.

Note: You will sometimes have to "rearrange" the words in each independent clause in order to apply Subject-Auxiliary Inversion. An example is done for you, illustrating how you might do this.
Example:

1. Of course I was staring, registering the shifting expressions of her face, the flickering play of the light.
        . . .

- Omitting *of course*, the subject is *I*, based on the following evidence from Subject-Auxiliary Inversion.*Was I* staring, registering the shifting expressions of her face, the flickering play of the light?
- The predicate is: *staring, registering the shifting expressions of her face, the flickering play of the light.*

---

a) A handsome, well-preserved man of sixty, in mufti, came to the hall door to greet his guests.
b) It was von Rabbeck.
c) And though he shook their hands and apologized and smiled, it was plain that he was not half as glad to see them as was last year's Count.
d) The officers climbing the soft-carpeted steps and listening to their host understood this perfectly well.

Source: The Kiss, by Anton Chekhov.

---

a) The love affair began in the summer in those dark days when young men and women did not have love affairs.
b) It was one of those summers when it rained in torrents.
c) Almost every afternoon towards sunset the low-hanging, rain-filled clouds would sweep across the sky in packed masses and suddenly, with barely a warning, the rain would pour down in blinding sheets.

Source: The Lovers, by Bessie Head.

3. More Subjects and Predicates

Identify all independent clauses in the following text excerpts. Identify the subject and predicate of each. Label any pleonastic subjects, and identify cases in which the syntactic subject is not also the logical subject.

> Dwight drove in a sullen reverie. When I spoke he answered curtly or not at all. Now and then his expression changed, and he grunted as if to claim some point of argument. He kept a Camel burning on his lower lip. Just the other side of Concrete he pulled the car hard to the left and hit a beaver that was crossing the road. Dwight said he had swerved to miss the beaver, but that wasn't true. He had gone out of his way to run over it. He stopped the car on the shoulder of the road and backed up to where the beaver lay.
>
> *Source: This Boy's Life,* by Tobias Wolff.

> As soon as the pound notes were placed in his palm Jonathan simply closed it tight over them and buried his fist and money inside his trouser pocket. He had to be extra careful because he had seen a man a couple of days earlier collapse into near-madness in an instant before that oceanic crowd because no sooner had he got his twenty pounds than some heartless ruffian picked it off him. Though it was not right that a man in such an extremity of agony should be blamed yet many in the queues that day were able to remark quietly at the victim's carelessness, especially after he pulled out the innards of his pocket and revealed a hole in it big enough to pass a thief's head. But of course he had insisted that the money had been in the other pocket, pulling it out too to show its comparative wholeness. So one had to be careful.
>
> *Source: Witnesses to War,* by Chinua Achebe.

4. Subordination and Coordination

Write out the main clauses that you find in each of the following texts. Identify any subordinate clauses. Identify any coordinate clauses. Are they also subordinate? How do subordination and coordination contribute to the overall tone or style of the texts, and how might you compare them in terms of their use of coordination and subordination?

> Gramps says that I am a country girl at heart, and that is true. I have lived most of my thirteen years in Bybanks, Kentucky, which is not much more than a caboodle of houses roosting in a green spot alongside the Ohio River. Just over a year ago, my father plucked me up like a weed and took me and all our belongings . . . and we drove three hundred miles straight north and stopped in front of a house in Euclid, Ohio.
>
> *Source: Walk Two Moons,* by Sharon Creech.

> But poor Jo never got her laugh, for she was transfixed upon the threshold by a spectacle which held her there, staring with her mouth nearly as wide open as her eyes. Going to exult over a fallen enemy, and to praise a strong-minded sister for the banishment of an objectionable lover, it certainly *was* a shock to behold the aforesaid enemy serenely sitting on the sofa, with the strong-minded sister enthroned upon his knee, and wearing an expression of the most abject submission.
>
> *Source: Little Women,* by Louisa May Alcott.

5. More Practice

List the independent clauses in the following text. Then identify any suibordinate or coordinate clauses. Label them as tensed, (bare or *to-*) infinitival, or participial.

> If anyone had prophesied before his marriage that he would find it difficult to tell this to Undine he would have smiled at the suggestion; and during their first days together it had seemed as though pecuniary questions were the last likely to be raised between them. But his marital education had since made strides, and he now knew that a disregard for money may imply not the willingness to get on without it but merely a blind confidence that it will somehow be provided.
>
> *Source: The Custom of the Country,* by Edith Wharton.

6. More Coordination and Subordination

Find two texts of your choice, each about four or five sentences long. One should use predominantly coordination, and the other predominantly subordination. Analyze each syntactically, identifying main, subordinate, and coordinate clauses; other types of coordination, and so on. Compare the rhetorical effect of each. Is one "easier" to understand than the other? Why or why not? (Children's books are good places to look for examples, because we assume their syntactic structure will be "simple," but this is not always the case.)

LANGUAGE DIVERSITY EXERCISES

1. Coordination in Languages Other Than English

Not all languages, quite obviously, rely on the FANBOYS to form coordinate structures. Do some research on a language you do not know, to determine how that language forms coordinate structures. What are the conjunctions in the language? How do they differ from their English counterparts? Does the language have equivalents of the conjunctive adverbs you find in English? Illustrate your answer with examples.

2. Punctuation

Grammar handbooks typically discuss the punctuation of different coordinate and subordinate structures. Consult a few different handbooks and try to determine whether they are consistent in their treatment of punctuation of coordinate and subordinate constructions. If you wish, create a minilesson on punctuation for your classmates, in which you analyze punctuation rules in the context of the approach to syntax we have taken here. (You might use phrase structure diagrams to illustrate where certain punctuation marks occur, for example.)

3. Language and Gender

The well-known linguist Otto Jespersen claims in his book *Language: It's Nature, Development and Origin* (1922) that the language of women differed from that of men in crucial ways. One such difference was in the use of coordination. He claimed that women used more coordination (*parataxis*) and men more subordination (*hypotaxis*). Research his argument and write a short essay about it (two pages or so). What were his grounds for this claim? What do you think about it given your knowledge of coordination and subordination?

4. Complementizers in Other Languages

In English, the complementizer *that* introduces tensed subordinate clauses, and the complementizer *for* introduces some infinitival clauses. These complementizers are for the most part optional. In other languages, however, complementizers are obligatory. Choose a language and provide some examples of the complementizers in that language. Do complementizers differ depending on the tense of the subordinate clause they introduce? Are they optional or obligatory? You can look this information up in grammar books (it won't be under *comple-*

mentizers, but you can usually find it in discussions of *subordination*). Another way to find out about the complementizer system in a language is to interview a native speaker, or someone who speaks the language fairly fluently.

CHAPTER REVIEW TERMS

subject, predicate, Subject-Auxiliary Inversion, pleonastic subjects, logical and syntactic subjects, clause, sentence, independent (or main) clause, subordinate and coordinate clauses, conjunctive adverbs, tensed, (bare and to-) infinitival and participial clauses, fragments, Extraposition

CHAPTER REVIEW EXERCISE

Choose from among the following options to create a chapter exercise. You may wish to add options from previous chapter exercises to make this exercise more comprehensive.
In the following text:

1. List all the independent clauses.
2. Identify any fragments (incomplete sentences).
3. Identify any coordinate or subordinate clauses. Label each as tensed, bare infinitival, to-infinitival, or participial.
4. Identify the subject of each independent clause.
5. Identify any pleonastic subjects and any examples of syntactic subjects that are not also logical subjects. Identify the logical subjects in such cases.

I ran back from Miyagawa-cho and was relieved to find the okiya as quiet as I'd left it. I crept inside and knelt in the dim light of the entrance hall, dabbing the sweat from my forehead and neck with the sleeve of my robe and trying to catch my breath. I was just beginning to settle down, now that I'd succeeded in not getting caught. But then I looked at the door to the maids' room and saw that it stood open a bit, just wide enough to reach an arm through, and I felt myself go cold. No one ever left it that way. Except in hot weather it was usually closed all the way. Now as I watched it, I felt certain I heard a rustling sound from within. I hoped it was a rat; because if it wasn't a rat, it was Hatsumomo and her boyfriend again. I began to wish I hadn't gone to Miyagawa-cho. I wished it so hard that if such a thing had been possible, I think time itself would have begun to run backward just from the force of all my wishing.

Source: Memoirs of a Geisha, by Arthur Golden.

11

Complements

Sentence structure is innate but whining is acquired.
From *Remembering Needleman* by Woody Allen

Introduction

In the second part of the book we discussed the internal structure of phrases of each lexical category: noun, verb, adjective, adverb, and preposition. In Chapter 10 we began our discussion of how those phrases function within the sentence. We saw that noun phrases, for example, can function as subjects and that verb phrases can function as predicates. These two phrases together form a syntactic unit, the clause. In this chapter and the next we consider some additional functions of phrases, including clauses, as *complements* and *adjuncts*.

Complementation is the syntactic relationship between a phrase and the head that *subcategorizes*, or selects, it. Put more simply, a complement *completes* a phrase. For example, the complement of the verb *believe* in (1) is the noun phrase *John*. Together, *believe* and *John* make up the verb phrase, *believed John*.

(1) Mary [believed John].
         VP

In English, complements typically occur to the immediate *right* of the head, as illustrated in (2).

(2)   phrase

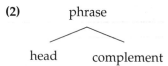

       head   complement

According to the abstract phrase structure in (2), a head and the complement it selects together form a larger phrase. In the event that the head is a verb, such as *believe*, and the complement in (2) a noun phrase, such as *John*, the head and its complement form a larger unit, the verb phrase.

Phrase structure allows us to express a number of important generalizations about heads and complements, but as we find below, certain facts about complementation are not expressed by phrase structure rules alone.

For example, consider the possible phrase structure rule for verb phrase in (3).

(3) $VP \Rightarrow V \begin{Bmatrix} NP & (PP) \\ S \end{Bmatrix}$

According to (3), a verb can be followed by both a noun phrase complement and a prepositional phrase complement, or by just a noun phrase complement. A verb can also, according to (3), take a clausal, or S, complement. These options are illustrated in (4).

(4) a. Mary believed [John].
             NP
   b. Mary gave [a present] [to John].
             NP   PP
   c. Mary thinks [that John is intelligent].
             S

All of the sentences in (4) are possible, given the phrase structure rule in (3). The phrase structure rule in (4) does not tell us, however, that only *certain* verbs can be followed by clauses, and only *certain* others by noun phrases, prepositional phrases, and so on. For example, although *give* in (4b) can occur with noun phrase and prepositional phrase complements, *think* in (4c) cannot occur with these complements, as we see in (5).

(5) *Mary thinks [the story] [to John].
             NP   PP

Think, unlike *give*, selects a clausal complement. *Give*, on the other hand, does not select a clause, as we see in (6).

(6) *Mary gave [that John is intelligent].
             S

We see, then, that certain crucial syntactic information, namely the types of complements a particular head selects, is not captured by phrase structure rules alone. We express our knowledge of the distribution of complements by proposing that this information is encoded not in phrase structure rules, but rather in our mental dictionary, or lexicon. We can think of this lexicon as being made up of different vocabulary entries for all the words we know in our language. The entry for each lexical head includes information about the kinds of complements it takes. That some such repository of information exists makes sense from the point of view of our unconscious knowledge of syntax. As English speakers we somehow "know" that *believe* can take a clause complement but that *give* cannot. This knowledge must be "listed" somewhere, and a logical place for it is in our mental dictionary.

Subcategorization

We will borrow a term from linguistics, **subcategorization,** to describe the idea that a head, such as *believe* or *give,* selects, or "subcategorizes," a particular phrase as a complement. Entries encoding this information for each head are called *subcategorization frames.* An example is given in (7) for *believe* and in (8) for *give.* (The _____ is the "slot" in which the verb occurs.)

(7) *believe,* V_____ $\left(\begin{array}{c} NP \\ S \end{array}\right)$

(8) *give,* V_____ NP PP

According to (7), *believe* selects a noun phrase or clause complement, optionally. This means that *believe* can also occur with no complement at all. The kinds of verb phrases possible with *believe* as a head are illustrated in (9).

(9) a. Mary believes.
     b. Mary believes [John].
                        NP.
     c. Mary believes [that John is intelligent].
                        S

The subcategorization frame in (8) for *give,* on the other hand, expresses quite different information. *Give* must occur with both a noun phrase complement and a prepositional phrase complement. *Give* thus occurs in contexts such as (10).

(10) Mary gave [a present] [to John].
                 NP   PP

    Some of you may be wondering, given our discussion throughout the book of movement rules such as Indirect Object Movement, why we do not write the subcategorization frame for *give* as (11) rather than (8).

(11) *give,* V_____ $\begin{array}{cc} NP & PP \\ NP & NP \end{array}$

The frame in (11) indicates that *give* can be followed by a noun phrase and a prepositional phrase or by two noun phrases, as a result of Indirect Object Movement. Recall that this rule applies to sentences such as (10), to derive sentences such as (12).

(12) Mary gave [John] [a present].
                 NP   NP

There exist other examples of sentences in which word order is changed by movement, raising a similar question: should these different orders of complements, derived through movement, also be encoded in subcategorization frames?

If we take subcategorization frames to express the kinds of complements a head selects, either before or after a movement rule has applied, then we essentially make movement rules obsolete. Word orders would be encoded in our mental lexicons, rather than being derived through movement rules. Linguists argue, for a number of independent reasons that we will not pursue here, that the more explanatory model of grammar is one which includes movement rules, and in which subcategorization frames provide information about the "base" structure of a phrase, *before* movement applies. We will assume, then, that the appropriate subcategorization frame for *give* is (8) rather than (11).

Complements also occur with lexical heads other than verbs. Prepositions can also take complements, as can adjectives, adverbs, and nouns. Some possibilities are illustrated in (13), where we see that the preposition *by*, the adjective *proud*, the adverb *fortunately*, and the noun *destruction* all select complements.

(13) a. The painting was [by [Andrew Wyeth]].
                                     PP NP
          b. She was [proud [of her achievements]].
                         AP   PP
          c. [Fortunately [for Mary]], the bus was on time.
               ADVP   PP
          d. They witnessed [the destruction [of the city]].
                               NP   PP

We begin our discussion below with a detailed overview of the possible complements of verbs, because verbs select the widest variety of complements. In later sections we turn to the complements of prepositions, adjectives, adverbs, and nouns.

Before we begin our discussion of the complements of verbs, one caveat is in order. A possible source of confusion in the discussion is that complements can often have more than one label. We will try to clearly differentiate between *semantic* labels, such as direct object, indirect object, and subjective complement, and *syntactic* labels, such as noun phrase, verb phrase, adjective phrase. Throughout, we will diagram complements using phrase structure rules, which clearly express the syntactic labels of complements. We will add semantic labels to the trees when possible, to provide a visual representation of the correspondence between semantic labels and syntactic category.

Complements of Verbs

Direct Objects and Subjective Complements

The most common kind of complement a verb can take, one that you have probably heard of, is a **direct object.** Semantically, a direct object takes the action of the verb. Syntactically, direct objects are noun phrases that occur to the immediate right of the verb in the verb phrase. We call verbs that select direct object complements *transitive* verbs, and verbs that do not select direct objects, *intransitive* verbs.

You have already been introduced to the notion of **transitivity** in Chapter 9. There, we saw that prepositions can be transitive, meaning that they take a noun phrase object. Prepositions can also be intransitive, occurring without an object. We called these intransitive prepositions *particles*. A transitive preposition is illustrated in (14a), where *to* is followed by *Lancelot*, the noun phrase object of the preposition. An intransitive preposition, or particle, is illustrated in (14b), where *up* is followed by nothing at all.

(14)   a. The knight spoke *to* Lancelot.
       b. The knight gave *up*.

Some examples of transitive verbs and their direct objects are given in (15), and of intransitive verbs in (16).

(15)   a. The old woman swallowed *a fly*.
       b. Her daughter plays *basketball*.
       c. The pirates found *the loot*.

(16)   a. The old woman laughed.
       b. Her daughter slept.
       c. The pirates appeared.

Not all noun phrases that occur to the right of the verb are direct objects. For example, contrast the direct objects in (15) with the noun phrases that occur to the right of *linking* verbs, verbs that express states, in (17). (You may remember linking verbs from Chapter 7 in the discussion of adjective phrase positions.)

(17)   a. Hortense **became** *a famous physicist*.
       b. Hortense and Lionel **remained** *friends*.
       c. The students **were** *fun people to be around*.
       d. Queen Elizabeth **is** *Queen of England*.

The italicized noun phrases in (17) do not "take the action of the verb," as there is no action to take. Rather, these noun phrases *describe* the subject noun phrase. They are thus semantic predicates, assigning a *property* to the subject noun phrase. The semantic label for this type of complement is **subjective complement.** Syntactically, the complements in (17) are, like direct objects, noun phrases.

Subjective complements can also be adjective phrases, as in (18).

(18)   a. Hortense became *sick*.
       b. Hortense and Lionel remained *happy*.
       c. Playing the zither is *fun*.

Other examples of linking verbs (in this case, "sense" verbs) that select adjective phrase subjective complements are given in (19).

(19)   a. The soup tastes *salty.*
       b. The music sounds *interesting.*
       c. Hortense feels *good.*

In addition to noun phrases and adjective phrases, subjective complements can also be prepositional phrases. Such prepositional phrases often have idiomatic, adjectival interpretations. For example, the prepositional phrases *in good health, in great spirits,* and *out to lunch* in (20) all function as subjective complements.

(20)   a. Howard Stern seems *out to lunch* most of the time.
       b. The pets were *in good health* when we returned.
       c. Harry appeared *in good spirits.*

We can diagram the syntactic position of subjective complements as in (21), where a verb takes a noun phrase, adjective phrase, or prepositional phrase complement. The complement functions semantically as a subjective complement, when selected by a linking verb. (Subjective complement is abbreviated here as SC for convenience.)

(21)

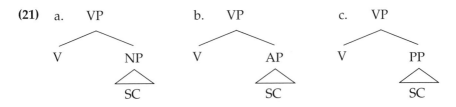

Observe that the subjective complement noun phrase in (21a) and the noun phrase direct object in (22), are syntactically identical.

(22)

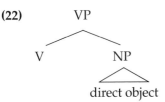

We can distinguish these different noun phrase complements semantically; direct objects take the action of the verb, and subjective complements assign a property to the subject.

There is another way to distinguish direct object and subjective complement noun phrases; only the former undergo the Passive movement rule. Passive can apply, for example, to the direct objects in (15), repeated in (23). The application of Passive produces the sentences in (24).

(23)   a. The old woman swallowed *a fly.*
      b. Her daughter plays *basketball.*
      c. The pirates found *the loot.*

(24)   a. *A fly* was swallowed by the old woman.
      b. *Basketball* is played by her daughter.
      c. *The loot* was found by the pirates.

Passive fails in sentences with subjective complement noun phrases, as illustrated in (25–26).

(25)   a. Hortense became *a famous physicist.*
      b. Hortense and Lionel remained *friends.*
      c. The students were *fun people to be around.*

(26)   a. **A famous physicist* was become by Hortense.
      b. **Friends* were remained by Hortense and Lionel.
      c. **Fun people to be around* were been by the students.

The above patterns illustrate that Passive cannot apply in sentences with subjective complements, but rather is restricted to applying to direct objects. Applying the Passive movement rule is therefore a useful way to differentiate between these two types of complements, both of which are noun phrases that occur to the immediate right of the verb.

Objective Complements

As we might expect, we find complements that are predicated of the direct object noun phrase, rather than of the subject noun phrase. These complements, called **objective complements,** can be noun phrases, adjective phrases, or prepositional phrases. Like subjective complements, they assign a property to a noun phrase, in this case the direct object noun phrase. Some examples of noun phrase, adjective phrase, and prepositional phrase objective complements are given in (27–29).

(27)   Noun phrase objective complements
      a. His eloquence made the speech *a work of art.*
      b. The senator considers the bill *a good thing.*

(28)   Adjective phrase objective complements
      a. His eloquence made the speech *poetic.*
      b. The senator considers the bill *completely fair.*

(29)   Prepositional phrase objective complements
      a. Some listeners consider Howard Stern *out to lunch.*
      b. We found the pets *in good health* when we returned.

Notice that objective complements are selected by action verbs rather than by linking verbs; this is to be expected, since verbs that select objective complements must also, by definition, select direct object complements, noun phrases that take the action of the verb. Observe as well that objective complements are sometimes optional. For example, *make, consider,* and *find* typically select objective complements, as in the above sentences. These verbs can also occur without these complements, as in (30).

(30) a. He made the speech.
      b. The senator considered the bill.
      c. We found the pets.

We can diagram objective complements as in (31) (where objective complement is abbreviated as OC).

(31) a.   b.   c.

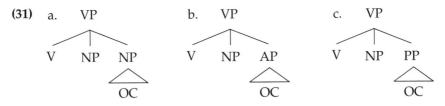

As you can see in (31), there is no possible way to confuse objective complement noun phrases with direct objects, because objective complements, by definition, occur *after* direct object noun phrases. There is also no confusion between subjective complements and objective complements, because the former occur after linking verbs and the latter after direct objects.

We have so far discussed three different kinds of complements of verbs. The semantic labels for these complements are direct object, subjective complement, and objective complement. Syntactically, direct objects are noun phrases, and the other two types of complements can be noun phrases, adjective phrases, or prepositional phrases. We have discussed a number of ways to distinguish among these complement types both syntactically and semantically.

Prepositional Phrase Complements

We saw above that verbs can take two different kinds of prepositional phrase complements, namely prepositional phrase subjective and objective complements. These complements have a convenient semantic label, but other types of prepositional phrase complements have no particular semantic label. We will simply refer to them as **prepositional phrase complements.** Some examples are give in (32).

(32) a. The lion went *to the waterhole.*
      b. Jim talked *to Pam.*
      c. He comes *from Scotland.*
      d. The Hunchback lurked *near the cathedral.*
      e. The farmer blamed the crop failure *on the lack of rain.*
      f. The child put the toy *in the box.*

   g. The dog snuck *into the kitchen*.
   h. The buyer asked *about the plummeting house prices*.

    Determining whether a prepositional phrase is a complement or not, that is, whether it is selected by a verb or not, is not always easy, since prepositional phrases can occur with almost any verb at all. For example, consider the sentences in (33).

   (33) a. The Hunchback lurked *near the cathedral*.
         b. The Hunchback saw Esmerelda *in the belfry*.
         c. The Hunchback rang the bell *after dark*.

Though each sentence in (33) includes a prepositional phrase, only *near the cathedral* in (33a) is a complement. This is because the verb *lurk* typically selects a complement that expresses information about either location or direction—we don't just *lurk*, we *lurk somewhere*. The verbs *see* and *ring*, on the other hand, are not verbs that *typically* select prepositional phrases. We *see someone*, or *ring something*, but where the seeing or ringing takes place is "extra information," rather than something that must be specifically encoded in the subcategorization frame of the verb. For that matter, prepositional phrases of location and direction can occur indiscriminately in almost any sentence. Such truly *unselected* prepositional phrases are distinct from those selected by verbs such as *lurk, sneak*, or the other verbs in (32), verbs that we think of as *typically* occuring with a complement of location or direction.
    Prepositional phrase complements are thus selected by a number of different verbs and have a number of different meanings. Though some prepositional phrase complements have semantic labels, such as *subjective complement* or *objective complement*, most we will refer to simply as *prepositional phrase complements*, with the structure in (34). (We include an optional noun phrase to account for cases such as (32e) and (32f), where a direct object noun phrase precedes the prepositional phrase complement.)

   (34)   VP

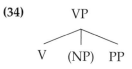

      V   (NP) PP

    Recall from Chapter 9 that some verbs can occur in construction with particles, or intransitive prepositions, with which they form an idiomatic, semantic unit. Particles have the interesting property of undergoing Particle Shift, moving to the right over the direct object noun phrase of the verb.
    Some examples of sentences with particles are given in (35) for review. We can see that the verb-particle forms a semantic unit, when we compare the particle constructions with sentences with transitive prepositions, as in (36).

   (35) a. John put *out* the garbage.
         b. The robber handed *over* the jewels.
         c. They picked *up* Tina.

(36) a. John ran *out* the door.
      b. The robber jumped *over* the fence.
      c. They drove *up* the street.

In (35), *put out/hand over/pick up* have idiomatic meanings that are not shared by the verbs and following prepositional phrases in (36). *Hand over* in (35b), for example, means to *relinquish*. *Jump over* in (36b), in contrast, forms no such idiomatic unit with the verb: *over* is in this case purely directional.

On the basis of evidence that particles form a semantic unit with the verb, we will assume that they are selected by, and thus are complements of, the verbs with which they occur. They are typically selected by verbs that also select direct object noun phrases, as in (35). They can also, as we see in (37), be selected by verbs that select no other complements.

(37) a. They ran *out*.
      b. She felt put *off*.
      c. We jumped *up*.
      d. I wish they would get *out*, so we could move *in*.

The phrase structure we will assume for particle complements is illustrated in (38), where the verb also sometimes selects a direct object that occurs to the right of the particle.

(38)

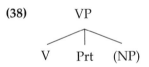

Prt   (NP)

Indirect Objects

In addition to being subjective complements, objective complements, and direct object complements, noun phrases can also be **indirect objects,** yet another kind of complement. Indirect objects are noun phrases that follow the verb in sentences such as (39).

(39) a. Hortense gave *the gorilla* the banana.
      b. Juliet sent *Romeo* a letter.

Indirect objects are, semantically, the *receiver, beneficiary,* or *goal* of a direct object. In (39a) for example, *the gorilla* is the beneficiary of the direct object *the banana,* and in (39b), *Romeo* is the goal of the direct object *a letter* (though as you may know, the tragedy is that he never receives it). Indirect objects occur with a class of verbs that also select direct objects, called **dative** verbs.

Syntactically, indirect objects are noun phrases that originate as complements of the prepositions *to* and *for,* as in (40a) and (41a). Indirect Object Movement applies to derive the (b) sentences in (40–41) from the (a) ones.

(40)   a. Hortense gave a banana to *the gorilla*. =>
         b. Hortense gave *the gorilla* a banana.

(41)   a. Juliet sent a letter to *Romeo*. =>
         b. Juliet sent *Romeo* a letter.

The status of indirect objects as complements raises some interesting questions for our formulation of subcategorization frames for dative verbs such as *give, send, write, bake,* verbs whose complements can be reordered by Indirect Object Movement to derive the (b) order from the (a) order in (42).

(42)   a. V NP PP =>
         b. V NP NP

Given the two possible orders of complements after verbs such as *give, send,* how do we formulate the subcategorization frame for such verbs? We proposed earlier in the chapter that in a grammar that includes movement rules such as Indirect Object Movement, it is reasonable to list in subcategorization frames the order of complements only *before* movement rules apply; otherwise, movement rules become superfluous. We thus proposed that the subcategorization frame for *give* is (43a), rather than (43b).

(43)   a. *give,* V_____ NP PP

         b. *give,* V_____ $\begin{bmatrix} \text{NP NP} \\ \text{NP PP} \end{bmatrix}$

According to (43a), dative verbs such as *give* are actually subcategorized for noun phrase and prepositional phrase complements, where the prepositional phrase *dominates* an indirect object noun phrase. Indirect Object Movement can apply, deriving the order *verb + indirect object + direct object,* as illustrated in (40–41). Syntactically then, the indirect object noun phrase in the sentences discussed above is not directly selected by the verb. Rather, the verb selects a prepositional phrase complement that *dominates* the indirect object, as expressed by the subcategorization frame in (43a). The phrase structure in which indirect objects originate is therefore (44). (Direct object is abbreviated as DO and Indirect Object as IO.)

(44)

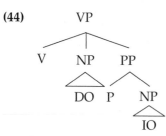

After Indirect Object Movement applies, we derive the phrase structure in (44a).

(44a)

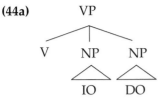

We will assume, then, that dative verbs such as *give* subcategorize noun phrase and prepositional phrase complements. Indirect objects originate as a specific type of object of a preposition, namely the only kind that can undergo Indirect Object Movement.

Once again, movement provides us with a useful way to distinguish between different kinds of complements that are otherwise syntactically indistinguishable. For example, (44) is also the structure of a sentence in which the verb selects a direct object and a prepositional phrase complement that does not dominate an indirect object, as in (45).

(45)   a. Hortense walked [the dog] [to the store].
                          NP   PP
          b. Lionel danced [the macarena] [for the crowd].
                          NP   PP

We might expect *the store* and *the crowd* to be indirect objects in (45), as they are objects of prepositions *to* and *for*, in a configuration identical to (44). When we apply Indirect Object Movement, however, we can see that neither *the store* nor *the crowd* is an indirect object, as Indirect Object Movement gives rise to the ungrammatical sentences in (46).

(46)   a. *Hortense walked [the store] [the dog].
                          NP   NP
          b. *Lionel danced [the crowd] [the macarena].
                          NP   NP

Indirect objects are thus a particular kind of object of a preposition that undergoes Indirect Object Movement. We can test whether an object of a preposition is an indirect object or not by applying Indirect Object Movement. We also see here that again, syntactically parallel structures can be semantically distinct; though an indirect object is syntactically an object of a preposition, it crucially differs semantically from other such objects.

Adverb Phrase and Adverbial Noun Phrase Complements

You may recall from Chapter 8 that adverb phrases express information about time, manner, reason, possibility, speaker intention, and so on. They occur in a wide range of positions and can be inserted into almost any sentence, to add more information and detail. Adverb phrases are thus typically modifiers rather than complements; verbs and other heads do not typically *select* adverbs. Rather, adverb phrases can occur fairly indiscriminately in any sentence.

There are a few cases in which adverb phrases appear to be selected by verbs. One is given in (47).

(47)   The official worded the bill *carefully.*

Typically, we don't just *word* something, we *word something in a particular way.* Consequently, (47) sounds oddly incomplete if we omit the adverb phrase *carefully.* Some other examples of what appear to be **adverb phrase complements** are in sentences such as those in (48).

(48)   a. The bread cuts easily.
       b. The new Volkswagen handles beautifully.

These constructions, called *middle verb* constructions, are interesting not only because they appear to require adverb phrases, as we see by the ungrammaticality of (49), but also because the syntactic subject is actually the logical object of the verb. This is illustrated in (50).

(49)   a. *The bread cuts.
       b. *The new Volkswagen handles.

(50)   a. Someone cuts the bread.
       b. Someone handles the new Volkswagen.

There also exist complements that have adverbial interpretations, though they are not of the syntactic category Adverb. **Adverbial noun phrase complements,** for example, occur with a variety of different kinds of verbs. These complements are labeled *adverbial* because they express information about *time/manner/place,* or in other cases *measurement,* such as height, weight, age, cost. Some adverbial noun phrase complements selected by the verbs *drive, lurk, go,* and *glance* are given in (51).

(51)   a. We drove *home.*
       b. The Hunchback lurked *downtown.*
       c. The lion went *uphill.*
       d. Dorothy glanced *outside.*

Adverbial noun phrases can sometimes be interchanged with adverbial prepositional phrase complements, as we see by comparing (51) and (52).

(52)   a. We drove *to our house.*
       b. The Hunchback lurked *near the cathedral.*
       c. The lion went *to the waterhole.*
       d. Dorothy glanced *out the window.*

This is not surprising, since prepositional phrases often express adverbial information of time (*at 6 p.m.*), manner (*with a crash*), or place (*at home*).

Verbs such as *measure/weigh/cost* also take adverbial noun phrase complements that express measurement of some kind, as in the examples in (53).

(53)   a.   The Hunchback weighed *300 pounds,* and measured *five feet.*
        b.   The car cost *many thousands of dollars.*

Adverbial noun phrase complements occur to the immediate right of the verb, in the same position as direct object noun phrases and subjective complement noun phrases, as in (54).

(54)

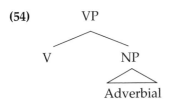

We can distinguish adverbial noun phrase complements from other noun phrase complements by using some of the diagnostics we developed above.

First, adverbial noun phrase complements can be distinguished from direct objects by failing to undergo Passive. This is demonstrated by the ungrammaticality of the passives of the sentences in (53), given in (55).

(55)   a.   **300 pounds* was weighed by The Hunchback.
        b.   **Many thousands of dollars* was cost by the car.

We can also distinguish adverbial noun phrases from subjective complements. Adverbial noun phrase complements do not occur with linking verbs, as we can see in (56).

(56)   a.   **The Hunchback remained *300 pounds.*
        b.   **The car became *many thousands of dollars.*

We are thus able to differentiate adverbial noun phrase complements from others in the same syntactic configuration by investigating their other properties. We can determine whether they undergo a particular movement rule, for example, or identify them by the type of verb that selects them.

Participial Phrase Complements

Complements of verbs can also be verb phrases, or what we will call **participial phrase complements.** Recall from Chapter 6 that a verb phrase can have the structure in (57).

(57)

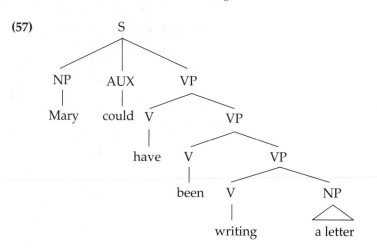

The phrase structure rules that generate (57) are given in (58).

(58) a. S => NP (AUX) VP.

b. AUX => $\left| \begin{array}{l} \text{tense} \\ \textit{have/be/modal/do} \end{array} \right|$

c. VP => V (VP)

We might say that auxiliary verbs and modals select verb phrase complements, though recall that the category Auxiliary is *grammatical* rather than *lexical*. Members of the category Auxiliary invariably introduce lexical verbs, just as members of the grammatical category Determiner invariably introduce nouns. It thus makes little sense to say that members of Auxiliary or Determiner *select* complements, when their position, and what follows them, are fixed.

Restricting the discussion to complements of lexical categories, there exist lexical verbs that clearly select verb phrase complements, and they are of interest to us here. These verb phrase complements are headed by a participial verb, as illustrated in (59).

(59) a. Hortense began *getting nervous.*
b. Lionel keeps *pursuing his degree.*
c. The students started *studying grammar.*

The participial phrases in (59) are complements of **temporal aspect verbs,** verbs that select complements headed by present participles. Thus, such constructions typically express habitual or durative (progressive) aspect.

Other types of verbs also select participial phrase complements, as illustrated in (60).

(60) a. The child loves *playing in the sandbox.*
b. Lionel denied/loathed/regretted/resented *being chosen.*
c. They usually don't mind/dislike/like/dread *eating squid.*
d. I can't imagine/bear *eating squid.*

Both a complete and more abbreviated phrase structure for a participial phrase complement are given in (61).

(61)

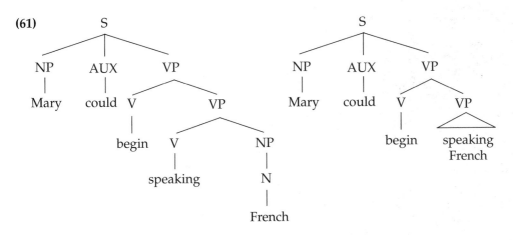

Participial phrase complements are easy to identify, as they cannot be confused with any other kind of complement we have discussed so far.

Tensed Clause Complements

From Chapter 10 you are already familiar with subordinate clauses and how they occur inside larger, independent clauses, as in (62).

(62) The stockbrokers hoped [that the market would improve].
               S

The subordinate clause in (62) is a complement of the verb *hope*. Notice also that the subordinate clause is tensed; the main verb of the subordinate clause is *was*, a past tense form of the verb *be*. The clausal complement in (62) is therefore what we refer to as a **tensed clause complement,** one of the several kinds of clausal complements that verbs select. Additional examples are given in (63).

(63) a. They thought [that Garth Brooks was singing tonight].
                 S
       b. No one knows [that Trisha Yearwood will also be there].
                 S
       c. The fans decided [that this concert surpassed all others].
                 S

In (63), the verbs *think, know,* and *decide* all select tensed clause complements. We know these clausal complements are tensed because they contain tensed verbs (*was, will,* and *surpassed*). The tensed clause complements in (63) are also all introduced by (optional) *that*, the complementizer that in English introduces only tensed subordinate clauses, as we discussed in Chapter 10.

We can diagram clausal complements using triangle notation or more articulated structure as in (65).

(65)

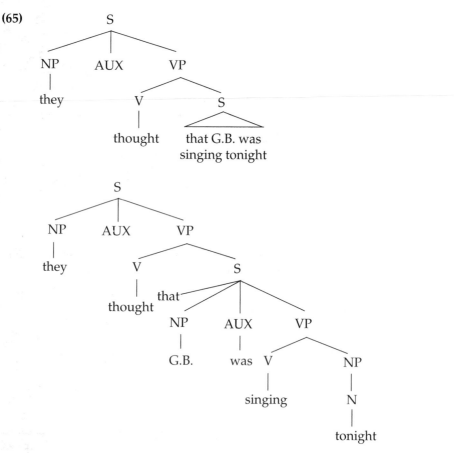

Infinitival Complements

Recall that another kind of subordinate clause introduced in Chapter 10 is the *infinitival* clause. An example of an infinitival clause is given in (66).

(66) The stockbrokers hoped [to make money for their clients].
                                    S

The complement of *hope* in (66) is an infinitive; the uninflected main verb of the complement is *make*, preceded by *to*. We can say, then, that *hope* takes an infinitival clause as a complement, what we will call an **infinitival complement.**

Other examples of infinitival complements of verbs are given in (67).

(67)   a.   They want [the singers to do an encore].
                   S

       b.   Garth expects [to sing a ballad or two].
                     S

As you can see in (67), infinitival complements can have expressed noun phrase subjects, as in (67a), or unexpressed subjects, as in (67b). We might also encounter infinitival complements of the form in (68), where they are introduced by the complementizer *for*.

(68)   a.   They want [for the singers to do an encore].
                   S

       b.   Garth expects [for to sing a ballad or two].
                    S

Infinitival complements have the same basic structure as tensed clausal complements in (65), with the difference that we will assume they lack an AUX position, given their lack of a tensed auxiliary verb. Infinitival complements can therefore be diagrammed as in (69), where *to* is assumed to be part of the verb.

(69)

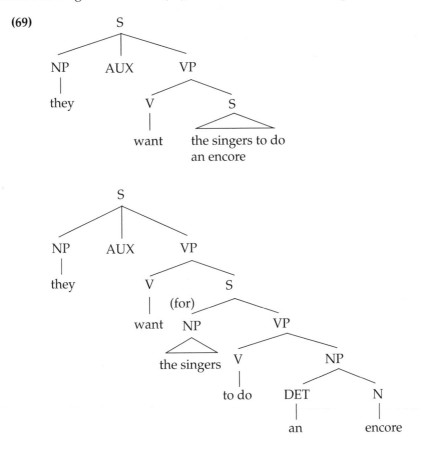

WH-Complements

Another type of clausal complement is the **WH-complement,** a clausal complement in which WH-Movement has occurred. WH-complements can be either tensed or infinitival, and are typically selected by verbs such as *wonder, know,* and *ask.* Because of their interrogative form, they are sometimes referred to as *indirect questions.* Some examples of such complements are given in (70).

(70)   a. I wonder [why Garth Brooks likes singing at the fair].
                   S
          b. The fans asked [which star would be singing first].
                   S
          c. Trisha Yearwood doesn't know [which song to sing].
                   S
          d. Garth Brooks decided [where to put his guitar].
                   S

The clausal complements in (70a–b) are tensed, and the ones in (70c–d) are infinitival. In each case, WH-Movement has applied to move some constituent to clause-initial position.

An interesting fact about WH-complements is that, because they involve WH-Movement, they appear to lack complementizers; they are introduced by neither *that* nor *for,* the two complementizers we have discussed above and in Chapter 10. There do exist, however two possible WH-complementizers, namely *whether* and *if,* that occur in WH-complements, as in (71).

(71)   I wonder [if/whether Garth Brooks likes singing at the fair].
                   S

Whether and *if* in (71) do not appear in their positions as a result of WH-Movement; there is no obvious position in the clause they could have originated in and been moved from. Rather, they appear to originate in "complementizer position," just like *that* and *for* above. Because we interpret them as WH-words, we consider the clauses they introduce WH-complements, distinct from other types of tensed or infinitival complements. This distinction is further supported by evidence that neither *whether* nor *if* can introduce tensed or infinitival complements of verbs that do *not* select indirect questions, such as *think* and *prefer.*

(72)   a. *I think [whether Garth Brooks likes singing at the fair].
                   S
          b. *I prefer [if Garth Brooks likes singing at the fair].
                   S

Similarly, neither *that* nor *for* can introduce indirect questions, as we see in (73), where these complementizers are ungrammatical in complements selected by *wonder,* a verb that always selects a WH-complement.

(73)   a. *I wonder [that Garth Brooks likes singing at the fair].
                   S
          b. *I wonder [for Trisha to sing an encore].
                   S

We can see from the above discussion and examples that verbs clearly *select* not only the category of their complement, namely S, but also the complementizer that introduces it.

Finally, observe that *whether* and *if* are distinct from each other with respect to the kinds of WH-complements they introduce. As we see in (74), *whether* introduces both tensed and infinitival WH-complements.

(74)   a. I wonder whether John left.
       b. *I wonder whether to leave.

The sentences in (75) show, in contrast, that *if* introduces only tensed WH-complements.

(75)   a. I wonder if John left.
       b. *I wonder if (John) to leave.

Another interesting point about WH-complementizers is that they are not optional, as we see by the ungrammaticality of the sentences in (76–77). *Whether* and *if* thus contrast with the optional English complementizers *that* and *for*.

(76)   a. I wonder whether Garth Brooks likes singing at the fair.
       b. *I wonder Garth Brooks likes singing at the fair.

(77)   a. I wonder if John left.
       b. *I wonder John left.

We can diagram WH-complements as in (78), where we assume that WH-Movement has taken place within the subordinate clause, to move a WH-phrase to sentence-initial position. Alternatively, this position can be filled with a WH-complementizer, *whether* or *if*, as in (79).

(78)

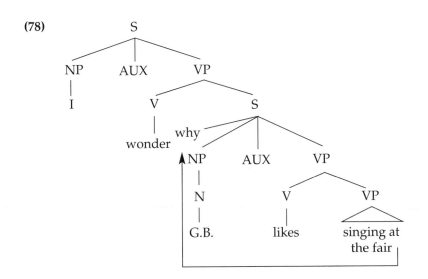

(79)

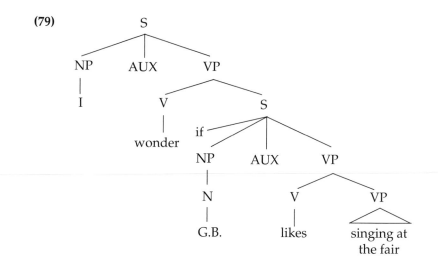

The above data suggest that English complementizers *that, for, if,* and *whether* have very distinct properties regarding the types of clausal complements they introduce. *That* introduces tensed, non-WH-complements, and *for,* infinitival, non-WH-complements. *Whether* and *if,* on the other hand, introduce *only* WH-complements; furthermore, *whether* introduces either tensed or infinitival WH-complements, but *if* only tensed WH-complements. Finally, both *that* and *for* are optional in English, but *whether* and *if* are obligatory in indirect questions without WH-movement.

Verbs therefore appear to select the clauses introduced by certain complementizers. The distribution of complementizers in English is represented in Table 11.1.

We turn now to two types of subordinate clauses we discussed in Chapter 10, clauses that take no complementizers at all.

Bare Infinitival and Participial Clause Complements

Recall from the discussion in Chapter 10 that bare infinitival or participial clauses follow certain kinds of verbs, namely **perception verbs,** such as *watch* and *hear,* and the verbs *make* and *let.* Some examples of participial clauses (in

Table 11.1
English Complementizers

	+WH	−WH
Tensed complements	whether/if (obligatory)	that (optional)
Infinitival complements	whether (obligatory)	for (optional)

which the verb is either in its *-ing* or *-en/-ed/-t* form) are given in (80), and of bare infinitival clauses in (81).

(80) a. We watched [the squirrel climbing the tree].
                          S
      b. The child heard [her mother shouting].
                          S
      c. They found [the campers drenched by the rain].
                     S
      d. The committee members heard [the bill discussed at the meeting].
                                      S

(81) a. He made [Cary clean her room].
                  S
      b. The dog let [the cat walk by].
                     S
      c. We watched [the squirrel climb the tree].
                     S
      d. The child heard [her mother shout].
                          S

We will not repeat all the arguments here for analyzing the bracketed constituents as subjects and predicates, and hence as clauses. We can diagram such **bare infinitival** and **participial clause complements** as in (82).

(82)

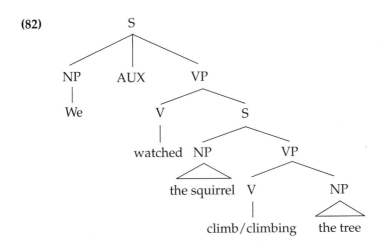

In terms of phrase structure, bare infinitival and participial complements are basically identical in position to tensed, infinitival, and WH-complements. They occur to the right of the verb, and consist of a subject noun phrase and verb phrase predicate. They differ from tensed clauses (and are similar to *to-*infinitival clauses) in lacking an AUX position, as they have no tense. They differ from each other in the form of the verb heading the verb phrase complement.

This concludes our discussion of the wide range of complements of verbs. In the following section we turn to the complements of other lexical categories, including adverbs, adjectives, prepositions, and nouns.

Complements of Other Lexical Categories

Beginning the discussion with adverbs, this lexical category is unique in taking virtually no complements at all. A few cases I am aware of are given in (83).

(83)   a. [Unfortunately [for our hero]], Superman was captured by
          ADVP   PP
          Lex Luthor.
       b. He ran [quickly [for a nonathlete]].
               ADVP   PP

The adverbs *unfortunately* and *quickly* in (83) appear to select a prepositional phrase complement. (83b) is illustrated in (84).

(84)

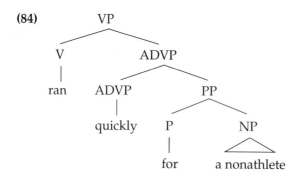

Adjectives take a broader range of complements than adverbs. Some select different prepositional phrase complements, as in (85), illustrated in (86).

(85)   Mary is   a. [fond [of chocolate]].
                      AP   PP

                  b. [proud [of her heritage]].
                      AP   PP

                  c. [happy [about the promotion]].
                      AP   PP

(86)

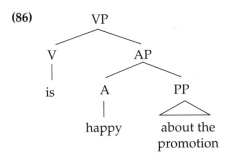

Adjectives can also occur with either infinitival or tensed clause complements, as in (87), with the corresponding phrase structure in (88).

(87) She was   a. [able [to leave]].
              AP   S

          b. [happy [that her daughter won the award]].
             AP   S

(88)

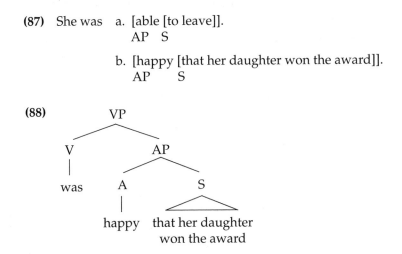

Turning next to complements of prepositions, we have already discussed the fact that transitive prepositions select noun phrase complements, what we have referred to as objects of prepositions. An example is given in (89).

(89)   The kitten jumped [off [the bed]].
                              PP NP

We also briefly discussed in Chapter 9 how prepositions can select another prepositional phrase as a complement.

(90) a. John is [from [near Toronto]].
                     PP   PP
          b. They'll judge me [as [without qualifications]].
                              PP PP
          c. Sue is [in [for a surprise]].
                     PP PP

Prepositions also occur in a number of other more complex, idiomatic constructions, in which they appear to select a noun phrase and prepositional phrase
complement. Some examples are given in (91).

(91)   in aid of/in accordance with/in common with/by virtue of/on
       account of/at variance with

We won't analyze constructions such as in (91) further here. Prepositions can
also take verb phrase (participial) complements, and in some cases, adjective
phrase complements.

(92)   a. [while/after/before/since [eating breakfast]]
          PP   VP
          (participial complement).
       b. She went [from [happy to sad]]. (adjective phrase complement).
                    PP   AP
       c. He strikes me [as [unbalanced]]. (adjective phrase complement).
                         PP AP

Prepositions can also select participial clause complements, as in (93), or tensed
clause complements, as in (94).

(93)   [With [John gone]], there was no reason to continue the conversation.
        PP   S

(94)   There was no reason to continue the conversation
       [because [John had left]].
        PP   S

Recall that there is in fact a large class of prepositions, aptly named **subordinating prepositions,** which select clauses as complements quite regularly.
Other examples, in addition to *because* and *with* in (93–94), are given in (95).

(95)   a. [*Although/when/because/even though/while*
          PP
          [he had made his decision]],
          S
          John almost changed his mind at the last minute.
       b. [*If* [she could], Mary wanted to see the play.
          PPS
       c. It had been a long time [*since* [she had been to the theater]].
                                   PP   S
       d. She wore black, [*as* [it was appropriate]].
                           PP S

We return to the functions of subordinating prepositional phrases in Chapter 12
in more detail. We can diagram the range of complements that prepositions
select as in (96).

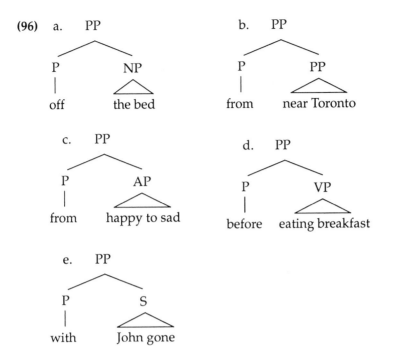

(96) a. PP — P | off — NP the bed

b. PP — P | from — PP near Toronto

c. PP — P | from — AP happy to sad

d. PP — P | before — VP eating breakfast

e. PP — P | with — S John gone

The complements of nouns, the final type of complement we will discuss here, is a complex issue, as it is not always clear whether phrases following nouns are actually selected by the noun or not. For example, consider (97), in which a prepositional phrase or a clause can follow the noun *student*, and thus is a potential candidate for being analyzed as a complement of the head noun.

(97) a. the student *of linguistics*.
b. the fact *that the earth is round*

It is difficult to see how a noun such as *student* selects a complement, such as *of linguistics*, given that nouns typically do not appear "incomplete" when they occur without complements. Nouns thus differ from verbs, many of which seem odd or ungrammatical without their selected complements (**Mary kissed*, versus *Mary kissed her daughter*). On the other hand, adjectives can occur as freely without complements as with them, as in *Hortense is proud* versus *Hortense is proud of her achievements*. It may be that nouns simply pattern more closely with adjectives in having completely optional complements, than with verbs, whose complements are often obligatory.

One argument for analyzing the prepositional phrase in (97a) and the clause in (97b) as complements of nouns is that semantically, they form an integral part of the description of the nouns, *student* and *fact*, respectively. These phrases thus might be argued to "complete" the noun phrase in the way that a complement of the verb completes the verb phrase.

There is also some syntactic evidence that the phrases in (97) form a constituent with the head noun in a way that modifiers of nouns do not. This evidence comes from *one* **pronominalization.** To illustrate, consider the contrast between (98) and (99).

(98) a. this student of linguistics and that *one*.
  b. *this student of chemistry and that *one* of linguistics

(99) a. this student from Seattle and that *one*.
  b. this student from Boston and that *one* from Seattle

We see in (98a) that the noun *student,* together with the prepositional phrase *of linguistics,* can be replaced by the pronoun *one.* The ungrammaticality of (98b) shows that *of linguistics* in fact *must* form a constituent with *student,* the constituent that is replaced by the pronoun *one.* We can diagram the noun phrase *the student of linguistics* as in (100), and where pronominalization operates on the entire noun phrase, rather than on the noun *student* alone.

(100)

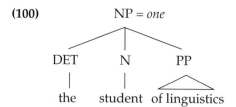

Considering now (99), we see that the prepositional phrase *from Seattle* does not appear to form a syntactic constituent with the noun *student* in the same way as *of linguistics* in (98). We can represent the relevant difference between the prepositional phrases in (98) and (99) by giving (99) the phrase structure in (101).

(101)

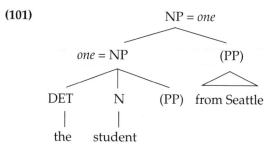

In (101), *one* can replace either the higher or lower noun phrase, deriving either (99a) or (99b), both of which are grammatical. Crucially, the prepositional phrase *from Seattle* occurs in a higher position than the phrase *of linguistics*

(which would occupy, if present in (101), the PP position in the lower NP). Because *one* pronominalization can operate on either the higher or lower noun phrase in (101), it follows that *of linguistics* will always be replaced by *one,* along with *student.* The phrase *from Seattle,* on the other hand, is only optionally replaced by *one.*

In Chapter 12, we provide additional arguments that unselected phrases, such as the prepositional phrase *from Seattle* in (101), occupy higher "adjoined" positions in a phrase than do complements, such as *of linguistics.* For now, observe that we can use *one* pronominalization as a diagnostic for what we will assume are complements of nouns. Complements must be included in the constituent replaced by *one.* Modifiers of nouns, on the other hand, need only optionally be included, as they are adjoined outside the lower NP that *one* replaces.

Summary

Summarizing this chapter, we have examined in detail the **complements** of verbs and other lexical heads, finding that lexical categories differ with respect to the range of phrases they select as complements. We discussed how selection can be formalized as **subcategorization,** a notation devised to express our unconscious knowledge of complementation encoded in our mental lexicon.

We have seen that syntactically, complements of different heads are sometimes indistinguishable; many different verbs take noun phrase complements that appear to be syntactically identical. We found, however, that complements of the same syntactic category can nevertheless differ semantically quite dramatically. Some of the semantic labels for different noun phrase complements, for example, are **direct object, subjective complement, objective complement, indirect object, object of a preposition,** and **adverbial noun phrase.** We discussed a number of ways to differentiate among syntactically identical complements, using movement (such as Passive and Indirect Object Movement) and by identifying the type of verb the complement is selected by (choosing among, for example, **linking verbs, transitive verbs,** and **dative verbs, temporal aspect verbs,** and **perception verbs.**

We have provided phrase structure diagrams for each type of complement, illustrating the different NP, PP (including Particles and subordinating prepositional phrases), AP, VP, (**participial phrase complements**) and clausal (S) complements selected by different lexical heads. S complements can be divided into three different types. **Tensed clausal complements** are introduced by the complementizer *that.* **Infinitival complements** can be introduced by the complementizer *for,* and **WH-complements** are introduced by an interrogative WH-phrase or by the complementizers *whether/if.* **Bare infinitival** and **participial clause complements** lack tense (and hence an AUX position), and are not introduced by complementizers.

Finally, we discussed the complements of nouns, finding that these complements are syntactically, but not necessarily semantically, distinguishable from modifiers of nouns. That is, complements of nouns appear to be included in the lowest noun phrase, to the right of the head noun. Modifiers are adjoined in higher positions. Either the higher or lower noun phrase can be replaced by *one* through the process of *one pronominalization*, with the result that complements will always be included in the constituent replaced by *one*, but modifiers will be only optionally.

DISCOVERY PROBLEMS

Problem 1. Complements

Suppose you want to explain to someone how to use the following English words. You might explain that a particular word is a verb or a preposition, and then you might use the word in context. When you do this, you are essentially defining the word by its syntactic category and providing examples of the complements it takes.

For this exercise, write out sentences that illustrate as many different kinds of complements for each of the following heads as you can. Also, identify the syntactic category of the head.

decide arrange certain observe ready begin because without under when

For example, suppose you need to determine the complementation of the verb *like*. You come up with the following complements:

a) They like [snowboards].
         NP
b) They like [going snowboarding].
         VP

You conclude from the data in (a–b) that *like* selects the following complements: a direct object or a participial complement

$$\text{like, V} \underline{\qquad} \begin{vmatrix} \text{NP} \\ \text{VP} \end{vmatrix}$$

Try to devise an informal subcategorization frame for each head, one that encodes all the possible complements you describe.

Problem 2. Noun Phrase Complements

As we have seen, identifying complements can be confusing because complements often have more than one label. For example, there are a number of complements of the syntactic category noun phrase that have different semantic labels (direct object, objective complement, etc.). For this exercise, create sentences with different kinds of noun phrase complements using the verbs provided. You should come up with a cross section of noun phrase complements that have different semantic labels. Provide the semantic label for each noun phrase complement and iIllustrate how you used the different diagnostics discussed in the chapter to differentiate among them.

a) *consider, elect, make:* objective complements
b) *remain, appear, become:* subjective complements
c) *adore, make, throw:* direct objects
d) *weigh, cost, grow:* adverbial noun phrases

Problem 3. Indirect Objects

We have assumed that indirect objects are dominated by prepositional phrases prior to Indirect Object Movement. They are thus not strictly noun phrase complements of the verb. Nevertheless, after Indirect Object Movement they occur in the same syntactic position as other noun phrases: to the immediate right of the verb, as illustrated below:

Sasha sent a package to *her sister.* => Sasha sent *her sister* a package. With this in mind, answer the following questions:

a) How do you know that the indirect object on the right in the sentence is not a subjective complement?
b) How do you know it is not a direct object?
c) How do you know it is not an objective complement?
d) How do you know it is not an adverbial noun phrase complement?

Use the diagnostics we have discussed in the text to answer these questions. Illustrate your answers with clear examples.

Problem 4. Passive Practice

Now that you have seen that not all active sentences can be passivized, for one reason or another, try to explain why Passive fails in the following sentences. Be as specific as you can, using the information about differences among complements discussed in the chapter.

a) The smoke vanished.
b) Al has become a nuisance.
c) John remained Mary's dance partner.
d) That package weighs ten pounds.
e) We went home.
f) The defendant lied about the incident.

*Problem 5. Complements and WH-movement

We have discussed WH-Movement in several different contexts in previous chapters. For this exercise, apply WH-Movement to the following italicized noun phrases. Identify the semantic type of complement in each case. Do noun phrase complements differ in any way with respect to how WH-Movement

applies to them? Can we use WH-Movement as a diagnostic for differentiating among different kinds of noun phrase complements? In particular, think about the WH-word that replaces the noun phrase. Is it the same for all noun phrase complements? Explain why or why not.
Example:

    a) Hortense visited *her relatives.*
    b) Hortense visited *who?*
    c) *Who* did Hortense visit?

Her relatives = direct object noun phrase

    a) Mary is *my friend.*
    b) The parents named their son *Tiger.*
    c) John became *a firefighter.*
    d) Dogs consider cats *incredible nuisances.*
    e) Mike and Betty remained *our dear friends.*

    f) Mary met *her mother.*
    g) The children sang *the national anthem.*
    h) Mary baked her mother *a cake.*
    i) Mary baked a cake for *her mother.*

Now apply WH-Movement to the following sentences to complements that are not noun phrases. Identify the italicized complement in each sentence (syntactically and semantically, if you can). What kinds of conclusions can you draw about the effects of WH-Movement on these complements and on those above? How do subjective and objective complements pattern together versus, for example, direct objects? Can we use WH-Movement as a diagnostic for different complement types?

    a) Mary is *extraordinarily content.*
    b) The parents find Tiger *very mature.*
    c) We found Sue *in bad shape.*
    d) We returned to find our dog *in a bad way.*

Make up additional sentences in which you apply WH-Movement to different complement types to test your hypotheses.

Problem 6. Indirect Object Movement and Passive

In our discussions of movement in this chapter, we saw that direct objects can undergo at least two different movement rules, Passive and Indirect Object Movement. Indirect objects also undergo movement when they change places with the direct object by Indirect Object Movement. Now, consider the sentences in (a–b).

a) Juliet sent a letter to Romeo.
b) Juliet sent Romeo a letter.

In (a), no movement rule has applied, but in (b), Indirect Object Movement has applied. Apply Passive to *each* of the above sentences. What is the result? Create three or four examples of this same pattern of movement on your own, following the instructions below.

- Formulate a sentence in which a dative verb takes a direct object noun phrase and a prepositional phrase (that dominates an indirect object).
- Apply Indirect Object Movement, deriving the order *verb + indirect object + direct object*.
- Apply Passive in *each* sentence in the pair.

You should find that sentences with direct and indirect objects have two different passives, depending on whether Indirect Object Movement has applied or not.

*Problem 7. Idioms

There are phrases in English called *idioms,* which are interpreted nonliterally. Some examples are given below.

a) That guy kicked the bucket.
b) She bought it on that test.
c) Lionel kept a stiff upper lip.

What happens when you attempt to make the active sentences passive? Can you apply WH-Movement, or any other movement rule we have discussed so far? If the rules apply, does the phrase keep its idiomatic interpretation? Why or why not? Find at least three more examples of idioms and apply some movement rules to them. What is the result, and can you explain why?

TEXT ANALYSIS

1. Identifying Complements

List the complements of each of the boldface heads in the following sentences. Label each complement by syntactic category (as a noun phrase, verb phrase, etc.). If the complement has a particular semantic label, include that label as well. (Choose from the list in the chapter summary.) What makes this exercise difficult is that not all material that follows a head is a complement. You must therefore distinguish between phrases *selected* by the head, and unselected phrases.

1. The next day she *went* downtown *by* herself, *leaving* Ryukichi at home.
2. When she *came* to the bomb site she *noticed* that a fire was *burning* inside the cabin.
3. She *ran* to the door and *walked* in.
4. The room *was* full of smoke and it was *billowing* out the window.
5. Ryo turned *without* a word and *hurried* off.
6. She had *thought* of asking for the address of Tsuruishi's sister and of going to burn a stick of incense in his memory, but suddenly this *seemed* quite pointless.

Source: Downtown, by Fumiko Hayashi.

2. More Complements

Do the same as above in the following sentences.

1. The cold *passed* reluctantly from the earth, and the retiring fogs *revealed* an army stretched out *on* the hills, resting.
2. As the landscape changed *from* brown to green, the army *awakened,* and *began* to tremble *with* eagerness at the noise of rumors.
3. It *cast* its eyes upon the roads, which were *growing* from long troughs of liquid mud to proper thoroughfares.
4. A river, amber-tinted in the shadow of its banks, *purled* at the army's feet; and at night, when the stream had *become* of a sorrowful blackness, one could see *across* it the red, eye-like gleam of hostile camp fires set *in* the low brows of distant hills.

Source: The Red Badge of Courage, by Stephen Crane.

3. Clausal Complements

In texts of your choice, find at least two examples each of the following:

- tensed clausal complements
- infinitival complements
- bare infinitival complements
- participial clause complements
- WH-complements

Bring your sentences to class to exchange with another student. See whether you can identify the types of clausal complements in each other's sentences.

LANGUAGE DIVERSITY EXERCISES

1. *Ser* and *Estar*

Spanish has two different words for main verb *be: ser* and *estar*. These two verbs differ, however, in terms of the complements they take. Spanish grammar books discuss this difference in some detail, providing examples of the different uses of *ser* and *estar*. On the basis of what you now know about complementation, analyze the syntactic differences between *ser* and *estar*. Do they systematically select different complements? Do the verbs differ in meaning? Provide examples to support your conclusions, and compare your findings with the syntax of English main verb *be*.

2. Complements in Other Languages

In a language of your choice, analyze at least three different kinds of complements. Give examples, and show how the complementation of a particular head differs from its English counterpart. Indirect objects in other languages often exhibit interesting differences from their English counterparts—you may wish to investigate them. (Other good things to look for are indirect questions, infinitival complements, direct objects, etc.)

3. Earlier English Complements

Analyze three or four sentences in a passage in an earlier version of English (Old, Middle, or Early Modern) in terms of complementation. Identify the complements you find, and the heads that select them. What syntactic differences between complementation in this earlier version of English and modern English do you find?

4. Subordination in Pidgin Languages

Pidgins are claimed to lack subordination and to rely primarily on coordination to form longer and more complex sentences. Find a passage of written pidgin, and analyze it from this point of view. Do you find any subordinate clauses? If you do, label them according to whether they are tensed, infinitival, or participial. Also identify the head that selects them. Identify examples of coordination. Is it true from what you find that pidgin languages lack subordination? Rewrite the passage in some variety of American English, using as much (additional) subordination as you can. What changes?

CHAPTER REVIEW TERMS

Complements, subcategorization, and our mental lexicon

Semantic complement types: direct object, subjective complement, objective complement, indirect object, adverbial noun phrase, object of a preposition

Syntactic complement types: noun phrase, prepositional phrase (including particles, subordinating prepositional phrases), adverb phrase, adjective phrase, participial phrase (verb phrase)

Clausal complements: tensed, infinitival (bare and *to-*), participial, WH-complement

transitive verbs, perception verbs, dative verbs, temporal aspect verbs

Complementizers: *that, for, whether/if*

one pronominalization

CHAPTER REVIEW EXERCISE

Choose from among the following options to create a chapter exercise. You may wish to add options from previous chapter exercises to make this exercise more comprehensive.

1. List the complements of each of the verbs in the text excerpt.
2. Label the syntactic category of each complement (as NP, VP, PP, S, and so on).
3. Provide the semantic label of the complement if it has one (direct object, subjective complement, indirect object and so on).
4. Label any clausal complements as tensed, infinitival (bare or *to-*), or participial.
5. Identify any WH-complements.
6. Identify any transitive verbs.
7. Identify any perception verbs, temporal aspect verbs, and dative verbs.
8. Identify any complementizers.

Because she was such a methodical house-keeper, my mother had plenty of time to read her beloved books, walk to the corner stores, or visit with neighbors. I never sensed that she was bored or lonely. She always took special pains to put on fresh lipstick and to comb her hair when she knew that my father was on his way home. As soon as she saw him coming down the street, she began preparing the Manhattan cocktails which they shared every single night of their married life as they sat together on our porch and talked about their day. She seemed to grow more vibrant as they talked, asking him questions about work, and listening with unwavering interest and sympathetic understanding. He in turn asked her what she had done, whom she had talked with, and what she had read. When, occasionally, I listened to them talk, I could sense their love for one another, which made me happy, though I felt jealously excluded from their conversation. Indeed, so special was their ritual cocktail hour that my father never drank another Manhattan after my mother's death.

Source: Wait Till Next Year, by Doris Kearns Goodwin.

12

Adjuncts in the Verb Phrase

Language ought to be the joint creation of poets and manual workers.
George Orwell

Introduction

In the previous chapter we investigated how heads and their complements make up larger phrases. We relied both on our intuitions about selection and on syntactic tests for constituency, to show that heads and complements form a syntactic unit. We have yet to discuss, however, the syntax and semantics of phrases that are *not* selected, what we will call *adjuncts*. These phrases are typically either modifiers or predicates, providing additional information beyond that supplied by complements. Adjuncts in the verb phrase, which we discuss in this chapter, are also *moveable*, occurring in both sentence-initial and sentence-final position.

Some examples of adjuncts are given in (1).

(1) a. Mary believed John, *with some trepidation.* (PP adjunct).
     b. Mary talked to John, *upset and distracted.* (AP adjunct)
     c. Mary thinks that John is intelligent, *fortunately.* (ADVP adjunct).
     d. Mary laughed, *pretending she was happy.* (VP adjunct)

Adjuncts, like complements, can be of any category, as you can see in (1). That they can occur in either sentence-initial or sentence-final position is illustrated by comparing (1) and (2).

(2) a. *With some trepidation,* Mary believed John. (PP adjunct).
     b. *Upset and distracted,* Mary talked to John. (AP adjunct)
     c. *Fortunately,* Mary thinks that John is intelligent. (ADVP adjunct).
     d. *Pretending she was happy,* Mary laughed. (VP adjunct)

Adjuncts can also be clauses, as you can see in (3).

(3) a. Mary talked to John, *her eyes sparkling with anger.* (participial
        clause).
     b. Mary talked to John, (in order) *to hear his side of the story.*
        (infinitival clause)

284

That adjuncts in the verb phrase are unselected by the verb may seem in some ways obvious; the verb *believe* in (1a), for example, selects a noun phrase, prepositional phrase, or clausal complement. We typically believe *something*, or we believe *in something*, or we believe *that something*. We don't, however, typically think of *believe* as also requiring a phrase expressing *how* or *the manner in which* we believe. Similarly, the adjunct adjective phrase in (1b), *upset and distracted*, is not selected by the verb *talk*; we talk *to someone*, or we talk *about something*, or we just talk. *Talk* therefore optionally selects a prepositional phrase complement. It makes no sense to say, however, that *talk* also optionally selects an adjective phrase complement that describes the mood we are in when we talk.

Adjuncts in VP therefore occur fairly indiscriminately with *any* verb, and thus do not appear to be selected. This is further illustrated in (4) by the evidence that the adjunct prepositional phrase *on Tuesday* can occur in any number of different sentences, regardless of the verb in the sentence.

(4) a. We considered John happy *on Tuesday*.
     b. John wanted Mary to leave *on Tuesday*.
     c. Mary watched John play the violin *on Tuesday*.
     d. John put the car in the garage *on Tuesday*.
     e. Mary gave a book to John *on Tuesday*.

In the following sections we will discuss other evidence, beyond our intuitions about selection, that allows us to distinguish adjuncts in VP from complements of verbs. In particular, we will discuss syntactic evidence based on movement and the order of constituents in the sentence. We find, for instance, that with respect to the order of constituents in a sentence, adjuncts always occur *outside* (to the right of) complements. Further, adjuncts are *moveable*, originating in sentence-final position, but able to move to sentence-initial position.

We will assume that in terms of phrase structure, adjuncts occur in adjoined position in the verb phrase, as illustrated in (5).

(5)
```
                 VP
              ┌───────┴───────┐
            VP               adjunct
       ┌─────┴─────┐
     head      complements
```

(5) illustrates the principle of *adjunction*. Adjuncts are adjoined to a phrase higher than the one dominating the head and its complements. It follows from this assumption that adjuncts form a constituent with the head and its complements, but always occur to the *right* of complements in English. Further, we will assume that constituents in adjoined position can move to sentence-initial position, in contrast to complements, which do not occur in adjoined position.

Prepositional Phrases Adjuncts

We saw above that syntactically, adjuncts differ from complements in two important ways. **Adjuncts** are typically *moveable*, occurring in either sentence-initial or sentence-final position, as illustrated in (1–2). Adjuncts also occur outside the complements of a particular head. This means that in English adjuncts occur to the right of all complements. Crucially, adjuncts never occur *between* a head and its complements.

We saw that the prepositional phrase *on Tuesday* in (4) is a good example of an adjunct. It is not selected, occurring optionally with any number of different verbs. This **prepositional phrase adjunct** can also move to the front of the sentence, as we see in (7).

(7) a. *On Tuesday,* we considered John happy.
     b. *On Tuesday,* John wanted Mary to leave.
     c. *On Tuesday,* Mary watched John play the violin.
     d. *On Tuesday,* John put the car in the garage.
     e. *On Tuesday,* Mary gave a book to John.

Recall from the previous chapter that prepositional phrases can also be complements. Some examples from that chapter are given below.

(8) a. The lion went *to the waterhole.*
     b. Jim talked *to Pam.*
     c. He comes *from Scotland.*
     d. The Hunchback lurked *near the cathedral.*
     e. The farmer blamed the crop failure *on the lack of rain.*
     f. The child put the toy *in the box.*
     g. The dog sneaked/snuck *into the kitchen.*

The prepositional phrases in (8) are *prepositional phrase complements,* with no distinct semantic label. Other prepositional phrase complements, on the other hand, can be *subjective* or *objective complements,* or the prepositional phrase complements of *dative* verbs. This latter type of prepositional phrase complement dominates an *indirect object.* Examples of these complements are given in (9).

(9) a. Mary is *out of sorts.* (subjective complement).
     b. Mary considers John *out of sorts.* (objective complement)
     c. Mary gave a book *to Sue.* (prepositional phrase dominating an indirect object)

Given what we have assumed above about the syntactic distinction between adjuncts and complements, we expect two things. First, we expect an adjunct prepositional phrase, such as *on Tuesday,* to occur only *outside* of complements. Second, we expect only the adjunct to move to sentence-initial position.

Restricting the discussion to the examples in (9), we can see that the first expectation is borne out. To illustrate, compare (10–11).

(10) a. *Mary is *on Tuesday* out of sorts.
 b. *Mary considers John *on Tuesday* out of sorts.
 c. *Mary gave a book *on Tuesday* to Sue.

(11) a. Mary is out of sorts *on Tuesday*.
 b. Mary considers John out of sorts *on Tuesday*.
 c. Mary gave a book to Sue *on Tuesday*.

As you can see, the sentences in (10) are "worse" than those in (11), where the prepositional phrase adjunct is sentence-final (you may not find the sentences in (10) crashingly ungrammatical, but I think we would all agree that those in (11) certainly sound more natural). We explain this by proposing the structure in (12) for adjunct prepositional phrases, in which they occur outside, rather than inside, complements.

(12)

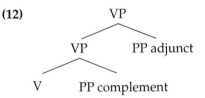

Turning next to the second prediction, that only adjuncts freely move from sentence-final to sentence-initial position, we see that this prediction too is correct. We have seen in (7) that adjunct prepositional phrases such as *on Tuesday* can freely occur in sentence-initial position. Notice, however, that the same is not true of the prepositional phrase complements in (13) (compare with (7)).

(13) a. *Out of sorts Mary is.
 b. *Out of sorts Mary considers John.
 c. *To Sue Mary gave a book.

((13c) has a "literary interpretation" that is grammatical. The sentence sounds odd, however, in casual speech.)

We might expect, given the syntactic distinction between complements and adjuncts we have found evidence for here, that there would also be a clear semantic difference between complement and adjunct prepositional phrases. This is not always the case, however, as illustrated in (14).

(14) a. Pam put Rover in the garage.
 b. Pam saw Rover in the garage.

In (14), the prepositional phrase *in the garage* means the same thing in both sentences; it expresses location. In (14a), however, *in the garage* is a complement of the verb *put*, and in (14b) it is an adjunct. We know this because *put*, but not *see*, subcategorizes a prepositional phrase. We must put something *somewhere*, which suggests that *put* requires a prepositional phrase complement of location. As for *see*, we see *something*, but *where* we see it is not required to complete the verb phrase. *See* thus subcategorizes a direct object noun phrase, but not also a prepositional phrase. The prepositional phrases in (14) thus differ with respect to their complement/adjunct status, but this difference is not also reflected semantically, as both express location.

Another type of prepositional phrase adjunct that you have already been introduced to, but that we have not discussed specifically as an adjunct, is the *subordinating* prepositional phrase. Some examples are given in (15).

(15) a. *Before/after/when* he sang his latest hit, Garth hugged some fans.
      b. Garth hugged some fans *before/after/when* he sang his latest hit.

Subordinating prepositional phrases, in which the complement of the preposition is a subordinate clause, freely occur in sentence-initial or sentence-final position, as you can see in (15). Such prepositional phrases also occur outside of all complements of the verb, in the adjunct position in (12). This is illustrated in (16), where *before he sang his latest hit* precedes the complement *some fans*, with an ungrammatical result.

(16) *Garth hugged [*before* he sang his latest hit] some fans.

We thus have evidence for a syntactic distinction between selected and unselected phrases, or between complements and adjuncts. We have also seen that complements and adjuncts are not necessarily distinguishable on the basis of their semantics.

Adverb Phrase and Adverbial Noun Phrase Adjuncts

As we saw in Chapter 8, **adverb phrases** occur in a number of positions, and in Chapter 11 we discussed some of the few ways in which adverb phrases show up as complements. Some examples of adverb phrase complements are repeated in (17).

(17) a. She worded the letter *carefully*.
      b. The bread cuts *easily*.

Adverb phrases also occur quite freely as unselected phrases, or as what we know now to be adjuncts, as illustrated in (18).

(18) a. *Fortunately*, we don't *often* have exams.
      b. She runs five miles *daily*, and *lately* she finishes her workout *quite quickly*.
      c. You should *probably* go to the dentist *soon*.

As for position, we know that adverb phrases can occur in either sentence-initial or sentence-final position; indeed, they can occur in five different positions in the sentence, as discussed in Chapter 8. The phrase structure illustrating those positions is repeated in (19).

(19)

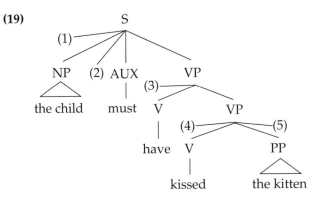

Given our current assumptions about adjunction, we can assume that adverbs are adjoined to VP (in positions 3, 4, and 5), or that they occur in sentence initial position, (position 1), or between the subject noun phrase and AUX (position 2). Though this last position is the only one that is not necessarily an *adjoined* position in the way we have described above, it is nevertheless clearly not a *complement* position.

The possible adjunct positions for adverb phrases can now be illustrated as in (20–21).

(20)

(21)

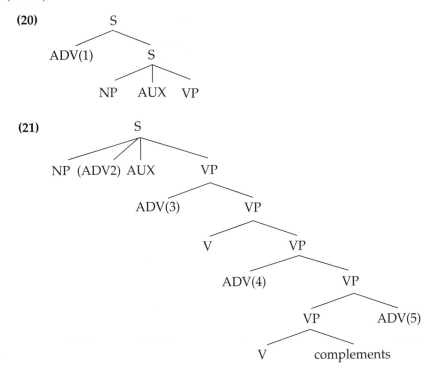

According to (20–21), we do not expect adverbs to intervene between the verb and its complements. This is for the most part the case, as we see in (22).

(22) a. She dropped the vase *clumsily.*
      b. *She dropped *clumsily* the vase.

(23) a. Frankie *always* thought that Johnny was a nice guy.
      b. *Frankie thought *always* that Johnny was a nice guy.

Adverb phrases thus fit the pattern of adjuncts, which is what we might expect, given the evidence that they occur in different noncomplement positions in the sentence. Also, they are rarely selected by verbs or other heads.

Turning now to adverbial noun phrases, these can appear as adjuncts, unselected by the verb, as in (24).

(24) a. He bought a gift for Julia *downtown.*
      b. Griffey hit a home run *yesterday.*

The **adverbial noun phrase adjuncts** in (24) differ from adverbial noun phrase complements in (25).

(25) a. They put the new office *downtown.*
      b. The Hunchback weighed *300 pounds.*

The verbs *buy* and *hit* in (24) select direct objects, and dative *buy* also selects a prepositional phrase that dominates an indirect object. The adverbial noun phrases provide additional information: in (24a) about *where* he bought the gift, and in (24b) *when* Griffey hit the home run. The verbs *put* and *weigh* in (25), on the other hand, select adverbial complements, as we put something *somewhere,* and we say that something weighs *some amount.* Both of these adverbial complements are also noun phrases.

The adverbial noun phrase adjuncts, but not the adverbial noun phrase complements, can, as we might expect, occur in sentence-initial position.

(26) a. *Downtown,* he bought a gift for Julia.
      b. *Yesterday,* Griffey hit a home run.

(27) a. **Downtown* they put the office.
      b. **300 pounds* the Hunchback weighed.

The adverbial noun phrase adjuncts also must occur outside complements, which is what we expect if adjuncts occur in adjoined position as in (12).

(28) a. *He bought *downtown* a gift for Julia.
      b. *Griffey hit *yesterday* a home run.

The syntactic distribution of adverb phrases and unselected adverbial noun phrases thus supports an analysis of these phrases as adjuncts, rather than complements. We can diagram adverbial noun phrase adjuncts as in (29).

(29)

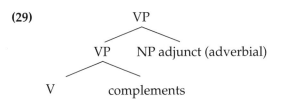

Participial Phrase Adjuncts

Recall that verb phrases, or participial phrases, can be complements of a number of different verbs, including temporal aspect verbs such as those in (30).

(30) a. Sue began *eating lunch.*
  b. The puppy kept *chewing the sock.*

Participial phrases can also occur in adjunct position, as in (31).

(31) a. The child grabbed the cookie, *caught by surprise.*
  b. Romeo searched for Juliet, *consumed by desire.*

The **participial phrase adjuncts** in (31) are unselected; neither *grab* nor *search* selects a participial phrase that expresses adverbial information of *manner*. Further, observe that the participial phrases in (31) can occur in sentence-initial position as well as in sentence-final position, patterning in yet another way with adjuncts rather than complements.

(32) a. *Caught by surprise,* the child grabbed the cookie.
  b. *Consumed by desire,* Romeo looked for Juliet.

(33) a. **Eating lunch,* Sue began.
  b. **Chewing the sock,* the puppy kept.

Participial phrase adjuncts can also not intervene between complements and heads, as we see in (34).

(34) a. *The child grabbed *caught by surprise* the cookie.
  b. *Romeo searched *consumed by desire* for Juliet.

We can diagram participial phrase adjuncts as in (35).

(35)

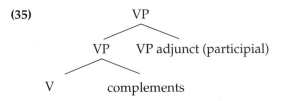

Adjective Phrase Adjuncts

Adjective phrases as complements occur in sentences such as those in (36).

(36)   a. Sally Field was *ecstatic*.
       b. He seems *completely happy*.

Recall that the complements in (36) are called *subjective complements,* because the adjective phrase is a predicate which assigns a property to the subject noun phrase. Adjective phrases can also be *objective* complements, as in (37),

(37)   a. They painted the room *a pretty lavender*.
       b. The wind blew the door *closed*.

and can be adjuncts, as in (38).

(38)   a. Sally Field accepted her Oscar, *ecstatic*.
       b. He ran through the woods, *completely happy*.

In (38), an **adjective phrase adjunct** has been added to the sentence. In neither case is the adjective phrase selected by the verb. *Accept* is a transitive verb that selects the direct object *her Oscar,* and *run* selects a prepositional phrase of location or direction. The adjective phrases *ecstatic* and *completely happy* are thus unselected by the verbs, and thus are adjuncts.

Further evidence for the adjunct status of the adjective phrases in (38) is that they can occur in sentence-initial position. They contrast with adjective phrase complements, which cannot occur in this position. These contrasts are given in (39–41).

(39)   a. *Ecstatic,* Sally Field accepted her Oscar.   (adjuncts).
       b. *Completely happy,* he ran through the woods.

(40)   a. **Ecstatic,* Sally Field was.   (subjective complements).
       b. *Completely happy, he seemed.

(41)   a. **A pretty lavender,* they painted the room.(objective complements).
       b. **Closed,* the wind blew the door.

As expected, adjunct adjective phrases cannot intervene between the verb and its complement.

(42)   a. *Sally Field accepted *ecstatic* her Oscar.
       b. *He ran *completely happy* through the woods.

We can once again diagram adjective phrase adjuncts as adjoined to VP as in (43).

(43)

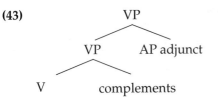

We have discussed above both adjective phrase and prepositional phrase adjuncts, contrasting them with both adjective phrase and prepositional phrase subjective and objective complements.

Clausal Adjuncts

Infinitival, tensed, and participial clauses can all be complements, as we saw in Chapter 11. They can also occur quite productively as adjuncts. In this section we discuss how each type of clause functions as an adjunct within the verb phrase.

Infinitival Adjuncts

Infinitival clauses can be complements, as in (44).

(44)   a. Lionel wants *to eat bagels for lunch.*
   b. Lionel expects *Mary to be there.*
   c. Lionel arranged *for his mother to take a cab.*

Infinitival clauses can also be adjuncts, as we see in (45).

(45)   a. Lionel sets his alarm for 6 a.m. *(in order) to be on time.*
   b. Linda commutes sixteen miles to work *to keep her job.*

The **infinitival adjuncts** in (45) are unselected by the verbs, *set* and *commute*, respectively. These infinitives always have an *in order to* interpretation, and for this reason are sometimes called *rationale clauses*, as they express reason. As you can see in (45), these *to*-infinitives can have "empty" subject positions, just as infinitival complements do. They can also have expressed subjects, as in (46).

(46)   Lionel leaves his door open *(in order) for the cat to get in.*

Infinitival adjuncts are fairly easy to distinguish from infinitival complements. They always have an "in order to" interpretation, whether or not this introductory prepositional phrase is present. They can also, as illustrated in (47), occur in sentence-initial position.

(47) a. *In order to be on time,* Lionel sets his alarm for 6 a.m.
     b. *To keep her job,* Linda commutes sixteen miles to work
     c. *In order for the cat to get in,* Lionel leaves his door open.

This is an impossibility for infinitival complements, as we see in (48).

(48) a. **To eat bagels for lunch,* Lionel wants.
     b. **(For) Mary to be there,* Lionel expects.

Further, infinitival adjuncts always occur outside of complements, as illustrated in (49).

(49) a. *Lionel sets *in order to be on time* his alarm for 6 a.m.
     b. *Linda commutes *to keep her job* sixteen miles to work.
     c. *Lionel leaves *in order for the cat to get in* the door open.

(These sentences are grammatical only with a strong "parenthetical" intonation. What is crucial is that if we do not interpret the rationale clauses as parenthetical, the sentences sound very odd, if not completely ungrammatical.)

We can diagram adjunct infinitival clauses as in (50), the basic position of other adjunct clauses, discussed below.

(50)

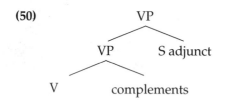

Participial Clause Adjuncts

Recall that participial clauses can be complements, as in (51).

(51) a. Holyfield had *his fists clenched in anger.*
     b. Tyson saw *his face betraying no emotion.*

Participial clauses also occur as adjuncts, as in (52).

(52) a. Holyfield stormed from the arena, *his fists clenched in anger.*
     b. The referee stopped the fight, *his face betraying no emotion.*

The **participial clause adjuncts** in (52) are called *absolute phrases* in some traditional approaches to grammar. These phrases can, as we see by comparing (52) and (53), occur in sentence-initial or sentence-final position.

(53) a. *His fists clenched in anger,* Holyfield stormed from the arena.
     b. *His face betraying no emotion,* the referee stopped the fight.

Participial clause adjuncts differ from participial clause complements in by now predictable ways. These complements cannot occur in sentence-initial position, as we see by comparing (53) with (54), sentences in which participial clause complements have been preposed.

(54) a. **His fists clenched in anger* Holyfield had.
b. **His face betraying no emotion* Tyson saw.

Participial clause adjuncts must, as we also by now expect, follow complements, as we see in (55).

(55) a. Holyfield had his fists clenched in anger, *his face betraying no emotion.*
b. **Holyfield had *his face betraying no emotion* his fists clenched in anger.*

We can conclude that infinitives and participial clauses can occur as adjuncts within the verb phrase, occurring in the same position as other clausal adjuncts, diagrammed in (50).

Summary

In this chapter, we have discussed the difference between complements and **adjuncts** in the verb phrase, unselected phrases that occur in adjoined positions. Unlike complements, adjuncts can move to sentence-initial position, and always follow complements. Evidence from movement supports the claim that adjuncts are constituents of the verb phrase, though they occur in a position different from that occupied by complements. We saw that adjuncts in the verb phrase can be **prepositional phrase adjuncts, adverbial noun phrase adjuncts, adjective phrase adjuncts,** and **participial phrase adjuncts. Adverb phrases** can also be adjuncts in the verb phrase, and can occur in other adjoined positions as well. We also discussed infinitival and participial clause adjuncts. The former are sometimes known as *rationale clauses,* and the latter as *absolute phrases.*

DISCOVERY PROBLEMS

Problem 1. Creating Adjuncts

Below is a list of verbs. For each, do the following.

- Use it in a sentence with one of its complements.
- Label the category and semantic type of the complement.

- Add an adjunct to each sentence (use as many different kinds as you can in this exercise).
- Label the syntactic category of the adjunct you add

Example:

meet

John met Mary   *Mary* = NP complement, direct object

John met Mary *on Tuesday. On Tuesday* = PP adjunct

> *hope pray beg desire read page consider teach*

Problem 2. Functions of Participial Phrases

We have now seen that participial phrases and clauses occur as both complements and adjuncts. Participial phrases can also occur in subject position. They can also form the predicate of a clause, but we will leave this function aside here for this exercise.

Below is a list of sentences, all of which contain participial phrases. Identify the syntactic category of each participial phrase as verb phrase, noun phrase, or adjective phrase. Then determine the function of each phrase as complement, adjunct, or subject.

a) *Reading* makes the children happy.
b) *Reading the Cat in the Hat* makes the children happy.
c) The children really enjoy *reading books.*
d) The kids played for hours, *pretending they were Star Wars characters.*
e) *Spurred on by the spirit of competition,* Hortense completed the race with a sprained ankle.
f) Rosanne's *singing of the national anthem* made a lot of people mad.
g) Rosanne left in a huff, after *singing the national anthem.*
h) Because *her singing* was criticized, Rosanne became furious.
i) *Singing the national anthem* is a difficult task.
j) Rosanne started *singing the national anthem.*

*Problem 3. Dangling Participles

A common writing "error" involving participles is the (in)famous *dangling* participle, exemplified below.

a) *Walking down the trail,* the cliff surprised the hikers.
b) *Drinking a martini,* the dog approached the woman.

These sentences seem odd because the subject of the participial phrase is *not* the same as the subject of the sentence, though this is how we tend to try to interpret them. Notice that if we move the participial phrases to the end of the sentence, (to a position in which they presumably no longer "dangle"), we get a more natural sounding sentence in which the subject of the participial phrase is the object, rather than subject, of the main clause.

  c) The cliff surprised the hikers, *walking down the trail.*
  d) The dog licked the woman, *drinking a martini.*

For this exercise create 4 sentences in which participial phrases are dangling modifiers. Explain how you can "fix" each sentence. (You may want to do this exercise in the form of a minilesson, if you are a teacher or prospective teacher.)

TEXT ANALYSIS

I. Finding Adjuncts

In the following passage, identify any adjuncts. Label the syntactic category of each, and include any other labels that apply. Some sentences will have no adjuncts, so be careful!

> a) I think it's time to redefine crime.
> b) When the individuals running a savings and loan loot the life savings of an elderly couple, that should be a crime.
> c) When corporate executives approve the dumping of pollution into the air or water, causing untold environmental damage and eventually killing thousands of people, that should be a crime.
> d) When a CEO defrauds the federal government on a defense contract, stealing our tax money, that, too, should be a crime.
> e) And when the automaker decides to save eleven dollars on a safety part, the omission of which causes the deaths of dozens of people, that should definitely be considered a major crime.
>
> Source: *Downsize This!*, by Michael Moore.

2. Distinguishing Complements and Adjuncts

Identify the bracketed phrases in the following text as complements or adjuncts. Label each according to syntactic category, and any other labels that apply. Also, identify the syntactic category of the heads selecting the phrases you label as complements. (There is one kind of adjunct below with which you are not yet familiar. Try to pick it out and label its syntactic category.)

a) Elizabeth Middleton, [twenty-nine years old] and [unmarried], [overly educated] and [excessively rational], [knowing right from wrong and fancy from fact], woke [in a nest of marten and fox pelts] to the sight of an eagle [circling overhead], and saw [at once] that it could not be far [to Paradise].

b) [All around her] was a world of [intense green and severe white mountains], [a wilderness of deep and bountiful silence], [magnificent beyond all imagining].

c) This was not [England], that was clear enough.

d) Nor was it the port at New-York where she had waited for months for the long trip north [to begin], nor any of the settlements [between New-York and Albany].

Source: Into the Wilderness, by Sara Donati.

a) [At work] she drank [her coffee] [from Rick's valentine mug] and kept [their engagement party picture] on her desk in [a charming country blue ceramic frame].

b) [In the picture] Rick wore [his Winning Team Smile] and Emily beamed [in her Laura Ashley party dress].

c) [In the messy sprawl of welfare paperwork], Emily [sometimes] eyed [that picture], [wishing she could crawl back inside that framed moment], [just about a year ago now at the Laguna Hills Country Club].

f) No one had had [a more splendid engagement party] than Rick and Emily.

g) Right out [of *Gatsby*].

Source: Graced Land, by Laura Kalpakian.

3. Participial Phrases

The text excerpt below contains a number of participles with different functions. Label them, choosing from the following options:

- participial phrase complements
- gerunds
- participial clause complements
- prenominal participial adjective phrases
- participial phrase adjuncts
- participial clause adjuncts

a) The horse bolted over the pool of ice toward Peter Lake, and lowered his wide white neck.
b) Peter Lake took possession of himself and throwing his arms around what seemed like a swan, sprang to the horse's back.
c) He was up again, exulting even as the pistol shots rang out in the cold air.
d) Having become his accomplice in one graceful motion, the horse turned and skittered, leaning back slightly on his haunches to get breath and power for an explosive start.
e) In that moment, Peter Lake faced his stunned pursuers, and laughed at them.
f) His entire being was one light perfect laugh.
g) He felt the horse pitch forward, and then they raced up the street, leaving Pearly Soames and some of the Short Tail Gang backed against the iron rails, firing their pistols and cursing—all twelve of them save Pearly himself, who bit his lower lip, squinted, and began to think of new ways to trap his quarry.

Source: Winter's Tale, by Mark Helprin.

4. Sentence Combining

Find an example in a text of a number of sentences that you can combine, using adjuncts. Combine the sentences, and label each adjunct you create. Bring your "uncombined" sentences to class and exchange them with someone else. See if your classmate combine your sentences in the same way as you did, and discuss any differences. What did you choose to do in the same way? (Education majors may want to do this exercise as a minilesson.)

5. Sentence Uncombining

Find a text in which there are at least four examples of adjuncts such as we have discussed in this chapter. Label the syntactic category of each adjunct. Rewrite the sentences, making separate sentences of the adjunct phrases. In effect, do *sentence combining* in reverse. What is the effect on the overall flow and tone of the text? (This exercise can also be done as a minilesson.)

LANGUAGE DIVERSITY EXERCISES

1. Adjuncts in Other Languages

All languages have adjuncts, but they do not necessarily syntactically parallel those we find in English. Choose a language other than English and investigate the syntax and semantics of adjuncts in that language. Does the language have participial clauses or phrases? Adjunct adjective phrases, prepositional phrases, and so on? Give some examples, and show how they are the same or different from their English counterparts.

2. Adjuncts in Other Varieties of English

Adjuncts in earlier versions of English differ from their modern counterparts. Examine a few lines of text in Old or Middle English. What adjuncts do you find, and how do you know that is what they are? Discuss any differences between these earlier versions and modern English with respect to the adjuncts you find.

CHAPTER REVIEW TERMS

adjuncts, prepositional phrase adjuncts, adverbial noun phrase adjuncts, adverb phrase adjuncts, adjective phrase adjuncts, and participial phrase adjuncts, infinitival and participial clause adjuncts (rationale clauses and absolute phrases).

CHAPTER REVIEW EXERCISE

Choose from among the following options to create a chapter exercise. You may wish to add options from previous chapter exercises to make this exercise more comprehensive.
In the following text:

- Find all the adjuncts.
- Label them by syntactic category.

- Write out two sentences from the text and show how an adjunct contained in it can move from sentence-initial to sentence-final position (or vice versa).
- Write out two sentences from the text and show how adjuncts cannot precede complements.

> Elizabeth was sitting with her mother and sisters, reflecting on what she had heard, and doubting whether she were authorized to mention it, when Sire William Lucas himself appeared, sent by his daughter to announce her engagement to the family. With many compliments to them, and much self-gratulation on the prospect of a connection between the houses, he unfolded the matter— to an audience not merely wondering but incredulous; for Mrs. Bennet, with more perseverance than politeness, protested he must be entirely mistaken, and Lydia, always unguarded and often uncivil, boisterously exclaimed,
>
> "Good Lord! Sir William, how can you tell such a story? Do not you know that Mr. Collins wants to marry Lizzy?"
>
> Source: *Pride and Prejudice,* by Jane Austen.

> The history of mankind is a history of repeated injuries and usurpations on the part of man toward woman, having in direct object the establishment of an absolute tyranny over her. To prove this, let facts be submitted to a candid world.
>
> He has never permitted her to exercise her inalienable right to the elective franchise.
>
> He has compelled her to submit to laws, in the formation of which she had no voice.
>
> He has withheld from her the rights which are given to the most ignorant and degraded men— both natives and foreigners.
>
> Source: *Declaration of Independence,* by Elizabeth Cady Stanton.

13

Adjuncts in the Noun Phrase

*Language is the road map of a culture. It tells you where its people
come from and where they are going.*
From *Starting from Scratch* by Rita Mae Brown

Introduction

In the previous chapter we discussed a number of different kinds of adjuncts
that occur in verb phrases, including prepositional phrase, adjective phrase,
verb phrase (participial), and clausal adjuncts. These adjuncts form a natural
class of phrases that are unselected by heads, and they occur in both sentence-
initial and sentence-final position. They also occur outside of complements, and
can be distinguished from complements in this way.

We conclude this section of the book on the function of phrases with a discussion of adjuncts in noun phrases. Adjuncts that appear in noun phrases differ from those that occur in the verb phrase in certain ways. They are similar,
however, in being unselected by a head and in occurring outside complements.
By virtue of their status as constituents of the noun phrase, adjuncts in the noun
phrase do not occur in sentence-initial position; rather, they occur in final position within the noun phrase of which they are a constituent.

The two types of adjuncts within the noun phrase we will discuss here
include *appositive* noun phrases and *relative clauses*, illustrated in (1–2).

(1) Wolfgang Amadeus Mozart, a musical genius, was born in Salzburg,
      Austria.

(2) One serenade that was often played in the pleasure garden of the
      Mirabell Palace was called *Eine Kleine Nachtmusik*.

In (1), *a musical genius* is an appositive noun phrase that *renames* and forms a
constituent with the noun phrase *Wolfgang Amadeus Mozart*. In (2), the clause
that was often played in the pleasure garden of the Mirabell Palace is also an adjunct
within a larger noun phrase, in this case the phrase *one serenade that was often
played in the pleasure garden of the Mirabell Palace*. This type of clausal adjunct is
called a *relative clause*. We will discuss below three different types of relative

clauses, and also the distinction between *restrictive relative clauses,* such as in (2), and *nonrestrictive relative clauses,* as in (3).

(3) One serenade, which was often played in the pleasure garden of the Mirabell Palace, was *Eine Kleine Nachtmusik.*

In (3), the nonrestrictive relative clause is set off by commas and differs both syntactically and semantically from the restrictive relative clause in (2), in ways we discuss below. We conclude the chapter with a discussion of *free relative clauses,* such as *I'll do whatever you want.* These clauses share certain properties with relative clauses but differ from them in functioning as full noun phrases rather than as adjuncts within noun phrases.

Appositive Noun Phrases

You are by now familiar with a number of different ways in which noun phrases occur as complements of verbs and prepositions. Recall, for example, that subjective and objective complement noun phrases assign a property to another noun phrase, and are thus predicates, as illustrated in (4).

(4) a. Kevin Costner is *a well-known actor.* (subjective complement).
  b. Some call Hollywood *the home of the American film industry.* (objective complement)

Noun phrases can also be adjuncts, as we can see in (5).

(5) a. Kevin Costner, *a well-known actor,* has made some pretty bad movies.
  b. We visited Hollywood, *the home of the American film industry.*

The noun phrases in (5) are called **appositive noun phrases,** noun phrases that "rename" another full noun phrase. They are thus by definition adjuncts, as they are not selected by the noun phrase they rename (only heads select, phrases don't). Notice also that appositive noun phrases are not predicates; they rename, rather than assign a property to, another noun phrase.

The subjective complement in (4a) can be distinguished from its appositive counterpart in (5a) fairly easily; appositive noun phrases immediately follow the noun phrase they rename. The appositive noun phrase in (5a) is thus not in a position to the right of a linking verb, the position in which subjective complements occur.

The objective complement in (4b) might, however, be confused with the appositive noun phrase in (5b). There are some ways to clearly distinguish objective complements from appositive noun phrases, however. First of all, notice that the noun phrase *Hollywood* in (4b) does not form a constituent with *the home of the American film industry.* In (5b) on the other hand, *Hollywood* does form a constituent with *the home of the American film industry*. This becomes evident when we consider the way in which pronominalization works in these sentences. To illustrate, consider (6) and (7).

(6)   a. Some call *Hollywood* the home of the American film industry.
      b. Some call *it* the home of the American film industry.

(7)   a. We visited *Hollywood, the home of the American film industry.*
      b. We visited *it.*

As you can see in (6b), the noun phrase *Hollywood* can be replaced by a pronoun, *it*. The following noun phrase, *the home of the American film industry* is not also pronominalized by *it*, which suggests that this noun phrase is a separate constituent. The phrase structure of (6a) is thus (8), where the noun phrase *Hollywood* can be replaced by the pronoun *it*.

(8)
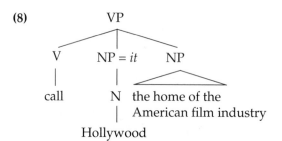

In (7b), on the other hand, the entire noun phrase *Hollywood, the home of the American film industry,* has been replaced by *it*. The structure in this case is (9).

(9)
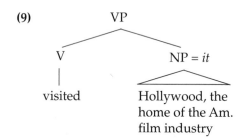

We can therefore propose, on the basis of evidence from pronominalization, that appositive noun phrases form a constituent with the noun phrase they rename. We can diagram them as in (10).

(10)
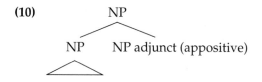

    Appositive noun phrases differ somewhat from the other adjuncts we have discussed in that they don't move away from the noun phrase they are adjoined to. For example, the following (b) sentences are ungrammatical, where the appositive noun phrase occurs in sentence-final or sentence-initial position, separate from the noun phrase it renames.

(11) a. Kevin Costner, *a well-known actor,* made a new baseball movie.
      b. *Kevin Costner made a new baseball movie, *a well-known actor.*

(12) a. They interviewed Kevin Costner, a well-known actor.
      b. *A well-known actor,* they interviewed Kevin Costner.

Appositive noun phrases are thus a type of adjunct that does not exhibit the same kinds of movement possibilities as adjuncts in the verb phrase discussed in Chapter 12. This difference is not surprising, as appositive noun phrases occupy a different adjunct position: they occur within noun phrases. Appositive noun phrases are also unique in their semantics, as adjuncts that *rename* another noun phrase.

Restrictive Relative Clauses

Relative clauses, or clausal adjuncts within the noun phrase, semantically modify nouns and have three different syntactic forms—*tensed, infinitival,* or *reduced.* They can also, as we shall see, be *restrictive* or *nonrestrictive,* and they differ in certain important ways from complements of nouns, discussed briefly in Chapter 11. We begin the discussion with tensed relative clauses.

Tensed Relative Clauses

Some examples of tensed restrictive relative clauses are given in (13).

(13) a. We love [the puppy [that we brought back from Montana]].
                   NP   S
      b. [The woman [who John met at the party]] turned out to be a spy.
          NP   S

As you can see from the labeled brackets in (13), each noun phrase contains a clause that modifies the head noun, *puppy* and *woman,* respectively. The information expressed by these clausal modifiers contributes to the description of the noun; *the puppy* in (13a), for example, is "restricted" to being the one we brought back from Montana. *The woman* in (13b) is distinguished from other women by being the one who John met at the party. The relative clauses in (13) are consequently referred to as **restrictive relative clauses**—they restrict the set of members a particular noun refers to.

We can also see that the relative clauses in (13) are tensed, because they contain a tensed verb. They may, at first glance, look something like clausal complements of verbs discussed in the previous chapter, but they differ from such complements in a number of ways.

The most obvious way in which a **tensed relative clause** differs from a clausal complement of a verb or some other head is that the former follows a noun. Relative clauses also semantically differ from the tensed clausal complement of a verb, such as *think* in (14).

(14)   The voters thought *that the new mayor would do a good job.*

The clausal complement in (14) does not modify a noun, but rather completes the verb phrase headed by *think*.

Perhaps the most telling distinction between clausal complements and relative clauses is that relative clauses form a syntactic constituent with the noun they modify. They can thus be pronominalized along with the noun, and can move along with it as well. Clausal complements do not share these properties, as we see below.

To begin, consider the tensed relative clause in (15a) and the tensed clausal complement in (15b).

(15)   a. I met [the woman [who ran the race]].
                   NP   S
           b. I [wonder [who ran the race]].
                VP   S

In (15a), the relative clause *who ran the race* modifies *woman*, a noun. The same clause in (15b) follows the verb *wonder* and is a complement of that verb, rather than a modifier. We know this because *wonder* is a verb that selects a WH-complement to complete the verb phrase it heads.

Notice further that the phrase *the woman who ran the race* appears to form a constituent, namely a noun phrase, that we can in turn replace with the pronoun *her.*

(16)   John met [the woman who ran the race] and I met *her* too.
                   NP

We cannot replace a clausal complement with a pronoun, which is what we expect. Clausal complements such as in (15b) form a constituent with a verb, rather than with a noun. Pronominalization in (15b) thus yields (17), where the proform *so* replaces the verb phrase.

(17)   I [wonder who ran the race], and *so* does John.
              VP

Assuming that the relative clause in (15a) forms a constituent with the noun, we also expect this constituent to be able to undergo the same kinds of movement rules that other noun phrases do. For example, we expect a noun modified by a relative clause to undergo Passive. This is the case, as we can see in (18).

(18) a. The judges approached [the woman who ran the race].
                                NP

   b. [The woman who ran the race] was approached by the judges.
        NP

A clausal complement of a verb, on the other hand, does not undergo Passive, as we see in (19).

(19) a. I wonder [who ran the race].
                           S

   b. *[Who ran the race] was wondered by me.
        S

Another distinction (and possible source of confusion, in some cases) between relative clauses and clausal complements is that relative clauses are introduced by **relative pronouns,** rather than complementizers. Relative pronouns *who/when/why/where/which,* and *that* link the relative clause with the noun it modifies. Some examples are given in (20). (The relative pronoun *that* is in some prescriptive approaches taken to be "incorrect" in relative clauses that modify human nouns; in such cases, it is assumed that only *who(m)* is correct. Descriptively, however, *that* with human nouns is widely used.)

(20) a. [the person [*who/that* she met]].
         NP   S

   b. [the person [*who/that* met her]].
      NP   S

   c. [the reason [*why* she met him]].
      NP   S

   d. [the moment [*when* she met him]].
      NP   S

   e. [the place [*where* she met him]].
      NP   S

   f. [the car [*that/which* she drove]].
      NP   S

As you may have noticed, we can sometimes omit relative pronouns. For example, we can say *the person who she met,* or *the person she met.* Others cannot be omitted; we cannot, for example, omit *who* in *the person who met her;* the phrase *the person met her* has a completely different meaning.

As we can see in (20), the relative pronoun refers to the noun head of the noun phrase. Relative pronouns are also identical to interrogative pronouns, except for *that.* The resemblance between relative pronouns and the interrogative pronouns is not in fact accidental; in both relative clauses and WH-complements of verbs, WH-Movement has applied.

To illustrate, consider the WH-complement of the verb *wonder* below.

(21) I [wonder [who she met _____]].
       VP   S

In (21), WH-Movement has taken place in the clausal complement, moving interrogative *who* to clause-initial position. WH-Movement also takes place in relative clauses, in English (but not in all languages, as languages form relative clauses in different ways). WH-Movement in relative clauses is distinct from WH-Movement in clausal complements such as (21) in that it has the result of linking a noun with a restrictive clausal modifier.

To illustrate, consider (22), where an interrogative pronoun moves to initial position in a relative clause.

(22)   a. the person [she met the person]
         b. the person [she met *who*]
         c. the person [*who* she met_____]

In (22), the relative pronoun, moved by WH-Movement, refers to the head of the noun phrase. This is not the case in (21), where *who* does not have an antecedent in the sentence at all.

To further illustrate the distinction between relative clauses and clausal complements of verbs, consider (20f), where the relative pronoun, *that*, does not appear to be interrogative. We might think, then, that the pronoun is not a pronoun at all, but rather a complementizer, identical to the complementizer *that* we find in tensed clausal complements of verbs such as *think*, in (23).

(23) I think [that she met the person].
             S

In (23), no WH-Movement has taken place, and *that* is not an interrogative pronoun on a par with *who* in (21). In the relative clause in (20f), on the other hand, WH-Movement has taken place. *That* refers to the noun *car*, and is fronted to clause-initial position as illustrated in (24).

(24)   a. [the car [she drove the car]]
             NP   S
         b. [the car [she drove *that*]]
             NP   S
         c. [the car [*that* she drove_____]]
             NP   S

To summarize, we distinguish relative clauses from clausal complements of verbs in the following ways. Relative clauses form a constituent with a noun and can be replaced by a pronoun. Clausal complements, on the other hand, cannot be replaced by pronouns in this way, but rather are replaced by proforms such as *so* that pronominalize clauses, rather than noun phrases. Relative clauses in English are also formed by WH-Movement within the clause, fronting to clause-initial position a relative pronoun that corresponds to the head of the noun phrase. Clausal complements, on the other hand, may involve WH-Movement, but the clause-initial WH-phrase does not correspond to a preceding noun, nor are such clauses modifiers. Rather, clausal complements semantically complete a phrase (a verb phrase, in the examples we have discussed), and are selected by a head (in our examples, a verb).

We can now diagram relative clauses as in (25), where the relative clause occurs in adjunct position. The phrase structure of a clausal complement of a verb is given for comparison in (26).

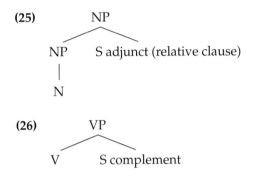

(25)

NP

NP   S adjunct (relative clause)

|

N

(26)

VP

V   S complement

We further elaborate and justify the phrase structure of relative clauses in the following section, where we oppose them to complements of nouns.

Relative Clauses Versus Complements of Nouns

We suggested in Chapter 11 that nouns form constituents with other phrases, phrases that we analyzed as complements of nouns, mainly on the basis of syntactic evidence. Semantically, it is not always clear whether a constituent is a complement of the noun or not.

Recall that complements of nouns occur immediately to the right of the head noun and form a constituent with the noun, a constituent that can be replaced by the pronoun *one*. Some examples of complements of nouns are repeated in (27).

(27) a. the student [of linguistics]
                    PP
         b. the fact [that the earth is round]
                  S

We concluded in Chapter 11 that the prepositional phrase in (27a) and the clause in (27b) are complements of the nouns *student* and *fact*, on the basis of evidence that both of these constituents must be replaced by the pronoun *one*. This is illustrated in (28) and (29).

(28)   a. *This student of chemistry met that *one* of linguistics.
        b. This student of chemistry met that *one*.

(29)   a. *The fact that the earth orbits the sun is better accepted than the *one* that the earth is round.
        b. This fact that the earth orbits the sun is better accepted than that *one*.

In contrast to (28), other prepositional phrases do not seem to form a constituent with the noun *student* in the same way. The prepositional phrase *from Seattle*, for example, can, but need not, be replaced by *one*.

(30)   a. This student from Boston met that one *from Seattle*.
        b. This student from Boston met that one.

We proposed the following structural distinction between the two prepositional phrases in (31).

(31)

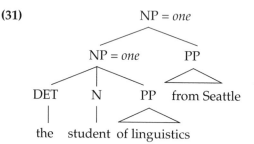

If we adopt (31), and assume that *one* replaces NP, we account for the evidence regarding prepositional phrases discussed above. Prepositional phrase complements will always be replaced by *one* along with the head noun, given that *one* pronominalizes a noun phrase, either the higher or lower one in (31). A prepositional phrase adjunct can also be replaced by *one* along with the head noun, as *one* may replace the higher noun phrase in (31). *One* can also replace the lower noun phrase, leaving the adjunct prepositional phrase outside. We thus derive the patterns involving prepositional phrases in noun phrases in (28–30).

We are now in a position to oppose clausal complements of nouns, such as in (29), with relative clauses. That is, we expect a clausal complement to differ both semantically and syntactically with a relative clause. As we see below, this is in fact the case.

First, observe that the clausal complement in (29) tells us what the *fact* actually *is*, namely, that the earth is round. The clause thus does not modify the noun, providing more descriptive information; rather, it tells us what the noun *is*. The relative clause in (32), on the other hand, modifies the noun *fact*.

(32)   The fact *that scientists proved many years ago*

The relative clause in (32) provides descriptive information about *the fact*, namely that it was proven many years ago. It does not, however, tell us what the fact *is*. The relative clause in (32) is thus semantically quite different from the clausal complement of the noun *fact* in (29).

The relative clause differs from the clausal complement syntactically as well; observe that WH-Movement applies in the relative clause but not in the clausal complement. This is illustrated by the contrast between the noun phrase in (29), where there is no WH-Movement, and (32), where WH-Movement occurs, as illustrated in (33).

(33) a. The fact [scientists proved *the fact* many years ago]
         S
     b. The fact [scientists proved *that* many years ago]
         S
     c. The fact [*that* scientists proved _____ many years ago]
         S

Further support for this distinction comes from the status of *that* in complements and relative clauses. In (29), *that* does not function as an interrogative pronoun but rather as a complementizer. (Interestingly, complementizers that introduce clausal complements of nouns cannot be omitted.) Tensed clausal complements of nouns thus are syntactically parallel to tensed clausal complements of other heads, such as verbs, prepositions, and adjectives; they are introduced by a complementizer, namely *that*, and do not involve WH-Movement. The relative pronoun *that* in (32), on the other hand, results from WH-Movement, and can also be omitted, as we see by the grammaticality of *the fact scientists proved many years ago*.

Relative clauses and clausal complements of nouns both form part of the noun phrase. As we might expect, both complements of nouns and relative clause adjuncts move as part of the noun phrase. This is unsurprising, since both are constituents of the noun phrase and differ only in occurring in complement or adjunct position, respectively. The grammaticality of the sentences in (34–35) is to be expected, where a noun phrase dominating a relative clause, and one dominating a clausal complement, undergo Passive.

(34) a. [The fact that the earth is round] surprised the scientists.
        NP
     b. The scientists were surprised by [the fact that the earth is round].
                                          NP

(35) a. [The fact that the scientists supported with evidence] caused an
        NP
        uproar.
     b. An uproar was caused by
        [the fact that the scientists supported with evidence].
        NP

A final, and also by now predictable, difference between clausal complements of nouns and relative clauses is that the latter must occur outside the former, as we see in (36) and (37).

(36)   a.   The fact that the earth is round that scientists proved many years
              ago
         b.   *The fact that scientists proved many years ago that the earth is
              round

(37)   a.   This student of linguistics from Seattle
         b.   *This student from Seattle of linguistics

As you can see in (36–37), adjuncts (a relative clause in (36) and a prepositional
phrase in (37)), must occur outside of complements of nouns. We represent this
distinction in terms of phrase structure as in (38), where an adjunct in a noun
phrase can be, as we have now seen, a relative clause, a prepositional phrase, or
an appositive noun phrase.

(38)

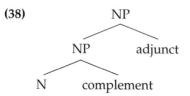

adjunct = relative clause (S), PP, or NP (appositive)

Relative Clause Extraposition

One final issue we need to raise here is the difference between adjuncts in
the noun phrase and adjuncts in the verb phrase with respect to movement. Relative clauses can sometimes be *extraposed* to sentence-final position, but only
under certain circumstances. This is illustrated by the contrast between (39),
where **relative clause extraposition** is possible, and (40), where it is not.

(39)   a.   [The student [that Mary knows from geometry class]] came in.
              NP   S
         b.   [The student] came in [that Mary knows from geometry class].
              NP   S

(40)   a.   [The student [that Mary knows from geometry class]] met Bill.
              NP   S
         b.   *[The student] met Bill [that Mary knows from geometry class].
              NP   S

We will not pursue the particulars of relative clause extraposition further here.
Notice, however, that the movement options for relative clauses are more
restricted than those for adjuncts in the verb phrase. Recall that adjuncts adjoined

to VP occur in sentence-final position, and can move to sentence-initial position, as illustrated in (41) with the prepositional phrase adjunct *with great glee.*

(41) a. Mary ran along the beach *with great glee.*
        b. *With great glee,* Mary ran along the beach.

Relative clauses, on the other hand, can move only under restricted conditions by extraposition. This is not surprising, as relative clauses are constituents of noun phrases, rather than of verb phrases. We therefore expect them to pattern somewhat differently.

In the following two sections we turn to some of the different forms restrictive relative clauses can take. We then turn to distinctions between restrictive and nonrestrictive relative clauses.

Infinitival Relative Clauses

Infinitives show up quite productively as adjuncts in noun phrases, as restrictive relative clauses. They differ from their tensed clause counterparts, however, in a few important ways. Consider, for example, (42).

(42) a. [The person _____ *to do the job*] is Tony.
        b. [Hawaii is *the place to go* _____] on your vacation.
        c. [The reason *for you to leave* _____] was clear.

As you can see in (42), infinitival relative clauses differ from their tensed counterparts not only with respect to the form of the verb, but also in completely lacking relative pronouns. We can tell, however, that infinitival relatives, like tensed relatives, are formed through some kind of WH-Movement, as the sources for the noun phrases in (42) are those in (43).

(43) a. the person [*the person* to do the job]
        b. the place [to go *to this place*]
        c. the reason [for you to leave *for this reason*]

Some linguists suggest that infinitival relative clauses involve a form of "unexpressed" WH-Movement; the relative clauses in (42) are derived by "covert" WH-Movement in the clauses in (43). Because movement is covert, no relative pronouns "show up" after movement occurs. Nevertheless, the relative clauses in (42) have "gaps" indicating a position from which movement has taken place, as illustrated by the blank lines in (42).

Syntactically, infinitival relative clauses have all the other properties of tensed relative clauses. They form a constituent with the noun, as we can see by the evidence from pronominalization in (44). They also undergo movement as part of the noun phrase, as in (45), an example of passivization of a noun phrase dominating an infinitival relative clause.

(44) a. [The person [to do the job]] said *he* would be late.
            NP   S

          b. Linda chose [the place [to go]], because *it* has such nice weather.
                          NP   S

          c. [The reason [for you to leave]] was clear. But I can't really
             NP   S
             describe *it*.

(45) a. The company called [a person [to do the job]].
                                NP   S

          b. [A person [to do the job]] was called by the company.
             NP   S

Infinitival relative clauses also differ from infinitival complements of verbs in the same ways that tensed relative clauses do. Infinitival relatives, but not infinitival complements, involve "covert" WH-Movement, and modify a noun. They thus cannot be confused with infinitival WH-complements of verbs, such as in (46), where WH-Movement is "overt."

(46) I wonder [who to see].
                   S

Infinitival relatives can also, along with the noun they modify, be replaced with a pronoun. Infinitival complements of verbs, on the other hand, complete the verb phrase and cannot be replaced with a pronoun.
   Consider, for example, the sentence in (47).

(47) Bill expects [Mary to do the job].

The clausal complement in (47) cannot be replaced by a pronoun, as we see by the evidence that it does not have the meaning in (48).

(48) Bill expects *her.*

Rather, the verb phrase *expects Mary to do the job* can be replaced by the pro-form *so*, as in (49).

(49) Bill expects Mary to do the job, and *so* does the boss.

When we compare the pronominalization data in (48–49) with that in (44), we can conclude that infinitival relative clauses form part of a larger noun phrase and are as such distinct from infinitival complements of verbs.
   With this in mind, consider (50), which is ambiguous. We can now explain this ambiguity in syntactic terms.

(50) Bill expects [the person to do the job].

(50) can mean either that Bill expects *someone,* or that he expects *someone to do something.* In other words, the bracketed material in (50) can be analyzed as a noun phrase dominating a relative clause as in (51a), or as a clause as in (51b).

    (51)   a. Bill expects [the person [to do the job]].
                        NP   S
           b. Bill [expects [the person to do the job]].
                    VP   S

Correspondingly, we can replace the noun phrase in (51a) with a pronoun, and the clause in (51b) with *so,* deriving the results in (52).

    (52)   a. Bill expects [the person [to do the job]] to show up any minute.
                        NP   S
          She is always late.
           b. Bill [expects [the person to do the job]] and *so* does Jim.
                    VP   S

We can conclude that there are two different syntactic structures for (50), namely (53a–b).

(53)

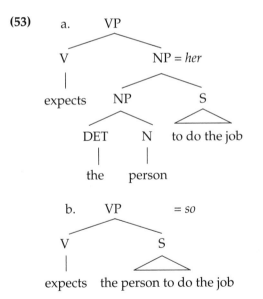

In (53a), *the person to do the job* is a noun phrase, referring to a particular person, and in (53b), it is a clause, denoting an event. We thus represent the ambiguity in (50) with two different syntactic structures, one in which *expect* selects a noun phrase complement and the other in which *expect* selects an infinitival clause complement.

Reduced Relative Clauses

In addition to being tensed and infinitival, restrictive relative clauses can also be **reduced,** deriving from tensed relative clauses by omission of the relative pronoun and the verb *be*. This is illustrated in (54–55).

(54)   a.   Mary talked with [a scholar [who was visiting the English
                              NP   S
           Department]].
       b.   Mary talked with [a scholar [visiting the English Department]].
                              NP   VP

(55)   a.   [The book [that is going on sale]] is by Noam Chomsky.
            NP   S
       b.   [The book [going on sale]] is by Noam Chomsky.
            NP   VP

As you can see in (54–55), reduced relative clauses are derived by omission of the relative pronoun and a form of *be* in a tensed relative clause. These relative clauses are as a result sometimes called *participial* relative clauses, because the remaining verb is in it participial form, originally introduced by auxiliary *be*. We will call them *reduced* relative clauses, though, because they do not always include a participle, as you can see in the examples in (56).

(56)   a.   Mary talked with [a scholar [who was sick with the flu]].
                              NP   S
       b.   Mary talked with [a scholar [sick with the flu]].
                              NP   AP

In (56), after deletion of *be* and the relative pronoun *who*, we are left with the phrase *sick with the flu*, an adjective phrase. It is thus not the case that all reduced relative clauses are participial phrases.

To preserve the generalization that reduced relative clauses derive from tensed ones, and to allow us to diagram all relative clauses consistently, we will assume that reduced relative clauses originate as tensed relative clauses and therefore occur in the same adjunct position as other tensed relatives, as in (57).

(57)

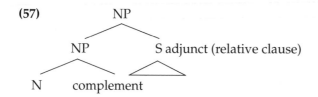

A deletion rule of some kind then applies to them, omitting the relative pronoun and the verb *be,* leaving a verb phrase or adjective phrase. We will diagram reduced relative clauses as S, just as other relative clauses, for clarity.

One potential snag in identifying reduced relative clauses is that they can sometimes be confused with participial clause complements of verbs. For example, consider (58).

(58) The journalists found *the fighter walking back to his locker.*

The phrase *The fighter walking back to his locker* in (58) is actually ambiguous between being a participial clause complement of *find* and a noun phrase containing a participial relative clause, derived by reduction of the tensed relative clause in *the fighter **who was** walking back to his locker.* These two interpretations suggest that there are two structures for (58), namely (59–60).

(59)

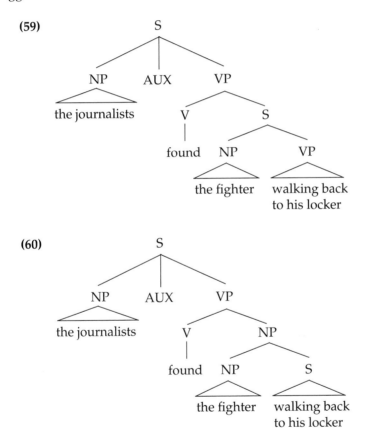

According to the phrase structure in (59), *the fighter walking back to his locker* is a clause, and in (60), it is a noun phrase. We thus interpret the subordinate clause in (59) as depicting an *event*. As we might expect, the subject noun phrase of that subordinate clause can be replaced by a pronoun, as in (61).

(61) a. The journalists found *the fighter* walking back to his locker.
   b. The journalists found *him* walking back to his locker.

In (60), on the other hand, we interpret the sentence as meaning the journalists found *someone,* namely *the fighter* (who was) *walking back to his locker.* As we by now expect, the entire noun phrase, *the fighter walking back to his locker,* can be replaced by a pronoun, as in (62).

(62)   a. The journalists found *the fighter walking back to his locker.*
       b. The journalists found *him.*

We can also apply Passive in (59–60) with different, expected, results. Passive applied in (59) derives (63), where the noun phrase subject of the subordinate clause moves.

(63)   [The fighter] was found [_____ walking back to his locker]
       NP   S
       by the journalists.

Passive applied to (60), moving the object of *find,* derives (64):

(64)   [The fighter walking back to his locker] was found _____ by the
       NP
       journalists.

We can therefore distinguish reduced relative clauses from participial clause complements of verbs by their status as constituents of noun phrases. As such, they undergo movement as part of a larger noun phrase, and can, as part of a noun phrase, be replaced by a pronoun. Semantically, reduced relative clauses, like other relative clauses, modify a noun rather than express an event.

Nonrestrictive Relative Clauses

So far, we have limited the discussion of the syntax of relative clauses to restrictive relative clauses. Relative clauses can also be **nonrestrictive,** differing from restrictive relative clauses in certain important ways. An example of a restrictive and contrasting nonrestrictive relative clause is given in (65).

(65)   a. The man who I know came to the party.
       b. The man, who I know, came to the party.

As you can see illustrated in (65), nonrestrictive relative clauses differ from restrictive ones in being set off by commas in written text, and by comma *intonation* in oral speech. Otherwise, however, their syntax appears to be similar in the relevant respects to that of restrictive relatives; they involve WH-Movement, and appear to modify a noun. They also form a constituent with the noun, as we can see from evidence involving pronominalization and movement.

Taking movement first, observe that a nonrestrictive relative clause must be dominated by a larger noun phrase, as it must move along with the head noun. This is illustrated by the example of passive in (66).

(66)   a.   The Smiths bought that house, *which we would really like to live in.*
           b.   That house, *which we would really like to live in,* was bought by the Smiths.

Nonrestrictive relative clauses can also be extraposed, as we see in (67).

(67)   a.   The man, who I know, came in.
           b.   The man came in, who I know.

Nonrestrictive relative clauses can be pronominalized, along with the rest of the noun phrase, suggesting that like their restrictive counterparts, nonrestrictive relative clauses are constituents of a larger noun phrase. This is illustrated by pronominalization of the noun phrases in (68), as in (69).

(68)   a.   The house, *which we would really like to live in,* is too expensive.
           b.   Any student, *who isn't afraid of hard work,* can apply for the job.
           c.   Lionel, *who is often gloomy and negative,* can be a tough person to get along with.
           d.   The Badlands, *where the sunsets are gorgeous,* is one of her favorite places.

(69)   a.   *It* is too expensive.
           b.   *He/she* can apply for the job.
           c.   *He* can be a tough person to get along with.
           d.   *It* is one of her favorite places.

Also, nonrestrictive relative clauses can remain outside of the part of the noun phrase pronominalized by *one,* as in (70). This is unsurprising, if nonrestrictive relatives are adjuncts.

(70)   a.   this man, who I know, and that *one,* who I've never met
           b.   this man, who I know, and that *one*

What then, if anything, differentiates nonrestrictive relative clauses from restrictive ones, other than comma intonation?

One difference between restrictive and nonrestrictive relative clauses is that nonrestrictive relative clauses do not modify the head noun in the same way as restrictive relative clauses. We can see this distinction when we compare the examples in (71).

(71)   a.   The author, who has just written a new novel, walked in.
           b.   The author who has just written a new novel walked in.

In (71a), the nonrestrictive relative clause provides "extra" information about the noun phrase *the author*. More specifically, the noun phrase *the author* denotes a set of one member, say, *Alice Walker*. This is not the case in (71b), where the restrictive relative clause provides information essential to the description of the noun *author*. Here, the member of the set in question is *the author who has just written a new novel*.

This difference in restrictive versus nonrestrictive modification is further illustrated by the evidence that only nonrestrictive relative clauses can modify proper names.

(72) a. Alice Walker, who has just written a new novel, walked in.
          b. *Alice Walker who has just written a new novel walked in.

The grammaticality of (72a) follows, given that a nonrestrictive relative clause is not part of the description of a noun. Proper nouns pick out a specific referent, and as such can take no restrictive modifiers that contribute information affecting what the noun refers to. The phrase in (72b) is therefore ungrammatical; in this case, a restrictive relative clause modifies a proper noun. For (72b) to be grammatical, we have to interpret it as meaning that there is more than one Alice Walker, and that the one in question is the one who has recently written a novel. In other words, we have to turn *Alice Walker* into a common rather than proper noun, one that can take a restrictive modifier. No such interpretation is forced in (72a).

Restrictive relative clauses thus differ semantically from nonrestrictive ones in terms of their modification properties. Restrictive relative clauses express information included in the denotation of the noun, and nonrestrictive relative clauses do not.

Restrictive and nonrestrictive relative clauses differ syntactically as well. Nonrestrictive relative clauses can only be tensed. As illustrated in (73), they cannot be infinitival.

(73) a. *The man, *to do the job,* came in.
          b. *Larry, *for Mary to talk to,* was at the party.

Nonrestrictive relative clauses might be argued to be able to be reduced, based on the grammaticality of sentences such as (74a). Here, we might assume that the nonrestrictive, reduced relative clause derives from its tensed counterpart in (74b).

(74) a. Alice Walker, *beaming with pride,* accepted the award.
          b. Alice Walker, *who was beaming with pride,* accepted the award.

Notice that participial phrases that are identical to the one in (74a) can occur as verb phrase adjuncts, as in (75).

(75) a. *Beaming with pride,* Alice Walker accepted the award.
          c. Alice Walker accepted the award, *beaming with pride.*

We know that the participial phrase *beaming with pride* in (75) is a verb phrase adjunct because it can occur in both sentence-initial and sentence-final position. Recall that nonrestrictive relative clauses do not occur in such positions, as the ungrammaticality of (76) indicates.

(76)   a.   Alice Walker, who has just written a new novel, accepted the award.
       b.   *Alice Walker accepted the award, who has just written a new novel.

We can therefore keep from confusing the nonrestrictive (participial) relative clauses as in (74a) with the participial phrase adjuncts as in (75), because they occur in different positions.

Nonrestrictive relative clauses also differ from restrictive relative clauses in terms of order; nonrestrictive relative clauses must *follow* restrictive relative clauses, as illustrated in (77–78).

(77)   a.   The house that looks out over the bay, *which we would really like to live in*
       b.   *The house, *which we would really like to live in* that looks out over the bay

(78)   a.   Any student who is taking Math 250, *who isn't afraid of hard work*
       b.   *Any student, *who isn't afraid of hard work* who is taking Math 250

The patterns in (77–78) suggest that there must be more than one possible adjunct position inside the noun phrase. We can diagram this position, one where a nonrestrictive relative clause can occur, as in (79).

(79)

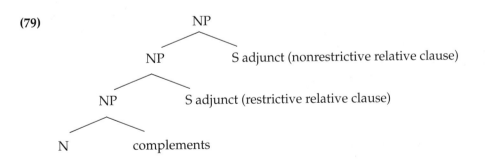

This concludes our discussion of relative clauses. We end the chapter with a brief discussion of a type of clause that has certain properties of relative clauses but other properties in common with full noun phrases. These phrases are called *free relative clauses*.

Free Relative Clauses

Sometimes, phrases that resemble relative clauses appear without a preceding noun and thus do not appear to be dominated by a larger noun phrase. These constructions have various names, and we will call them **free relative clauses** following linguistic convention. Some examples are given in (80).

    (80) a. I'll eat *whatever you want.*
             b. We can meet John *whenever you want.*
             c. She goes *wherever she pleases.*

Free relative clauses are WH-phrases introduced by the complex relative pronouns *whenever, wherever, whatever, however,* and others. They are called *free* relative clauses because they are not contained in larger noun phrases, and thus do not follow noun heads as other relative clauses do. Free relative clauses do, however, seem to be derived by WH-Movement, as illustrated in (80–82).

    (80) a. I'll eat [you want to eat *something*].
             b. I'll eat [you want to eat *whatever*].
             c. I'll eat [*whatever* you want (to eat)_____].

    (81) a. We can meet John [you want to meet John *at some time*].
             b. We can meet John [you want to meet John *whenever*].
             c. We can meet John [*whenever* you want (to meet John)_____]

    (82) a. She goes [she pleases to go *somewhere*].
             b. She goes [she pleases to go *wherever*].
             c. She goes [*wherever* she pleases (to go) _____].

Free relative clauses are thus distinct from other kinds of relative clauses in not following a noun. They are also distinct in not occurring strictly as adjuncts. The free relative clause in (81), for example, is an adjunct, telling us *when* we can meet John. (The free relative clause in this case has an *adverbial* interpretation.) They can also be complements of verbs, as in (80), where a free relative clause functions as the direct object position of the verb *eat,* or in (82), where the clause functions as the complement of *go* (as we typically *go somewhere*).

    Other examples of free relative clauses in complement positions are given in (83).

    (83) a. She will become *whatever she wants.* (subjective complement)
             b. She will give the book to *who(m)ever you wish.* (indirect object)
             c. We can swim until *whenever you want to go home.* (object of a
                preposition).
             d. You can paint the wall *whatever you want.* (objective complement)

Free relative clauses can also occur as subjects, as in (84), which is what we would expect if these phrases are noun phrases.

(84) *Whatever you want* is fine with me.

Free relative clauses can be pronominalized just as noun phrases can be, and they also undergo movement rules that apply to noun phrases. For example, Indirect Object Movement applies to the phrase *who(m)ever you wish* in (85a), deriving (85b).

(85) a. She will give the book to *who(m)ever you wish.*
b. She will give *who(m)ever you wish* the book.

Similarly, Passive applies in (86–87), to derive the (b) sentences from the (a) ones.

(86) a. Your grandmother will buy *whatever you want.*
b. *Whatever you want* will be bought by your grandmother.

(87) a. The officials can meet *who(m)ever you wish* at the airport.
b. *Who(m)ever you wish* can be met (by the officials) at the airport.

There exist several good reasons to analyze free relative clauses as noun phrases, distinct from relative clauses that occur as *parts* of noun phrases. As noun phrases, free relative clauses can be complements, adjuncts, or subjects, undergoing the same processes of pronominalization and movement as other noun phrases do. We will assume that these clauses are noun phrases, and diagram them using triangle notation as in (88).

(88) NP

whenever you want

Summary

In this chapter, we have discussed two types of adjuncts that occur in noun phrases, namely **appositive noun phrases** and **relative clauses.** Appositive noun phrases are adjuncts that rename another noun phrase and form a constituent with that noun phrase. Relative clauses pattern semantically with other adjuncts in being modifiers, and occur in adjunct position outside of complements of nouns.

Because relative clauses are constituents of noun phrases, they do not occur in both sentence-initial and sentence-final position as adjuncts in the verb phrase do. They do, however, undergo a limited type of movement called **relative clause extraposition,** and differ in expected ways from clausal complements of both verbs and nouns. Relative clauses form a constituent of the noun phrase, and thus move as part of the noun phrase (as we have seen from evidence from Passive). They can also be replaced by a pronoun that also replaces the head noun, again indicating they form part of the larger noun phrase. They involve WH-Movement, which has the effect of deriving a **relative pronoun** linked to the head noun. Clausal complements, on the other hand, are not noun phrases, and thus do not exhibit the same movement and pronominalization properties as relative clauses. Clausal complements may involve WH-Movement, but this movement does not result in a structure in which a relative pronoun is linked to a noun.

Relative clauses can be **tensed, infinitival,** or **reduced,** the latter derived by omitting the relative pronoun and a form of *be* from a tensed relative clause. Infinitival relatives differ from tensed ones in lacking relative pronouns, though they are, like their tensed counterparts, formed through ("covert" rather than "overt") WH-Movement. We saw that relative clauses can be **restrictive** or **non-restrictive;** restrictive relative clauses "restrict" the set of members to which a noun refers, but nonrestrictive relative clauses do not. For this reason, nonrestrictive relative clauses, but not restrictive ones, can occur with proper names. Nonrestrictive relative clauses differ from restrictive relative clauses in other ways as well; they occur outside restrictive relative clauses, and can be tensed or reduced, but not infinitival. We concluded that there are at least two different adjunct positions within the noun phrase, a lower one for restrictive relative clauses and a higher one for nonrestrictive relative clauses.

Finally, we considered **free relative clauses,** or clauses that function as adjunct, complement, or subject noun phrases. These clauses, though formed through WH-Movement, differ from relative clauses in functioning as noun phrases themselves, rather than as clausal modifiers of nouns.

DISCOVERY PROBLEMS

Problem 1. Creating Appositive Noun Phrases

By using appositives, we can often turn a number of abbreviated sentences into one longer one. Rewrite the following sentences using appositive noun phrases as much as you can.

Example:
Dwight Yoakum is in town. He is my favorite country singer.
Dwight Yoakum, my favorite country singer, is in town.

a) The Super-Mall has everything. It is a new mall in Auburn. It has the best shopping in the city.
b) *The Wizard of Oz* is not really a kid's book. It was turned into a very successful film. *The Wizard of Oz* is my daughter's favorite novel.
c) The winner had everything going for him. He was a young man with charm and talent. He was a student at the university.
d) They finally got the garbage trucks running again in New York. New York is a city that has had many problems with sanitation.
e) Dr. Chuck is a great guy. He is our dentist. He is a funny person, with brown hair and blue eyes.

f) Elvis Costello is from England. He is a rock and roll singer. He just made a CD with Burt Bacharach.

Problem 2. "Breaking Out" Relative Clauses

Relative clauses, like appositives, provide us with a means of combining sentences and ideas into a single phrase. For example, we can combine the two sentences below into one sentence by forming a relative clause.

(1) a. The collie was barking furiously.
      b. The collie belongs to my sister.
=> The collie that belongs to my sister was barking furiously.

Alternatively, we can "break out" relative clauses to create two sentences from one, as below.

Six people who had applied for the job showed up for the interview.

(2) a. Six people had applied for the job.
      b. Six people showed up for the interview.

For this exercise, make up four or five sentences, each of which includes at least one noun phrase with a tensed relative clause. Then "break out" each relative clause into a separate sentence. Next find three or four examples of relative clauses in texts of your choice. Write down the sentences they occur in, and then rewrite the sentences with the relative clauses "broken out," as above. How does this affect the tone and style of each sentence?

Problem 3. WH-movement in Relative Clauses

We discussed in the text how WH-Movement applies to create relative clauses from clausal modifiers. WH-Movement has the effect of moving a phrase, replaced by a relative pronoun, to clause-initial position. This relative pronoun corresponds to the noun head of the noun phrase. An example is given below.

a) the boy [the girl saw *the boy* at the beach]
b) the boy [the girl saw *who* at the beach]
c) the boy [*who* the girl saw _____ at the beach]
(WH-Movement of the direct object noun phrase in the relative clause)

Apply WH-Movement in the following examples, in the steps illustrated above. Remember that WH-Movement from the subject position involves movement that we can't really see, but we posit that movement occurs, in order for this type of WH-Movement to be consistent with others. Is the noun phrase that undergoes movement a subject, direct object, subjective complement, objective complement, adverbial noun phrase, indirect object, object of a preposition?

a) the cat [no one likes the cat]
b) the cat [the cat eats pancakes]
c) the cat [Mary is sitting on the couch with the cat]
d) the cat [we gave a bath to the cat]
e) the cat [we gave the cat a bath]
f) the cat [the cat became very lazy]
g) the cat [we left our dog with the cat]
h) the cat [we saw the cat's kittens]
i) the cat [they talked to John about the cat]

Which relative pronouns in the relative clauses you created above are optional? Try to write an informal statement about how we might predict the optionality of a relative pronoun, based on what we now know about the operation of WH-Movement in relative clauses.

Problem 4. One Pronominalization Again

Recall that one way to determine the status of an adjunct or complement in a noun phrase is to try to replace that phrase, along with the head of the noun phrase, with the pronoun *one*. *One* is a pronoun that obligatorily replaces the noun and its complements. Adjuncts, on the other hand, may remain outside the constituent replaced by *one* because they occur above complements in adjoined position.

Below are examples of noun phrases that include clausal complements or clausal adjuncts (relative clauses). Use the *one* replacement test to determine whether the bracketed clause is a complement or an adjunct.

a) The claim [that shocked the world]
b) The claim [that the theorem was false]
c) The belief [that she found upsetting]
d) Her belief [that pigs have wings]
e) The idea [that sparked great controversy]
f) The idea [that you could get in free]
g) Andy's guess [that ruined the surprise party]
h) Andy's guess [that the party was on Saturday]

Do the same for the following examples, which do not include clauses but rather prepositional phrases following the noun. Are these phrases complements or adjuncts, based on the *one* test?

a) the destruction [of the city]
b) the notion [of justice]
c) the notion [with broad implications]
d) the student [with brown hair]
e) The Queen [of Denmark]

Diagram two examples each of adjuncts and complements from the data above.

Problem 5. Reduced Relative Clauses

You have seen that reduced relative clauses are derived by omission of a relative pronoun and a form of *be*. We thus derive the reduced relative clause in (a) from the tensed counterpart in (b).

a) The person who was arrested for theft
b) The person arrested for theft

Make up three or four other examples of reduced relative clauses, in which the main verb in the relative clause is a past participle. What observations can you make about reduced relative clauses with such participles? In particular, how do you account for the difference between these clauses and independent clauses in which a past participle is typically introduced by auxiliary verb *have*, rather than the auxiliary *be?*

Problem 6. The Functions of Noun Phrases

Identify any noun phrases you find in the following sentences as complements, subjects, or adjuncts. Identify them using of the following labels that apply: direct object, object of preposition, indirect object, subjective complement, objective complement, adverbial noun phrase, appositive noun phrase, free relative clause (noun phrase).

1. We have hundreds of farms in the county—dozens in the immediate area—but we've gridded everything off with some help from the forces in Salisbury, Marlborough, and Swindon, and we'll be canvassing all of them, looking for some evidence the kid was there.
2. Unlike Ophelia, most girls recover from early adolescence; it's not a fatal disease, but an acute condition that disappears with time.
3. As the hypodermic needle slid into my arm, I wondered if the doctor, who seemed no more than an overlarge child, was old enough to have qualified professionally.
4. We got off the freeway once, between the tiny communities of Greycliff and Reedpoint, to look for the graves of Bill Thomas, his son, Charley, and Joe Schultz, a mule driver.
5. John Romm, the Acting Assistant Secretary for the Office of Energy Efficiency and Renewable Energy, called the contract signing "an exceptional moment of the solar energy program."
6. The police know of the criminal operation of the Black Muslim movement because they have thoroughly infiltrated it.
7. Jacob Branowski, one of the most eloquent commentators on the relationship of science to other human activities, always reminded us that scientific theories are a fiction.

TEXT ANALYSIS

I. Finding Adjuncts in Noun Phrases

List all restrictive and nonrestrictive relative clauses you find in the following text. Also list any appositive noun phrases, and any free relative clauses.

a) Maple grew up in the Richmond Hill section of Queens.
b) He is one of seven children.
c) His father, who was a mail carrier on the New York-to-Buffalo run, died in a veteran's hospital three years ago.
d) His mother, who died two years ago, was a nurse's aide.
e) Jack went to Catholic schools "with nasty nuns" and then attended Brooklyn Tech, a prestigious school for math and science wonks.
f) He failed the exam in aeronautics, among other subjects.
g) Mainly, he was a truant who spent his time at the Museum of Natural History.
h) Brooklyn Tech did not choose to confer on him the honor of a diploma.
i) Eventually, he got one from a less distinguished outfit: the Fort Greene Night School.

Source: "The Crime Buster," by David Remnick, *The New Yorker*, February 24 & March 3, 1997.

2. More Practice

Do the same as in (1) in the following sentences. In addition, identify any noun phrase complements and give their semantic label if they have one.

a) David WalksAlong, the Spokane Tribal Council Chairman, showed up at the band's rehearsal a few times.
b) He was a tall, light-skinned Indian with brown eyes and a round face.
c) He'd been a great basketball player in his youth, a slashing, brutal point guard who looked almost like an old-time Indian warrior.
d) But he spent most of his time playing golf now and had grown fat in the belly and thighs.
e) WalksAlong had long, dark beautiful hair twenty years ago but had cut it shorter and shorter as it grew more gray.

Source: Reservation Blues, by Sherman Alexie.

3. Class Exercise

Find at least two examples of each of the following constructions in texts of your choice. Type out a list of your sentences (without any telltale labels) and bring them to class to exchange with a classmate. See if your classmate analyzes the text the same way that you do, and discuss any differences you may have.

- Restrictive relative clauses: at least one example each of tensed, infinitival, and reduced relative clauses
- Nonrestrictive relative clauses
- Appositive noun phrases
- Free relative clauses

4. Punctuation Minilesson

Create a minilesson on punctuation of appositive noun phrases and restrictive and nonrestrictive relative clauses. You might look at a selection of writing/grammar handbooks to see what kinds of conventions they recommend. Are they all consistent? Why or why not? Try to explain the punctuation of these constructions in syntactic terms on the basis of what has been discussed in the chapter. Create some exercises for your classmates to illustrate your points.

LANGUAGE DIVERSITY EXERCISES

1. Relative Clauses in Other Languages

As you probably might expect, although relative clauses exist across languages, their syntactic properties differ in certain ways from those we have discussed above. (Not all involve the "overt" WH-Movement that you see in English relative clauses, for example.) Investigate some of the similarities and differences between English relative clauses and those in other languages. Can they be restrictive and nonrestrictive? Tensed, infinitival, and reduced? What is the inventory of relative pronouns in the language? Illustrate your claims with clear examples.

2. Relative Clauses in Earlier English

Investigate the syntax of relative clauses in an earlier form of English (Old or Middle English yield the best results). How do relative clauses in these earlier versions differ from their modern counterparts? Can they be restrictive and nonrestrictive? Tensed, infinitival, and reduced? What is the inventory of relative pronouns in the language? Illustrate their properties, using clear examples.

CHAPTER REVIEW TERMS

adjuncts in the noun phrase

appositive noun phrases, relative clauses (tensed, infinitival, and reduced), relative clause extraposition, relative pronouns, restrictive and nonrestrictive relative clauses, free relative clauses

CHAPTER REVIEW EXERCISE

Choose any number of the following options to create a chapter exercise. You may wish to add options from previous chapter exercises to make this exercise more comprehensive.

In the following text excerpts, identify all:

- Restrictive relative clauses (label each as tensed, infinitival, or reduced)
- Nonrestrictive relative clauses
- Appositive noun phrases
- Free relative clauses

> It was the she-wolf who had first caught the sound of men's voices and the whining of the sled dogs; and it was the she-wolf who was first to spring away from the cornered man in his circle of dying flame. The pack had been loath to forego the kill it had hunted down, and it lingered for several minutes, making sure of the sounds; and then it, too, sprang away on the trail made by the she-wolf.
>
> Running at the forefront of the pack was a large gray wolf—one of its several leaders. It was he who directed the pack's course on the heels of the she-wolf. It was he who snarled warningly at the younger members of the pack or slashed at them with his fangs when they ambitiously tried to pass him. And it was he who increased the pace when he sighted the she-wolf, now trotting slowly across the snow.
>
> *Source: White Fang*, by Jack London.

AWE!—awe of a man whose whiskers you have trimmed, whose hair you have cut, whose cravats you have tied, whose shirts you have "put into the wash," whose boots and shoes you have kicked into the closet, whose dressing gown you have worn while combing your hair; who has been down cellar with you at eleven o'clock at night to hunt for a chicken-bone; who has hooked your dresses, unlaced your boots, fastened your bracelets, and tied on your bonnet; who has stood before your looking glass, with thumb and finger on his proboscis, scraping his chin; whom you have buttered, and sugared, and toasted, and tea-ed; whom you have seen asleep with his mouth wide open! Ri—diculous!

Source: Awe-ful Thoughts, by Fanny Fern.

Glossary

Acronyms words formed by combining the first letters of a series of words: *NOW = National Organization for Women, ZIP* (code) = *zone improvement plan*

Adjectival modifiers see *Prenominal adjective phrases.*

Adjective phrase adjunct adjective phrase in adjoined position: *They returned from the hike* **hungry.** Adjective phrase adjuncts modify a noun phrase in the sentence, and can occur in either sentence-initial or sentence-final position. See also *Adjunct.*

Adjunct unselected phrases that occur in adjoined position, outside the level of a phrase that dominates the head and its complements. Evidence from the syntactic properties of adjuncts (they follow complements, and can, if they are adjoined to VP, front to sentence-initial position) supports the claim that these phrases are adjoined "higher" in the phrase than complements are. Adjuncts can be of any category, including clauses, and can adjoin to either a verb phrase or a noun phrase.

Adjunction process of adjoining to another constituent. See *Adjunct.*

Adverbial noun phrase noun phrase that expresses adverbial information of time, manner, reason, place, or cause. An example of an adverbial noun phrase complement is *home* in *The boy walked* **home.** Adverbial noun phrases also express measurement (height, weight, etc.) as in *The baby weighed* **eleven pounds.** Adverbial noun phrases can also be adjuncts, as in **Downtown,** *the traffic is terrible.*

Adverbial noun phrase adjunct See *Adverbial noun phrase.*

Adverbial noun phrase complement See *Adverbial noun phrase*

Adverb phrase adjunct phrase that occurs in non-complement position within and at the periphery of the sentence. **Obviously,** *the party was a success/The party was a success* **obviously**/*The party was* **obviously** *a success.* Because adverb phrases are unselected, move around relatively freely, and occur in non-complement positions we classify them as *adjuncts.*

Adverb phrase complement phrases that are selected by a very small number of verbs, and that occur obligatorily only under restricted conditions. An example of an adverb phrase complement is *carefully* in *She worded the letter* **carefully,** where the verb *word* appears to select an adverb phrase. Other positions in which adverb phrases obligatorily occur are *middle constructions,* such as *The new Volkswagen drives* **beautifully.**

Affixation   process of adding suffixes or prefixes to a word in English. Affixation can also involve adding *infixes,* or affixes that occur within words, but this process is not productive in English. See also *Derivational affixation* and *Inflectional affixation.*

Ambiguity   having more than one meaning. Words can be ambiguous, as in *He won the suit,* where *suit* can mean a type of clothing or a legal proceeding. Sentences can also be ambiguous, as in *They saw the man with the binoculars,* where the prepositional phrase *with the binoculars* modifies either *the man* or the verb *see.* Word level ambiguity is called "lexical" ambiguity, and sentence level ambiguity is referred to as "syntactic" ambiguity.

Anomaly   nonsense sentence or word. The sentence *colorless green ideas sleep furiously* is anomalous, as is the word *Jabberwocky.*

Antecedent   (pragmatic and linguistic) See *Pronominalization*

Appositive noun phrase   adjunct in a noun phrase. The noun phrase *a famous scientist* in *Madame Curie, a famous scientist* is an appositive noun phrase. Appositive noun phrases rename and form a constituent with the noun phrase they adjoin to. They therefore do not move as freely as adjuncts adjoined to verb phrases.

Aspect   duration, completion, or habitual occurrence of an event, typically expressed semantically or morphologically by verbs in English. Aspect is morphologically expressed by the participial forms of the verb; the past participle (*eaten, brought, cried*) expresses completion, or perfect aspect, while the present participle (*eating, crying*) expresses duration, or progressive aspect. Aspect can also be semantic, and not correspond to verbal morphology. For example, *John continued to speak* has progressive aspect, though there is no present participle. Habitual aspect is not expressed morphologically in English, but rather semantically or syntactically. In some varieties of English, *Mary works hard all the time* expresses habitual aspect. In other varieties of English, habitual aspect is syntactic, expressed by the addition of the verb *be,* as in *Mary be working hard.* See also *Participle.*

Auxiliary   grammatical category with a cluster of specific properties differentiating members from main verbs. Members include the auxiliary verbs *have/be/do* and the modals *will/would/shall/should* etc. Tensed auxiliary verbs and modals undergo Subject-Auxiliary Inversion, Tag Question Formation, and *Not* Contraction. They also have grammatical meanings (tense and sometimes aspect, and also sometimes number and person), but lack lexical content, in contrast to main verbs. Members of the category Auxiliary, when tensed, occur in the AUX position in the phrase structure tree. See also *AUX position, Do-Insertion* and *Modal.*

Auxiliary verb   see *Auxiliary, AUX position,* and *Modal.*

AUX position   position in which tensed auxiliary verbs and modals occur in the phrase structure tree. AUX is also the position to which a verb may raise via Verb Raising, and it is the position to which rules such as Subject-Auxiliary Inversion and Tag Question Formation apply. Tense features also occur in AUX, in the absence of an auxiliary verb, giving rise under certain conditions to *Do*-Insertion. The negative morpheme *not* contracts only with elements in AUX. See also *Auxiliary, Do-Insertion,* and *Modal.*

Bare infinitival complement   See *Infinitival complement.*

Blending   morphological process by which we combine two words to form a new one: *electronic + mail = email, skirt + shorts = skort*

Case   morphological or syntactic means of expressing grammatical function of a noun phrase, as a subject (with subjective or nominative case), direct object (with objective or accusative case), indirect object (with dative or sometimes accusative case), possessor (with genitive case), and so on. Case in English is expressed morphologically in a limited way; pronouns (*I/me, she/her,* etc.) have different forms that reflect their different grammatical functions as subjects and objects, and genitive case is expressed by the -*'s* affix or the form of a possessive determiner, as in *Martin Luther King Jr.*'s *speech* and **his** *speech.* Case in English is primarily syntactic, or *structural,* meaning that noun phrases in the subject position are interpreted as having structural nominative case and in the direct object position as having structural accusative case, and so on.

Clause   phrase consisting of a noun phrase (subject) and verb phrase (predicate), generated by the phrase structure rule S => NP (AUX) VP. Clauses can be *tensed, infinitival* (either *bare* or *to-*), or *participial,* depending on the form of the verb heading the verb phrase predicate, and on whether AUX (and hence tense) is present. See also *Independent clause* and *Subordinate clause.*

Clipping   morphological process by which we abbreviate words, creating new ones: *prof* for *professor, rad* for *radical*

Coining   morphological process by which we create entirely new words, unrelated to existing words: *quiz* and *kleenex*

Communicative competence   Linguist Dell Hymes' term for our understanding of language use in social situations. For some, communicative competence is included in the definition of *grammar,* as it is part of what speakers know about their language. Others consider knowledge of language use in context separate from the grammatical system including rules of syntax, semantics, morphology, and phonology.

Complement   phrase selected by a lexical head. A complement "completes" a phrase. Complements can be analyzed either in terms of their syntactic category or in terms of their semantics. For example, a verb might select a noun phrase complement that can semantically function as either a *direct object, objective complement,* or *subjective complement.* See also *Subcategorization.*

Complementizers   words that introduce subordinate clauses. Complementizers, *that, for, whether,* and *if,* appear to in some sense *select* the tense of the clause with which they occur. For example, *that* and *if* introduce only tensed subordinate clauses, and *for* introduces only infinitival clauses. *Whether* introduces either tensed or infinitival subordinate clauses.

Complex prepositional phrase   prepositional phrase in which a preposition selects a prepositional phrase complement. (*Out around the house, over under the tree*)

Compounding   morphological process by which we create a single word out of two or more words. Compounds can be recognized by compound stress, where the first word of the compound is accented. Some examples include: *scapegoat, browbeat, underside.*

Conjunction   See *Coordination.*

Conjunctive adverbs   See *Coordination.*

Constituent   word or phrase that forms part of a larger phrase. For example, a verb is a constituent of a verb phrase, as is any complement of the verb. Adjuncts are also constituents of the phrases to which they adjoin, namely verb phrases and noun phrases.

Contradiction   a sentence that cannot be true because the truth of one part implies the falsity of another. For example, *John was killed but he didn't die* is a contradiction, because the truth of the first clause implies the falsity of the second.

Coordination   process by which two words or phrases are connected by a *conjunction* (*for, and, nor, but, or, yet, so*). Independent clauses can also be conjoined by conjunctive adverbs (such as *therefore, however, etc.*). Coordination can often cause ambiguity (as in *big men and women*) and is a useful tool for determining the status of a word or a group of words as a phrase. Coordination also is most acceptable when it involves "like" categories, and thus helps us identify the category of a phrase or word (if we know the category of one of the coordinate phrases or heads, we can usually infer that the other will be of the same category). Conjunctions (that we can remember by the acronym FANBOYS) form a closed class of words with grammatical meanings, and thus form a grammatical category. This category differs from other grammatical categories such as Determiner or Degree, as conjunctions do not syntactically introduce a particular lexical head.

Dative verbs   class of transitive verbs that select both a direct object and a prepositional phrase that dominates an indirect object (*Linda sent a package to her son.*) Dative verbs include *give/send/write/bring/buy/bake/throw* among others. *Indirect Object Movement* applies only in sentences with dative verbs, to derive from the example above *Linda sent her son a package.*

Definiteness   property of noun phrases to refer to something known to both the speaker and hearer. The noun phrase *the class* in the sentence *The class is really fun,* is assumed to refer to a class known to both speaker and hearer. In the sentence *I signed up for a class,* it is not the case that the referent for *a class* is known to the hearer, or to the speaker either, for that matter. The determiner *the* is thus definite, and *a* is indefinite. Other definite determiners include *the/this/these/those,* and quantifiers, such as *all, each,* and *every* are also definite. The quantifiers *some/several/many/few* are indefinite.

Degree   grammatical category that includes the closed class of words expressing degree such as *too/so/more/very/less.* Degree words introduce the lexical categories Adjective and Adverb (*very tall/more quickly*). We included adverbs such as *extraordinarily/amazingly/incredibly* in this class when they introduce adjectives or adverbs, as in this position they express degree. In other positions we analyze them as manner adverbs, as in *She plays the piano amazingly.*

Degree adverbs   See *Degree.*

Derivational affixation   process by which we form new words by adding suffixes and prefixes in English. Derivational affixes typically change the syntactic category of the word they attach to. For example, the noun *friend* becomes the adjective *friendly* when affixed with *-ly.* Derivational prefixes, on the other hand, do not change the category, but do significantly alter the semantics of the word they attach to, and thus in this sense allow us to derive a "new" word. For example, *happy* and *unhappy* have entirely different (in fact opposite) meanings. Derivational affixes provide clues to the category of a word; for example, words ending in *-ment* or *-ity* are nouns (*excitement, serenity*) and those ending in *-ate* or *-ize* are verbs (*pontificate, regularize*).

Descriptive grammar   our unconscious knowledge of language, composed of semantic, phonological, syntactic, and morphological rules.

Determiners   grammatical category of prenominal elements that express definiteness, number, and sometimes case in English. *A/the/this/that/these/those* are all determiners that differ in terms of definiteness and number. *A* is singular and indefinite, while the others are definite. *This/that/a* are singular, and *these/those* are plural. *The* is unspecified for number, and can be followed by a singular or plural noun (*the dog/dogs*). *His/her/my,* and so on are *possessive* determiners (*her book*) that express possessive (genitive) case. English also has WH-determiners such as *whose/which/what* (*whose book*). See also *Case* and *Definiteness.*

Direct object   noun phrase complement of a transitive verb that semantically takes the action of the verb. We can test for direct objects by using the Passive movement rule, which applies only to such phrases. For example, we know that the noun phrase *the movie* in *The students watched* **the movie** is a direct object, because it can be passivized, as in **The movie** *was watched by the students.*

***Do*-Insertion**   operation that inserts the pleonastic auxiliary *do* into the AUX position in the absence of another auxiliary element (*have/be* or a modal). *Do* is inserted to realize tense inflection when *not* occurs to the right of AUX. *Do* is also inserted in order for Subject-Auxiliary Inversion, Tag Question Formation, or *Not* Contraction to apply if no other auxiliary is present. See also *Auxiliary* and *AUX position*.

Dominate   describes the phrase structure relationship among constituents whereby one constituent can be contained inside another, larger phrase. A verb, for example, is *dominated* by a verb phrase, as is the complement of the verb and also any adjuncts in the verb phrase. S dominates the subject and the predicate, NP and VP, and also the AUX position, if present.

Ellipsis   process by which a word or phrase can be "missing," but interpreted under identity to an antecedent in the preceding discourse. For example, we interpret the quantifier *many* in the sentence *Some people came to see the show, but **many** left before it was over* to precede an "empty" noun, *people*. The head of the noun phrase is in this case "ellipted." See also *Verb Phrase Ellipsis*.

Extraposition   movement rule that applies to clauses, to move them to sentence-final position. Extraposition can apply to clauses in subject position, as in [*That Mary smokes*] *bothers me*, to derive *It bothers me* [*that Mary smokes*]. In this case, pleonastic *it* is inserted in the subject position when the clause is extraposed. Relative clauses can also be extraposed; *the teacher* [*who we had heard so much about*] *walked in* becomes *the teacher walked in* [*who we had heard so much about*], after extraposition.

Flat adverbs   adverbs that are not affixed with *-ly* and which typically have adjectival counterparts. For example, in *She threw the ball hard, hard* is a flat adverb, as it modifies *threw*. In the sentence *The test was hard, hard* is an adjective, describing *the test*. We sometimes create flat adverbs from *-ly* adverbs, as in *She walks so slow/slowly*, or *He left quick/quickly*.

Fragments   phrases that do not form full clauses, and which in writing are considered "incomplete sentences." For example, *People who like a bad storm* is a noun phrase and hence a fragment, if it is not included in a clause such as *People who like a bad storm should live on the Gulf*. Fragments can be a useful literary device, and are often employed by writers for stylistic effect.

Free relative clauses   clauses that are syntactically noun phrases, and that have the structure of relative clauses without a head noun. Some examples include *I'll do whatever you want*, or *She'll leave whenever she can*. These phrases appear to involve WH-Movement like relative clauses, but they are not modifiers of nouns. See also *Relative clause*.

Future tense   See *Tense*

Gender   inflection that expresses grammatical gender as feminine, masculine, or neuter. Grammatical gender does not necessarily correlate with the *biological* gender of a word (nouns, verbs, and/or adjectives can all have grammatical gender, depending on the language). For example, in French the noun *mond* "earth" is masculine (*le mond*) but in German "earth," *Welt*, is feminine (*die Welt*). Grammatical gender is an "agreement" feature; in a language in which nouns have grammatical gender, for instance, the determiner must "agree" in gender with the noun it precedes. For this reason, the determiner *the* in such languages, for example, has different forms depending on the gender of the following noun (*le* = masculine singular in French, *la* = feminine singular, *der* = masculine singular in German, *die* = feminine singular, *das* = neuter singular). Pronouns, on the other hand, express the biological gender of the noun to which they refer (*he/she/it*, and *his/hers*). Possessive determiners (*his/her/its*) also express biological, but not grammatical, gender, as they do not "agree" with the noun they introduce; *his* in *his books* does not agree in gender with *books*, but rather refers to some male antecedent in the previous discourse.

Gerund   word that functions as a noun though it has verbal morphology, namely an -*ing* affix. *Competitive swimming is a very tough sport.*

Grammar   this term has many different definitions, but in this book *grammar* refers to the linguistic system comprising semantic, phonological, syntactic, and morphological rules. See also *Descriptive grammar* and *Prescriptive grammar*.

Grammatical categories   syntactic categories with a particular cluster of characteristics that differentiate them from "lexical" categories. Grammatical categories are members of closed morphological classes (we do not add new members) with grammatical, rather than intrinsic, meaning. Syntactically, they typically introduce lexical categories, though there exist grammatical categories, such as conjunctions, that have other functions. There are also other categories whose status as grammatical categories as we have defined them here is subject to debate, namely proforms and prepositions. See also *Degree, Determiner, Lexical categories, Modifiers of prepositions, Numerals,* and *Pronominalization.*

Grammaticality   in the approach taken in this book, whether a sentence is possible in a particular language (here, English) or not. This concept of grammaticality is thus different from the definition in prescriptive grammar, as a sentence that adheres to prescriptive grammatical rules.

Habitual aspect   See *Aspect.*

Head   phrase structure term for the main word of a larger syntactic unit, a phrase. In the context of this book heads are restricted to being members of the lexical categories Noun, Verb, Adjective, and Adverb. Prepositions, whose status as to lexical or grammatical category remains unclear, are also heads. See also *Phrase* and *Phrase structure.*

Hierarchical structure   property of syntactic structure that a phrase can dominate another phrase. Syntactic structure is therefore much more complex than a simple linear string of words. Hierarchical structure can be illustrated using phrase structure rules in which, for example, a verb and its noun phrase complement form a larger verb phrase. In this case, the verb phrase dominates another phrase (the noun phrase complement), creating hierarchical structure. See also *Phrase structure.*

Independent clause   clause that is not dominated by a dependent constituent, such as a verb phrase, noun phrase, etc. Also called a *main clause.* See also *Clause, Sentence* and *Subordinate clause.*

Indirect object   noun phrase complement of a preposition *to* or *for* that can undergo Indirect Object Movement. For example, *Mary* is an indirect object in *John gave a book to* **Mary** because we can also say *John gave* **Mary** *a book.* Semantically, an indirect object is the beneficiary or goal of the direct object. See *Indirect Object Movement*

Indirect Object Movement   movement rule that applies to both direct and indirect object noun phrases in a sentence, deriving from *Mary gave a book to John* the sentence *Mary gave John a book.* This rule also involves omitting the preposition *to* or *for* that originally introduces the indirect object noun phrase. Indirect Object Movement provides evidence for phrases, because only noun phrases can undergo this operation. It also provides a way to determine whether the object of a preposition is an indirect object, because only indirect objects can undergo this operation. See also *Indirect object.*

Infinitive   form of the verb that lacks all inflection (tense, number, person). Infinitives are sometimes called the "base" form of the verb. We refer in the text to *bare infinitives (eat)* and *to-infinitives (to eat).* See also *Infinitival adjunct* and *Infinitival complement.*

Inflectional affixation   process by which affixes (prefixes or suffixes in English) that express grammatical information (such as number, case, gender, person, etc.) are added to words. Inflectional affixes, unlike derivational affixes, do not change the category of the word they attach to. For example, the adjective *tall* remains an adjective when affixed by inflectional *-est* in *tallest.* Inflectional affixes also often provide clues to the syntactic category of a word. For example, third person singular *-s* is an affix we find on verbs (*she walks*), and *-er/-est* appear on adjectives (*tallest*) and adverbs (*She ran faster than John.*). Plural *-s*, on the other hand, affixes only to nouns (*knights*). See also *Case, Gender, Number,* and *Person.*

Infinitival adjunct   *to*-infinitival clauses that occur in adjoined position, either sentence-initial or sentence-final. **To learn another language,** *you have to study hard/You have to study hard* **to learn another language.** Infinitival adjuncts can also be distinguished from infinitival complements by their "in order" interpretation. For example, the infinitival adjunct *to learn another language* has this interpretation, as we see by the grammaticality of *In order to learn another language, you have to study hard.* The infinitival complement *to study hard* in *I want to study hard,* on the other hand, cannot have an "in order" interpretation, as the ungrammaticality of *I want in order to study* illustrates.

Infinitival complement   clausal complement in which the verb is infinitival, lacking any tense, person, or number inflection. Infinitival complements may be *to*-infinitives, in which case the complement may or may not have an expressed subject, as in *I want* **to go home**/*I want* **Mary to go home.** *Bare* infinitival complements have expressed subjects, and are typically selected by perception verbs and the verbs *make* and *let. When the earthquake hit, she felt* **the walls shake.**

Infinitival relative clause   relative clause in which the verb is infinitival, as in *the person* **to do the job.** Infinitival relative clauses differ from *tensed* relative clauses in two important ways. One is in the form of the main verb (infinitival versus tensed) and the second is in relative pronouns (infinitival relatives lack relative pronouns altogether, but tensed relatives omit them only under certain conditions). Infinitival relative clauses thus do not appear to be derived by WH-Movement in the same way as tensed relative clauses, unless such movement is "covert." See also *Relative clause* and *Tensed relative clause.*

Intransitive   See *Transitivity*

Lexical categories   syntactic categories that share characteristics that distinguish them from "grammatical" categories. Lexical categories are members of open morphological classes (we productively add new members to lexical categories), and have intrinsic meanings. They head phrases, and can be introduced by grammatical categories. The lexical categories include Noun, Adjective, Adverb, and Verb. We have also discussed how Prepositions share certain characteristics of lexical categories, yet in other ways appear to be grammatical categories. For example, Prepositions head phrases, and can be introduced by a grammatical category such as the modifier *straight,* as in *straight up the hill.* Prepositions are a closed morphological class, however, and have grammatical meanings. In these ways they pattern with other grammatical categories such as Degree, Determiner, etc. See also *Grammatical categories.*

Linking verbs   set of verbs, including *be, become, remain, seem, appear,* that select subjective complements. Linking verbs are semantically "stative" rather than active, and provide a way (using the *linking verb test*) to help us distinguish between adjective phrases and adverb phrases, since only the former can be subjective complements. (*The process seems slow/*slowly.*)

Logical subject   See *Subject.*

Main clause   See *Independent clause.*

Metaphor   nonliteral meaning created by equating two things that do not appear to have properties in common. *This car is a lemon. Love is a rose.*

Modal   members of the grammatical category Auxiliary. Modals express modality (necessity, possibility, etc.) and have present and past tense forms. Modals occur in the AUX position and undergo the operations that apply to that position. See *AUX position* and *Auxiliary*.

Modifier   see *Adjuncts, Modifiers of prepositions, Prenominal adjective phrases, Prenominal noun modifiers, Relative clause*.

Modifiers of prepositions   members of a closed grammatical class of words, including *right/straight/clear*, etc., that introduce prepositions (*right/straight/ clear* into the room). In that capacity, these words do not function as lexical categories, as they do in *She is right*, or *It was a clear day*, for example, where they function as adjectives. Prepositions are therefore introduced by a grammatical category just as other lexical categories are, which suggests that in this way they pattern with lexical categories Noun, Verb, Adjective, and Adverb. See also *Grammatical categories* and *Lexical categories*.

Morphology   word structure and the rules we use to form words. See *Acronyms, Affixation, Blending, Clipping, Coining, Compounding, Derivational affixation, Inflectional affixation*.

Movement   syntactic operations that reorganize words and phrases in sentences under certain restricted conditions. Movement rules provide evidence for phrases and heads, as both of these elements move. Movement cannot, however, apply to *parts* of phrases. See also *Indirect Object Movement, Particle Shift, Passive, PP Preposing, Subject-Auxiliary Inversion,* and *WH-Movement*.

Nominalization   noun formed by derivational affixation. For example, we form the nominalization *excitement* by affixing the verb *excite* with the derivational affix *-ment*.

Nonrestrictive relative clause   See *Relative clause*.

Not Contraction   operation in which the negative morpheme *not* contracts with an element in the AUX position (*have/be/do* or a modal). This gives rise to forms such as *didn't, haven't, wouldn't*, etc. See also *AUX position, Auxiliary,* and Do-*Insertion*.

Noun modifiers   See *Prenominal noun modifiers*.

Number   grammatical feature or inflection that is expressed morphologically in a number of ways, by affixation or by the form of a word. Some examples of number expressed through affixation are the third person singular *-s* affix on verbs (*She walks/They walk*), the plural affix *-s* on count nouns (*horses*) and irregular affixes such as *-en* on *oxen* or *-a* on *ova*. Examples of word forms that express number are proforms (*he/they*), members of the category NUM (*six* people, *eight* goats), and determiners *this/these*. Number can also be expressed without a change in a word's form, as in "zero plurals" such as *sheep, deer*.

Numeral   grammatical category of prenominal elements including cardinal (*one, two*) and ordinal (*first, second*) numbers, and "general" ordinals such as *last, sole, next.*

Objective complement   complement of a verb that also selects a direct object. Objective complements are predicates that assign a property to the direct object, as in *We considered the election unfair.* Objective complements can be noun phrases, prepositional phrases, and adjective phrases. See also *Predicate.*

Object of a preposition   the noun phrase complement of a preposition, as in *up* **the tree** or *down* **the stairs**. Also called a *prepositional object.*

One **pronominalization**   process by which the pronoun *one* replaces part of a noun phrase. This process tells us that noun phrases can have different "levels" within a larger phrase. *One* replaces the lowest level, including the head and its complements, but adjuncts, adjoined to a higher level of the noun phrase, can optionally remain outside the pronominalized constituent.

Participial adjectives   See *Participle.*

Participle   verb form in which the verb ends in *-ing* or *-ed/-en/-t*. The *-ing* form of the verb is called the **present participle** (*walking, eating*), and the *-ed/-en/ -t* form is called the **past participle** (*walked, eaten, bought*). The present participle can typically be recognized by the preceding auxiliary verb, a form of *be.* The past participle typically follows auxiliary *have.* Participles occur in a variety of other positions, however, in which they are not preceded by auxiliary verbs (**Walking** *down the street, I met Mary/***Eaten** *by mosquitos, we ran home*). Participles often express *aspect,* or the duration or completion of an event. Present participles typically express **progressive aspect,** or duration, and past participles express **perfect aspect,** or completion. Participles can also function as other syntactic categories, namely as adjectives, as in *the* **disgusted/disgusting** *visitor,* or as nouns (**gerunds**) as in **Writing** *can be difficult.* See also *Aspect.*

Participial clause adjunct   untensed clause in which the main verb is a past or present participle, as in **Her horse rearing in fright,** *Mary clung to the saddle.* Participial clause adjuncts occur in either sentence-initial or sentence-final position, and are sometimes referred to as *absolute phrases* in traditional grammars. They differ from *participial clause complements,* such as *They saw* **her horse rearing in fright** in not being selected by a verb, and in not occurring in complement position.

Participial clause complement   clause complement, in which the main verb is participial, and the clause itself lacks tense (and an AUX position). Perception verbs such as *hear/watch/feel* typically select participial clause complements, as in *We heard* **Mary talking to John.**

Participial phrase adjunct   verb phrase adjunct headed by a participial verb, as in **Leaping for joy,** *the dog greeted her owner.* Participial phrase adjuncts lack subjects, and differ from *participial phrase complements* in being unselected, and in occurring in adjunct positions (sentence-finally and sentence-initially) rather than in complement position. An example of a participial phrase complement is *the dog began* **leaping for joy.**

Participial phrase complement   verb phrase complement that is headed by a participial verb, as in *We began* **understanding grammar.** Participial phrases lack subjects (and hence are simply verb phrases), and are typically selected as complements by *temporal aspect verbs* such as *begin/commence/start/finish.*

Particle   intransitive preposition, or a preposition that lacks a noun phrase object. Particles thus occur in sentences such as *I give* **up!**, and *The salesperson handed* **over** *the merchandise.* In the first example, it is clear that the preposition *up* is a particle (and thus intransitive) as there is no noun phrase object. In the second example, although *over* is followed by a noun phrase *the merchandise,* this noun phrase is the object of the verb, rather than the object of the preposition. We know this because this object can undergo Passive, an operation that does not apply to objects of prepositions. Particles also semantically differ from transitive prepositions in forming a semantic unit with the verb. For example, *hand over* in the above example has an idiomatic meaning "to relinquish." *Over* in its use as a transitive preposition lacks this idiomatic interpretation (as in *knock* **over** *the vase*). See also *particle shift* and *Transitivity.*

Particle Shift   movement rule in which a particle, or intransitive preposition, moves to the right over the direct object of the verb (*She picked* **up** *her daughter* => *She picked her daughter* **up.**) Particle Shift provides evidence for phrases, because movement of the particle must be over a noun phrase. It also provides evidence that certain prepositions are *intransitive,* and others *transitive.* That is, particles do not select noun phrase objects, and can occur in constructions such as *She jumped up.* Particles thus differ from transitive prepositions that do select noun phrase objects, such as the preposition *up* in *up the tree.* Transitive prepositions, unlike their intransitive counterparts, do not undergo Particle Shift. See also *Transitivity.*

Passive   movement rule in which both the subject noun phrase and the direct object noun phrase move, creating a passive sentence from an active one. For example, we can turn the active sentence *The lion ate the zebra* into the passive sentence *The zebra was eaten by the lion* by moving the subject noun phrase to the right and the object noun phrase to the left. Passive has the rhetorical effect of foregrounding the direct object (by virtue of relocating it in the subject, or topic, position) and by suppressing the subject (by "demoting" it to a position to the right of the verb). Passive also involves changing the main verb into a past participle introduced by a form of *be.* Passive provides us with a test for the status of a noun phrase as a *direct object,* since it applies exclusively in sentences with active verbs that select direct object noun phrase complements.

Past participle   See *Participle.*

Past tense   See *Tense.*

Perception verbs   class of verbs (*see, hear, watch, feel* and so on) that typically select bare infinitival or participial clause complements. For example, the perception verb *see* selects a bare infinitival complement in *Hortense saw* **the kids ride their bikes,** or a participial clause complement, as in *Hortense saw* **the kids riding their bikes.**

Perfect aspect   See *Aspect* and *Participle.*

Person   agreement inflection expressed by three different pronoun forms in English that distinguish between the speaker (first person: *I,* etc.), the individual addressed (second person: *you,* sg./pl.), and the individual or thing being spoken about (third person: *she/they,* etc.).

Phonetics   the study of the set of sounds in a language. Different languages have different inventories of sounds that speakers know unconsciously. Speakers of a language are therefore able to recognize which sounds, or *phonemes,* are part of their language's inventory and which are not. For example, a Spanish speaker recognizes a trilled [r] as a sound in Spanish. An American English speaker, on the other hand, knows that this sound is not part of the set of sounds she recognizes as "English."

Phonology   the set of grammatical rules that guide our pronunciation (creating our different *accents*), word and sentence stress, intonation, etc. For example, English has a phonological rule that leads us to pronounce the affix *-ed* in *kicked* as [t], but in *climbed* as [d].

Phrase   syntactic unit headed by a lexical category Noun, Verb, Adjective, Adverb, or Preposition (recall, however, that we left the status of Preposition as a lexical or grammatical category open). Evidence that syntactic structure is organized into phrases comes from movement, pronominalization, and coordination. See *Coordination, Movement,* and *Pronominalization.*

Phrase structure   the notation linguists use to express syntactic structure. The fundamental properties of phrase structure are that syntactic structure is organized into phrases and that all phrases have heads, giving rise to *phrase structure rules* such as VP => V NP, etc. Phrase structure also allows us to express the generalizations that syntactic structure is hierarchical and recursive. Properties of phrase structure are expressed in terms of lists of phrase structure rules for each phrase (noun phrase, verb phrase, sentence, etc.). See also *Hierarchical structure* and *Recursion.*

Phrase structure rules   See *Phrase structure.*

Pleonastic *do*   See Do-*Insertion.*

Pleonastic subject   See *Subject*.

Possessive case   See *Case*.

Possessive noun phrase   full noun phrase that precedes the head noun in a larger noun phrase. Possessive noun phrases are affixed with inflectional -'s, and thus have morphological possessive, or genitive case. (*The civil rights leader from Atlanta's speech*) See also *Case*.

Postnominal adjective phrases   adjective phrases that follow the noun in the noun phrase. These adjective phrases modify the noun, as in *all things* **bright and beautiful,** and *something* **wicked.** Only certain adjective phrases occur in this position in English, as we can see by the ungrammaticality of **the ball* **red.**

PP Preposing   movement rule that fronts a prepositional phrase to sentence-initial position, and also "inverts" the subject and verb. For example, when we apply PP Preposing to the sentence *The boulder rolled down the hill* we derive *Down the hill rolled the boulder.* PP Preposing provides us with a tool to distinguish particles, or intransitive prepositions, from transitive prepositions, since only the latter undergo PP Preposing.

Pragmatic antecedent   See *Pronominalization*.

Predicate   phrase that assigns a semantic property to a noun phrase. The verb phrase of a clause is a predicate, assigning a property to the subject. Adjective phrases, noun phrases, and prepositional phrases can also be predicates, when they assign a property to a noun phrase. Such predicates are typically **subjective complements** (*Nina seems* **upset and dejected**) or **objective complements** (*We consider Nina* **upset**) or **adjuncts** (*Nina,* **upset and dejected,** *left the party.*) See also *Adjunct, Objective complement,* and *Subjective complement*.

Prenominal adjective phrases   adjective phrases that precede and modify the head of the noun phrase (*the* **elegant** *party*). Prenominal adjectives can also be participial, as in *some* **boring/bored** *speakers.*

Prenominal noun modifiers   nouns that occur in prenominal position and modify the head of the noun phrase, as in **brick** *wall,* **nylon** *stocking,* and **student** *demonstrator.* We distinguish noun modifiers from adjectival ones by performing, for example, the *very* test for adjectives; **the very student demonstrator* is ungrammatical, indicating that *student* is not an adjective. See also *Prenominal adjective phrases*.

Prepositional phrase complement   prepositional phrase selected by a head. For example, in *put the car* **in the garage,** the complement *in the garage* is selected by the verb *put.* We can tell this prepositional phrase is a complement by the evidence that *put* sounds ungrammatical without the prepositional phrase, as in **We put the car.* The status of a prepositional phrase as a complement is not always clear; many verbs can occur with optional prepositional phrases following them. For example, we *talk*, but we also *talk* **to Pam.** One test for a prepositional phrase complement is whether it can move to sentence-initial position, a property we associate with adjuncts, rather than complements. So for example, ***In the garage** *we put the car* sounds predictably odd, as does ***To Pam** *we talked*, given that *in the garage* and *to Pam* are complements of *put* and *talk*, respectively. **On Sunday** *we put the car in the garage*, however, is grammatical, as *on Sunday* is a prepositional phrase adjunct rather than a complement. Adjectives also select prepositional phrase complements, as in *proud* **of his country,** and *happy* **about the decision.** Prepositions that select other prepositional phrases as complements we call *complex prepositional phrases,* as in *up* **over the top.** We also saw that nouns can select prepositional phrases, as in *the student* **of linguistics.** In this case, we determined the status of the prepositional phrase *of linguistics* as a complement based on evidence from *one* pronominalization.

Prepositional objects See *Object of a preposition.*

Prepositional phrase adjunct unselected prepositional phrase that occurs in either sentence-initial or sentence-final position, as in **For fun,** *they skipped stones in the river/They skipped stones in the river* **for fun.** Prepositional phrase adjuncts, like prepositional phrase complements, can be of different types. They can be, for example, *complex prepositional phrases,* as in **Out under the eaves,** *we found a swallow's nest,* or *subordinating prepositional phrases,* as in **Although it was very dark,** *they started home.*

Prescriptive grammar grammatical rules we consciously learn in order to speak or write in a way we perceive to be "correct" or "proper."

Present participle See *Participle.*

Present tense See *Tense.*

Presupposition facts whose truth is required in order to understand a sentence, based on our assumptions about the world. For example, we understand the sentence *Would you like another cookie?* to be true in a world in which the following presupposition holds: *you have already had at least one cookie.*

Proform See *Pronominalization.*

Progressive aspect See *Aspect* and *Participle.*

Pronominalization process by which a phrase is replaced by a grammatical word that serves as its "placeholder." These grammatical words, or *proforms,* typically refer to antecedents in the previous discourse. (The label *proform* includes *pronouns,* words that replace only noun phrases.) For example, the antecedent of the proform *so* in *John is very tall and so is Mary* is the adjective phrase *very tall,* and the antecedent of the proform *himself* in *John shaves himself* is the noun phrase *John.* Proforms can also have pragmatic antecedents, antecedents that are not linguistically expressed but rather taken from context. For example, after walking into a room a teacher might say, pointing out the window, *I bet* **she** *is glad she's not in this class!* The hearer understands the unexpressed antecedent to be a (female) person the teacher sees out the window. Proforms express various inflectional features, such as number, person, gender, and case, which give rise to their different forms. Proforms are sometimes designated as a grammatical category, because the members of this set of words forms a closed class. Proforms also have no intrinsic meaning, and thus appear to be similar to grammatical categories in this way as well. Proforms, however, also *replace* full phrases of various lexical categories (including noun phrases, verb phrases, and adjective phrases, among others). In this way they differ from the other grammatical categories discussed in the text. We will thus leave their status as a grammatical category open here. See also *Case, Gender, Number, One Pronominalization* and *Person.*

Pronoun   See *Pronominalization.*

Quantification   complex semantic relationships created by the interplay of quantifiers such as *all/both/each/every/some,* etc. For example, the sentence *Everybody loves somebody* is ambiguous because of the interaction of the quantificational properties of *everybody* and *somebody.* This *scope* ambiguity disappears when we replace a quantified phrase with a noun phrase without quantificational properties, as in *Alisa loves somebody,* or *Everybody loves Alisa.* See also *Quantifier.*

Quantifier   grammatical category of prenominal elements including *all/both/some/each/every/several/many/few.* Quantifiers differ semantically from other categories expressing quantity in also having *scope* properties that sometimes give rise to interesting ambiguities. Quantifiers, like determiners, can be definite or indefinite, and singular or plural. The quantifier *all* is definite, for example, because it picks out every member of a particular set. The quantifier *several* is indefinite, as it picks out unspecified members of a set. See also *Definiteness* and *Quantification.*

Recursion   property of phrase structure that allows a phrase to generate another phrase of the same category. As a result, a recursive phrase structure rule can generate a phrase of infinite length. For example, the phrase structure rule for noun phrase, NP => N (PP), is recursive, because the optional prepositional phrase can itself also dominate a noun phrase as indicated by the phrase structure rule PP => P (NP). Noun phrases with such structure can therefore have indefinite length. Speakers are constrained, however, by memory limitations, which encourage them to limit the length of their utterances so that they can be understood.

Reduced relative clause   tensed relative clause in which the relative pronoun and a form of *be* have been omitted, leaving a participle. For example, *the women who were playing soccer* can be "reduced" to *the women playing soccer.* Sometimes, after *be* and the relative pronoun are omitted, a participial adjective remains, as in *the women who were upset about the game => the women upset about the game.*

Relative clause clausal adjunct in the noun phrase that modifies the head noun. Relative clauses can be restrictive or nonrestrictive modifiers. For example, *the director who won an Oscar* refers to a particular person, a set of one member. In this case, the relative clause is restrictive—it is included in the description of the noun phrase. In *the director, who won an Oscar,* we understand [the director] to refer to a set of one member whose description does not include the relative clause; the clause in this case provides only incidental information, and is thus nonrestrictive. Relative clauses are derived in English by WH-Movement, and are introduced by *relative pronouns (that, which, when, where, who, why).* Relative clauses can be *tensed, reduced* or *infinitival,* depending on the form of the verb. Relative clauses have several properties that distinguish them from clausal complements of nouns and verbs, one of which is that restrictive relative clauses can move under certain circumstances by relative clause extraposition. See also *Adjunct, Extraposition, Infinitival relative clause, Reduced relative clause,* and *Tensed relative clause.*

Relative clause extraposition See *Extraposition* and *Relative clause.*

Relative pronoun interrogative *(which/why/who/when/where)* pronoun that introduces a relative clause, as in *the teacher who the students like. That* can also be a relative pronoun, as in *the teacher that the students like.* Relative pronouns result from WH-movement of a phrase within the relative clause. *The teacher [the students like* **who**] => *the teacher [***who** *the students like_____].*

Relative pronouns See *Relative clause.*

Restrictive relative clause See *Relative clause.*

Semantics grammatical component that includes rules by which we understand word and sentence meaning. See *Ambiguity, Anomaly, Contradiction, Metaphor, Presupposition, Quantification,* and *Semantic shift.*

Semantic shift creating a new word by assigning a new meaning to an existing word. The adjective *kosher* at one time described food prepared according to the dietary requirements of Jewish law. Now it has semantically shifted to also have the more general meaning *acceptable,* as in *It's kosher to do it that way.*

Sentence a clause or larger constituent, informally defined as "everything between the capital and the period." A sentence can therefore consist of a single independent clause as in *Lions eat zebras,* or *I think that lions eat zebras,* where the independent clause dominates a subordinate clause. A sentence can also be made up of two or more independent clauses, as in *Lions eat zebras and zebras eat grass.* A "sentence" can therefore consist of a (simple or complex) clause, or a number of independent clauses. See also *Independent clause* and *Subordinate clause.*

Standard English   forms and usage of language perceived to be "correct" and "proper" by a particular speech community. What is considered standard can vary from speech community to speech community, making "standard" English difficult to define. Many of us nevertheless assume it exists in some "pure" form.

Strong verbs   verbs that express inflection by internal vowel changes. Examples from English include *sing/sang/sung*, and *find/found*.

Subcategorization   syntactic principle of selection. A head subcategorizes, or selects, a particular syntactic category as a complement. For example, *adore* selects a noun phrase complement (*adore* **her friends**), and *put* selects a noun phrase and prepositional phrase complement (*put* **the car in the garage**). Linguists propose that the subcategorization "frames" for lexical heads form an important component of our mental lexicon, or dictionary, representing information a speaker must "know" unconsciously in order to speak his/her language. See also *Complement*.

Subject   syntactically defined as the noun phrase position in a clause, as expressed by the phrase structure rule S => NP (AUX) VP. For example, *the bagels* is the subject of the sentence *The bagels were in the box*. The syntactic subject is often distinct from the semantic, or *logical*, subject of a sentence. For example, in *There were some bagels in that bag*, the noun phrase *some bagels* is the logical subject, but not also the syntactic subject, which is *there*. Syntactic subjects can therefore be semantically "empty," or *pleonastic*. Another such example is *it* in *It is raining*.

Subject-Auxiliary Inversion   movement rule that fronts a tensed auxiliary element (*have/be/do* or a modal) over the subject noun phrase to sentence-initial position in order to form a *yes/no* question (*Is the professor leaving?*). Subject-Auxiliary Inversion provides evidence that the subject of a sentence is a phrase, and also that tensed auxiliary verbs and modals occur in a position distinct from that dominating main verbs, as only the former undergo certain operations, one of which is Subject-Auxiliary Inversion. See also *AUX position, Auxiliary,* and Do-*Insertion*.

Subjective complement   complement of a linking verb, which can be either a noun phrase, adjective phrase, or prepositional phrase. Such complements are semantic predicates and assign a property to the subject noun phrase (*Mary remained* **president of the company**). See also *Complement* and *Predicate*.

Subordinate clause   clause that is dependent, or dominated by a phrase that is itself dependent (and thus can't stand alone). A clausal complement of a preposition or verb or any other head will thus always be subordinate, since prepositional phrases, verb phrases, etc. are also always dependent. A relative clause is also subordinate, as it is dominated by a (dependent) noun phrase. Subordinate clauses can be *tensed, infinitival* or *participial* depending on the form of the verb. See also *Independent clause* and *Subordinating preposition*.

Subordinating preposition   class of prepositions including *when/because/with/ while/though* and so on that select clauses as complements. Such clauses are by definition subordinate, because the prepositional phrase that dominates them is always dependent. For example, the subordinating preposition *because* selects a clausal complement in the sentence *Mary left work because* **she felt sick.** The clause *she felt sick* is a subordinate clause, as it is dominated by a prepositional phrase that is dominated by a verb phrase. See also *Subordinate clause.*

Subordination   See *Subordinate clause.*

Suppletion   morphological form of a word that expresses inflection and that is historically unrelated to other forms of the word. For example, the past tense form of *go*, namely *went*, is historically unrelated to *go*, and thus a suppletive form of *go* used to express past tense inflection. Some adjectives have suppletive forms that express comparative/superlative distinctions, such as *good/better/best, bad/worse/worst.*

Syntactic categories   divisions among word classes (such as Noun, Verb, Determiner, Degree, etc.) based on syntactic, morphological, and to some extent semantic characteristics. Morphology tells us, for example, that the word *walks* is either a noun or a verb, as the -s affix marks third person singular inflection on verbs and number on nouns. In *Walks are therapeutic,* syntactic clues tell us that *walks* is a noun, as it occurs in the subject position, a noun phrase position. We also know from semantics that *walks* here is a particular type of noun, namely a concrete, common, count noun. Syntactic categories can be "lexical" or "grammatical," depending on their morphological, semantic, and syntactic properties. See also *Grammatical categories* and *Lexical categories.*

Syntactic subject   See *Subject.*

Syntax   word order and the operations that apply to syntactic units, or constituents. See *Coordination, Movement,* and *Pronominalization.*

Tag Question Formation   syntactic operation that applies only to tensed auxiliaries and modals in AUX, to form a question at the end of a sentence (*The bus is coming now, isn't it?*). Tag questions are opposite in polarity to their sources: *John left, didn't he?/John didn't leave, did he?* Tag Question Formation provides a means of distinguishing between tensed auxiliary verbs and modals, on the one hand, and main verbs on the other, because only the former undergo this process. See also *AUX position, Auxiliary,* and *Do-Insertion.*

Temporal aspect verbs   class of verbs that typically select participial phrase complements, as in *They began/commenced/started/finished watching the movie.*

Tense   time frame in which an event or state occurs. Tense can be morphologically expressed in English by past or present tense affixes on the verb (*I walked, she walks*). Tense can also be semantic, in which case the tense of a sentence may not necessarily correlate with verbal morphology. For example, in the sentence *I would like my dinner now, would* has past morphology, but tense is interpreted as present. Future tense is expressed in English syntactically by the addition of *will* or *shall* to a sentence (*I will go*), and can also be semantic, as in *I am leaving tomorrow,* where *am* is morphologically present tense but the sentence is interpreted in future tense.

Tensed clause complement   clausal complement in which the verb is tensed. Tensed clause complements are optionally introduced by the complementizer *that: I think* **(that) John is smart.** Heads other than verbs also select tensed clause complements, including adjectives, as in *It is certain* **that Mary will be there,** and (subordinating) prepositions, as in *John left because* **the party was dull.** Tensed clause complements are by definition subordinate clauses, as they are dominated by another constituent (either a verb phrase, an adjective phrase, or a prepositional phrase).

Tensed relative clause   relative clause in which the verb is tensed, as in *any book* **that you find at the corner bookstore,** or *the student* **who talked to the principal.** Tensed relative clauses are introduced by relative pronouns that can under certain circumstances be omitted, as in *any book* **(that) you find at the corner book store.** Tensed relative clauses appear to be derived by WH-Movement, the process by which an interrogative pronoun is moved to clause-initial position. For example, the relative clause *who George met* in the noun phrase *the teacher who George met* appears to derive from the source: *the teacher [George met* **who].**

To-infinitival complement   See *Infinitival complement.*

Transitivity   property of verbs and prepositions that they select noun phrase complements that function semantically as *objects* (a "direct" object in the case of verbs, and an "object of a preposition" in the case of prepositions). For example, the verb *throw* is transitive, and selects a noun phrase direct object complement, as in *She threw* **the frisbee.** The preposition *with* is also transitive, selecting a noun phrase object in *with* **the knife.** Verbs and prepositions can also be intransitive in English: *laugh* is intransitive in *She laughed,* and *up* is intransitive (and thus a particle) in *She looked the number up,* or in *Shut up!* See also *Direct object, Object of a preposition, Particle* and *Particle Shift.*

Verb Phrase Ellipsis   syntactic operation in which the verb phrase is omitted, and interpreted as referring to an antecedent verb phrase in a preceding clause. For example, in *Mary likes apples but John doesn't* _____, the verb phrase *likes apples* is omitted in the second clause and is interpreted as referring to *likes apples* in the first clause. Verb Phrase Ellipsis provides us with a way to determine which elements in a sentence occur in the verb phrase and which in the AUX position, as elements in AUX (such as *doesn't* in the above example) are not omitted along with the verb phrase.

Verb Raising   movement rule that applies to auxiliaries *have* and *be* in English to "raise" untensed forms of these verbs from V position to AUX position. This explains the fact that auxiliary *have* can occur to either side of *not,* as in *Hortense might have* **not** *eaten the salmon/Hortense might* **not** *have eaten the* *salmon*. By proposing that main verb *be* also raises from V to AUX, we explain why main verb *be* can, like tensed auxiliary verbs, undergo processes that apply to elements in AUX, such as Subject-Auxiliary Inversion, Tag Question Formation, etc. See also *AUX position*.

Weak verbs   verbs that express inflection by regular affixation. Verbs affixed by *-ed/-t/-en* in English are weak verbs, as are verbs affixed with *-s* and *-ing*.

WH-complement   clausal complement introduced by a WH-word, as in *We wonder* **where Mary bought her hat.** WH-complements occur after a class of verbs that includes *wonder, ask,* and *decide*. These complements can be either infinitival or tensed; compare, for example, *We wonder* **where Mary bought her hat** with *We wonder* **where to go today for lunch.** WH-complements, like relative clauses, are derived by WH-Movement, the operation which moves an interrogative phrase (a WH-phrase) to clause-initial position. WH-complements can also be introduced by WH-complementizers, *if* and *whether,* as in *I asked* **if Mary liked her hat,** and *We must decide* **whether to go.**

WH-Movement   movement rule in which a phrase is replaced by an interrogative proform and then moved to sentence-initial position, as in *What did Cary eat* _____? WH-Movement applies to phrases, and thus provides evidence for phrase structure organized into such syntactic units. WH-Movement is also a movement rule that involves pronominalization.

Appendix: Guide to Language Diversity Exercises

Below are some bibliographical references for various topics addressed by the Language Diversity Exercises at the end of each chapter. Both print and electronic resources are provided. This list is not meant to be comprehensive, but rather to give you some ideas of where to begin your research.

GENERAL LINGUISTICS

The following are good resources to use for general questions about morphology, semantics, and syntax. They will also be of interest to those of you who want to further research topics from the point of view of a "linguistic" approach to grammar and syntax.

Books

Crystal, David. (1995). *The Cambridge Encyclopedia of the English Language.* Cambridge, England: Cambridge University Press
Finegan, E. and N. Besnier. (1989). *Language: Its Structure and Use.* New York Harcourt, Brace, Jovanovich.
Fromkin, V. and R. Rodman. (1998). *Introduction to Language* (6th ed.). New York Harcourt Brace.
Napoli, Donna Jo. (1993). *Syntax: Theory and Problems.* New York: Oxford University Press.
Napoli, Donna Jo. (1996). *Linguistics: An Introduction.* New York: Oxford University Press.
Pinker, Steven. (1994). *The Language Instinct.* New York: William Morrow.

Websites

http://linguistlist.org/~ask-ling/threads.html
(Ask a Linguist, from the Linguist website)

LANGUAGE VARIATION/PIDGINS/CREOLES

The following are good sources of information about different dialects (of American and other varieties of English). Some of these references specifically target pidgin and creole languages, should you wish to focus on these varieties. The history of English language textbooks listed in the History of English section below, and the introductory general linguistics textbooks listed above can also be useful resources for researching dialect variation, pidgins, and creoles.

Books

Burling, Robbins. (1973). *English in Black and White.* New York: Holt, Rinehart and Winston.

Carver, Craig M. (1987). *American Regional Dialects: A Word Geography.* Ann Arbor: University of Michigan Press.

Cassidy, Frederick G. (1985). *Dictionary of American Regional English.* Cambridge, Mass.: Belknap Press, Harvard University.

Dillard, J. L. (1972) *Black English; Its History and Usage in the United States.* New York: Random House.

Dillard, J. L. (1992). *A History of American English.* London New York: Longman.

Ferguson, C. A. and S. B. Heath (eds.) (1981). *Language in the USA.* Cambridge, England: Cambridge University Press.

Folb, Edith. (1980). *Runnin' Down Some Lines: The Language and Culture of Black Teenagers.* Cambridge, Mass.: Harvard University Press.

Hendrickson, Robert (1986). *American Talk: The Words and Ways of American Dialects.* New York: Viking Penguin Inc.

Holm, John (1988–1989). *Pidgins and Creoles.* Vols. 1–2. Cambridge, England: Cambridge University Press.

Labov, William. (1972). *Language in the Inner City; Studies in the Black English Vernacular.* Philadelphia: University of Pennsylvania Press.

Marckwardt, Albert Henry. (1980). *American English.* Revised by J. L. Dillard. New York: Oxford University Press.

Mulhausler, Peter. (1986). *Pidgin and Creole Linguistics.* Oxford, England: Basil Blackwell.

Preston, Dennis R. (ed.) (1993). *American Dialect Research.* With the assistance of the members of the committee, John G. Fought . . . et al and the distinguished honorary members of the committee, Dwight Bolinger and Charles F. Hockett. Amsterdam Philadelphia: John Benjamins.

Rickford, John. (1999). *African American Vernacular English: Features, Evolution, Educational Implications.* Malden, Mass.: Blackwell.

Romaine, Suzanne. (1988). *Pidgin and Creole Languages.* London/New York: Longman.

Smitherman-Donaldson, Geneva. (1977). *Talkin and Testifying: The Language of Black America.* Boston: Houghton Mifflin.

Todd, Loreto. (1984). *Modern Englishes: Pidgins and Creoles.* Oxford, England: Basil Blackwell.

Wolfram, Walt and Natalie Schilling-Estes. (1998). *American English: Dialects and Variation.* Malden, Mass.: Blackwell.

Zentella, Ana Celia. (1997). *Growing Up Bilingual.* Malden, Mass.: Blackwell.

Journals

American Speech
Language in Society

Websites

http://www.americandialect.org/ (American Dialect Society)
http://www.sil.org/ethnologue/ethnologue.html (Ethnologue)

LANGUAGE POLICY AND PRESCRIPTION

The following are good resources for further study of language prescription, notions of standard versus nonstandard English, and language discrimination (such as the official English controversy, etc.).

Baron, Dennis E. (1990). *The English-Only Question: An Official Language for Americans?* New Haven, Conn.: Yale University Press.

Crawford, James (ed.). (1992). *Language Loyalties: A Source Book on the Official English Controversy,* with an afterword by Geoffrey Nunberg. Chicago: University of Chicago Press.

Daniels, Harvey A. (ed.). (1990). *Not Only English: Affirming America's Multilingual Heritage.* Urbana, Ill: National Council of Teachers of English.

Lippi-Green, Rosina. (1997). *English with an Accent: Language, Ideology, and Discrimination in the United States.* New York: Routledge.

McKay, Sandra Lee and Sau-Ling Cynthia Wong (eds.). (1988). *Language Diversity, Problem or Resource? A Social and Educational Perspective on Language Minorities in the United States.* New York: Newbury House.

Milroy, James and Lesley Milroy. (1985). *Authority in Language: Investigating Language Prescription and Standardisation.* London: Routledge & Kegan Paul.

Pinker, Steven. (1994). *The Language Instinct.* New York: William Morrow.

Websites

http://ourworld.compuserve.com/homepages/JWCRAWFORD/home2.htm

HISTORY OF ENGLISH

Many of the current textbooks on the history of the English language are organized chronologically and provide similar information regarding the various grammatical changes the language has gone through during stages labeled Old, Middle, Early Modern, and Modern English. These textbooks also provide a good overview of borrowing into English from Latin and French, and from Celtic and Scandinavian languages. Most include examples of original text translated into modern English. Many of the language diversity exercises are modeled on the information available in these texts; topics introduced in these exercises are all easily researched in the textbooks given below. Also included below are a number of additional resources about language change, to supplement your research.

Books

Aitchison, Jean. (1985). *Language Change: Progress or Decay?* New York: Universe Books.
Bailey, Richard W. (1991). *Images of English: A Cultural History of the Language.* Ann Arbor: University of Michigan Press.
Baugh, Albert C. and Thomas Cable. (1993). *A History of the English Language.* 4th ed. Englewood Cliffs NJ: Prentice-Hall, Inc.
Bolton, W. F. (1982). *A Living Language: The History and Structure of English.* New York: Random House.
Burrow, J. A. and Thorlac Turville-Petre. (1995). *A Book of Middle English.* Malden, Mass.: Blackwell.
Comrie, Bernard. (1990). *The World's Major Languages.* New York: Oxford University Press.
Graddol, D. D. Leith and J. Swann. *English: History, Diversity and Change.* London: Routledge.
Hogg, Richard M. (ed.). (1992). *Cambridge History of the English Language.* Cambridge: Cambridge University Press.
Hughes, Geoffrey. (1988). *Words in Time: A Social History of the English Vocabulary.* New York: Blackwell.
Millward, C. M. (1988). *A Biography of the English Language.* 2nd ed. Boston: Holt, Rinehart and Winston, Inc.
Mitchell, Bruce. (1994). *An Invitation to Old English and Anglo-Saxon England.* Malden, Mass.: Blackwell.
Pyles, Thomas and John Algeo. (1993). *The Origins and Development of the English Language.* 4th ed. New York Harcourt Brace Jovanovich, Inc.
Traugott, E. C. (1972). *A History of English Syntax.* New York: Holt, Rinehart and Winston.

Websites

http://www.georgetown.edu/labyrinth/labyrinth-home.html
http://www.lonestar.texas.net/~jebbo/learn-as/contents.html
http://www.georgetown.edu/cball/oe/old_english.html

ENGLISH EDUCATION

The following are basic resources for use in creating minilessons, practice lesson plans, or research papers on grammar and syntax in the secondary and elementary school curriculum.

Books

Cummings, D. W. (1988). *American English Spelling.* Baltimore, Md.: Johns Hopkins University Press.
Cleary, Linda Miller and Michael Linn. (1993). *Linguistics for Teachers.* New York McGraw-Hill, Inc.
Noguchi, Rei R. (1991). *Grammar and the Teaching of Writing: Limits and Possibilities.* Urbana, Ill.: National Council of Teachers of English.
Strong, William. (1996). *The Writer's Toolbox: A Sentence-Combining Workshop.* New York: McGraw-Hill, Inc.

Weaver, Constance. (1996) *Teaching Grammar in Context.* Portsmouth, N.H.: Boynton/ Cook Publishers, Heinemann.

Journals

College Composition and Communication: National Council of Teachers of English
College English: National Council of Teachers of English
English Journal: National Council of Teachers of English
Syntax in the Schools: National Council of Teachers of English
Teaching English in the Two-Year College: National Council of Teachers of English

Websites

http://www.note.org/
http://www.aitech.ac.ip/~siteslj/
http://www.beavton.k12.or.us/vose/resources/humanities.html#humanities
http://www.mcrel.org/resources/links/language.asp
http://www.pct.edu/courses/evavra/ATEG

TEACHING ENGLISH AS A SECOND LANGUAGE

Some resources for researching language diversity exercises from the point of view of teaching English as a second language are given below.

Books

Anderson, Paul S. (1971). *Linguistics in the Elementary School Classroom.* [Compiled by] Paul S. Anderson. New York: Macmillan (TESOL).
Azar, Betty Schrampfer. (1995). *Chartbook: A Reference Grammar.* Englewood Cliffs, N.J.: Prentice-Hall.
Boyd, Gertrude A. (1976). *Linguistics in the Elementary School.* Itasca, Ill.: F.E. Peacock (TESOL).
Celce-Murcia, Marianne. (1983). *The Grammar Book: An ESL-EFL Teacher's Course.* Boston, MA. Heinle & Heinle Publishers, Inc. (TESOL).
Celce-Murcia, Marianne (ed.). (1991). *Teaching English as a Second or Foreign Language.* Boston: Newbury House (TESOL).
Harmer, Jeremy. (1987). *Teaching and Learning Grammar.* London/New York: Longman (TESOL).
Ur, Penny. (1988). *Grammar Practice Activities: A Practical Guide for Teachers.* Cambridge/ New York: Cambridge University Press (TESOL).

Journals

TESOL Quarterly

Websites

http://www.tesol.edu/index.html
http://www.pacific.net/~sperling/eslcafe.html

INDEX

Note: Page numbers followed by *g* indicate glossary definitions.